Music and Power at the Court of Louis XIII

What role did sacred music play in mediating Louis XIII's grip on power in the early seventeenth century? How can a study of music as "sounding liturgy" contribute to the wider discourse on absolutism and "the arts" in early modern France? Taking the scholarship of the so-called ceremonialists as a point of departure, Peter Bennett engages with Weber's seminal formulation of power to consider the contexts in which liturgy, music, and ceremonial legitimated the power of a king almost continuously mired in religious conflict. Numerous musical settings show that David, the psalmist, musician, king, and agent of the Holy Spirit, provided the most enduring model of kingship; but in the final decade of his life, as Louis dedicated the kingdom to the Virgin Mary, the model of "Christ the King" became even more potent – a model reflected in a flowering of musical publications and famous paintings by Vouet and Champaigne.

PETER BENNETT is Associate Professor of Musicology at Case Western Reserve University, Cleveland. He previously spent fifteen years working as a harpsichordist, organist, and director, performing and recording several CDs to critical acclaim in the UK and Europe.

Music and Power at the Court of Louis XIII

Sounding the Liturgy in Early Modern France

PETER BENNETT

Case Western Reserve University

CAMBRIDGE
UNIVERSITY PRESS

University Printing House, Cambridge CB2 8BS, United Kingdom

One Liberty Plaza, 20th Floor, New York, NY 10006, USA

477 Williamstown Road, Port Melbourne, VIC 3207, Australia

314–321, 3rd Floor, Plot 3, Splendor Forum, Jasola District Centre, New Delhi – 110025, India

79 Anson Road, #06-04/06, Singapore 079906

Cambridge University Press is part of the University of Cambridge.

It furthers the University's mission by disseminating knowledge in the pursuit of education, learning, and research at the highest international levels of excellence.

www.cambridge.org
Information on this title: www.cambridge.org/9781108830638
DOI: 10.1017/9781108902588

© Peter Bennett 2021

This publication is in copyright. Subject to statutory exception and to the provisions of relevant collective licensing agreements, no reproduction of any part may take place without the written permission of Cambridge University Press.

First published 2021

A catalogue record for this publication is available from the British Library.

Library of Congress Cataloging-in-Publication Data
Names: Bennett, Lewis Peter, 1965–, author.
Title: Music and power at the court of Louis XIII : sounding the liturgy in early modern France / Peter Bennett.
Description: New York : Cambridge University Press, 2021. | Includes bibliographical references and index.
Identifiers: LCCN 2020058188 (print) | LCCN 2020058189 (ebook) | ISBN 9781108830638 (hardback) | ISBN 9781108822435 (paperback) | ISBN 9781108902588 (epub)
Subjects: LCSH: Music–Political aspects–France–History–17th century. | Church music–France–17th century. | Church music–Catholic church–17th century. | France–History–17th century. | Louis XIII, King of France, 1601-1643.
Classification: LCC ML3917.F8 B45 2021 (print) | LCC ML3917.F8 (ebook) | DDC 781.71/20094409032–dc23
LC record available at https://lccn.loc.gov/2020058188
LC ebook record available at https://lccn.loc.gov/2020058189

ISBN 978-1-108-83063-8 Hardback

Cambridge University Press has no responsibility for the persistence or accuracy of URLs for external or third-party internet websites referred to in this publication and does not guarantee that any content on such websites is, or will remain, accurate or appropriate.

Contents

List of Figures [*page* vi]
List of Tables [ix]
List of Music Examples [x]
Acknowledgments [xii]
Note on the Texts [xiv]

Introduction: Music, Liturgy, and Power [1]

1 David's Harp, Apollo's Lyre: Psalms, Music, and Kingship in the Sixteenth Century [17]

2 Accession: The Coronation, the Holy Spirit, and the Phoenix [46]

3 The Sword of David and the Battle against Heresy [88]

4 The Penitent King [123]

5 Pillars of Justice and Piety: The *Entrée*, the Te Deum, and the *Exaudiat te Dominus* [150]

6 Plainchant and the Politics of Rhythm: The Royal Abbey of Montmartre and the Royal Congregation of the Oratory of Jesus Christ [195]

7 Succession: The Vow of 1638 and Christ the King [238]

Epilogue and Conclusion: Continuity and Change under Louis XIV [274]

Bibliography [289]
Index [319]

Figures

1.1 Pierre Courtilleau, *The Capture of La Rochelle*. Musée d'Orbigny-Bernon, La Rochelle/Bridgeman Images. [*page* 18]
1.2 Superius part to Jacques Mauduit's setting of Baïf's translation of Psalm 67, "Dieu se lèvera soudain." Marin Mersenne, *Quaestiones celeberrimae in Genesim* (Paris, Sebastien Cramoisy, 1623). Bibliothèque nationale de France. [29]
1.3 Bodin's marginal illustration of the Unity of the King: "The image of the King, and the three estates conform to nature." Jean Bodin, *Les Six livres de la République* (Paris, Jacques du Puy, 1576). [31]
2.1 Abraham Blondet, *Lauda Jerusalem*, fragment, bass part. Abraham Blondet, *Officii Divae Ceciliae virgo et martyr Musicorum patronae musici concentibus expressi* (Paris, Pierre Ballard, 1611). Bibliothèque nationale de France. [62]
2.2 Coronation of Louis XIII. Anointing of the head, with Marie de Médicis and musicians in the background. Engraving, Thomas de Leu, c. 1610. Bibliothèque nationale de France [63]
2.3 Musicians with shawm and *cornet* (the *écurie*) and a lute and flute (the *chambre*) at the coronation of Louis XIII. Engraving, Pierre I Firens, 1610. Bibliothèque nationale de France. [72]
2.4 Arms of Henri III with the *collier* of the Knights of the Holy Spirit. André Favin, *Le Théâtre d'Honneur* (Paris, Robert Foüet, 1620). Bibliothèque nationale de France. [79]
2.5 Celebration of Mass for the Holy Spirit, 1703. *L'Office des chevaliers de l'Ordre du St. Esprit* (Paris, Imprimerie Royale, 1703). Bibliothèque nationale de France. [80]
2.6 Recitation of *Laudate Dominum* accompanied by the Lyre. Marin Mersenne, *Harmonie universelle* (Paris, Sebastien Cramoisy, 1636), *Livre quatrième des instruments*. Bibliothèque nationale de France. [83]
3.1 Louis IX portrayed as the root of a dynastic tree. Engraving of unknown origin. Bibliothèque nationale de France. [92]
3.2 Fireworks on the Seine for the octave of the feast of Saint Louis. Matthias Mérian, *La Représentation des artifices de feu, & autres triomphes faits à Paris sur le gué des Célestins & en l'isle Louviers, le lundy deuxiesme*

	septembre 1613 en l'honneur de la feste de S. Louys (Paris, Nicolas de Mathonière, 1613). Bibliothèque de l'INHA. [96]
3.3	Caignet's monophonic setting of Desportes's translation of Psalm 126 in *vers mesurez*. Denis Caignet, *Cinquante psaumes de David mis en vers François par Ph. Desportes, Abbé de Thiron, et les chants en musique* (Paris, Pierre Ballard, 1625). Bibliothèque municipale Bourges. [109]
3.4	The Hôtel de Bourbon and its chapel. As seen in the map by Matthias Mérian (Paris, Nicolas de Mathonière, 1615). Bibliothèque nationale de France. [113]
3.5	Illustration of the internal arrangement of the chapel of the Petit-Bourbon. After F-Pn MS nouv. acq. fr. 9740. [114]
3.6	Henri III dining "en public" in 1584. Richard Cooke, *La Première partie du compte de Richarde Cooke de Kent pour son voyage et temps employé en France*, Folger Shakespeare Library, MS V.a.146. [117]
4.1	*Dessus* part of *Domine salvum fac regem*. Charles d'Ambleville, *Harmonia sacra ... cum quatuor vocum* (Paris, Pierre Ballard, 1636). Bibliothèque nationale de France. [148]
5.1	The *entrée* of Louis XIII into Paris in 1614 (Paris?, 1614?). Bibliothèque nationale de France. [155]
5.2	First arch at Arles, 1622. *Entrée de Loys XIII, Roy de France et de Navarre dans sa ville d'Arles, le XXIX. octobre M. DC. XXII* (Avignon, Jean Bramereau, 1623). Bibliothèque nationale de France. [163]
5.3	Final arch at Arles, 1622. *Entrée de Loys XIII, Roy de France et de Navarre dans sa ville d'Arles, le XXIX. octobre M. DC. XXII* (Avignon, Jean Bramereau, 1623). Bibliothèque nationale de France. [165]
6.1	View of the Martyrium at Montmartre in the later seventeenth century. Engraving by Israel Silvestre. Bibliothèque nationale de France. [210]
6.2	Chant for second verse of *Dionysii martyris* (*Ad Gallos missi*). Paris manuscript. Bibliothèque nationale de France. [215]
6.3	Chant for *Dionysii martyris*. *Antiphonier Bénédictin ... de Montmartre* (Paris, Louis Sevestre, 1646). Bibliothèque nationale de France. [215]
6.4	Chant for *Stabat mater*. *Antiphonier Bénédictin ... de Montmartre* (Paris, Louis Sevestre, 1646). Bibliothèque nationale de France. [219]
6.5	Chant for *Et exultativit* in mensural notation. Paris manuscript. Bibliothèque nationale de France. [219]
6.6	Chant for *Magnificat* and *Et exultavit*. *Antiphonier Bénédictin ... de Montmartre* (Paris, Louis Sevestre, 1646). Bibliothèque nationale de France. [220]

6.7 *Fauxbourdon* for *Credidi propter*. Paris manuscript. Bibliothèque nationale de France. [220]

6.8 Chant for *Credidi propter. Antiphonier Bénédictin . . . de Montmartre* (Paris, Louis Sevestre, 1646). Bibliothèque nationale de France. [220]

6.9 Chant for *Credidi propter*, v.2, *Ego dixi in excessu meo*. Paris manuscript. Bibliothèque nationale de France. [221]

6.10 Arithmetic proportion according to Descartes. René Descartes, *Excellent Compendium of Music with Necessary and Judicious Animadversions Thereupon* (London, Thomas Harper and Humphrey Moseley, 1653). [222]

6.11 Geometric proportion according to Descartes. René Descartes, *Excellent Compendium of Music with Necessary and Judicious Animadversions Thereupon* (London, Thomas Harper and Humphrey Moseley, 1653). [223]

6.12 Versicle and Response, *Deus in adiutorium meum intende*. François Bourgoing, *Brevis psalmodiae ratio ad usum presbytorium congregationis oratorii Domini nostri Jesu Christi instituta* (Paris, Pierre Ballard, 1634). Bibliothèque nationale de France. [230]

7.1 Simon Vouet, *Le Vœu de Louis XIII*, Charenton-le-Pont, Médiathèque de l'Architecture et du Patrimoine. Photo © Ministère de la Culture – Médiathèque de l'architecture et du patrimoine, Dist. RMN-Grand Palais / Archives photographiques (Saint-Quentin-en-Yvelines). [242]

7.2 Philippe de Champaigne, *Le Vœu de Louis XIII*. Caen, Musée des Beaux-Arts. Photo © akg-images. [247]

7.3 Abraham Bosse, *Les Vœux du Roy et de la Reyne a la Vierge*. Bibliothèque nationale de France. [250]

Tables

2.1 Text, translation, and source of Jean Mouton's setting of *Domine salvum fac regem*. [*page* 55]

2.2 Text, translation, and source of Guillaume Costeley and Jean Maillard's settings of *Domine salvum fac regem*. [53]

3.1 Text and translation of Psalm 128, *Qu'Israel maintenant*, and *Leandre estant dessus le bord de l'Elespont* (verse 1). [106]

4.1 Psalm-texted and Songs-texted "motets" from the repertoire of the *musique de la chambre* preserved in the Paris manuscript. [130]

4.2 Text, translation, and source of *Domine multiplicati sunt*. [131]

4.3 Text, translation, and source of *Adiuva nos Deus salutaris*. [131]

4.4 Text, translation, and source of *Egredimini filiae Sion*. [133]

4.5 Text and translation of Psalm 19, *Exaudiat te Dominus*. [140]

5.1 Text and translation of *Recueil de vers du Sr. G. de Baïf, mis en Musique par N. Métru, chantez en allégresse de l'heureux retour du Roy* (Paris, Pierre Ballard, 1628). [160]

5.2 Text and translation of Guillaume Bouzignac (attrib.), *Omnes gentes plaudite manibus*, Tours manuscript. [177]

5.3 Text and translation of Guillaume Bouzignac (attrib.), *Cantate Domino, omnis Francia*, Tours manuscript. [177]

5.4 Psalms identified in the *entrée* ceremony. [179]

5.5 Psalms identified in the "Te Deum" ceremony. [180]

5.6 Psalms identified in the "Te Deum"/*entrée* ceremony. [181]

5.7 Text, translation, and source of *Exaudiat te Dominus*, Newberry/Avignon manuscript. [190]

7.1 Text, translation, and source of Nicolas Formé, *Ecce tu pulchra es* (Paris, Pierre Ballard, 1638). [272]

7.2 Text, translation and source of anonymous, *Veni sponsa mea*, Paris manuscript. [272]

8.1 Text and translation of *Pulsate, pulsate tympana*, Pierre Perrin, *Cantica pro Capella Regis* (Paris, Christophe Ballard, 1665). [282]

Music Examples

2.1 Didier Le Blanc, *Te Deum*, opening. *Octo cantica divae Mariae Virginis* (Paris, Adrian Le Roy and Robert Ballard, 1584). [*page* 69]

2.2 Eustache Du Caurroy *Te Deum*, opening. *Preces ecclesiasticae* (Paris, Pierre Ballard, 1609). [71]

2.3 Eustache Du Caurroy, *In exitu Israel*, opening, showing psalm tone in tenor. *Preces ecclesiasticae* (Paris, Pierre Ballard, 1609). [84]

3.1 *Qu'Israel dise maintenant*, set to the melody of *Leandre estant dessus le bord de l'Elespont*. *Airs de différents auteurs mis en tablature de luth par Gabriel Bataille* (Paris, Pierre Ballard, 1609/1614). [107]

3.2 Artus Auxcousteaux, reconstruction of Psalm 80, *Exultate Deo adjutori nostro*. *Psalmi aliquot ad numeros musices IIII, V et sex vocum redacti* (Paris, Pierre Ballard, 1631). [120]

4.1 Artus Auxcousteaux, reconstruction of *Deus, Deus meus, respice in me*. *Psalmi aliquot ad numeros musices IIII, V et sex vocum redacti* (Paris, Pierre Ballard, 1631). [129]

4.2 Anonymous, *Domine salvum fac regem*. Paris manuscript. [136]

5.1 Jacques Mauduit, "Ode à la Reyne," *Soit que l'œil pourveu de nouvelle clairté*, in reconstructed version for four voices. *Airs de différents auteurs mes en tablature de luth par Gabriel Bataille. Cinquiesme livre* (Paris, Pierre Ballard, 1614). [158]

5.2 Extant *cinquiesme* voice part of Nicolas Métru, *Vive le Roy*. *Recueil de vers du Sr. G. de Baïf, mis en Musique par N. Métru, chantez en allégresse de l'heureux retour du Roy* (Paris, Pierre Ballard, 1628). [159]

5.3 Anonymous, opening of *Vivat Rex in aeternum*, surviving superius voice. Newberry/Avignon manuscript (MS 5123). [161]

5.4 Guillaume Bouzignac (attrib.), opening of *Omnes gentes plaudite manibus*. Tours manuscript. [174]

5.5 Anonymous, *Domine salvum fac regem*. Paris manuscript. [185]

5.6 Nicolas Le Vavasseur, *Exaudiat te Dominus* (vv. 1–2). Nicolas le Vavasseur, *Airs a III. IIII. et V. parties* (Paris, Pierre Ballard, 1626). [187]

5.7 Anonymous, *Exaudiat te in die dolentis animae tua*, surviving superius part. Newberry/Avignon Manuscript (MS 5123). [189]

6.1 Opening verse of Antoine Boësset, *Dionysii martyris*. Paris manuscript. [213]
6.2 André Péchon, *Pange lingua gloriosi*. Paris manuscript. [216]
6.3 Antoine Boësset, *Stabat mater dolorosa*, v. 1. Paris manuscript. [217]
7.1 Nicolas Formé, opening of Magnificat in Tone 1. *Le Cantique de la Vierge Marie selon les Tons ou Modes usités en L'église*, F-Pn MS fonds fr. 1870. [251]
7.2 Nicolas Formé, *O salutaris hostia*, for low voices. *Musica simplex quatuor vocum* (Paris, Pierre Ballard, 1638). [254]
7.3 Nicolas Formé, *O salutaris hostia*, "pour les voix plus hautes." *Musica simplex quatuor vocum* (Paris, Pierre Ballard, 1638). [255]
7.4 Charles d'Ambleville, Psalm 121, *Laetatus sum*, concluding doxology: four-voice and six-voice publications combined. *Harmonia sacra . . . cum quatuor [sex] vocum* (Paris, Pierre Ballard, 1636). [261]
7.5 Nicolas Formé, conclusion of Gloria. Mass *Aeternae Henrici Magni* (Paris, Pierre Ballard, 1638). [263]
7.6 The dialogue between the Sirens and the gilded vault. *Balet comique de la royne* (Paris, Adrian le Roy, Robert Ballard, and Mamert Patisson, 1582). [267]
7.7 Nicolas Formé, opening and second section of *Ecce tu pulchra es*. Mass *Aeternae Henrici Magni* (Paris, Pierre Ballard, 1638). [269]

Acknowledgments

Although I had been thinking about this book for several years, the impetus and means to complete it came from a year's fellowship at the Centre d'Études Supérieures de la Renaissance, Tours, in 2015–16, supported by Le STUDIUM, the Loire Valley Institute for Advanced Studies. For that, I am grateful to Philippe Vendrix, director of the CESR as I arrived, Benoît Pierre, director as I left, and to all in the Le STUDIUM and CESR administrations who made the experience so enriching for me as a scholar and so rewarding for my family. In particular I would like to thank my colleagues in the CESR musicology office David Fiala, Vasco Zara, and the late Xavier Bisaro for their kind welcome and their generosity in helping me navigate a wide range of scholarly and practical challenges. I am also grateful to Bernard Dompnier for his wise counsel and assistance in organizing *Sacred/Secular Intersections in Early Modern Ceremonial: Text, Music, Image, and Power*, a conference that took place at the CESR in July 2016, and to all those from across France and the UK who attended and shared their work and ideas so productively. I would also like to thank Isabelle His and Theodora Psychoyou for the opportunities to present my own work in the wider French musicological community, Thierry Favier for his welcome and collegiality, and Jean Duron and Thomas Leconte at the Centre de Musique Baroque de Versailles for their support, unrivaled knowledge of the field, and shared fascination with the subject of this book.

Closer to home, I would also like to thank the department and college administration at Case Western Reserve University, Cleveland, for supporting my year away so wholeheartedly, and my colleagues and former colleagues in the department from whom I have learned so much – especially Georgia Cowart, Susan McClary, and Ross Duffin. John Hajdu Heyer, Kate van Orden, and Don Fader have also been constantly reassuring presences, offering support and encouragement whenever called upon, as well as incisive and frequently transformative suggestions. And I would also like to thank Darren Keefe for his assistance with the Latin translations and scansion, Timothy Beale for advice on and translation of the Hebrew psalms, Erin Benay for her insights into the paintings discussed in Chapter 7, and Megan Long for advice with the musical reconstructions.

On a personal note, I would like to acknowledge the role that my Anglo-French godparents Jean and Bernard Lefèvre played twenty years ago as I set out on this Louis XIII adventure, providing a room to sleep in in Paris and enabling me to get to grips with the Paris manuscript in a way that has served me well ever since. Finally, I will forever be grateful to my wife and children for their love, constant support, and willingness to move across the world more than once as I followed the winding trail to (I hope) a satisfactory conclusion.

Note on the Texts

Latin Biblical texts are taken from the Clementine Vulgate edition and retain the verse numbering of the original: psalms therefore begin at either v. 1 or v. 2. English translations of Biblical texts are, unless otherwise stated, taken from the 1750 Challoner revision of the Douai–Reims edition of 1609. All quotations of French and Latin texts follow the original spelling, although modern accentuation has been added to improve legibility.

Music examples are provided with prefatory staves showing the original clefs to indicate the approximate range of each voice (since many of the musical sources used do not provide voice designations). Voices without a prefatory clef are editorial reconstructions. Editorial barlines have been added to works transcribed from printed sources where such barlines are necessary to clarify the polyphonic texture: otherwise the absence of barlines follows the source. Transcriptions from the Paris and Tours manuscripts include the original barring. All note values are original, and chant incipits and versets reflect the notational practice of the source as closely as possible.

Introduction

Music, Liturgy, and Power

> Nature leads us to observe Ceremonies. Ceremony is the external act of Religion, the witness to the worship and private devotion that man renders to God; like joining the hands, lifting the eyes to Heaven, it is a visible sign that one recognizes God ...[1]
> Claude Villette, *Les Raisons de l'Office, et cérémonies qui se font en l'Église Catholique* (Paris, Guillaume de Rues, 1611)

This book considers the role that the liturgy and music of the Roman Catholic church played in mediating Louis XIII's grip on power during the first half of the seventeenth century. It is hard to overstate the far-reaching influence of both the church and its ecclesiastical structures, not just on the king, but on the people, cities, and the state of France during this period. The daily life of a typical urban resident would have been punctuated by the regular rhythms, sounds, and actions of the church calendar – the cathedral bells ringing to call the faithful to Mass, processions of clergy and singers through and around the city on feasts such as Corpus Christi or Easter, and the regular processions of any number of religious houses or confraternities on feasts related to their orders.[2] The city dweller would have also experienced other processions and ceremonies for extraordinary events – the plague, harvest, or perhaps a Te Deum to celebrate a military victory by the king. If they were fortunate, they might even receive a visit from the king himself as he made a ceremonial *entrée*, led through the streets by the city dignitaries to the cathedral, where he would be presented with a crucifix to kiss, be blessed by the Bishop, and take an oath to uphold the liberties of the church, before entering to give thanks for his latest victory.[3] In some cities, such as Angers, Le Mans, and others, the king was

---

[1] "Nature nous conduit à faire Cérémonies. Cérémonie, est l'œuvre de Religion extérieure, en témoignage du culte, & service intérieur que l'homme rend à Dieu: comme joindre les mains eslevant les yeux au Ciel, est un signal visible que l'on recognoist Dieu ..."

[2] See, for example, the diaries of the cleric Jean Louvet describing ecclesiastical life in Angers between 1560 and 1634 in *Revue de l'Anjou et de Maine et Loire*, 3/1 (1854), 257–304; 3/2 (1854), 1–64, 129–92, 257–320; 4/2 (1855), 130–320; 4/3 (1855), 1–320.

[3] For a broad overview of the concept of "sacred space" or "ceremonial space," see for example Andrew Spicer and Sarah Hamilton (eds.), *Defining the Holy: Sacred Space in Medieval and Early*

even considered to be a member of the chapter, and on entering the cathedral he was presented with the hood and surplice that signified his role as an honorary canon. His status as "sacral" monarch, a *rex christianissimus*, was, of course, a long tradition in France: in a coronation rite dating back centuries, the king was anointed with holy oil that had (so it was told) been brought down from heaven by a dove for the baptism of Clovis, and that had served at almost every coronation since.[4] The court itself was also effectively an ecclesiastical institution, with almost all the bishops of France simultaneously holding court positions, and with the most powerful figures at court, and even some of the most renowned military commanders (most notably Richelieu), being churchmen.[5] Even more than that, however, the developing notion of the absolute monarch was inextricably linked to the sacral nature of the king: in the early years of the seventeenth century, as a response to the assassination of his two predecessors, and to the new doctrines curtailing his temporal authority being embraced by the Pope and the Jesuits, jurists and courtiers around Louis XIII began to construct an identity for the king that would almost immediately refer to him as ruling "absolutely," although the full political and financial facets of the concept would only come later.[6]

Modern Europe (Aldershot, Ashgate, 2005) and Juliusz Chrościcki, "Ceremonial space", in Allan Ellenius (ed.), *Iconography, Propaganda, and Legitimation* (Oxford, Clarendon Press, 1998), pp. 193–216. For an exploration of these issues as they pertain to music history, see for example Iain Fenlon, *The Ceremonial City: History, Memory and Myth in Renaissance Venice* (New Haven and London, Yale University Press, 2007), and the essays in Fiona Kisby (ed.), *Music and Musicians in Renaissance Cities and Towns* (Cambridge, Cambridge University Press, 2001). Growing out of a consideration of how sacred spaces might be defined, and the burgeoning field of sound studies, the concept of the "soundscape" has also become an important focus of recent musicological scholarship. See for example Robert Kendrick, *The Sounds of Milan, 1585–1650* (Oxford, Oxford University Press, 2002); Alexander Fisher, *Music, Piety, and Propaganda: The Soundscapes of Counter-Reformation Bavaria* (Oxford, Oxford University Press, 2015); and the essays in Daniele Filippi and Michael Noone (eds.), *Listening to Early Modern Catholicism* (Leiden, Brill, 2017).

[4] For an overview of the concept of the sacral monarch from a broad anthropological perspective, see Sergio Bertelli, *The King's Body: Sacred Rituals of Power in Medieval and Early Modern Europe*, trans. R. Burr Litchfield (University Park, Pennsylvania State University Press, 2001); and Sergio Bertelli, '*Rex et sacerdos*: The holiness of the king in European civilization', in Ellenius (ed.), *Iconography*, pp. 123–46.

[5] See Benoist Pierre, *La Monarchie ecclésiale: le clergé de cour en France à l'époque moderne* (Paris, Champ Vallon, 2013). The dominance of the clergy at court was much diminished under Louis XIV, but until then the so-called *prélats d'état* had occupied central roles in government; see Joseph Bergin, *The Politics of Religion in Early Modern France* (New Haven and London, Yale University Press, 2014), pp. 14–16.

[6] For an overview of this process, see Fanny Cosandey and Robert Descimon, *L'Absolutisme en France: histoire et historiographie* (Paris, Seuil, 2002).

If, then, the daily life of the French people – from urban artisan to the king himself – was closely bounded by, and operated within, the framework of the Catholic church as derived from the Bible and the teachings of the Church Fathers, at the same time another ideological and philosophical frame of reference also held sway. While of course the sixteenth century (the "High Renaissance" or the "Age of Humanism") saw the educated elite turn to the models of antiquity for inspiration in the political, literary, and other artistic spheres, in France such models were particularly influential. In political terms, the belief that the country was entering a new era that would rival both the historical reality of the Roman Empire and the mythical Golden Age had been widely embraced under Francis I, but in the second half of the sixteenth century too, such ideas were espoused by those around Henri III and Henri IV, and were reflected not just in the poetry of writers such as Ronsard and the other members of the Pléiade, but in many different aspects of court-centered artistic production.[7] According to such a framework, Charlemagne himself had descended from Francus (son of Hector), a mythical figure who had escaped after the fall of Troy and whose descendant Pharamond had supposedly been the first king of France, a narrative that was celebrated by Ronsard in his *Franciade* (a reimagining of the *Aeneid*) in a clear attempt to frame the French monarchy as the descendants of the heroes of antiquity.[8] Likewise, Guy le Fèvre de la Boderie's *La Galliade* endeavored to link all the great civilizations of the past – ancient Gaul, Egypt (home of the Hermetic tradition), Greece (classical antiquity), Judea (the Judaeo-Christian tradition), Rome (the Roman Empire), and Italy – into a continuous descent (or ascent) that culminated in France.[9] The whole of the sixteenth century had thus seen the French monarchy equated with the mythical (Hercules, Perseus, or Apollo) and real (Pompilius, Vespasian, or Attalus) warriors of antiquity, a practice that survived well into the seventeenth century and that was brought to life in, for example, the *entrée* at Arles in 1622, in which the whole program was based on the legend of Perseus (Louis) rescuing Andromeda (France) from the sea monster (Heresy), the same narrative that underpinned *Persée*, Lully's *tragédie en musique*, some fifty

---

[7] Emmanuel le Roy Ladurie, *The French Royal State, 1460–1610*, trans. Juliet Vale (Oxford, Blackwell, 1994), pp. 109–23.
[8] Frances Yates, *Astraea: The Imperial Theme in the Sixteenth Century* (London and Boston, Routledge, 1985), pp. 121–6.
[9] Frances Yates, *The French Academies of the Sixteenth Century*, Studies of the Warburg Institute, 15 (London, Warburg Institute, 1947), p. 43.

years later.[10] (We should of course remember that in Arles and many other cities of southern France, genuine Roman antiquities frequently dominated the cityscape.) In philosophical terms, this enthusiasm for all things classical was also reflected in the embrace of a Neoplatonic worldview in which, following Marsilio Ficino and his later French disciple Pontus de Tyard, music and poetry were the first of the four steps by which man might ascend to a more perfect state, and in which profane love was a preparation for a love of the divine.[11] The poets and musicians of the court were therefore required to do more than just allude to a mythical past: their creations, be it poetry, measured music, a *balet de cour*, or some other kind of court festival, were themselves the vehicles by which France's prosperity and well-being would be assured. Events such as the Balet comique de la Reine of 1581, or any number of royal *entrées* (which were celebrated until the 1660s) or other festivals, were thus replete with hidden symbolism (emblems, mottos, and devices) or recreations of ancient poetry and music – all in an attempt to invoke the powers that the ancient and occult worlds possessed and bring them to bear on the nation.

In this study I explore how the music produced as a response to Louis XIII in the context of these ideological frameworks – classical, biblical/ ecclesiastical, and Neoplatonic – might contribute to the wider discourse on ceremonial, power, and absolutism in early modern France. In particular I focus on how the liturgy – typically transmitted to us as a text in normative printed sources, but in reality consisting of a much broader set of practices, beliefs, and actions that were either universally applied across Catholic Christendom or specially developed for particular circumstances – might be brought to life as an act and "read" or interpreted through the musical practices or compositions associated with it.[12] Music, as "sounding liturgy," could highlight liturgical acts or facets of a liturgical text that were considered significant; composers could set liturgical texts in ways that reflected underlying ideologies; and texts could be troped, centonized, modified, translated, or glossed in a musical composition to clarify and

---

[10] For classical allusion in the *entrée*, see Ralph Giesey, 'Models of rulership in French royal ceremonial', in Sean Willentz (ed.), *Rites of Power: Symbolism, Ritual, and Politics since the Middle Ages* (Philadelphia, University of Pennsylvania Press, 1985), pp. 41–64. More generally, see Françoise Bardon, *Le Portrait mythologique à la cour de France sous Henri IV et Louis XIII. Mythologie et politique* (Paris, Éditions A. et J. Picard, 1974).

[11] Yates, *French Academies*, pp. 77–94.

[12] I interpret the concept of liturgy broadly to include not just "official" authorized texts, but all Latin texted chant or music performed in some kind of formalized ceremony. I exclude devotional texts in French and their musical settings, usually performed in a less formal setting.

emphasize a particular meaning or reading. At the same time, within this musical and liturgical discourse, various "voices" or subject positions might also emerge: as Carolyn Abbate has suggested, expanding on Edward Cone's initial formulation of a single "composer's voice," music can be thought of as being "animated by multiple, decentered voices located in several invisible bodies."[13] Although the music central to this study (including chant) was at one level performed by a variety of voices (the singers concerned, who might be paid employees of the court, priests, members of a religious confraternity, a member of an adoring crowd at a public ceremony, or a private individual in their own house), these literal, sounding voices also interacted with at least two other, underlying authorial voices: the composers of the music itself, and – central to this study – the authors of the texts they set: the Church Fathers, the Old Testament prophets, the ancient kings of France, or (most relevant) King David, the psalmist, musician-king, author of a significant proportion of the texts that make up the liturgy, and the model for the Western Christian conception of the monarchy itself.[14] The psalms, while of course regularly performed as part of the regular cycle of church Offices, also took on particular meanings when set to music in a way that reflected a particular ideology. In the biblical framework, music itself – created by Jubal according to the account in Genesis, handed down to David, and preserved in the psalmody and chant of the universal Catholic church – could trace its existence to the very beginning of the Judaeo-Christian world. In this case, the authorial voice frequently belonged to David himself, inspired by the Holy Spirit and probably mediated by Saint Jerome's translation of the Vulgate. On the other hand, in the classical or Neoplatonic framework, music was a creation of Apollo, lost during the Middle Ages but finally revived in the 1570s by the scholar performers of Charles IX's Académie de poésie et de musique.[15] In this framework, the psalms, as the most poetic and musical of all biblical texts, could still serve an important devotional role, but would now need to be considered as part of the syncretic musical-humanist tradition most

---

[13] Carolyn Abbate, *Unsung Voices: Opera and Musical Narrative in the Nineteenth Century* (Princeton, Princeton University Press, 1996), pp. 11–13; Edward Cone, *The Composer's Voice* (Berkeley, University of California Press, 1974), especially p. 69.

[14] The literature on David's reception in the Renaissance is extensive; see for example, Elise Boilet, Sonia Cavicchioli, and Paul-Alexis Mellet (eds.), *Les Figures de David à la Renaissance* (Geneva, Droz, 2015); Dominique Vinay, *La Couronne et la lyre: présence du roi David dans la littérature française de la Renaissance* (PhD dissertation, Université François Rabelais – Tours, 2002).

[15] Yates, *French Academies*, pp. 36–76.

famously exemplified in Mersenne's 1623 *Quaestiones celerribimae in Genesim*, a tract that reconciled the Platonic and Mosaic accounts of creation and preserved some of the most important examples of psalms translated from the Hebrew and set anew in the rhythmic meters of antiquity.[16] Here, David was mediated by a different voice – that of a contemporary imitator of Cicero or Horace, standing in for an ancient, humanist approach to musical composition that would have spoken to an educated audience as loudly as the musical content itself.

But how, specifically, might a "musical reading" of the liturgy or the psalms, and an exploration of the ideological framework in which it was conceived, relate to wider issues of monarchical power? The concept of "representation" has come to dominate much of the thinking around the French monarchy in the seventeenth century, a period undoubtedly overshadowed by Louis XIV and the extravagances of his artistic patronage. In this conceptual framework, while Louis XIV was widely considered to rule with divine authority, those around the king were nevertheless concerned with "representing" him to the populace in ways that enhanced his glory and power – through analogies with the heroes of antiquity or mythology, with the ancient kings of France, or with the kings of Israel, in particular David. (These analogies could be executed visually in the form of portraits, medals, sculpture; in literature; and in sacred music, opera, and ballet.) Certainly for the early and middle part of his reign, as Burke, Marin, Apostolides, and Sabatier have argued (albeit from different perspectives), the king's absolute power was intrinsically tied up with the process of representation itself, even if, as is frequently claimed, in later years Louis's greatness was so widely accepted and self-evident that allegorical representations were no longer required (indeed detracted from his power).[17] In the realm of sacred music, Favier has also identified representational strategies at work in the *grand motet* produced for Louis XIVs *chapelle royale*, in this case located in a new aesthetic, the sublime,

---

[16] While the Church Fathers, such as Origen, Eusebius, and Jerome, and many others, referred to the psalms as poetry or lyric verse, and while they are certainly organized into lines (one of the defining features of poetry), psalm texts do not typically obey any metrical pattern. It is partly this lack of number and organization that prompted the production of numerous metrical translations in the sixteenth and seventeenth centuries; see F.W. Dobbs Allsop, 'Poetry of the psalms', in William Brown (ed.), *The Oxford Handbook of the Psalms* (Oxford, Oxford University Press, 2014). See also the discussion in Chapter 1.

[17] Peter Burke, *The Fabrication of Louis XIV* (New Haven and London, Yale University Press, 1992); Louis Marin, *Le Portrait du Roi* (Paris, Éditions de Minuit, 1981); Jean-Marie Apostolides, *Le Roi-machine: spectacle et politique au temps de Louis XIV* (Paris, Éditions de Minuit, 1981); Gerard Sabatier, *Versailles ou la figure du Roi* (Paris, Albin Michel, 1999).

introduced into the motet by Lalande and taken up by his successors well into the eighteenth century.[18] In this approach, according to Favier, the older linear, rhetorical compositional technique that dutifully worked through successive verses of the psalm text was replaced with a dazzling and overwhelming presentation of ideas, a painting-like image of the battles, conquests, and the greatness of King David that the psalm texts frequently recounted. Yet the mechanism by which the 'representation' described by Favier (and indeed Burke et al.) actually confers *real* power is not clear, especially as he points out that Lalande's motets presented many situations that "illustrate not so much David's temporal power but rather God's power over David's destiny and that of his nation."[19] Favier's discussion is also bounded primarily by a concern for the "musical work," an approach that leaves less room for a consideration of the role of the liturgy and practices of the *chapelle royale* more broadly, or for the role of liturgy across the church and nation of France, in which the liturgical performance of a *grand motet* was a relative rarity.[20] Montagnier's study of the *grand motet*, by contrast, is situated in a more explicit reading of the psalter, but again, in both this article and his other contributions, the mechanism by which the representational strategy he also sees functions, is largely taken for granted.[21]

To explore the relationship between music, liturgy, and power during the reign of Louis XIII, then, we might profitably turn to one of Max Weber's formulations – that the concept of power is a social construct, the

---

[18] Thierry Favier, 'The French *grand motet* and the king's glory: A reconsideration of the issue', in Reinhard Strohm, Ryszard Wieczorek, Robert Kendrick, Helen Geyer, and Zofia Fabianska (eds.), *Early Music Context and Ideas, II* (Krakow, Institute of Musicology, Jagellonian University, 2008), pp. 188–97. This material was subsequently expanded in Thierry Favier, *Le Motet à grand chœur (1660–1792): Gloria in Gallia Deo* (Paris, Fayard, 2009), pp. 141–214. See also Favier's extensive survey of the musicological literature in this field in Thierry Favier, 'Musique religieuse et absolutisme sous le règne de Louis XIV: essai de bilan critique', in Peter Bennett and Bernard Dompnier (eds.), *Cérémonial politique et cérémonial religieux dans l'Europe modern: échanges et métissages* (Paris, Garnier, 2020), pp. 19–38.

[19] Favier, 'The French *grand motet*', pp. 195.

[20] For the provincial reception of the *grand motet*, see John Hajdu Heyer, *The Lure and Legacy of Music at Versailles: Louis XIV and the Aix School* (Cambridge, Cambridge University Press, 2014); Lionel Sawkins, 'En province, à Versailles et au Concert Spirituel: réception, diffusions et exécution des motets de Lalande au XVIIIe siècle', *Revue de musicologie*, 92/1 (2006), 13–40; and Favier, *Le Motet à grand chœur*, pp. 379–435.

[21] Jean-Paul Montagnier, 'Chanter Dieu en la chapelle royale: le grand motet et ses supports littéraires', *Revue de musicologie*, 86/2 (2000), 217–63; see also Jean-Paul Montagnier, 'Le Te Deum en France à l'époque baroque: un emblème royal', *Revue de musicologie*, 84/2 (1998), 199–233. Jean-Paul Montagnier, 'Sacred music and royal propaganda under Louis XIV (ca. 1661–ca. 1686)', *Rivista internazionale di musica sacra*, new series 27/2 (2006), 83–94.

"chance, within a social relationship of enforcing one's own will."[22] As Weber explains, while it is possible that those in a subordinate position might acquiesce to the dominance of the ruler through fear, self-interest, or affection for the monarch, rulers typically attempt to foster the idea that their power is "legitimate" – that the conceptual framework that supports the power relation is accepted by those in the subordinate position so that they obey appropriate commands from the dominant. The concept or mechanism of "representation" clearly falls under Weber's category of "charismatic rule" – that the ruler is considered to be legitimate through the possession of exceptional personal qualities (often military prowess) or supernatural abilities (the royal touch, for example).[23] Yet, as David Beetham has argued, Weber's definition of the three different types of rule ("charismatic," "rational," and "traditional") fails to recognize the significance of the actions of the subordinate in the legitimizing process.[24] In particular, situating his critique in the broader observation that Weber focused solely on whether those in subordinate positions *believed* in the legitimacy of the system (rather than any rational assessment of whether it was indeed legitimate), Beetham instead argued *not* that there are three different types of legitimate rule, but that there are three interlinked factors (nevertheless related to Weber's categories) that are all necessary to render power legitimate: viz., that it conforms to established rules; that the rules are justified by reference to belief systems *shared* by both dominant and subordinate; and that there is evidence of consent between the ruler and people, typically shown through action. Specifically, "It is in the sense of the public actions of the subordinate, expressive of consent, that we can properly talk about the 'legitimation' of power, not the propaganda or public relations campaigns, the 'legitimations' generated by the powerful themselves."[25]

In this revised model, then, the representation or portrayal of the monarch as a charismatic leader with supernatural powers (and the belief in those powers by the people) is not in itself sufficient to grant legitimacy to that monarch: indeed, if such representation is simply an attempt to

---

[22] Max Weber, trans. Keith Tribe, *Economy and Society* (Cambridge, Massachusetts and London, Harvard University Press, 2019), p. 134.
[23] Weber, *Economy and Society*, p. 342. The persistence of the "royal touch" documented by Bloch is testimony to the role that the supernatural played in the identity of the king; see Marc Bloch, trans. J.E. Anderson, *The Royal Touch: Sacred Monarchy and Scrofula in England and France* (London, Routledge and Kegan Paul, 1973), pp. 223–8.
[24] David Beetham, *The Legitimation of Power* (Basingstoke, Palgrave Macmillan, 2013), pp. 10–12.
[25] Beetham, *Legitimation*, p. 19.

persuade the subordinates of something that the dominant does not actually believe in, such rule is, on the contrary, illegitimate. In that sense, as Burke cautioned, the representational strategies around Louis XIV, some of which may well have been put into place cynically, with rituals of state seen merely as calculated theatrical performances, and with the king "playing" his part, may not (in Beetham's framework) have granted legitimacy to his rule.[26] And in a similar way, both Marin's and Apostolides's formulations, that either the "portrait" of the king or a "machine" that takes his place (both of which are controlled by others) were in reality the driving force of power, also point to a disconnection or lack of legitimacy that is perhaps reflected in subsequent critiques of these representational strategies themselves.[27]

But it also alerts us to numerous observations that scholars have made about ritual and ceremonial *before* the reign of Louis XIV – that such ceremonies were, by contrast, not "representational" or intended to persuade, but, in the eyes of those present, "performative," i.e. they made what they enacted real. More than that, however, they also reflected a world in which resemblance and analogy were not, as Foucault argues, just simple linguistic, rhetorical, or logical processes, but a boundless and complex array of relationships and symbols that fundamentally underpinned the thought and epistemologies of the sixteenth century.[28] In this magical world, those present at court or religious ceremonies were not part of an asymmetrical relationship, either active "players" on a stage or part of a passive audience observing the representation: on the contrary, all were participants, all had to genuinely subscribe to the underlying belief system, and all were necessary for the ritual to have meaning. In that sense, as Gomes has argued, such ceremonies can be considered as "reminiscent," an opportunity for all those present (across the entire spectrum of power) to

---

[26] Burke, *Fabrication of Louis XIV*, pp. 12–13.

[27] Referring to the demise of Neoplatonic ideology in the 1660s, Cowart argues that "With that rupture came a profound crisis in the role of the arts vis-à-vis the king, as the arts could now be perceived as serving a degraded form of propaganda in the modern sense, rather than the eternal truth they had been believed to reflect." See Georgia Cowart, *The Triumph of Pleasure* (Chicago, Chicago University Press, 2007), p. 48.

[28] See Michel Foucault, *The Order of Things: An Archeology of the Human Sciences* (New York, Pantheon, 1971), pp. 17–45; originally published as *Les Mots et les choses* (Paris, Gallimard, 1966). For this "crisis of metaphoricity," see Sabatier, *Versailles*, pp. 550–9. Burke describes the same process in Peter Burke, 'The demise of royal mythologies', in Ellenius (ed.), *Iconography*, pp. 245–54. For a musicological perspective on these issues see Gary Tomlinson, *Music in Renaissance Magic: Toward a Historiography of Others* (Chicago, University of Chicago Press, 1993), especially pp. 52–61.

reflect on and work through the reality of their beliefs, rather than necessarily to admire their leader.[29]

If then (as will become apparent in the rest of this book), the reign of Louis XIII at least partially fell into such a "magical" (or to use a musical cognate, "enchanted") age, the way that we might understand the role that liturgy and music played in legitimating royal power is clear.[30] Liturgy – as a reflection of the teachings and practices of the universal Catholic church (or perhaps more accurately, the Gallican church) – is a manifestation of the shared conceptual framework that unites the king with his people (and, just as importantly, the nobility and bishops who make up his court) and which teaches that the anointed king reigns with God's express consent.[31] Liturgy structures the extraordinary ceremonies and actions (the coronation, the funeral, the *entrée*, the Te Deum, the induction of the Knights of the Holy Spirit, and many others) that, through their participation, indicate the consent of the people and their acceptance of that framework – in Villette's contemporary words, events that are "the external act of religion, the witness to ... the private devotion that man renders to God." Liturgy also provides numerous opportunities to restate a common trope – though one which we should now reinterpret through Beetham's framework as simply another shared belief rather than as "representation" – that the temporal king could be identified with the biblical King David (or as Foucault would put it, there was a fundamental "resemblance" between the two), since both were chosen by God, and that the psalms (which make up the bulk of texts performed in a liturgical context) spoke not just for David, their author, but for Louis himself, especially when (as King David had famously done) these psalms were performed to musical settings by the king's musicians or when Louis himself sang them.[32]

---

[29] See Rita Costa Gomes, *The Making of a Court Society: Kings and Nobles in Late Medieval Portugal* (Cambridge, Cambridge University Press, 2003), pp. 356–69. Favier's identification of *grand motet* texts that reveal David's faults or weaknesses imply that this model was still in play in at least one sphere during the latter part of Louis XIV's reign; see Favier, 'The French *grand motet*', p. 196.

[30] The whole of this period can be seen in terms of Max Weber's famous process of "disenchantment" and Crouzet's conflicting state of "overenchantment"; see Denis Crouzet, *Les Guerriers de Dieu* (Paris, Champ Vallon, 1990), Vol. 1, p. 143.

[31] The concept of Gallicanism – essentially a measure of independence from Rome and the Pope – though reaching its apogee in 1682, dated back to the Concordat of Bologna of 1516. For still the most comprehensive history see William Jervis, *The Gallican Church: The History of the Church of France from the Concordat of Bologna to the Revolution* (London, John Murray, 1872).

[32] Foucault, *The Order of Things*, p. 17.

Such an analysis also prompts any scholar of ceremonial in the early seventeenth century to re-engage with the so-called ceremonialist or neo-ceremonialist school exemplified by the work of Ralph Giesey, Lawrence Bryant, Richard Jackson, and Sarah Hanley, and, in a similar vein in the Francophone world, Michèle Fogel, Bernard Guenée, and Françoise Lehoux.[33] Jackson, Hanley, and Giesey all identify the 1610 succession of Louis XIII as a turning point between a conception of the monarchy centered around the great ceremonies of state in the sixteenth century (the coronation, the funeral, the *lit de justice*), and one centered around court ritual (essentially secular) in the later seventeenth century.[34] Nevertheless, even for this early period and before, Giesey argued that such ceremonial events were part of an image-making process (the creation of the "king imagined," who "by reenacting a set of tradition-laden dramas" paid homage to his ancestors in ceremonies that "constitute a set of images"), a process that did not depend on any religious or liturgical dimension for its efficacy.[35] Likewise, the studies of the *entrée* by Guenée and Lehoux and by Bryant, while both acknowledging that the ceremony was probably derived from the Corpus Christi procession and noting the concluding ceremony in the cathedral, also relegated the liturgical dimension to a minor side issue.[36] Even more strikingly, Fogel's study of the Te Deum ceremony – a ceremony centered around the liturgical performance of one of the ancient hymns of the church – declined to engage directly with the liturgical act itself, adopting a broad historical/anthropological approach and framing the event as part of a royalist communication strategy. Such studies, then, while certainly documenting the actions that testify to a shared belief system, overlook an essential point of access into

---

[33] Giesey, 'Models of rulership', pp. 41–64; Ralph Giesey, *Cérémonial et puissance souveraine: France, XVe–XVIIe siècle* (Paris, Colin, 1987); Ralph Giesey, 'The King imagined', in Keith Michael Baker (ed.), *The French Revolution and the Creation of Modern Political Culture, Vol. 1: The Political Culture of the Old Régime* (Oxford, Pergamon Press, 1987), pp. 41–59. Lawrence Bryant, *The King and the City in the Parisian Royal Entry Ceremony: Politics, Ritual and Art in the Renaissance* (Geneva, Droz, 1986); Richard Jackson, *Vive le Roi! A History of the French Coronation from Charles V to Charles X* (Chapel Hill, University of North Carolina Press, 1984); Sarah Hanley, *The Lit de Justice of the Kings of France: Constitutional Ideology in Legend, Ritual, and Discourse* (Princeton, Princeton University Press, 1983); Michèle Fogel, *Les Cérémonies d'information dans la France du XVIe au XVIIIe siècle* (Paris, Fayard, 1989); Bernard Guenée and Françoise Lehoux, *Les Entrées royales françaises de 1328 à 1515* (Paris, Éditions du CNRS, 1968).

[34] This is the type of court described by Norbert Elias, trans. Edmund Jephcott, *The Court Society* (New York, Pantheon, 1983). See also Giesey, 'The King imagined', p. 47

[35] Giesey, 'Models of rulership'; 'The King imagined', p. 46.

[36] Guenée and Lehoux, *Entrées royales*, p. 18; Bryant, *King and the City*, pp. 17–18.

what that shared belief system might consist of: such an approach is surely especially called for when we consider that such ceremonies were often framed by, and responded to, some of the most extreme religious violence France had ever seen. By contrast, Kate van Orden's musicological study of the Te Deum ceremony and processions in late sixteenth-century France (a study that my own work is indebted to) focuses both on the action and the underlying belief system, exploring in broad terms some of the meanings that liturgical items such as the Te Deum and Psalm 19, *Exaudiat te Dominus*, held for the participants and those observing, and how they were used to bind groups together, to "discipline" the nobility in support of the king.[37] Yet how much more might we gain by exploring even more deeply the broader religious, ceremonial, and liturgical framework in which the king – in this case Louis XIII – was embedded, and approaching all these events not just from the anthropological/performative perspective of act, but by reintroducing an explicitly textual dimension, supplemented by a musical reading?

This study, then, aims to revisit the terrain of both the ceremonialists and others concerned with "the arts" and power by centering an investigation of legitimizing strategies around the specifics of liturgical texts and the musical and ideological response to them. An exploration of liturgical practices during the reign of Louis XIII is not intrinsically problematic. Numerous sources survive, many of which will feature in this study, both centrally mandated from Rome or locally developed at court, in religious houses, or in the provinces. The same, however, cannot be said for musical sources, nor does the current musicological literature help much with this endeavor. (The important work of Favier and Montagnier is primarily concerned with the later period.) There is little surviving or identifiable "repertoire" for the *musique de la chapelle royale* (it did not play the same dominant role that it would later in the century under Louis XIV), and until recently, apart from a handful of works by Nicolas Formé, very few surviving musical sources could be directly associated with the court at all.[38] Outside the court, the royal publishers Ballard focused mainly on volumes of *airs de cour*, though they did issue generic collections containing vespers psalms, simple Mass settings, and hymns by Charles

---

[37] Kate van Orden, *Music, Discipline, and Arms in Early Modern France* (Chicago, Chicago University Press, 2005), esp. ch. 1, 'The Cross and the Sword'.

[38] Although we can probably assume that the works of *sous-maître* Eustache Du Caurroy (d. 1609) continued to be performed into the reign of Louis XIII; see Marie-Alexis Colin (ed.), *Eustache Du Caurroy: Preces Ecclesiasticae* (Paris, Klincksieck, 2000).

d'Ambleville (1636, two volumes) and Jean de Bournonville (1612/25), produced primarily for use in cathedrals and collegiate churches with a moderately proficient *maîtrise*, alongside more ambitious publications such as the Requiem Masses by Eustache Du Caurroy (posthumous) and Étienne Moulinié, both in 1636.[39] Such publications have barely received more than a mention in now aging studies and surveys by Anthony, Dufourcq, and Launay, while the handful of publications that survive either incomplete (missing part-books, such as the psalms of Artus Auxcousteaux of 1631, the motets by Nicolas Le Vavasseur from the 1620s, or the street music by Nicolas Métru) or as fragments (such as the Office of Saint Cecilia by Abraham Blondet of 1611) do not feature at all.[40] The slightly later tradition of published polyphonic Mass settings has received a recent monograph-length study by Jean-Paul Montagnier (though most surviving works fall outside the reign of Louis XIII),[41] but apart from the works by Formé already mentioned, none of these "standard" publications (in that they were typically created to be generic, for a wide market) plays more than a passing role in this study. Instead, the majority of the most revealing and relevant musical sources are found either in the fragments described above or anonymously preserved in a handful of rich yet still mainly unexplored manuscripts, manuscripts that provide much of the musical foundation of this study. The first of these, which I explored in an earlier monograph (and which I will refer to as the Paris manuscript), is preserved in the Bibliothèque nationale de France and contains several hundred mainly anonymous works copied in score. Probably compiled by the composer André Péchon, *maître de musique* at the church of Saint-Germain-l'Auxerrois, the volume contains repertoire composed during the 1620s and 1630s from circles closely associated with the court, from

---

[39] For an overview of the publishing landscape and details of these works see Laurent Guillo, *Pierre I Ballard et Robert III Ballard, Imprimeurs du roy pour la musique (1599–1673)* (Liège, Mardaga, 2003).

[40] See James Anthony, *French Baroque Music from Beaujoyeulx to Rameau* (Portland, Amadeus Press, 1997); Denise Launay, *La Musique religieuse en France du Concile de Trente à 1804* (Paris, Klincksieck, 1993); Norbert Dufourcq, *La Musique française* (Paris, Picard, 1970), pp. 145–8; Catherine Massip, 'Paris, 1600–61', in Curtis Price (ed.), *The Early Baroque Era: Man & Music* (London, Palgrave Macmillan, 1993); Robert Isherwood, *Music in the Service of the King* (Ithaca, Cornell University Press, 1973). For an interesting overview that intersects with this study see Frédéric Gabriel, 'Chanter Dieu à la Cour: théologie, politique et liturgie', in Jean Duron (ed.), *Regards sur la musique au temps de Louis XIII* (Wavre, Mardaga, 2007), pp. 27–43.

[41] Jean-Paul Montagnier, *The Polyphonic Mass in France, 1600–1780: The Evidence of the Printed Choirbooks* (Cambridge, Cambridge University Press, 2017). Also intersecting with this study is Alexander Robinson, *Musique et musiciens à la cour d'Henri IV (1589–1610)* (PhD dissertation, University of Paris-Sorbonne, 2015).

the Abbey of Montmartre, and from the cathedral of Notre-Dame, in addition to preserving part of the repertoire of the church of Saint-Germain-l'Auxerrois itself.[42] A second manuscript, now preserved in Tours (I will refer to it as the Tours manuscript, although it was probably copied in Paris and contains works composed in the southwest of France), contains again largely anonymous pieces in score, some ninety of them concordant with pieces in the Paris manuscript.[43] Finally an incomplete set of part-books now preserved in the Newberry Library, Chicago, contains mainly anonymous repertoire associated with the cathedral of Saint-Sauveur, Avignon, dating from the 1620s (I will refer to this source as the Newberry/Avignon manuscript).[44]

Over the course of the next eight chapters, then, these sources will form the basis of an exploration of the various musical and liturgical responses to Louis XIII and the ideological frameworks encoded within them. Chapter 3, for example, shows how in 1618, shortly after Louis had begun his personal rule (after the assassination of Concini and the disgrace of his mother, Marie de Médicis), a liturgy was developed around the figure of the king's namesake and thirteenth-century ancestor Saint Louis, a liturgy that reframed the saint – long seen as a humble and devout favorite of the mendicant orders – as a model of divine kingship itself. And Chapter 6 shows how, at the Abbey of Montmartre, the liturgy, the chant declamation, and the music itself reflected the ideology of the Guise family who controlled it, through the promotion of Saint Denis and his conflation with Pseudo-Dionysius (symbols of kingship co-opted by the Guises during the Wars of Religion), and through the adoption of a classical or Neoplatonic

---

[42] Paris, Bibliothèque nationale de France, V^{ma} MS rés. 571; see Peter Bennett, *Sacred Repertories in Paris under Louis XIII: Bibliothèque nationale de France MS V^{ma} rés. 571*, Royal Musical Association Monographs, 17 (Farnham, Ashgate, 2009); and Denise Launay (ed.), *Anthologie du motet latin polyphonique en France (1606–61)* (Paris, Société française de musicologie, Heugel, 1963).

[43] Tours, Bibliothèque municipale, MS 168; see Peter Bennett, *Sacred Repertories in Paris, 1630–43: Paris, Bibliothèque nationale de France, V^{ma} rés. 571* (DPhil dissertation, Oxford University, 2004). See also Henri Quittard, 'Un musicien oublié du xviie siècle: G. Bouzignac', *Sammelbände der Internationalen Musik-Gesellschaft*, 6 (1904–5), 356–471, and Denise Launay, 'G. Bouzignac', *Musique et liturgie*, 21 (1951), 3–8. The manuscript is also the subject of an ongoing research project at the CMBV, led by Jean Duron and to be published online.

[44] Chicago, Newberry Library, Case MS 5136, 5123; see Laurent Guillo, 'Un recueil de motets de Sauvaire Intermet (Avignon, *c.* 1620–1625): Chicago, Newberry Library, Case MS 5136', *Dix-septième siècle*, 232 (2006/3), 453–75; Peter Bennett, 'The *entrée royale* and the *Exaudiat te Dominus* in early seventeenth-century France: Evidence from Chicago, Newberry Library, Case MS 5123', in Bernard Dompnier, Catherine Massip, and Solveig Serre (eds.), *Musique en liberté. Entre la cour et les provinces au temps des Bourbons* (Paris, École nationale des chartes, 2018), pp. 113–26.

musical ideology, both of which can be seen as strategies of opposition to the king. On the other hand, as we see in Chapter 7, by the end of his reign, as a reaction to the rising influence of the *dévots*, a Christocentric model of kingship took hold, reflected in the compositions by Nicolas Formé that were published as a response to the 1638 dedication of the kingdom of France to the Virgin Mary.

Dominant among these ideologies, however, is that of the Davidic/biblical model of kingship, embraced with new-found enthusiasm by those around the king following the assassination of Henri III and Henri IV, in what we might call the central track of the absolutist project, a track I introduce and explore (together with the parallel musical ideologies) in Chapter 1. But it is certainly not true to say that this ideology was uniform or only applied in the ways we might expect. Chapter 4, for example, shows how, at the heart of the court – in the *musique de la chambre* and the *musique de la chapelle royale* – music and liturgy brought the penitential and supplicatory character of the king to the foreground, a David who had betrayed Bathsheba and whose son Absalom had died in tragic circumstances. While such a "representation" is hard to understand if seen as propaganda, in the framework I am proposing instead, such a correspondence is unproblematic – indeed advantageous. David exhibited weakness and imperfection, yet was still chosen by God to lead the people of Israel: any weakness or imperfection in Louis, then, was not disqualifying – indeed it made him all the more similar to the model of all kings. Still at court, Chapter 2 shows how, by contrast, Louis's 1610 coronation ceremony invoked a conception of David as the unique vehicle of the Holy Spirit, whose anointing, confirmation, and induction as a Knight of the Order of the Holy Spirit at Reims were in fact the central theme in a much broader complex of ceremonial events than is usually considered as the "coronation." Outside the court, by contrast, a different set of motives came into play. In Paris and the other prosperous urban centers of France (as Chapter 3 shows) popular pamphlets and tracts presented the king as a David whose double-edged sword would defeat the heretics as it had Goliath: in the same way, composers closely associated with the court, such as Artus Auxcousteaux, dedicated their collections of psalm settings to the king, emphasizing his affinity with David the warrior, whose psalms celebrated military success and musical prowess. Finally, in the provinces of the south and southwest directly affected by the religious wars (Chapter 5), we see how the ceremonial *entrée*, although following a general plan handed down for centuries in which the king processed through a sequence of classical arches in imitation of a Roman triumph, was actually concluded by a ceremony in the city cathedral that invoked David in probably the most surprising way.

Louis XIII is, of course, often overlooked as a monarch – overshadowed by his son, ridiculed by Dumas and Tallemant de Réaux, and neglected by historians into the twenty-first century. Yet he lived at a moment in history that, almost by definition, makes his reign consequential. Coming to power at the dawn of the Age of Reason, yet still the beneficiary of a "magical" or "enchanted" worldview, Louis XIII occupied a position, to use a well-worn cliché, at the crossroads of history. While the larger political and historical issues fall outside the scope of this study, the music considered here, and its interaction with the liturgy, nevertheless have, I would argue, broader significance. Just, then, as images of Louis XIV in his *chapelle royale* might prompt us to ask questions about how music and "the arts" served that king, so too should our mental image of Louis XIII at prayer in his chamber after the assassination of Concini in 1617, singing psalms while camped out at the siege of La Rochelle in 1628, listening to the priests of the church of the Oratory imitating the singing style of David himself, or making his ceremonial *entrée* into Montpellier in 1622. In all these cases, it is the music, the sounding manifestation of the liturgy, that carries one of the essential messages about the event, conveys its underlying ideology, and – albeit in one circumscribed domain – sheds light on the process of legitimating power itself.

1 | David's Harp, Apollo's Lyre

Psalms, Music, and Kingship in the Sixteenth Century

On All Saints' Day, November 1, 1628, an elaborate sequence of religious processions and ceremonies celebrated the surrender of the port city of La Rochelle and the defeat of the Huguenot rebels who had occupied it since the previous year. After a brutal siege lasting some fourteen months, personally overseen by Cardinal Richelieu and often attended by Louis XIII himself, the rebels had finally capitulated and Louis's status as "most Christian" king was now assured after nearly two decades of religious and political unrest.[1] The day began with a Mass celebrated by Cardinal Richelieu at the Church of Sainte-Marguerite (the only Catholic church still standing in the city) in the presence of the priests of Congrégation de l'oratoire de Jésus-Christ (who had arrived the previous day from Bordeaux), together with other courtiers and military commanders.[2] A second Mass celebrated by the Archbishop of Bordeaux, Henri d'Escoubleau de Sourdis (who had also been an artillery commander at the siege), was followed by a procession through the crowded streets by the Capucins and Récollets carrying crosses and singing the Te Deum as they marched. At the same time, a group of sixty to eighty of the Frères religieux de la charité had set out from their *quartier* and also approached Sainte-Marguerite, this time singing psalms. The processions all met at the church where a third Mass was celebrated, ending at 1.00 p.m.

The day's celebrations culminated in the king's ceremonial entry to the city. In a typical "triumphal" *entrée*, Louis, dressed in his royal finery, would be met at the city walls by the civic dignitaries, process through a series of classically inspired triumphal arches, and be received by the ecclesiastical authorities at the city's main church. On this occasion, by contrast, the king arrived without overt display, dressed simply in his armor, receiving no civic ceremony or pomp.[3] Nevertheless, several

---

[1] A. Lloyd Moote, *Louis XIII, the Just* (Berkeley, Los Angeles, and London, University of California Press, 1989), pp. 194–8.

[2] For a complete account, see *Le Mercure françois*, 14 (1628/9), 708–9.

[3] For the distinction between a "victorious" and "triumphal" *entrée*, see Marie-Claude Canova Green, 'Warrior King or King of War? Louis XIII's Entries into his *bonnes villes* (1620–1629)', in J.R. Mulryne, Maria Ines Aliverti and Anna Maria Testaverde (eds.), *Ceremonial Entries in Early Modern Europe: The Iconography of Power* (Farnham, Ashgate, 2015), pp. 77–98.

Figure 1.1 Pierre Courtilleau, *The Capture of La Rochelle*. On the left is Louis, with Cardinal Richelieu, Michel de Marillac, and the Maréchal de Schomberg behind. On the right is Henri d'Escoubleau de Sourdis, Archbishop of Bordeaux elect, with the Oratorians of Bordeaux carrying the archiepiscopal cross behind. In the center, Sainte-Marguerite herself is portrayed in her standard yet highly appropriate iconography, trampling the head of the dragon/serpent of heresy.
Musée d'Orbigny-Bernon, La Rochelle/Bridgeman Images

hundred inhabitants of La Rochelle had been instructed to meet him at the gates of the city, and as he approached, in a cruel parody of the usual joyful response at an *entrée*, they threw themselves to their knees and cried out in a loud but trembling voice, "Vive le Roy qui nous a fait miséricorde" (Long live the king, who has shown us mercy). The king then continued on to the church of Sainte-Marguerite to cries of "Vive le Roy" (Long live the king) and "Vive le Roy qui nous a fait grâce" (Long live the king, who has given us grace), where he was greeted by the Archbishop of Bordeaux, accompanied by all the clergy of the city carrying their wooden crosses. (Figure 1.1 shows some of the main protagonists of this event, pictured with the city in the background.) Louis was led into the church, and, after a brief *harangue* from the archbishop, proceeded to a throne in front of the altar where, in a sign taken to reflect his great devotion, he enthusiastically led the singing of the Te Deum.

Kate van Orden has highlighted the significance of both Louis's own singing and his broader participation in the events of the following days that transformed him from "the source of a horrific siege into a beneficent monarch."[4] But those present would also have understood both the ceremony and the wider context in other ways too. After the archbishop had given his benediction, the king's confessor and preacher, Père Jean Souffran, gave a brief exhortation. Likening the king to a pilgrim who, undertaking a long journey through penitence and abnegation, is ultimately crowned in glory, Souffran praised the king for his perseverance in pursuing the Huguenots, continuing:[5]

It is why this great David, Patron and model of all Kings, seeing the disobedience of the Philistines, the enemies of God and his Estate, resolved to humiliate them, saying in Psalm 17, "I will pursue after my enemies, and overtake them: and I will not turn again till they are consumed."

This allusion to Louis's reenactment of David's own conquests was spelled out in a later account of the ceremony by the eighteenth-century ecclesiastical historian Jean-Louis Archon ("That which David did to the Philistines, so too the King has also done to the heretic rebels"),[6] but both this verse and the remainder of the psalm (which begins *Diligam te Domine fortitude meo* in the Vulgate) – though probably unspoken by Souffran – would also have been recognized by all those who heard it, albeit in different ways according to the confessional identity of the listener or, at one remove, the reader, since this information was also included in the widely disseminated published accounts of the ceremony.

For the Huguenots, whose own liturgy prioritized congregational psalm singing, and who would therefore probably have known Clément Marot's rhyming translation/paraphrase of the Hebrew by heart, Psalm 17 (18 in the Huguenot numbering) opens with the *quatrain* (emphasis mine):[7]

Je t'aimeray en toute obéissance	I will love you in all obedience
Tant que vivray, ô mon Dieu ma puissance.	As long as I live, O God my strength.
Dieu est mon *roc*, mon *rampart*, haut & seur,	God is my *rock*, my *rampart*, high and safe,
C'est ma rançon, c'est mon fort défenseur.	He is my ransom, he is my strong defender.

---

[4] Kate van Orden, *Music, Discipline, and Arms in Early Modern France* (Chicago, University of Chicago Press, 2005), pp. 182–5.

[5] *Le Mercure françois*, 14 (1628/9), 712–13: "C'est ainsi que fit ce grand David, Patron et modelle de tous les Roys, lequel voyant la désobéissance des Philistins ennemis de Dieu & de son Estat, se résolut de les humilier, disant au Pseaume 17. 'Persequar inimicos meos, & comprehendam illos: & non revertar donec deficient.'"

[6] Jean-Louis Archon, *Histoire ecclésiastique de la Chapelle des Rois de France* (Paris, Le Mercier, 1711), p. 757: "ce que David avoit fait à l'égard des Philistins, le Roy l'avoit fait aussi à l'égard des hérétiques rebelles."

[7] Clément Marot and Théodore de Bèze, *Les Pseaumes mis en rime françoise* (Lyon, Vincent, 1562), p. 68 (English translation my own).

Louis Budé's 1551 prose version, translated at Calvin's request and subsequently incorporated into revisions of Calvin's preferred biblical text, the Olivetan translation, adopts a similar strategy:[8]

3. Le Seigneur est mon *roc* & ma *forteresse*, & mon libérateur, mon Dieu, ma *roche* ...

The Lord is my *rock* and my *fortress*, and my liberator, my God, my *rock* ...

The Huguenots, who had just lost La Rochelle (a fortress known as "the (little) rock"), and whose worldview did not associate the psalms with the earthly monarchy, could therefore take comfort in the lines of the psalmist, King David, reassuring them that it was now God who was their rock and defender. For the Catholics, the corresponding verse in the Vulgate translation (the "official" Bible of the Catholic Church) did not allude to rocks or "La Rochelle" explicitly, but the remainder of the psalm nonetheless would have confirmed to them that it was their victory that the psalmist was describing. Among too many verses to quote in full are, for example:[9]

40. And thou hast girded me with strength unto battle; and hast subdued under me them that rose up against me.

...

44. Thou wilt deliver me from the contradictions of the people: thou wilt make me head of the Gentiles [i.e. the Huguenots].

But those more widely read clerics who took a particular interest in combating the heretical Huguenot translations would also have been familiar with the newer, "unofficial" Catholic versions of the psalms in prose. Plantin's so-called Polyglot Bible, based on the work of Hebrew scholar Sancte Pagnini (1470–1541), was reissued numerous times and available in France during the sixteenth century, with the psalms also receiving their own dedicated volume in subsequent editions:[10] the widely available interlinear *Psalmi Davidis hebraici* of 1615, for example, presented the Hebrew text alongside the Greek and Latin Vulgate, and provided a new Latin translation of the Hebrew.[11] Unlike

---

[8] Loys Budé, *Les Pseaumes de David traduicts selon la vérité Hébraïque* (Geneva, Jehan Crespin, 1551), pp. 30–1. Calvin's approved Bible, the Olivetan translation of 1535, was subject to continuous revision, with Calvin's preface to the 1553 edition crediting Budé and Bèze for help with the Psalms and the Apocrypha. See Pierre-Robert Olivetan, *La Bible, qui est toute la Saincte Escripture* (Geneva, Robert Estienne, 1553).

[9] English translation from the Challoner revision of the 1609 Douay–Reims Bible, *The Holy Bible Translated from the Latin Vulgate. Newly Revised and Corrected According to the Clementine Edition of the Scriptures* (Dublin, 1750).

[10] *Biblia Sacra hebraice, chaldaice, graece, & latine* (Antwerp, Christophe Plantin, 1569–73).

[11] *Psalmi Davidis hebraici, cum interlineari versione Xantis Pagnini* (Antwerp, Plantin, 1615).

the Vulgate, the Pagnini edition used the Latin *petra* (rock) to translate the Hebrew in verse 3 (*Dominus, petra mea*) but also, most notably, in the peroration of the psalm (verse 46 in the Vulgate, 47 in the Hebrew) where King David thanks God for his victory, once again in strikingly apposite language:[12]

46. Vivit Dominus & benedictus *petra* mea, & exaltet Deus salutis meae.

Jehovah liveth – and blessed is my *rock* [i.e. La Rochelle is mine, i.e. David's, i.e. Louis's]. And exalted is the God of my salvation.

. . .

50. Magnificans salutes regis sui, & facies misericordia uncto suo David, & semini eius; usque in seculum.

Magnifying the salvation of His King [Louis], and doing kindness to his anointed, to David, and to his seed – unto the age!

Both sides could thus appropriate the words of King David to lay claim to "the rock," although it was obviously the king and the Catholics who could overwhelmingly reap the military, political, and religious rewards: on hearing the news that La Rochelle had fallen, Pope Urban VIII processed with all his cardinals to the French national church of San Luigi dei Francesi in Rome, where he heard a Mass and a Te Deum.[13] And a papal brief to the king shortly afterward expressed the gratitude of the Holy See: "By your long siege of many months you have taught us that *Europe* oweth your *French* Legions no less commendation for their constancy, than for their expedition."[14] After a decade in which papal antipathy to the French monarchy had frequently reached crisis point, and in which the integrity of the kingdom of France had come under real threat, it is hard to overestimate the sense that Louis really was a new David, and that the kingdom of Israel/France had finally been delivered from its enemies.

---

[12] Latin translation of the Hebrew from *Psalmi Davidis, Proverbia Salomonis, Ecclesiastes et Canticum Canticorum Hebraicè, cum interlineari versione Santis Pagnini* (Paris, Cramoisy, 1632). English translation of the Hebrew (and Greek) from *Young's Literal Translation*. The Hebrew word used here and in verse 3/2 is *tsur*, which, together with *sela'*, translates directly to "rock." I am very grateful to Professor Timothy Beal for his translations and for his assistance in navigating the interlinear Hebrew and Latin text.

[13] *Le Mercure françois*, 15 (1629), 105–15.

[14] English translation in *A Breeve of Our Holy Father the Pope to the King upon the Taking of Rochell[e]* (London, Martin, 1629), p. 2.

Confessional Identity and Ideologies of the Psalms

The availability of numerous competing translations of the psalter, and the way in which they could subsequently be heard, quoted, and preached on, are, of course, simply reflections of the broader and longer history of the psalms in early modern France and their role in the religious, political, and cultural debates of the era. Under François I (r. 1515–47), the humanist orientation of the court had trumped any confessional disagreements over the role of biblical translations, and so the Protestant versions – those of Clément Marot, for example – were generally welcomed by virtue of their confessionally neutral, "classical" framing, even if, in practice, Marot's translations eschewed the elevated literary style that would shortly come to be associated with humanist poetry.[15] In his dedicatory letter to Francis I, for example, Marot draped the Holy Scriptures (and especially the psalms) in mythological garb, appealing:[16]

Thus, O King, take the work of David,
An earlier work of God, who takes delight in it,
Especially since God was his Apollo,
Who puts him and his harp in motion.
The Holy Spirit was his Calliope,
His Parnassus, the double-peaked mountain,
Was the summit of the high crystal heavens ...

With the court's enthusiasm for the culture of antiquity, an enthusiasm which persisted into the middle of the century and beyond, it was easy enough for the royal family to adopt Marot's translations, and even to become known for and identified with, their favorite psalms: in his posthumously published attack on the Huguenots, Florimond de Raemond describes how Henri II took Marot's version of Psalm 42/41 as his favorite, singing it while hunting ("Ainsi qu'on oyt le cerf bruire" [*Quemadmodum desiderat cervus*]), as well as apparently composing a melody for Psalm 128/127 ("Bien heureux est quiconque sert Dieu volontiers" [*Beati omnes*]);

---

[15] For François I's humanist orientation, see Emmanuel le Roy Ladurie, *The Royal French State, 1460–1610* (Oxford, Blackwell, 1994), pp. 109–23, and Franco Giacone, 'Les Lorraine et le psautier', in Yvonne Bellenger (ed.), *Le Mécénat et l'influence des Guises* (Paris, Champion, 1997), pp. 345–63.

[16] Clément Marot, *Cinquante-deux pseaumes de David, traduictz en rithme Françoyse selon la vérité Hébraïque* (Paris, Estienne Croulleau, 1556), n.p.: "O doncques Roy, prens l'œuvre de David / Œuvre plus tost de Dieu qui le ravit, / D'autant que Dieu son Apollo estoit, / Qui luy en train & sa harpe mettoit. / Le sainct esprit estoit sa Calliope, / Son Parnassus, montaigne à double croppe, / Fut le sommet du hault ciel cristallin ..."

while among other members of the court, Diane de Poitiers, Henri II's mistress, took Psalm 130/129 ("Du fond de ma pensée" [*De profundis clamavi*]).[17] Indeed, in the middle of the century, the pan-confessional and generally uncontroversial nature of Marot's paraphrases was reflected in the number of Catholic writers who attempted to complete his translations (he provided only around fifty of the 150 psalms in the psalter), ignoring the fact that Calvin and his congregation in Geneva had adopted and become closely identified with them.[18] But from around 1550, and into the 1560s, the reception, and subsequently execution, of psalm translations began to split along confessional lines – a "confessional divorce," as Jeanneret puts it.[19] The 1553 edition of the now completed Protestant psalter (Théodore de Bèze had contributed the remaining 100 psalms) included doctrinaire texts by Calvin that undermined the "confessional neutrality" of the paraphrases, rendering them unacceptable at a court that was at the same time becoming less and less tolerant of religious and confessional diversity. And yet, while de Bèze's own activism and associations with the psalms certainly made them less attractive from a Catholic confessional perspective, it was as much the literary quality of the paraphrases that condemned them to the newly emerging and highly influential Pléiade poets and those who followed their lead. While Marot had only half-heartedly invoked the poetry of antiquity as his inspiration, members of the Pléiade engaged in a genuine effort to elevate French poetry by returning to classical models (particularly the ode and the sonnet), by emphasizing the close connection of poetry to music (which they saw as inextricably linked), and by rejecting Marot's accessible and popular approach in a belief that poetry should be reserved for the aristocracy and that biblical text should be revealed only to those qualified and of appropriate moral standing to interpret it.[20]

Leading the charge of the Pléiade was Pierre de Ronsard, who in 1562, paraphrasing Plato's *Ion* and *Phaedrus*, urged Catholic poets to fight back

---

[17] Florimond de Raemond, *L'Histoire de la naissance, progrez et décadence de l'hérésie de ce siècle* (Paris, Veuve Guillaume de la Noue, 1610), p. 1043.

[18] Figures such as Maurice Scève, Jean Poictevin (who dedicated his translation to Charles, Cardinal de Lorraine), and lesser-known figures such as Gilles d'Aurigny and Louis de Masure all made steps toward completing the Marot psalter without any concern for its Geneva usage; see Michel Jeanneret, *Poésie et tradition biblique au xvie siècle* (Paris, J. Corti, 1969), p. 187; and Giacone, 'Les Lorraine et le psautier'.

[19] Jeanneret, *Poésie et tradition biblique*, ibid.

[20] Jeanneret, *Poésie et tradition biblique*, p. 188. For an overview of the Pléiade's relationship with music (from a secular perspective), see also Howard Mayer Brown, '*Ut musica poesis*: Music and poetry in France in the late sixteenth century', *Early Music History*, 13 (1994), 1–63.

against the Huguenot debasing of the language ("songs for the shopkeepers"),[21] while at the same time responding in kind to the effective literary proselytizing strategy that they had adopted:[22]

Just as the enemy has seduced by books
The errant peoples who falsely follow it,
We must in response confound them with books,
With books assault them, with books answer them.

Ronsard himself never responded to the psalms of Marot by producing his own translations (he provided only a paraphrase of the Te Deum), since, by the time of his ascendancy, much of Christian literature had effectively taken a different turn, leaving its biblical roots and the psalms behind.[23] Although numerous moralizing primers continued to appear for the instruction of children, many of which took their inspiration from the books of the Old Testament, for the educated elite the Bible now no longer represented a fashionable worldview.[24] Instead, it began to see the world through the lens of classical antiquity, seeking a Neoplatonic solution to the moral and religious problems of the day: and so, just as Plato had insisted that music (which he considered essentially poetry animated with rhythm and pitch) should be well-regulated for a state to prosper, so too should be the "music" (i.e. the lyric poetry of the by now semi-official Pléiade) of France (see below for more discussion on this). Nevertheless, the poetry the members of the Pléiade and its successors produced was still intended to counteract the destabilizing influence of the opponents of the Catholic church, even if reference to the church or the Bible was minimal. Ronsard himself certainly acknowledged this practice ("Ah! les Chrestiens devroient les Gentils imiter" [Ah! the Christians must imitate

---

[21] Pierre de Ronsard, *Response ... aux injures et calomnies de je ne sçay quell Predicantereaux et Ministreaux de Genève*, in *Discours des Misères de ce temps* in M. Prosper Blanchemin (ed.), *Œuvres complètes de P. de Ronsard* (Paris, A. Franck, 1866), Vol. 7, pp. 127–8: "chansons aux valets de boutique." See also Paul Laumonier, *Ronsard, poète lyrique: étude historique et littérarire* (Paris, Hachette, 1932) p. 302.

[22] Ronsard, *Discours à G. Des-Autels*, in *Discours des misères de ce temps*, in Blanchemin (ed.), *Œuvres*, p. 40: "Ainsi que l'ennemy par livres a séduit / Le peuple desvoyé qui faussement le suit, / Il faut en disputant par livres le confondre, / Par livres l'assaillir, par livres luy responder."

[23] Another approach, taken by Guy Le Fèvre de la Boderie, was to acknowledge that the Psalms were now Huguenot "property" and to focus on other texts – for him, the "Hymnes Ecclésiastiques, et autres Cantiques Spirituels composés par les Saints Docteurs"; see Jeanneret, *Poésie et tradition biblique*, p. 196.

[24] Most notably those by Guy du Faur de Pibrac; see Kate van Orden, *Materialities: Books, Readers, and the Chanson in Sixteenth-Century Europe* (Oxford and New York, Oxford University Press, 2015), pp. 228–66.

the Gentiles, i.e. the Greeks/Romans]),[25] as did Cardinal du Perron, who argued at Ronsard's funeral that he:[26]

> knew so well [how] to bring the riches and the treasures of Egypt to the Holy Land, that one recognizes immediately that all the elegance and all the sweetness of letters and of the humanities is not on the side of the heretics, as they pretend.

Despite the relative lack of interest in the Bible and the psalms from Ronsard himself, the 1560s saw other members of the Pléiade adopting a different strategy, attempting (as the wider religious situation deteriorated) to reconcile the biblical and humanist/Neoplatonic approaches to poetry. In their syncretic worldview, another lyric poet of antiquity – King David, author of the psalms, and a musician whose poetry, sung to the accompaniment of the harp, had calmed the afflicted Saul – could serve just as well, a new Apollo or Orpheus whose powers could be invoked to restore the religious harmony of the kingdom. Gabriel Dupuyherbault's translation of the psalms into French prose of 1554 (reprinted in 1563) had pointed out that David was a more excellent poet than Homer, Pindar, and Euripides, while observing that his own translation was "très nécessaire en ce temps," but the "resemblance" between the biblical king and the real and mythical poets of antiquity was, more broadly, already a familiar Renaissance trope.[27] Thus a new type of poetry developed, either taking David for overall inspiration (e.g. Du Bellay, *La Lyre chrestienne*), or using psalm texts as the basis for loose paraphrases that – when appropriate classical imagery could not be found – allegorized the successes of the king over his enemies and provided justification from both classical and biblical sources for his actions.[28]

None of these strategies or publications, however, can be considered as a direct or comprehensive Catholic response to the complete psalter of Marot and de Bèze. It thus famously fell to Jean-Antoine de Baïf to integrate the humanist/Neoplatonic principles of the Pléiade (in fact, to take them much

---

[25] Ronsard, *Les Hymnes*, in *Pièces posthumes*, in Blanchemin (ed.), *Œuvres*, Vol. 2, p. 652.

[26] Henri Chamard, *Histoire de la Pléiade* (Paris, Didier, 1939–40), Vol. 2, p. 372: "sceut si bien apporter les richesses et les trésors d'Aegypte en la Terre Saincte, que l'on recognut incontinent que toute l'élégance et toute la douceur des lettres et de l'humanité n'estoit pas du costé des hérétiques, comme ils prétendoient."

[27] Gabriel Dupuyherbault, *Psaumes de David, traduicts au plus près de leur sens propre & naturel* (Paris, Jehan de Roigny, 1563), n.p. The introduction to this volume recounts in detail the musical and poetic prowess of the poets of antiquity and the power to move the feelings of the listener, but reports that "Et bien, ores que tout ce fust vray, quel musicien avons nous en nostre David?" (Even so, while all that may be true, what a musician we have in our David).

[28] A. Gouverneur (ed.), *Œuvres complètes de Remy Belleau* (Paris, Franck, 1867), pp. 110–23.

further) with the texts of the psalms in an ambitious project undertaken under the patronage of Charles IX together with the composer Joachim Thibault de Courville and others – the Académie de poésie et de musique.

The Académie de poésie et de musique has long been recognized for its members' attempts to recreate the music of classical antiquity, most notably in the groundbreaking studies by Frances A. Yates and Daniel Pickering Walker.[29] Operating under a royal charter granted in 1570 and meeting in Jean-Antoine de Baïf's house just outside the walls of Paris near the Abbey of Saint-Victoire, the Académie attempted to bring back into use "both the kind of poetry and the measure and rule of music anciently used by the Greeks and Romans," something they hoped to achieve by completely integrating music and text in accordance with their readings of Plato, Plutarch, and others. Inspired by the famous accounts of the "effects" of ancient music (in which either the mode or the rhythm of a song was able to change behavior for the better), they also hoped to bring stability to the country and reconcile the opposing religious forces.

The mechanism by which this ancient music would act was described in great detail by the main theorist of the Académie, Pontus de Tyard (who in turn took most of his inspiration from the Neoplatonist Marsilio Ficino) in his *Solitaire premier* (1552). According to "the Platonic philosophers," during its descent into the body, the soul loses its unity with the sovereign One, that is, God. The task of mankind, therefore, is to return the soul to its initial state of perfection, a process that involves four steps of ascent, culminating in a state of "angelic understanding." While it is difficult to see how the three final steps could be executed, Tyard is crystal clear about the first: a "poetic fury" that awakens the drowsy parts of the soul:[30]

... by the tones of Music, and soothing the perturbed part by the suavity of sweet harmony: then, by the well-accorded diversity of musical accords, chasing away the dissonant discords, and finally reducing the disorder to a certain equality, well and proportionately measured, and ordered in the gracious and grave facility of verses regulated by the careful observance of number and measure.

---

[29] Frances A. Yates, *The French Academies of the Sixteenth Century*, Studies of the Warburg Institute, 15 (London, Warburg Institute, 1947); Daniel Pickering Walker, 'Musical humanism in the 16th and early 17th centuries', *The Music Review*, 2 (1941), 1–13; 3 (1942), 111–21, 220–7, 288–308; 4 (1943), 55–71. Yates drew much of her biographical information on Baïf from Mathieu Auge-Chiquet, *La Vie, les idées et l'œuvre de Jean-Antoine de Baïf* (Paris, Hachette, 1909, repr. Geneva, Slatkine, 1969).

[30] Quoted in Yates, *French Academies*, p. 80.

The practical way in which they achieved this integration of music and text was to go beyond the reforms of the poets of the Pléiade (who, while aspiring to many of the aims of the Académie, had not made such radical revisions to their conception of lyric poetry)[31] and to impose the long and short syllables used in Latin poetry – and the meters and poetic feet used by the poets of antiquity – to the French language, thereby creating what they called *vers mesurés à l'antique* which could then be completely integrated with its musical setting to produce *musique mesurée*.[32] Although some composers attempted to interpret the long and short syllables flexibly (notably Caietain), the archetypal musical setting would (in keeping with the rules of antiquity, and as preserved in the published musical settings of Baïf by Jacques Mauduit and Claude Le Jeune) treat a long syllable as exactly twice as long as a short syllable.[33] In further imitation of the Latin verse, rhyme was no longer a relevant consideration: thus a piece of *musique mesurée* would feature strophic verse, organized into rigidly structured poetic feet that were in turn organized into a higher structure (a "hyperfoot"), no rhyme, and a musical setting that exactly translated long and short syllables into the musical values of a minim and crotchet. Since the old imitative polyphony of the previous decades confused the declamation of the text and thereby lessened the "effects" of the music, *musique mesurée* was also completely homophonic, moving in block chords with no independence of voices.[34]

Although subsequent publications of *musique mesurée* prioritized secular works (Jacques Mauduit's settings of Baïf's *Chansonettes mesurées* published in 1586, and a few works in Caietain's *Airs mis en musique* of

---

[31] For the relationship of the Pléiade to lyric poetry, see Mayer Brown, '*Ut musica poesis*'.

[32] Baïf was not, in fact, the first to try and bring back the meters of antiquity; see Donat Lamothe, *Claude Le Jeune, le Psautier huguenot et la musique religieuse a la Cour pendant les règnes de Charles IX, Henri III et Henri IV* (PhD dissertation, University of Strasbourg, 1980), p. 79. Agrippa d'Aubigné reports that that Estienne Jodelle "en avait fait avant lui [Baïf] et meilleurs," and publications such as Jacques de la Taille, *Manière de faire des vers en français comme en grec et en latin*, 1573, confirm a broader interest in this approach to poetry. Looking back at the sixteenth century, Estienne Pasquier devotes several chapters to a comparison of Latin and French verse and declares that French is capable of adopting the measured verse of Latin and Greek; see Estienne Pasquier, *Les Recherches de la France* (Paris, Laurens Sonnius, 1621), pp. 651–2.

[33] For a discussion of this important issue, see Daniel Pickering Walker, 'Aspects and problems of *musique mesurée à l'antique*: The rhythm and notation of *musique mesurée*', *Musica Disciplina*, 4 (1950), 163–86.

[34] Pontus de Tyard argued for a monodic rendition of this new kind of music, while Claude Le Jeune thought it best to retain the advances made in harmony since the days of antiquity; see Walker, 'Musical humanism', 4 (1943), 55–71.

1578), reclaiming the psalm was undoubtedly central to the Académie's aims.[35] Baïf's first complete translation of the psalter from the Hebrew (rather than from the Vulgate or Greek) into measured French verse was executed between 1567 and 1569, during the Third Religious War and before the "official" foundation of the Académie in 1570.[36] Never published in its original form, the autograph manuscript describes the translation as a "psalter begun with the intention of serving good Catholics against the psalms of the heretics."[37] Yet, despite Baïf's outward confessional hostility, the Académie must still have been a tolerant organization, since it was this 1567–9 set of translations that the Huguenot composer Claude Le Jeune began to set (probably around 1570), and which he later published in modified form in his *Pseaumes en vers mesurez* of 1606.[38] Baïf's second translation of the psalter of 1573 (the year after the St. Bartholomew's Day Massacre of 1572) was set to music by another important composer associated with the Académie, Jacques Mauduit, although only a few settings survive, preserved by Marin Mersenne in his *Quaestiones celerrebimae in Genesim* of 1623.[39]

Unlike Le Jeune's settings, which show a much wider variety of scorings and a much more imaginative attempt to transcend the intrinsic limitations of *musique mesurée*, Mauduit's surviving psalms (only a handful, since Mersenne assumed that the remainder would shortly be published elsewhere) are provided with Baïf's phonetic spelling and embody what we have come to expect from *musique mesurée*: a texture entirely of "syllabic homophony," just two note values (long and short), no recognizable musical meter, and poorly comprehensible text unrelated to the natural poetic and syntactic structure of the original Hebrew psalms – all combining to produce a setting that depends entirely for its effectiveness on

---

[35] Yates demonstrates the complete compatibility of the ideals of *musique mesurée* with sacred music, but nonetheless treats the measured psalms as a corollary to the secular poetry; see Yates, *French Academies*, pp. 62–76. See also Marin Mersenne, *Quaestiones celeberrimae in Genesim* (Paris, Sebastien Cramoisy, 1623), cols. 1683–7.

[36] See Auge-Chiquet, *Vie de Baïf*, p. 400 and Yates, *French Academies*, p. 55. At the end of the source, F-Pn MS fonds fr. 19140, Baïf notes he was influenced by translations and commentaries on the Hebrew by Sancte Pagnini, Felix Pratense, Jean Compense, and François Valable.

[37] Ibid.: "Psaultier commencé en intention de servir aux bons catholiques contre les psalmes des hérétiques et fut commencé l'an 1567 au mois de Juillet, achevé ??? novembre 1569." Yates, *French Academies*, pp. 70–1.

[38] The published versions credit the text to the Protestant poet Odet de La Noue, but Noue's texts were clearly derived from Baïf's, reintroducing rhyme while otherwise making few changes. See the Introduction by Isabel His and Jean Vignes to Claude Le Jeune, *Pseaumes en vers mesurez*, ed. Isabelle His (Turnhout, Brepols, 2007). See also Yates, *French Academies*, pp. 66–7.

[39] Mauduit lived well into the seventeenth century and knew Mersenne well.

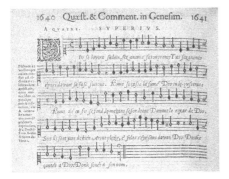

Figure 1.2 Superius part to Jacques Mauduit's setting of Baïf's translation of Psalm 67, "Dieu se lèvera soudain."

Marin Mersenne, *Quaestiones celeberrimae in Genesim* (Paris, Sebastien Cramoisy, 1623), cols. 1640–3. Bibliothèque nationale de France

a complete faith in the principles of the Académie.[40] (See Figure 1.2 for the superius part Mauduit's setting of Psalm 67.)[41]

Ideologies of Kingship

Presumably performed at the regular meetings of the Académie, probably in the presence of Charles IX himself, Mauduit's settings of Baïf's texts (even more than Le Jeune's) represent the high-water mark for the representation of Christian truths through the language of antiquity. At the same time, a figure moving in the same elite court circles, Jean Bodin, was constructing a theory of monarchy that shared common philosophical and ideological ground with Baïf's translations, formalizing, in his *Six livres de la république* (1576), the principles for a Christian monarch to operate in a judicial system bound by the rules of "harmony," i.e. within the numerically ordered and proportioned universe also built on Pythagorean principles.[42] Bodin's aim as a *politique* (i.e. he saw stability as more important than victory for either confessional faction) was to develop a theory to counteract attacks on the monarchy from several quarters: from "Monarchomachs" – Protestant theorists who favored an elected

---

[40] See Jeanneret, *Poésie et tradition biblique*, pp. 207–44 for a critique of Baïf's poetic style.
[41] Mersenne, *Quaestiones*, col. 1640.
[42] Jean Bodin, *Les Six livres de la République* (Paris, Jacques du Puy, 1576). See also John William Allen, *A History of Political Thought in the Sixteenth Century* (London, Methuen, 1960), pp. 394–444.

monarchy, most notably reflected in Hotman's *Francogallia* (1573), which envisaged a non-hereditary, elected monarchy harking back to the days of Gaul;[43] from a distrustful populace more widely, who had begun to have their doubts about a king who could so readily preside over the slaughter of so many citizens at the recent St. Bartholomew's Day Massacre; and from the earliest manifestation of the Sainte Ligue (the Catholic League; see below).

Most sixteenth-century theories of the monarchy had focused on the king as the embodiment of justice, with his primary role being to judge his subjects. Bodin, however, taking his justification from the Hebrew scriptures rather than civil law, centered his argument on the idea of "sovereignty," power granted by God which enabled the king to make law and to act without the consent of the people.[44] Nevertheless, as the culmination of his treatise, he returned to the concept of justice, addressing the issue in the final chapters, "Concerning Distributive, Commutative and Harmonic Justice and their relation to the Aristocratic, Popular, and Monarchial states."[45] Kate van Orden has persuasively pointed out the Pythagorean and musical connections in these chapters, but it is important not to overlook that Bodin ultimately deferred to biblical authority.[46] For Bodin, an egalitarian order, based on the principle of what he calls "commutative justice" (represented by an arithmetic sequence in which the interval between numbers remains constant), is natural to states where estates, honors, offices, and benefices are divided equally. On the other hand, an aristocracy would be based on "distributive justice" (represented by a geometric sequence in which the intervals between numbers are variable and unequal). For Bodin, the rigidity of the commutative system and the unpredictability of the distributive system led to a third preferred alternative, the "harmonic" system which could be represented by the sequence 4, 6, 8, 12 – neither an arithmetic nor a geometric progression, but one that nevertheless reflected many just proportions (4:8 = 6:12, 6:4 = 12:8, etc.).

Bodin explained why a harmonic system was most appropriate by making explicit use of musical concepts related to Pythagorean intervals. The Unity of the King (see Figure 1.3) indicated by the numeral 1,

---

[43] See Ladurie, *The French Royal State*, pp. 190–1, for the context in which Bodin conceived his work and a survey of monarchomach treatises. See also 'Bodin and the Monarchomachs', in John Salmon, *Renaissance and Revolt: Essays in the Intellectual and Social History of Early Modern France* (Cambridge, Cambridge University Press, 1987), pp. 119–35.

[44] See Herbert Rowen, *The King's State: Proprietary Dynasticism in Early Modern France* (New Brunswick, Rutgers University Press, 1980), pp. 27–47.

[45] Bodin, *Six livres*, p. 744   [46] Van Orden, *Music, Discipline, and Arms*, pp. 67–76.

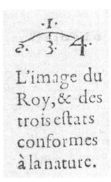

Figure 1.3 Bodin's marginal illustration of the Unity of the King: "The image of the King, and the three estates conform to nature."
Jean Bodin, *Les Six livres de la République* (Paris, Jacques du Puy, 1576), p. 756

encompassing the three estates, indicated by numerals 2, 3, and 4, is described in the following manner:[47]

The wise Prince will tune his subjects, one to the other, and all together with faith: thus, as one can see in the first four numbers, God has organized them in Harmonic proportion: to show us that the Royal state is Harmonic, and that he must govern Harmonically: because 2:3 makes the 5th, 3:4 makes the 4th, 2:4 the octave, and 1:4 the double octave, which contain the whole system of all the notes and consonances of music: and whoever wishes to pass on to 5, there will be an intolerable discord. (trans. Knolles, p. 790)

On the face of it, such an analysis – that number and harmony are at the root of all things – adopts the conceptual framework of Pontus de Tyard's *Solitaire second* (1555), and it is likely that Bodin (who would have moved in the same circles as Tyard) drew heavily on his work for this model:[48] Tyard's dialogue between *Solitaire* and *Curieux* reflects a worldview in which the internal and external worlds are described as a series of interlocking harmonies and, in turn, form the proportional and thus musical basis of the body, natural philosophy, and moral philosophy. Both Bodin

---

[47] Bodin, *Six livres*, p. 756: "le sage Prince accordera ses sugets les uns aux autres, & tous ensemble avec foy: tout ainsi comme on peut voir les quatre premiers nombres, que Dieu a disposez par proportion Harmonique: pour nous monstrer, que l'estat Royal est Harmonique, & qu'il se doit gouverner Harmoniquement: car 2. à 3. fiat la quinte, 3. à 4. la quarte, deux à quatre l'octave: & derechef, un à deux fait l'octave, 1. à 3. la douzième, tenant la quinte & l'octave, & 1. à 4. la double octave, qui contient l'entier système de tous les tons & accords de musique: & qui voudra passer à 5. il fera un discord insupportable."

[48] Pontus de Tyard, *Solitaire second, ou prose de la musique* (Lyon, Jean de Tournes, 1555). See also Yates, *French Academies*, pp. 85–8.

and Tyard would also have known, and been influenced by, one of the most important syncretic works of the sixteenth century, Francesco Giorgio's *Harmonia de mundi*, available in the original Latin (published in Venice in 1525 and in Paris in 1545), or in the translation by Guy Le Fèvre de la Boderie (published 1579 as *L'Harmonie du monde*), Bodin's colleague in the household of François, Duc d'Alençon.[49] Giorgio's monumental work, an exposition of Platonic philosophy tinged with astrology and magic, is built on a similar harmonic, musical framework: the entire volume is structured in "cantiques," each of which is divided into eight modes or "tons." The first cantique sets out a Platonic conception of the universe, the second a more biblical conception, and the whole volume concludes with twenty "motets" (conceptual categories) each of which is then considered in terms of its "accords."[50]

And yet, just like Tyard and the Franciscan Giorgio, Bodin did not give the final word to a Platonic conception of the universe and just governance. Going beyond the long-established tradition of medieval scholarship of the Chartres School and the Abbey of Saint Victor such as Thierry of Chartres and Hugh of Saint Victor (who had sought to unify the Platonic and Mosaic accounts of creation in their commentaries on Plato),[51] Bodin concluded his treatise by pointing out Plato's errors:[52]

---

[49] Francesco Giorgio, *De harmonia mundi totius cantica tria* (Paris, A. Berthelin, 1545); Francesco Giorgio, trans. Guy Le Fèvre de la Boderie, *L'Harmonie du monde divisée en trois cantiques* (Paris, J. Macé, 1579).

[50] For the relationship between Giorgio, Tyard, and la Boderie, see Daniel Pickering Walker, *Spiritual and Demonic Magic from Ficino to Campanella*, Studies of the Warburg Institute, 22 (London, Warburg Institute, 1958), pp. 112–26, and Yates, *French Academies*, pp. 87–8.

[51] Plato's *Timaeus* – which saw the universe in terms of number and musical proportion – was available in Latin translation throughout the Middle Ages, and became the object of intense study in the eleventh and twelfth centuries by figures associated with the cathedral of Chartres. The glosses produced by these members of the Chartres School – Thierry of Chartres, Bernard of Chartres, William of Conch, Hugh of Saint Victor – frequently added marginal diagrams in an attempt to explain Plato's complex geometric and mathematical concepts (often through the analogy of music) in the same way that Bodin did. See Anna Somfai, 'The Eleventh-Century Shift in the Reception of Plato's "Timaeus" and Calcidius's "Commentary"', *Journal of the Warburg and Courtauld Institutes*, 65 (2002), 1–21.

[52] Bodin, *Six livres*, pp. 771–2: "[Il] ... reste à voir s'il est vray ce que disoit Platon que Dieu gouverne ce monde par proportion Géométrique, par ce qu'il a prins ce fondement, pour monstrer que la République bien ordonnée à l'image de ce monde doit estre gouvernée par Iustice Géométrique. J'ay monstré tout le contraire par la nature de l'unité rapportée aux trois premiers nombres harmoniquement: & de l'intellect, aux trois parties de l'âme: & du point, à la ligne, à la superficie & au corps. Mais il faut passer plus outre: car si Platon eust regardé de plus près, il eust remarqué ce qu'il a oublié en son Timée, que ce grand Dieu de nature a composé harmoniquement le monde de la matière & de la forme."

It remains to be seen if it is true what Plato said, that God governs the world by Geometric proportion, because he took this basis to show that a well-ordered Republic in the image of this world must be governed by Geometric Justice. I have shown quite the opposite by the nature of the unity of the harmonious relationship of the first three numbers: and of the intellect, of the three parts of the soul: and of the point to the line, to the surface, and to the body. But one must go further: because if Plato had looked a little further, he would have noticed something he forgot in his *Timaeus*, that this great God of nature created the world harmonically in matter and form. (trans. Knolles, p. 792)

In keeping with the teachings of the Chartres school, Giorgio, too, acknowledged that the Platonic conception of the universe should be seen through the lens of the Bible, in particular the psalms ("Yet Pythagoras commands, that none timidly undertake to talk of these divine things without light: without the Light I say, of which the Writer of the Psalms sings, 'In your light we will see the Light'"),[53] but Bodin went further, ascribing the laws of a harmonious universe not to Pythagoras but to God himself.

It could thus be argued that, by the mid to late 1570s, the vogue for a Neoplatonic reading of the universe as the key to addressing its current concerns, and the preference emulating the rulers of antiquity, had passed. Indeed, during that decade and into the next, the country would be torn apart by religious divisions whose solutions, understandably, were felt to lie in the religious domain. After the St. Bartholomew's Day Massacre of 1572, and the death of Charles IX in 1574, Henri III's generous and amicable settlement with the Huguenots (the "Peace of Monsieur") in 1576 outraged hard-line Catholics to such an extent that in the same year Henri, Duc de Guise, formalized a group of clerics and nobles sympathetic to his cause into the so-called Sainte Ligue or Catholic League. While the League's founding purpose was ostensibly to fight against heresy, in fact their aims were much broader. In particular, they considered the Capetian line (and thus all its successors) to be usurpers, with the House of Lorraine (Guise) the rightful heirs of Charlemagne and accordingly to the crown of France. And since, to their mind, Henri III had also broken his coronation oath (to maintain the country as Catholic), the League's primary aims (though not overtly at first) were

---

[53] Giorgio, *L'Harmonie du monde*, p. 9: "Pourtant commande Pythagore, qu'aulcun témérairement n'entreprenne sans lumière de parler des choses divines: sans la Lumière dy-ie, de laquelle l'Escrivain des Pseaumes chante, En ta Lumière nous verrons la Lumière." The text refers to Psalm 35.

in fact to depose Henri III, to install a Guise as king, and to bring the church of France more closely under Papal control.[54]

In this context, it is not surprising, therefore, that those with a cultural and political stake in the new king Henri III began to reject the ideological framework of antiquity, arguing that a biblical model would more directly address the current political and religious realities. The Académie de poésie et de musique seems to have stopped its hyper-humanist experiments on Charles's death, and its successor – the so-called Académie du Palais, favored and hosted by Henri III – seems to have had different aims, focusing more on philosophy than poetry or music.[55] And as the Catholic League began to gain strength and the religious tensions began to boil over into what Crouzet has described as a state of "overenchantment" – a sense of eschatological fervor stoked by the predictions of Nostradamus – Henri III and his spiritual advisors also began to adopt a more overtly combative religious strategy, founding the Order of the Holy Spirit in 1578 (discussed in Chapter 2) and the Congregation of the Penitents of Notre-Dame in 1583 (Chapter 4), among other religious confraternities.[56] On the death of François d'Anjou, Henri III's only male heir, in 1584, the League broke cover – the Huguenot Henri of Navarre was now sole heir to the throne, and the League were determined to prevent his succession at all costs, lining up Cardinal Henri de Bourbon as a potential successor, and planning to release him from his priestly vows so he could marry the Duc de Guise's sister, the Duchesse de Montpensier.[57] Another series of religious wars then broke out, culminating in the assassination of Henri III in 1589, the abjuration and succession of Henri IV in 1593, and the dissolution of the League shortly afterward – although the sentiments that motivated them lived on into the seventeenth century and found a home both at court (as the *parti des dévots*) and in places such as the Abbey of Montmartre and the Church of the Congregation of the Oratory of Jesus Christ (see Chapter 6).

---

[54] For a detailed examination of the aims of the League from a religious perspective, see William Jervis, *The Gallican Church: The History of the Church of France from the Concordat of Bologna to the Revolution* (London, John Murray, 1872), pp. 172–5. See also Frederic Baumgartner, *Radical Reactionaries: The Political Thought of the French Catholic League* (Geneva, Droz, 1976).

[55] See Robert Sealy, *The Palace Academy of Henry III* (Geneva, Droz, 1981). This work supersedes Yate's observations in *French Academies*.

[56] See Denis Crouzet, *Les Guerriers de Dieu* (Paris, Champ Vallon, 1990), Vol. 1, p. 143.

[57] Jervis, *Gallican Church*, pp. 172–98.

More broadly, though, it was the religious turmoil of the late 1570s and 1580s, and a wish to defend the king against the League, that prompted royalist pamphleteers and judicial theorists to begin to modify the model espoused by Bodin, placing less emphasis on the "harmonical," natural dimension of kingship and more on the divine essence of the king – the concept of "absolutism," that the king acted as God's agent on earth.[58] As part of this change of tone, treatises immediately following Bodin's, such as Pierre Grégoire's *De Republica* of 1578, began to emphasize the idea of divine right and to clarify the relationship between the Pope and the king – both were God's agents, the king in the temporal domain, the Pope in the spiritual, also confirming a measure of Gallican independence and setting the stage for the conflicts with the Pope in the seventeenth century. But it was during the wars of 1585–93 that the biggest changes came about, particularly in the growing emphasis on the rights and qualities of the particular individual who occupied the office of the king, rather than on the office itself. Jacques Hurault's *Trois livres des offices d'estat* (1588), for example, outlined a relatively conventional theory of monarchy in the first of the three books, and claimed that his treatise was essentially a secular work.[59]

Much of Books 2 and 3 was dedicated to the personal traits of the king, and while the majority of his examples were indeed taken from "secular histories," the Bible and psalms were also called into play: in a chapter on *Les Passions de l'âme* (The Passions of the Soul), for example, a Prince may express his joy following the example of David in Psalms 31 and 9 – or his grief, following Psalm 68.[60] By contrast, the title of François Le Jay's *De la Dignité des rois, et princes souverains du droict inviolable de leurs successeurs légitime: et du devoir des peuples, et subiectz envers eux* (On the Dignity of Kings, and Sovereign Princes and the Inviolable Rights of Their Legitimate Successors: and the Duty of the People and Subjects toward Them) of 1589 is an obvious allusion to the issues surrounding the accession of Henri of Navarre, and its colophon "Craignez Dieu & Honorez le Roy" (Believe in God and Honor the King [1 Peter 2]) clearly identifies the volume as a religious treatise. And indeed, unlike Hurault, Le Jay took all his justification from the heavenly kingdom. Referencing

---

[58] For the history of these developments, see William Church, *Constitutional Thought in Sixteenth-Century France* (New York, Octagon, 1941).
[59] Jacques Hurault, *Trois livres des offices d'estat avec un sommaire des stratagèmes* (Lyon, François le Febvre, 1596).
[60] Hurault, *Trois livres*, p. 84.

Psalm 24, Deuteronomy 17, and Josiah 1, the first chapter of his book begins:[61]

> To lay the foundation, on which this whole work is built, the Holy Scripture teaches us that God all powerful is the builder who has made and constituted all the Princely Kingdoms and dominions of the earth. To him alone they belong as true possessions: for which he has oversight and leadership.

The preface to the chapter also makes clear the duties of the people toward kings:[62]

> That the people owe them honour, service and obeissance, they being lieutenants of God.

Numerous other treatises appearing in the 1580s and into the 1590s (those by Servin, Belloy, and others) continued this theme, culminating in du Rivault's *Les États, esquels il est discouru du prince, du noble et du tiers-état, conformément à nostre temps* (Lyon, 1596), a work that makes the strongest possible case for divine right of kings – that the king is now himself a God:[63]

> Finally, to conclude this present discourse on the Prince who is the Christ and the anointed of God, it will be very useful for him to always have before himself the description that Isaiah gave of the holy, perfect and immaculate Christ, which may not be misattributed to Kings, of whom it is written "You are Gods, and the sons of the most high."

David, the Ideal King

The process of reengaging with biblical models of kingship at the end of the sixteenth century closely parallels the "liturgifying" process that occurred in the Middle Ages, most famously described by Ernst Kantorowicz, in

---

[61] François Le Jay, *De la Dignité des rois, et princes souverains du droict inviolable de leurs successeurs légitime: et du devoir des peuples, et subiectz envers eux* (Tours, Mathurin le Mercier, 1589), p. 14: "Pour mettre le fondement, sur lequel toute ceste œuvre est bastie, l'escripture saincte nous enseigne: que Dieu tout puissant est l'ouvrier, qui a fait & constitué tous les Royaumes Principautez & dominations de la terre. Auquel seul ilz appartiennent en vraye proprieté: desquelz il a l'administration gouvernement & conduite."

[62] Ibid.: "Que le peuple leur doit honneur, service & obéissance, comme estans lieutenans de Dieu."

[63] David du Rivault, *Les États, esquels il est discouru du prince, du noble et du tiers-état, conformément à nostre temps* (Lyon, 1596), quoted in Church, *Constitutional Thought*, p. 137: "En fin pour conclure ce présent discours du Prince qui est le Christ et l'oint de Dieu, il luy seroit très-utile d'avoir tousiours devant les yeux la description qu'Esaie faict du sainct, parfaict et immaculé, Christ, laquelle ne peut ester mal attribué aux Roys, desquels il est escript Vous estes Dieux, et les fils du très-haut."

which the original secular coronations of the Merovingian dynasty were superseded by a ceremony of anointing.[64] Of course, both in the Middle Ages and in the sixteenth century, the ultimate anointed biblical king – Jesus Christ – did not always provide an ideal model of kingship for the realities of the monarchy, in which worldly strength and military might were more potent symbols than direct lineage with God. The Old Testament, however, was replete with anointed kings (in particular David, but also Solomon and Josiah) who faced the same kind of military and political challenges that the French kings faced and could provide more practical models for emulation. Thus, the Franks began to think of themselves as a chosen people in a continuous line not with the Emperors and citizens of Rome but with the prophets, kings, and people of Israel. Their kings were not a new Caesar, but, anointed with holy oil, they became the *christus Domini*, the *rex et sacerdos*, and the *rex christianissimum*.

The coronation ceremonies and rituals that developed to celebrate this anointing centered on Reims where the legend of the Holy Ampoule (as described in the ninth-century account by Hincmar, Archbishop of Reims) had originated. According to Hincmar, Clovis, the first king of the Franks, had been baptized and anointed by Saint Remi (409) using oil from an ampoule carried by a dove sent directly from God. This holy oil is subsequently recorded as being used for the coronations of Charles the Bald (869) and Louis the Pious (877), whilst Pope Innocent II invoked the same legend for the coronation of Louis VI (1131). (Charlemagne himself did not receive oil from the Holy Ampoule at his coronation because he was crowned in Rome. Nevertheless, the *Laudes regi* described by Kantorowicz highlight the importance of the anointing at this ceremony.)[65] It was the use of this holy oil from that point onward (as noted in the Reims and subsequent coronation *Ordines*) which enabled French monarchs to style themselves "most Christian" (i.e. most anointed), and it was the act of anointing itself which led to the use of the term *sacre* in preference to *couronnement*. Indeed, this emphasis on the religious, rather than the constitutional, character of the rite in France led to the coronation often being considered the eighth sacrament.[66]

---

[64] Ernst Kantorowicz, *Laudes Regiae: A Study in Liturgical Acclamations and Medieval Ruler Worship* (Berkeley, University of California Press, 1946), pp. 56–8.
[65] Ibid.
[66] See Marc Bloch, *Les Rois thaumaturges* (Strasbourg, 1924), pp. 224–9; trans. V.E. Anderson as *The Royal Touch* (London, 1973), pp. 130–3.

As the coronation ceremony developed, the role of David came into clearer focus, culminating in the rite preserved in the Last Capetian *Ordo* of 1250–70, a rite that was modified and expanded for the 1364 *Ordo* of Charles V.[67] In a striking parallel with that of Henri IV, Charles V's coronation had also been held in the wake of a problematic succession (following the death of Philip VI), and so the *Ordo* was explicitly crafted to reinforce the biblical heritage of the new king.[68] Subsequent coronations incorporated the essential features of both rites, and the Davidic nature of kingship thereafter underpinned every subsequent coronation until the end of the *ancien régime*. Nevertheless, as we have seen, other than at this ritual, by the sixteenth century Francis I, Henri II and Catherine de Médicis, and Charles IX all favored a more humanistic model, François seeing himself as a new Hercules, a pious Caesar, and a second Constantine.[69] Thus the revival that began in the 1580s and continued into the seventeenth century, while in some ways simply another turn of the wheel, nevertheless had something of a novelty about it, especially since – in line with the growing conception of the "individual" in early modern culture – the monarch himself (not just his office) was now increasingly personally identified with King David.[70]

A striking parallel emerges between this renewed interest in David as a model, his unique individual character, and the psalm translations that emerged from the 1580s onward. If Baïf's 1573 psalms represent the pinnacle of syncretic humanist endeavor, subsequent translations by him and others testify to an abandonment of the classical world and an embrace of the biblical. Philippe Desportes, closely associated with the court and the Palace Academy of Henri III, lodged with Baïf during the 1580s and was undoubtedly influenced by him, yet his translation of a substantial part of the psalter in rhymed verse, begun in 1587 and published in 1591 as *Soixante Pseaumes de David, mis en vers françois*, eschews all mention of antiquity.[71] Likewise Renaud de Beaune, Archbishop of Bourges, charged

---

[67] Richard Jackson, *Ordines Coronationis Franciae: Texts and Ordines for the Coronation of Frankish and French Kings* (Philadelphia, University of Pennsylvania Press, 1995–2000), **pp. 367-70**.

[68] See Chapter 2 for the literature concerning the coronation.

[69] Ladurie, *The French Royal State*, pp. 110–111.

[70] For the notion of the "sacred self" as it related to the monarchy, see Paul Kléber Monod, *The Power of Kings: Monarchy and Religion in Europe, 1589-1715* (New Haven and London, Yale University Press, 1999), pp. 9–24.

[71] Philippe Desportes, *Soixante Pseaumes de David, mis en vers François* (Rouen, Raphael du Petit Val, 1591). See also Yates, *French Academies*, p. 72. That said, a handful of the paraphrases are in *vers mesurés*.

by Henri IV with reestablishing music in the *chapelle royale* in 1589, republished an earlier 1563 set of prose translations at the request of Henri III in 1587, again making no reference to the literature or rulers of antiquity.[72] Instead, in his dedication to the king, he recounts the qualities of David, remarking in passing that he surpasses all the "poets and orators." In the following year, Blaise de la Vigenère published another complete translation, *Le Psaultier de David torné en prose mesurée ou vers libres* (1588), adopting a new poetic technique (effectively blank verse) that retained the syllable count of French verse while rejecting rhyme, at the same time providing another remarkable dedication to Henri III in which he confirmed the king's status as a sacral monarch of "le type & image d L'OINCT, du Seigneur, le Roy des Rois, le CHRIST ou MESSIHE" (the type and image of the anointed, of the Lord, of the King of Kings, the Christ or Messiah).[73] Others such as Dupuyherbault followed the same path, but most strikingly, Baïf himself produced a third and final translation of the complete psalter in 1587 at the command of Henri III, this time in rhymed verse, and, like the other translations produced that year, claiming no authority from classical sources or techniques.[74]

Although remaining in manuscript (as far as we know), this 1587 translation must have been widely known, since it features in an anecdote that strikingly reflects the ongoing rejection of classical literary (and more broadly cultural) models. In 1586 Baïf had been awarded a prize by the Académie de Jeux Floraux of Toulouse (a society of composer-poets with lineage back to the Troubadours) for his contribution to French poetry – he was now considered an equal of Ronsard – that consisted of a silver statue of Apollo.[75] But in 1587 the Académie met again to reconsider their decision: based on the new information that Baïf had recently translated the Psalms into rhyming French verse and that he had already published the seven penitential psalms, the records of the meeting describe how the Académie had been requested to change the silver Apollo (presumably not yet made?) for something else more appropriate.[76] For that reason, they

---

[72] Renaud de Beaune, *Les CL Pseaumes de David, Latins et François* (Paris, Gilles Robinot, 1587).
[73] Blaise de Vigenère, *Le Psaultier de David torné en prose mesurée ou vers libres* (Paris, Abel l'Angelier, 1588). Vigenère was known as a humanist, but in his dedication to Henri III he made absolutely clear Henri's status as a sacral monarch in the line of David.
[74] Gabriel Dupuyherbault, *Psaumes de David*; F-Pn MS fonds fr. 19140, f.186-310. Baïf provided no commentary or annotations to accompany this text.
[75] See Yates, *French Academies*, pp. 68–9.
[76] Baïf's preface to this volume of penitential psalms expresses the wish that the paraphrases will shortly appear with musical accompaniment, although no such publication is extant; see

decided to change the figure to a statue of King David, which was definitely made and presented to Baïf, since it was described shortly afterward, in 1589, by the poet Toussaint Sailly in a Latin poem praising Baïf's works. According to Sailly, paraphrased by Baïf's nineteenth-century biographer Auge-Chiquet:[77]

It represented the prophet king with his foot on the corpse of Goliath. On the giant's forehead could be distinguished the mark made by the pebble. The attitude of David was not that of a proud conqueror, but of a man who gives thanks to heaven for his triumph, and, conscious of his faults, supplicates Jehovah to withdraw his wrath from the people of Israel. At his feet was sculpted the lyre, which he was about to grasp, and the Book of Psalms open at one of the pages which sing the praises of the God of Abraham, Isaac, and Jacob.

This portrayal of David as a multifaceted character – a victorious warrior who, in the midst of his triumph, still remained humble – is, in fact, typical for much of this period, a period during which no king – Henri III, Henri IV, or Louis XIII – could claim absolute security or power, even in the midst of apparent military success.

David: King, Psalmist, Musician

In the sixteenth and early seventeenth centuries, then, numerous ideological threads converged on the figure of David. Contemporaries saw him as a lyric poet whose works – the Book of Psalms, often recounting his own deeds – took the form of "political" songs of praise, laments, prayers, and songs of victory for the kingdom of Israel; and as an ideal king, after whom the Western conception of the monarchy was itself modeled.[78] But his talents as a singer and instrumental performer – as much a key to his ability to bring harmony to the kingdoms of Israel and France as his poetic abilities – were also highly regarded: just, then, as Apollo's lyre represented celestial harmony (as in the Orphic Hymn, "with your resonant lyre you command the axis of the heavens, Placing all in harmony"), so too did

---

Alexandre Corianesco, 'Une nouvelle version des psaumes de Baïf', in *Mélanges d'histoire littéraire et de bibliographie offerts à Jean Bonnerot* (Paris, Nizet, 1954), pp. 93–6.

[77] *Davidis statua quam Tolosa misit praemium ad Janum Antonium Baiffium Floralionicem*, in Toussaint Sailly, *Varia Poemata* (Paris, Dionysii à Prato, 1589), p. 144. See also Auge-Chiquet, *Vie de Baïf*, p. 578. Translation from Yates, *French Academies*, p. 69.

[78] See the categories defined in Hermann Gunkel, *Introduction to the Psalms: The Genres of the Religious Lyric in Israel* (Macon, Mercer University Press, 1998).

David's harp, producing the same "effects" as the music of antiquity, exhibited most notably in the calming of Saul in I Samuel 16. According to Saint Hilaire of Poitiers (whose commentary on the psalms had first been published by Erasmus in 1523, but which also appeared in Paris in 1572, and which was adopted wholesale in Duranti's important *De ritibus ecclesiae catholicae* of 1596, reissued in 1606),[79] David composed and performed his psalms on the *psalterion*, a ten-stringed instrument shaped like the body of the Lord that transcended the earthly limitations of other instruments and reflected the harmonious order of heaven.[80] Saint Augustine, who famously also regarded the psalms as a reflection of divine order, argued for the superiority of the *psalterion* over the *cithara* (the ancient Greek equivalent), asserting that the *psalterion* praised God from on high (*de superioribus*) while the *cithara* praised God from below (*de inferioribus*).[81] Guillaume du Bartas adopted the same kind of approach in his much later *La Seconde sepmaine*, a widely read philosophical tract that (like the work of both the Chartres School and Giorgio) considered the creation of the universe and speculated on the events of the second week, after the account of the first seven days contained in the book of Genesis. As part of a discussion of the Hebrew language (created on the second day), du Bartas describes how, after Moses:[82]

David's the next, who with the melody
Of voice-matcht fingers, draws sphears harmony,
To his Heav'n-tuned harp, which shall resound
While the bright day-star rides his glorious Round:
Yea (happily) when both the whirling Poles
Shall cease their Galliard, th'ever-blessed soules
Of Christ his champions (cheer'd with his sweet songs)
Shall daunce to th'honor of the Strong of Strongs,
And all the Angels glory-winged Hostes
Sing Holy, Holy, Holy, God of Hoasts ["ô Sainct Dieu des armées" in the original French].

In du Bartas's formulation, David tunes his harp to the harmony of the spheres, and the music he plays animates the angels to dance as they sing

---

[79] Jean-Étienne Duranti, *De ritibus ecclesiae catholicae libri tres* (Lyon, Petri Landry, 1606).
[80] Hilaire of Poitiers, *Tractatus super Psalmos*, trans. Patrick Descourtieux as *Commentaires sur les Psaumes*, Sources Chrétiennes, 515 (Paris, Le Cerf, 2008), p. 141.
[81] Hilaire of Poitiers, ibid.
[82] English translation from Guillaume du Bartas, *Du Bartas His Devine Weekes and Works Translated: And Dedicated to the King's Most Excellent Majestie by Iosuah Sylvester* (London, Humphrey Lounes, 1611), p. 330. Original text in Guillaume du Bartas, *La Seconde sepmaine* (Rouen, Raphael du Petit Val, 1616).

the *Sanctus*, a song of praise closely related to the Trisagion from the Te Deum, and, like it, based on Isaiah 6:3 or Revelation 4:8.[83] The specific effects of David's harp were celebrated later, on the fourth day, dedicated to his achievements (*trophées*), in a discussion of the comfort he had given to Saul against the evil spirits:[84]

For that reason, it is spoken of the marvelous effects of Ancient Music, namely of that of David, whose instrument still divinely resounds in his Psalms, to the chaste ears and holy consciences, who hear it, an excellent remedy and alleviation for all sorts of ill.

If the harmonious "effects" of David's harp that "still resounded" were in some respects considered central, many commentaries also saw the main significance of the psalms in their status as Christological prophecies, prophecies of the coming of the Messiah, Jesus Christ, that had been given to David through the power of the Holy Spirit. David was recognized as being unique among Old Testament figures in that the Holy Spirit manifested itself to him directly as a result of his anointing. The Book of Samuel records:

Then Samuel took the horn of oil and anointed him in the midst of his brothers. And the Spirit of the Lord rushed upon David from that day forward. (1 Samuel 16:10–13)

and that the Holy Spirit acted through him as he wrote the psalms:

David the son of Jesse declares, the sweet psalmist of Israel, The Spirit of the Lord spoke by me, and His word was on my tongue. (2 Samuel 23:1–2)

This biblical truth was recognized in many psalm commentaries from this point onward. Hilaire of Poitiers, again, describing the *psalterion* declared:[85]

It is thus the Holy Spirit from above who sings [the praise of] God in the psalms, with the form of the body of the Lord, in which has spoken the Holy Spirit of heaven.

But beyond David's musical and poetic prowess, and the fact that the Holy Spirit acted through him and his psalms, his character and life more

---

[83] See Chapters 2 and 5 for further discussion of the Te Deum. The particular significance of the Trisagion in the later seventeenth and eighteenth centuries is addressed in Jean-Paul Montagnier, 'Le Te Deum en France à l'époque baroque: un emblème royale', *Revue de musicologie*, 84/2 (1998), 199–233.

[84] Du Bartas, *La Seconde sepmaine, Avis au Lecteur*, n.p.: "A raison dequoy est parlé des merveilleux effects de la Musique ancienne, nommément de celle de David, l'instrument duquel resonne encore divinement en ses Pseaumes, aux oreilles chastes & consciences sainctes, que en sentient, un excellent remède & allègement à toutes sortes de maux."

[85] Hilaire de Poitiers, *Commentaires sur les Psaumes*, p. 141.

generally were also held up as an ideal example of kingship itself. David's bravery and military prowess were obvious accomplishments that a contemporary king might aspire to emulate: best known for his personal bravery in the slaying of Goliath in I Samuel 17:17–37, he also commanded his armies in many victories in II Samuel 8:1–14. Less obvious characteristics for emulation were his humility and penitence, traits he exhibited after his infidelity with Bathsheba and the subsequent death of his son Absalom. Nevertheless, all these traits were considered relevant to the French/Frankish crown from its earliest days. Jonas d'Orléans's *De institutione regia*, written around 830 to serve as a guide to kingship for Pepin, Charlemagne's son, was not published in France until 1662, but his writings were nonetheless well known in the sixteenth century. In Chapter 3, "That which the King is, that which he must be, and that which he must avoid," d'Orléans quotes Saint Isidore's *Sententia*, where David – with all his imperfections, yet with his deep humility – is described as the ideal model of kingship:[86]

He who makes use of royal power justly distinguishes himself from all others in the following way: he shines all the more because of the grandeur of his rank as [much as] he humbles himself more deeply in his heart, taking to himself as a model the example of the humility of David, who did not boast of his merits, but who said, while abasing himself in humility "I will advance as a vile man, and vile will I appear before God, who has chosen me."

This sense of humility, already noted earlier in connection with Baïf's statue, is perhaps one of the most striking and unexpected facets of David's character to be highlighted in the context of kingship, but it is central to many other accounts of his life. Perhaps most notable is the analysis of David's attributes in Saint Ambrose's *Apologia prophetae David*, addressed to Emperor Theodosius Augustus and intended as a model for his contemplation. Here, David's characteristics – his strength, his respect for royal authority, his even greater respect for religion, his mercy, his patience, his temperance, his horror of cruelty, and his love for his people – are all framed in the context of his infidelity with Bathsheba, and are all seen in the context of a humility that compensated for and redeemed this sin.[87]

---

[86] Jonas d'Orléans, *De institutione regia*, trans. Alain Dubreucq as *Le Métier du roi*, Sources Chrétiennes, 407 (Paris, Le Cerf, 1995), p. 195 (English translation my own from Dubreucq's French).

[87] Saint Ambrose, *Apologia prophetae David*, trans. Marius Corder as *Apologie de David*, Sources Chrétiennes, 239 (Paris, Le Cerf, 1977), pp. 107–23 (English translation my own from Corder's French).

At the beginning of the seventeenth century, then, an educated subject would have been equipped with a deep and rich sense of the ideologies associated with kingship, David, and the psalms. So when we read of Louis XIII's actions at La Rochelle shortly before the siege was broken in 1628, paraphrased by Archon from Charles Bernard's much longer contemporary account, the cues that a contemporary reader would have picked up on shine through unmistakably:[88]

Since the King loved Music, but the serious and grave type of Music suitable for the Temples of Jesus Christ, where it must be simple and contemplative, in the moments of leisure which remained to him, having given his orders to those concerned with the progress of the siege, he kept up his spirits by composing motets; he had never learned music by rule, nevertheless there had never been any musician who lacked for less in his tones and measures. The Feast of Pentecost being the next day, and His Majesty not having brought with him his singers or musicians, he showed one of his ecclesiastics the manner of notating the psalms to be sung at first and second vespers, and so that everything would be made ready for the feast day, his zeal made him pass most of the night in this pleasurable task; one saw that day this pious Monarch, like a David in the midst of his singers, animating them by his voice, directing them with his movements in singing the psalms according to the notes which he had written: and all this with such just tuning, and such measured sounds, that everyone was charmed by their harmony.

Just as the Holy Spirit acted through David, so too – at first Vespers of the Feast of Pentecost – did it act through Louis, providing inspiration as he composed music for his biblical predecessor's psalms. Just as Louis had, at his coronation, taken his place as a sacral monarch, a *rex christianissimus*, a priest in the unbroken tradition of the Catholic church, so too could he lead the clerics and ecclesiastics through the Offices as first among equals.

---

[88] Charles Bernard, *Histoire du Roy Louis XIII* (Paris, Nicolas de Sercy, 1646), Book 12, p. 79. Bernard tells us that he was in Surgères, outside La Rochelle. Jean-Louis Archon, *Histoire ecclésiastique de la Chapelle des Rois de France* (Paris, Le Mercier, 1711), Vol. 2, p. 754: "Comme le Roy aimoit la Musique, mais de cette sorte de Musique grave & sérieuse, propres pour les Temples de J.C. où il faut de la simplicité & du recüeillement, dans les momens de loisir qui lui restoient, après avoir donné ses ordres à tout ce qui regardoit l'avancement du siège, il s'égayoit à composer des motets; il n'avoit jamais appris la Musique par règle; cependant il n'y voit point de Musicien qui manquât moins à ses tons & à ses mesures. La Fête de la Pentecôte étant prochaines, & Sa Majesté n'ayant pas mené avec Elle ni ses Chantres, ni ses Musiciens, Elle montra à un de ses Ecclésiastiques la manière de noter les Pseaumes qu'on chante aux premières & aux secondes Vêpres, & afin que tout fût prêt pour le jour de la Fête, son zèle lui fit passer la plupart d'une nuit à un travail où Elle prenoit plaisir; on vit ce jour-là ce pieux Monarque, comme David au milieu de ses Chantres, les animer par sa voix, les diriger par ses mouvemens en chantant les Pseaumes selon les notes qu'il avoit marquées; & tout cela avec des accords si justes, & des sons si mesurez, qu'on étoit charmé de leur harmonie."

And just as David's music not only calmed Saul but, by means of the *psalterion*, resonated with the universal harmonies of the world, so too did Louis's own compositions (clearly divinely inspired since he had received no training) as he directed his singers in the production of harmonious, measured, and even well-tuned sounds. Louis's humility and piety were also on display – he did not insist on a full complement of singers to accompany him and he required the music only to be simple and contemplative – but at the same time, his military prowess was also apparent, giving the orders to his soldiers that would shortly result in victory.

In this brief vignette, then, we see the liturgy, the psalms, the king's musical abilities, the king's accomplishment as a military commander, and music as model of universal harmony, all linking an apparently minor event to the broader ideological frameworks in which royal power was conceived. And yet, as the remainder of this book will show, the conception of the king framed by this isolated vignette was by no means unique. From his coronation in 1610, to the composition of supplicatory motets later in that decade, to celebratory pamphlets and songs published in the 1620s, to ceremonial *entrées* in the 1630s, to the reform of chant in royal institutions, and finally to the dedication of his kingdom to the Virgin Mary in 1638, these ideological threads were woven throughout his whole reign. To begin with, though, as Chapter 2 shows, it is as an agent of the Holy Spirit that we find Louis XIII first, at his coronation in Reims cathedral, following in David's footsteps as anointed king and "Christ."

2 | Accession

The Coronation, the Holy Spirit, and the Phoenix

The accession of Louis XIII to the throne of France was a dramatic and pivotal moment in French history. On May 14, 1610, just a day after his mother, Marie de Médicis, had been crowned regent in a ceremony at Saint-Denis (at which the eight-year-old Louis and his younger sister Élisabeth had helped to lift the crown onto their mother's head), the king himself, Louis's father, was struck down by François Ravaillac in the streets of Paris as he rode in a simple carriage, without escort, to meet with the Duke de Sully to discuss his upcoming military campaign on the borders of the Holy Roman Empire. The assassination of Henri IV, the second successive king of France to die in this manner, could not help but influence the nature of the monarchy and, through it, the process by which transitions of power were marked.[1]

In the years before his assassination, jurists drawn from the "talented bourgeoisie" had preemptively acted to protect both the king's person and his power by continuing the "liturgification" process of the sixteenth century, renewing and reinvigorating the focus on the king as an agent of God – the idea of absolutism in its simplest sense, in which a king's power is unarguable because it descends directly from God himself.[2] In particular, they aimed to establish the French king as an equal to the Pope, who, the Jesuits argued, exercised not just spiritual authority over the French crown, but also temporal authority: it was these views – and others such as

---

[1] For a short contemporary account of the coronation, the assassination, and the aftermath in which Louis was declared king, see *Les Cérémonies et ordre tenue au sacre et couronnement de la Royne Marie de Médicis le 13 mai 1610. Ensemble la mort du Roy, & comme Monsieur le Dauphin a esté déclaré Roy, & la Royne Régente par la Cour de Parlement* (Paris, 1610).

[2] For the political, religious, and juridical dimension of the period before the assassination, see Roland Mousnier, *The Assassination of Henri IV: The Tyrannicide Problem and the Consolidation of the French Absolute Monarchy in the Early Seventeenth Century*, trans. Joan Spencer (New York, Scribner, 1973), pp. 240–50; for the broader constitutional and religious context at the beginning of the seventeenth century, see William Church, *Constitutional Thought in Sixteenth-Century France* (New York, Octagon, 1941); W. Stankiewicz, *Politics and Religion in Seventeenth-Century France* (Berkeley, University of California Press, 1960); William Jervis, *The History of the Church of France from the Concordat of Bologna to the Revolution* (London, John Murray, 1872).

Mariana's *De rege et regis institute* (1599), which argued that it was lawful to remove a leader who held the Catholic religion in contempt – that were said to be the motivation for Ravaillac's attack.[3] Thus, the treatises on kingship that appeared either before or as Louis assumed the throne continued to develop and strengthen the idea of the divine right not just of the institution of the monarchy, but of the individual monarch himself. In language much stronger than that of Bodin or his immediate successors in the 1580s or 1590s (though not of Rivault), Pierre Mathieu's *Du devoir et obéissance des subjects envers le roy* of 1603 had claimed that the people of France were subject to the rule of the king of France because of his divine right to rule and his capacity as a vicar of God (i.e. as an equal to the Pope),[4] but du Boys went even further in his *De l'origine et autorité des Roys* of 1604, echoing the language of Psalm 90 and Psalm 17:[5]

Kings have been called gods because they are, by virtue of their power, the image of God. They are masters because of the obedience owed them by their subjects, overlords because they own men's lives and property, sovereign because there is no one above them, protectors because they are our shield and rampart.

Treatises such as this (and many others) continued to be produced into the reign of Louis XIII himself, but they rarely addressed the succession, an issue that has long intrigued scholars of political theology.[6] In the wake of Kantorowicz's seminal study, others such as Richard Jackson and Sarah Hanley have identified the coronation of Louis XIII, in particular, as a significant turning point in the broader history of dynastic continuity.[7]

---

[3] Mousnier, *Assassination*, p. 54.   [4] Church, *Constitutional Thought*, p. 305.
[5] Mousnier, *Assassination*, p. 243. See also Duchesne's 1609 assertion that kings are both images of God and enjoy priestly status: ibid.
[6] See Mousnier, *Assassination*, pp. 241–80 for the response in the immediate aftermath of the assassination
[7] Ernst Kantorowicz, *The King's Two Bodies: A Study in Medieval Political Theology* (Princeton, Princeton University Press, 1957/R 1997), especially pp. 383–450; Richard Jackson, *Vive le Roi! A History of the French Coronation from Charles V to Charles X* (Chapel Hill, University of North Carolina Press, 1984), pp. 15–23, 131–3; and Sarah Hanley, *The Lit de Justice of the Kings of France: Constitutional Ideology in Legend, Ritual, and Discourse* (Princeton, Princeton University Press, 1983), pp. 231–80. Hanley, in particular, considers the constitutional innovations of Louis XIII's coronation, the *entrée* into Reims, and the inaugural *lit de justice* in considerable depth. For an overview of the coronation rite in France more broadly, see Jacques le Goff, 'Reims, ville du sacre', in Pierre Nora (ed.), *Les Lieux de mémoire: II: La Nation* (Paris: Gallimard, 1986), pp. 89–184; Ralph Giesey, 'The King imagined', in Keith Baker (ed.), *The French Revolution and the Creation of Modern Political Culture, Vol. 1: The Political Culture of the Old Regime* (Oxford, Pergamon Press, 1987), pp. 41–59; Janos Bak, 'Coronation studies: Past, present and future', and the articles by Ralph Giesey, Jacques Le Goff, and others in Janos Bak (ed.), *Coronations: Medieval and Early Modern Monarchic Ritual* (Berkeley, Los Angeles,

By 1610, the complex medieval funeral ritual that preceded the coronation (in which an effigy of the late king was constructed to maintain the fiction that he was still alive as a "host" for the so-called *corpus mysticum* until his successor could be crowned) was beginning to fall out of use;[8] although a funeral effigy of Henri IV was made (the last time this would happen), and although his funeral took place in much the same way as that of his forebears had, Louis was nonetheless assumed to have taken power not at the coronation (which occurred months after his father's death) but, as Charles Loyseau described, at the very moment that "le Roy defunct a la bouche close."[9] Just twelve hours after the assassination, Louis had appeared at a *lit de justice* where Marie's regency was given legal justification for the first time in French history (as a precaution against political instability), and Louis himself was "declared and designated King of France … betrothing the Royalty that law and nature gave him."[10] The coronation, then, had been preempted as the mechanism by which the succession occurred, and, as Jackson puts it, "The King was now represented fully in the person of the individual who became king solely by biological accident of birth and right of succession. There was no need for a funeral ceremony to prevent a theoretical interregnum, and there was no need for a coronation to make a king."[11]

To the extent that music historians have engaged with the early modern French coronation (and ceremonial more generally), attention has typically focused on what we might assume would be the two most "musical" moments: the Te Deum, the ancient hymn of praise and thanksgiving that featured prominently in the ceremony for many centuries; and three so-called "coronation" motets from the sixteenth century that begin with the text *Domine salvum fac regem* ("O Lord save the King," the final verse of Psalm 19, though each has a different continuation) by Guillaume Costeley,

---

Oxford, University of California Press, 1990); and the articles in *Les Sacres des rois: actes du Colloque international d'histoire sur les sacres et couronnements royaux (Reims, 1975)* (Paris, Les Belles Lettres, 1985).

[8] This is the famous "two bodies" theory of the monarchy expounded in Kantorowicz, *The King's Two Bodies*. For a discussion of the medieval French funeral rite in general, see Ralph Giesey, 'Models of rulership in French royal ceremonial', in Sean Willentz (ed.), *Rites of Power: Symbolism, Ritual, and Politics since the Middle Ages* (Philadelphia, University of Pennsylvania Press, 1985), pp. 41–64. For the details of Henri IV's funeral, see Joël Cornette, *Henri IV à Saint-Denis: de l'abjuration à la profanation* (Paris, Belin, 2010).

[9] Ralph Giesey, 'The King imagined', p. 49.

[10] Ibid. See also Hanley, *Lit de Justice*, pp. 231–53, and Katherine Crawford, *Perilous Performances: Gender and Regency in Early Modern France* (Cambridge, MA and London, Harvard University Press, 2004), pp. 61–72.

[11] Jackson, *Vive le Roi*, p. 10.

Jean Maillard, and Jean Mouton.[12] Certainly, by the later seventeenth century and the reign of Louis XIV, numerous musical settings of both the Te Deum and the *Domine salvum fac regem* text (although without the sixteenth-century continuation) were composed and performed at court and more widely, becoming – it is argued or assumed – projections of royal power.[13] For the period under consideration here, too, the late sixteenth and early seventeenth century, Kate van Orden has proposed that the Te Deum, the *Domine salvum fac regem*, and Psalm 20, *Domine in virtute mea*, were incorporated into the so-called Te Deum ceremony, developed by Henri III in the 1580s and adopted by his successors into the seventeenth and even eighteenth centuries, as a means of recreating the most significant moments of the coronation and reasserting the king's authority.[14]

In this chapter, I reexamine the coronation of Louis XIII from a musical and liturgical perspective, taking Jackson's and Hanley's cue that the ceremony's primary function may not now have been to mark the succession. In particular, while laying out some of the groundwork and methodology for the remainder of the study and introducing some of the protagonist court ensembles, I challenge the notion that musical settings of the Te Deum and the *Domine salvum fac regem* were symbols of royal power central to the coronation of Louis XIII, and that subsequent performances (at a Te Deum ceremony or any other event or liturgy) thus "represented" or projected this power by alluding to this pivotal moment in a king's life. Instead, I consider the surviving musical evidence and the way in which music articulated or sounded the liturgy, and suggest that we should see such events in a much broader conceptual framework.[15]

---

[12] See Edward Lowinsky (ed.), *The Medici Codex of 1518*, Monuments of Renaissance Music, 3–5 (Chicago, University of Chicago Press, 1968), p. 157; Irwin Godt, *Guillaume Costeley: Life and Works* (PhD dissertation, University of New York, 1969).

[13] See Jean-Paul Montagnier, 'Le Te Deum en France à l'époque baroque: un emblème royal', *Revue de musicologie*, 84/2 (1998), 199–233; and Thierry Favier, *Le Motet à grand chœur (1660–1792): Gloria in Gallia Deo* (Paris, Fayard, 2009), especially Appendix 1, notices of performances of the Te Deum and *Domine salvum fac regem* for the birth of the Dauphin in 1729. The *Domine salvum fac regem* in the seventeenth and eighteenth centuries has received almost no scholarly attention, but see also Jean-Paul Montagnier, *The Polyphonic Mass in France, 1600–1780: The Evidence of the Printed Choirbooks* (Cambridge, Cambridge University Press, 2017); and Peter Bennett, 'Hearing King David in early modern France: Music and politics at the court of Louis XIII', *Journal of the American Musicological Society*, 69/1 (2016), 47–109.

[14] See Kate van Orden, *Music, Discipline, and Arms in Early Modern France* (Chicago, University of Chicago Press, 2005), p. 136.

[15] Jackson, for example, sees the overall plan of the coronation as featuring three key elements: a coronation, a baptism (the anointing), and a knighting (where the king is presented with his military regalia). On the other hand, Le Goff divides it into eight stages that include the entry,

Given the increased focus on the individual embodiment of the king that the theorists of absolutism reinforced, then, we should perhaps focus our attention more on the personal qualities of the model king, David, especially when we consider the role that the Holy Spirit played in both the life of the biblical king and in the events of 1610. Looking back at Louis's reign in his 1643 oration marking the king's death, Father Pierre Bourgoin of Metz described how the *spiritus Domini* – the Spirit of the Lord (the Old Testament term later taken to denote the Holy Spirit) – had guided Louis through his entire kingship, just as it had David: when Louis appeared to be acting under the influence of Concini, then of Luynes, then of Richelieu, it was in fact the invisible direction of the *spiritus Domini* that guided him then, and in all his subsequent deeds.[16] (We should also remember that, toward the end of his life, Henri IV was increasingly portrayed as an agent of the Holy Spirit.)[17] But it was at the coronation itself that the Holy Spirit began to act on the young king, a conventional understanding of the event that was reinforced and made explicit by the Parisian cleric Claude Villette in his 1611 *Les Raisons de l'Office*: according to Villette, it is the central act of the coronation, the anointing, that establishes the "convenance" (agreement or resemblance) between the kings of Judah and the French kings, and it is "by the Consecration of the Holy Spirit made to the person of our King, [that] the hearts of the French people are touched to render ... the obedience due to him ..."[18] It is for these reasons, then, that we should look at the coronation more broadly, beyond the contained ceremony itself, and realize that what we might consider a single "event" was in fact a complex sequence of rites, liturgies, and thus opportunities for music – not just a freestanding ceremony in which Samuel's anointing of David or Zadok's anointing of Solomon was reenacted (featuring, but not necessarily prioritizing, the performance of a Te Deum), but a series of liturgies focusing on the Holy Spirit: the ceremony of Louis's Confirmation (the

---

contracts, and other details. See Jackson, *Vive le Roi*, p. 134, and Jacques le Goff, 'A coronation program for the Age of Saint Louis: The Ordo of 1250', in János Bak (ed.), *Coronations: Medieval and Early Modern Monarchic Ritual* (Berkeley, Los Angeles, London, University of California Press, 1990), pp. 53–5.

[16] Pierre Bourgoin, *Éloges funèbres de Louys le Iuste sur le parallèle de David vivant et David mourant* (Metz, Jean Antoine, 1643), p. 29. Published funeral orations were widely read: in August 1610, Pierre de l'Estoile, for example, records buying the oration of P. Coeffeteau for the death of Henri IV. See *Mémoires-journaux de Pierre de L'Estoile: Journal de Henri IV* (Paris, Alphonse Lemerre, 1889), Vol. 10 (1609–10), p. 367.

[17] Mousnier, *Assassination*, p. 248.

[18] Claude Villette, *Les Raisons de l'Office, et cérémonies qui se font en l'église Catholique* (Paris, Guillaume des Rues, 1611), p. 212: "par le Sacre du sainct Esprit fait à la personne de nostre Roy, les cœurs des François sont touchez de luy rendre ... l'obéissance deuë ..."

Sacrament of the Holy Spirit), the *sacre et couronnement* itself (with its multiple anointings of oil brought by the dove of the Holy Spirit and by which the Holy Spirit was then bestowed on David/Solomon/Louis), and the culmination of the whole event, the final induction of the newly crowned king into the Order of the Knights of the Holy Spirit.

The *Entrée* and Confirmation

Louis had traveled to Reims, historic site of the coronation, from Paris, arriving on Thursday, October 14, 1610. As Théodore Godefroy (historiographer to both Louis XIII and Louis XIV) describes, he made a ceremonial *entrée*, entering the city in procession with all the dignitaries and forces of the city through a number of triumphal arches.[19] The first arch featured the figures of Francus, Samothes, and Remi, Bishop of Reims, who had crowned Clovis in 496. The king then passed through the gates of the city, where he encountered a tableau on which Saint Remi was again portrayed (this time receiving the Holy Ampoule from the dove of the Holy Spirit), before processing through other arches featuring David, Solomon, Josiah, and many other biblical and mythological characters. Nicolas Bergier, another chronicler of the event (and, incidentally, a notable theorist of musical and poetic rhythm), describes how elsewhere one tableaux represented Louis at his inaugural *lit de justice* with the caption *rex designatum* (king designate), while a second showed him making his *entrée* into Reims with the caption *rex susceptus* (king received), captions that Hanley has identified as again marking a shift in the role of the ceremonies surrounding the coronation.[20] Following the usual practices, the *entrée* culminated with the king being greeted at the door of the cathedral, where he prayed, kissed the Gospel presented by Cardinal de Joyeuse, and entered the building, processing up to the high altar where he knelt on a *prie-dieu* while "on chanta quelques Antiennes."[21]

Louis remained in Reims the following day, attending Mass at the Abbey of Saint-Remi, where he also viewed the Holy Ampoule and paid his respects at

---

[19] For several accounts of the coronation see Théodore and Denys Godefroy, *Le Cérémonial françois* 2 vols. (Paris, Sebastien de Cramoisy, 1649), Vol. I, beginning at pp. 52, 404, 419, 437, and 459. For an account in which the Latin text of the coronation liturgy is translated into French, see *L'Ordre et les cérémonies qui sont faictes au sacre et couronnement du très-Chrestien Roy de France* (Lyon, Nicolas Jullieron, 1610).

[20] Hanley, *Lit de Justice*, p. 260. See also Nicolas Bergier, *Le Bouquet royal, ou le parterre des riches inventions qui ont servi à l'entrée du roy Louis le Juste en sa ville de Reims* (Reims, Simon de Foigny, 1637), ff. 53v–57v: Bergier analyzes these two mottos and sets them in their broader constitutional context.

[21] Godefroy, I, pp. 449–50. The remaining liturgy of this event is not described, although it is possible that it was similar to the *entrée* described in Chapter 5.

the body of Saint Remi itself, before visiting the Abbey of Saint-Pierre, where, after lunch, the nuns sang a Te Deum as he sat in a throne in the center of the church.[22] On Saturday he was back in the cathedral, where he heard a Mass of Saint Nicaise and inspected relics, but it was later that day, the eve of the coronation itself, at 4.00 pm, that the first of the "coronation complex" of events began. Arriving at the west door, he was greeted by the Archbishop of Reims, Louis III de Lorraine, together with other bishops, suffragans, *pairs*, and the canons, all dressed in their pontifical robes. He then knelt on a tapestry rug and kissed a Gospel that he was then presented with, after which he was led to the altar as the *chantre* began to intone the Responsory *Ecce ego mitto Angelum* ("Behold, I send my messenger before your face, who will prepare your way," Jesus's words on John the Baptist in Luke 7:27, quoting Malachi 3:1), the chant conventionally specified by the 1615 *Pontificale Romanum* to be sung as an Emperor is received in procession in a church, in (we presume) monophonic chant sung by the clergy of the cathedral.[23]

After some more prayers and the singing of an antiphon to the Virgin Mary (most likely the *Salve Regina*, again simply chanted), the archbishop intoned a versicle and response taken from Psalm 19:10, followed by a prayer to the Virgin Mary.[24]

VERSUS: Domine salvum fac Regem.
RESPONSUM: Et exaudi nos in die qua invocaverimus te.
VERSUS: Dominus vobiscum.
RESPONSUM: Et cum spiritu tuo.
OREMUS: Concede nos famulos tuos . . .

It is this moment in the network of coronation liturgies that Edward Lowinsky identified with the three so-called coronation motets by Jean Mouton, Guillaume Costeley, and Jean Maillard, motets that all open with the final verse of Psalm 19, *Domine salvum fac regem*: in particular, Lowinsky suggested that Mouton's setting had been performed at this point in Francis I's coronation in 1515, the inference being that the other later settings were also somehow associated with subsequent coronations.[25]

---

[22] Godefroy, I, pp. 425–6.
[23] *Pontificale Romanum Clementis VIII Pont. Max* (Paris, Rolinum Thierry and Eustachium Foucault, 1615), p. 381.
[24] Godefroy, I, p. 53.
[25] Lowinsky asserted that "It is very likely that this motet was composed for the coronation of Francis I at the cathedral of Rheims on January 25 1515. In a contemporary account of the coronation the Archbishop of Rheims is reported to have recited the text of the motet as one of the official prayers." The reference Lowinsky provides points only to the performance of the equivalent versicle and response. See Lowinsky, *Medici Codex*, p. 157.

(See Tables 2.1 and 2.2 for the texts of these works.) But there is no evidence, certainly on this occasion, or at any previous coronation, that polyphony was performed, or that this moment (or this verse and response) had any special or "royal" significance. On the contrary, the versicle and response V. *Domine salvum fac regem. R. Et exaudi ...* is a standard part of the Offices, sung at ferial Lauds and Vespers during Advent, Lent, and Ember Days, after the Benedictus (Lauds) or the

Table 2.1 Text, translation, and source of Jean Mouton's setting of *Domine salvum fac regem*

Text	Source	Translation
Domine salvum fac regem et exaudi nos in die qua invocaverimus te.	Psalm 19:10	O Lord, save the King: and hear us in the day that we shall call upon thee.
Celestem dans ei rorem.	unidentified	Giving him heavenly dew.
Domine ...		O Lord ...
Tuum catholicum gregem salva defende protege.	unidentified	Save, defend and protect Your Catholic flock.
Domine ...		O Lord ...
Deus qui Moysi legem dedisti in Sinai monte, fac nos ad celum scandere post presentis vite cursum. Domine salvum fac regem.	unidentified	God who gave the law to Moses on Mount Sinai, make us to ascend to heaven after the course of the present life. O Lord, save the King.

Table 2.2 Text, translation, and source of Guillaume Costeley and Jean Maillard's settings of *Domine salvum fac regem*

Text	Source	Translation
Domine salvum fac regem.	Psalm 19:10	O Lord, save the King.
Desiderium cordis eius tribue ei, et voluntate labiorum eius noli fraudere.	Psalm 20:3	Thou hast given him his heart's desire: and hast not withholden from him the will of his lips.
Posuisti in capite eius coronam, et praevenisti eum in benedictionibus,	Psalm 20:4	For thou hast prevented him with blessings of sweetness: thou hast set on his head a crown of precious stones.
quoniam in misericordia tua speravit.	unidentified	For he puts his trust in your mercy.
Da ei victoriam contra hostes suos	unidentified	Give him victory against his enemies.
et longitudine dierum reple eum semenque eius maneat semper in saeculum et in saeculi.	Psalm 20:5	He asked life of thee: and thou hast given him length of days for ever and ever.

Magnificat (Vespers).[26] It is certainly true that by the late sixteenth century the complete Psalm 19 (which begins *Exaudiat te Dominus in die tribulationis*) became specifically identified as a prayer for the king and highly significant in royal liturgies – and indeed this psalm will feature prominently in the remainder of this study – but there are no conceivable circumstances in which an extensive polyphonic motet would substitute for a versicle and response, especially since the Maillard and Costeley settings do not even include the response *Et exaudi* ...[27] That is not to say that all three motets could not have been performed at some other, extraliturgical stage in the celebrations – as part of the king's *entrée* procession, or at the concluding dinner, where, for example, we know that motets were sung – especially since the Costeley and Maillard settings include highly appropriate verses from Psalm 20, *Domine in virtute tua*, which, in contrast with Psalm 19, was recited in full at the coronation (see below). Indeed, the Costeley and Maillard works have a much greater claim to royal associations than the Mouton, since Psalms 19 and 20 may have been combined in this way more generally, especially in connection with the king.[28] A liturgy to be celebrated at the Synod of Chartres in 1575, for example, includes the following prayer to be said by the bishop for the king.[29]

EPISCOPUS : Oremus pro Christiannissimo Domino nostro Rege.
CHORUS EX PSALM. 19 & 20: Domine salvum fac Regem, & desiderium cordis tribue ei.

That is not to suggest that these two pieces formed any part of the liturgy (simply that these lines may have more generally been thought of together), and we should certainly not conflate the group of three works with the tradition of performing Psalm 19 complete that developed later in the century, or imagine that, by virtue of these three motets, Psalm 19 somehow

---

[26] *Breviarium Romanum* (Rome, Typographica Vaticana, 1633), p. 49. The English version became part of the Anglican service of Evensong around this time.
[27] Jean Maillard, *Domine salvum fac regem*, first published in 1551[24] and 1553[7], ed. in *Recent Researches in the Music of the Renaissance*, 73 (1987). Guillaume Costeley, *Domine salvum fac regem*, first published in *Musique de Guillaume Costeley* (Paris, 1570), ed. in Godt, *Guillaume Costeley*, pp. 530–9.
[28] See John Brobeck, 'Some "liturgical" motets for the French royal court: A reconsideration of genre in the sixteenth-century motet', *Musica Diciplina*, 47 (1993), 123–57, for a discussion of the role and definition of the motet in France. Just as Cummings outlined for the Pope, psalm-based "motets" were performed at Henri III's dinner table; see Anthony Cummings, 'Toward an interpretation of the sixteenth-century motet', *Journal of the American Musicological Society*, 34/1 (1981), 43–59, and Chapter 3.
[29] Nicolas de Thou, *Norma pie vivendi* (Paris, Iacobum Kerver, 1575), f. 23v.

more generally evoked the coronation: none of these settings includes the essential opening verse of the Psalm 19 tradition *Exaudiat te Dominus*, and none of them actually formed part of the coronation liturgy itself.

Godefroy reveals nothing further about the liturgy or music, but he does tell us that this short ceremony was immediately followed by Vespers, at which Père Coton, the king's Jesuit confessor, preached on the divine institution of the *sacre et onction des Roys* and at which the king himself received the Sacrament of Confirmation from Cardinal de Joyeuse, a sacrament in which those already baptized receive the gift of the Holy Spirit through the imposition of hands and anointing.[30] The service was accompanied by the "Musique du Roy" – in this case the *musique de la chapelle royale*, the *musique de la chambre*, and probably the *musique de la grande écurie* – all presumably under the direction of Nicolas Formé (who had succeeded Eustache Du Caurroy as *sous-maître* at the *chapelle royale* on his death in 1609), Matthias Granier (who had taken on one of the roles in 1604), Eustache Picot, or possibly Étienne Le Roy (who would have been near the end of his career).[31]

The *musique de la chapelle* and the *musique de la chambre*, both parts of much larger organizations, the *chapelle* (about seventy clerics, servants, and musicians) and the *chambre* (hundreds of servants and courtiers), were relatively stable institutions during the late sixteenth and early seventeenth centuries.[32] In the early sixteenth century, the singers of the *chapelle* had been divided into a *chapelle de musique* (which performed polyphony, probably mainly outside the liturgy) and a *chapelle de plainchant*

---

[30] Godefroy, I, 407. For the Sacrament of Confirmation see *Pontificale Romanum Clementis VIII Pont Max.* (Paris, Rolinum Thierry and Eustachium Foucault, 1615), pp. 1–3.

[31] An inventory of *chapelle royale* personnel from 1610 (F-Pn MS fonds fr. 18512) lists Formé, Granier, and Le Roy as *sous-maîtres*, though it is possible that personnel changed over the course of the dramatic year. Certainly, Ernest Thoinan's edition of Annibal Gantez's *L'Entretien des musiciens* quotes a contemporary source that "Picot, qui avoit servi le roi défunt à son sacre, ..." See Annibal Gantez, *L'Entretien des musiciens* (Auxerre, Jacques Bouquet, 1643), ed. Ernest Thoinan (Paris, A. Claudin, 1878), p. 84. For occasions such as this, the king's musicians always took precedence over the musicians of the host church: see Jean-Louis Archon, *Histoire ecclésiastique de la Chapelle des Rois de France* (Paris, Le Mercier, 1711), Vol. II, p. 684. Archival accounts of the ceremony record the expenses for the erection of two platforms for the *chambre* and *chapelle*: see Archives nationales de France, K. 502, f. 4 and ff.57-8.

[32] See Michel le Moel, 'La Chapelle de Musique sous Henri IV et Louis XIII', *Recherches sur la musique française classique*, 6 (1966), 5–26; Isabelle Handy, *Musiciens au temps des derniers Valois (1547–1589)* (Paris: Champion, 2008); Jeanice Brooks, *Courtly Song in Late Sixteenth-Century France* (Chicago: University of Chicago Press, 2000), appendices 1 and 2. See also two important recent works: Alexander Robinson, *Musique et musiciens à la cour d'Henri IV (1589–1610)* (PhD dissertation, University of Paris-Sorbonne, 2015); and Jacques Szpirglas, *Dictionnaire de musiciens de la cour d'Henri IV et des maisons princières* (Paris, Garnier, 2019).

(which performed the Offices in chant), but under Henri III the *chapelle de plainchant* had been presented to Catherine de Médicis in 1585, then discontinued on her death in 1589.[33] The revised statutes of the *chapelle royale* drawn up in 1587 called for a total of six *basses-contres*, six *tailles*, six *hautes-contres*, six *enfants de chœur*, a *sous-maître* and two *dessus-mués*, though in reality these numbers may not have been so fixed.[34] By 1595, when court life had resumed some sense of normality after the end of the Wars of Religion, Henri IV attempted to bring back the personnel who had been part of the chapels of Henri III and Charles IX, wishing that "l'Office se fit dans sa Chapelle de la même manière qu'il s'étoit dans celle des Rois précédents":[35] the *États de la Maison* from this year shows that in doing so the number of singers had grown to eight *basses-contres*, eight *tailles*, and eight *hautes-contres*, though still only six boys, two *cornets*, and two *dessus-mués*, in addition to clerks and teachers of grammar.[36] And by 1610, a listing of the personnel in the *chapelle* appears to show that the numbers had grown even more, the account declaring that there were forty-three singers (not including boys) in the *chapelle*.[37] We can therefore assume the presence of a very substantial body of singers from the *chapelle* in the cathedral that day.[38]

The *musique de la chambre*, on the other hand, was a much smaller ensemble that served primarily in the *chambre*, although it performed all kinds of music, both sacred and secular. Often sharing personnel with the *musique de la chapelle* (although the singers of the *chambre* were more highly regarded and better paid), and generally performing alongside it at important ceremonial events, the *musique de la chambre* consisted of three boys, a group of male singers who would sing one to a part, and number of "soft" instruments: the 1610 listing includes figures such as Pierre Guédron (composer of *airs de cour*), Gabriel Bataille (the famous lutenist and arranger of *airs*), two flautists, and two other instrumentalists – Nicolas

---

[33] Abbé Oroux, *Histoire ecclésiastique de la Cour de France* (2 vols., Paris, Imprimerie Royale, 1776–7)., II, p. 181. Guillaume Du Peyrat, *Histoire ecclésiastique* de la cour ou les antiquitez et recherches de la chapelle, et oratoire du Roy de France (Paris, Henry Sara, 1645), p. 474, says the *chapelle de plainchant* was founded in 1543, but evidence presented in Brobeck, *The Motet at the Court of Francis I*, p. 21, suggests 1526.

[34] *L'Ordre que la Roy veut estre suivy et observé désormais pour le service Divin* ... This *règlement* is preserved in F-Pn MS 500 de Colbert 54, although several later (and more legible) copies exist. Quotations here are taken from MS fonds fr. 7008. The term *dessus-mué* may refer to adult falsettists, players of the "mute cornett," or falsettists who doubled as cornettists: see Simon Ravens, *The Supernatural Voice: A History of High Male Singing* (Woodbridge, Boydell, 2014), pp. 115–16.

[35] Archon, *Histoire ecclésiastique*, II, p. 660.

[36] États de la Maison, F-Pn MS fonds fr. 3994, f.226-8.   [37] F-Pn MS fonds fr. 18512.

[38] By 1619, the accounts list eight boys: Archives nationales de France, Z1a 486.

Doline and Jehan Nattie – who probably played viol or lute.[39] While the personnel certainly changed over the reign of Louis XIII, the disposition and numbers remained essentially fixed.[40]

For major events, the singers would be joined by the wind players of the *grande écurie*, and although Godefroy's account does not mention this group of musicians by name, illustrations of the coronation show multiple wind instruments participating (see Figure 2.3). The records of the *écurie* show the musicians divided into players of the "trompette," "fiffre, tabourin et musette" (who presumably did not perform in the cathedral), and "Hautbois, Saqueboutes, Cornet et Violle." It is probably this latter group that performed, doubling the musicians of the *chapelle* and *chambre*, and joining the two cornet players who were permanent members of the *chapelle*.[41]

As Louis approached the altar for his confirmation, then, these performers sang the Pentecost and Confirmation hymn *Veni creator spiritus*, supposedly written by Charlemagne himself.[42] We have no specific information as to who might have composed this piece, but Eustache Du Caurroy, who had been *sous-maître* at the *chapelle royale* until his death only a year before, seems a likely candidate: his Requiem had probably just been performed at the funeral of Henri IV, and his recently published *Preces ecclesiasticae*, dedicated to la Reine Marguerite (Henri IV's first wife, who was Louis's sponsor at the confirmation), provides two settings in imitative polyphony in the second volume of the collection.[43] (It is

---

[39] F-Pn MS fonds fr. 18512.

[40] The first year of Louis XIII's reign for which records survive is 1631. For that and all subsequent years, the ensemble consisted of three choirboys (presumably singing the *dessus* part together), a small group of men's voices (*haute-contre, taille, basse-contre*), two lutenists, a viol player, and a flutist; see 'État général des officiers de la Maison du Roy', Archives nationales de France, Z1^a 472, ff. 117r–18r (1631). For a complete listing of the personnel, see also Bennett, *Sacred Repertories in Paris under Louis XIII: Bibliothèque nationale de France MS V^{ma} res.571*, Royal Musical Association Monographs, 17 (Farnham, Ashgate, 2009), pp. 286–90.

[41] I am grateful to Dr. Szpirglas for sharing his work on the musicians at the court of Louis XIII in advance of publication. The account of the procession for the *États Généraux* on October 26, 1614, records that the procession featured "les haultsbois cornets à bouquins et sacquebouttes du Roy jouans et la Musique du Chapelle chantant": see F-Pn MS fonds fr. 18521.

[42] Archon, *Histoire ecclésiastique*, II, p. 711; Godefroy does not provide this information. *Veni creator* is ascribed to Charlemagne with confidence in, for example, Abbé Lebeuf, *Traité historique et pratique sur le chant ecclésiastique* (Paris, Jean-Baptiste Hérissant, 1741), p. 15.

[43] Eustache Du Caurroy, *Preces ecclesiasticae ad numerous musices redactae* (Paris, Pierre Ballard, 1609), 2 vols. For the history and structure of this collection, and for Du Caurroy's biography, see Marie-Alexis Colin, 'Eustache Du Caurroy. Un compositeur français aux confins du XVIe et du XVIIe siècle', *Acta Musicologica*, 73/2 (2001), 189–258, and Marie-Alexis Colin, *Eustache Du Caurroy: Preces ecclesiasticae* (Versailles, Éditions du CMBV, Klincksieck, 2000).

certainly possible that Formé or Granier or another past *sous-maître* provided the music, but no setting by them survives from this period.)[44] Of course, the text of *Veni creator* would not have been modified in any way for these circumstances, but as the first of the major musical items of the coronation "complex," its full and resonant sound, its call (in the voice of Charlemagne) for the Holy Spirit to come down to "visit your souls," and the observation that "You drive our enemy far away, And give us peace now: So with you as guide ahead We shall endure all danger" cannot but have been heard favorably by those present.

The ceremony proceeded with various prayers, invocations, anointings, signs of the cross, and the imposition of hands, followed immediately by the performance of the Antiphon *Confirma hoc Deus, quod operatus est in nobis a templo sancto tuo quod est in Jerusalem* (Confirm, O God, what thou hast wrought in us from thy temple in Jerusalem). Taken from Psalm 67, in which God is portrayed scattering his enemies, its text (verses 29 and 30) is an abbreviated version of the Offertory for the Mass of the Holy Spirit that was celebrated after the coronation (see below).[45] After the service was completed, Louis retired to the Bishops Palace for dinner, before returning to the cathedral to make his confession and retiring to his own lodgings.

The *Sacre*

The next day, Sunday, the day of the *sacre* itself, the king was woken at 6.00 a.m. by the Bishops of Laon and Beauvais (chosen from the twelve ecclesiastical peers of France) in the ritual of the sleeping king, in which Louis was considered to be resurrected from a lifeless body, represented in the past by the effigy of the former king.[46] He was then led in procession to the Cathedral, at the door of which the *Chantre* and Canons again sang the responsory *Ecce mitte angelum* in chant followed by more prayers, after which the canons led the king into the cathedral singing the "antienne" *Domine in virtute tuae laetabitur Rex* (Psalm 20) in *fauxbourdon*.[47]

---

[44] Granier published a collection of hymns in 1610, but this is lost. Jean de Bournonville's 1612 collection contained a setting of this hymn, but as he was a provincial composer without any royal appointment, his music was unlikely to have been performed. The Paris manuscript, which contains music from royal circles, does not contain a setting of the *Veni creator*.
[45] *Pontificale Romanum Clementis VIII Pont Max.*, pp. 1–3.
[46] See Jackson, *Vive le Roi*, pp. 131–54.
[47] Godefroy, I, p. 409, 58. In the first half of the eleventh century, the Royal *Ordo* specifies the singing of *Domine salvum fac regem* at this point, although the text also implies the singing of

2 In thy strength, O Lord, the king shall joy; and in thy salvation he shall rejoice exceedingly.

3 Thou hast given him his heart's desire: and hast not withholden from him the will of his lips.

4 For thou hast prevented him with blessings of sweetness: thou hast set on his head a crown of precious stones.

...

14 Be thou exalted, O Lord, in thy own strength: we will sing and praise thy power.

As sixteenth-century commentaries make clear, the psalm itself is a prophecy that the Messiah, the Christ (anointed one), will come, that God will crown him king, and that God will give him the strength to overcome all his enemies, a prophecy in which Louis, as a new "Christ," would now share. Gabriel Dupuyherbault's 1555 translation of the psalter prefaces the psalm with the observation that "The Prophet predicts the victory of Jesus Christ and his sempiternal reign" with a marginal note "Thanking God for the good prosperity of your good Prince";[48] while the Douay–Reims Bible observes that the psalm is "Praise to God for Christ's exaltation after his passion: and depression of his enemies."[49] The Douay–Reims commentary on v. 1, however, "Pertaining to the new Testament principally to Christ, partly to godly and victorious Kings, and generally to all the blessed, which overcome spiritual enemies," engages more with the earthly dimension, while Renaud de Beaune's translation of 1563, reissued in 1612, prioritizes the thanksgiving for the king: "Thanksgiving for the victory, safety, happiness and long life of the King. Mystically, to be sung to celebrate the victory of our Christ over his enemies, Sin, Death, and Satan."[50]

Even a musical technique as apparently simple as *fauxbourdon* could signal an ideological position, although in this case it is difficult establish exactly how the musical reading of this psalm would have been understood. The revised *règlement* for Henri III's *chapelle royale* of 1587 specified that

---

Psalm 20. The *Ordo* of 1250 has the performance of Psalm 19, *Exaudiat te Dominus* complete (with its antiphon *Domine salvum fac regem*), but this seems to be an exception. By the time of the coronation of Charles VIII in 1484, the pattern followed by Lous XIII was set. See Jackson, *Coronation Ordines*, pp. 204, 345, 572.

[48] Gabriel Dupuyherbault, *Psaumes de David, traduicts au plus près de leur sens propre & naturel* (Paris, Jehan de Roigny, 1555), p. 33: "Le Prophète predicte la victoire de Iesus Christ, & son règne sempiternel" and "Remerciant Dieu pour la bonne prospérité de ton bon Prince."

[49] *The Second Tome of the Holie Bible Faithfully Translated into English out of the Authenticall Latin. Diligently Conferred with the Hebrew, Greek, and Other Editions in Divers Languages* (Douai, John Cousturier, 1609/R1633), p. 45.

[50] Renaud de Beaune, *Les CL pseaumes de David, Latins et François, traduits par Mr Renaud de Beaune* (Paris, Gilles Robinot, 1612), f. 35r: "Action de grâces pour la victoire, salut, félicité & prorogation de la vie du Roy. Mystiquement se chanter la victoire de nostre Christ sur ses ennemis qui son, le Péché, la Mort, & Sathan."

many of the essential components of the liturgy were to be sung in *fauxbourdon*, with "musique" (i.e. polyphony) reserved for all but the most important occasions. (And we know that the practices of Henri III's *chapelle* were taken over by Henri IV and, subsequently, Louis XIII.)[51] Likewise, the two Masses later published by Nicolas Formé (who had just succeeded Eustache Du Caurroy as *sous-maitre* in 1609) "en contrepoint simple" (effectively *fauxbourdon*) also indicate that such simple music (to our ears) often played a key role in royal liturgies.[52] No notated setting of Psalm 20 survives, but settings of other psalms and directions for performing *fauxbourdon* are preserved in a number of relevant and important late sixteenth- and seventeenth-century sources – Benedic Macé's 1582 *Instructions pour apprendre à chanter à quatre parties*, a set of *fauxbourdons* of important psalms in Ballard's *Octo Cantica* of 1584 and 1599, and a fragment of the psalm *Lauda Jerusalem* in Abraham Blondet's 1611 *Officii Divae Ceciliae*.[53]

Macé's treatise provides four-voice settings, in choir-book format, of the eight psalm tones using notation that does not differentiate syllable length. Macé acknowledged this property of his settings, but justified it by asserting that chant and *fauxbourdon*, as he put it, "ne comprend en soy qu'une sorte de Notes plaines, & d'esgalle mesure & valeur"(consists of only one kind of plain notes, and of equal measure and value), and that differentiated note values were only appropriate for "musique figurée" (i.e. composed polyphony). Nevertheless, Macé attributed the "effects" of antiquity to these chants, describing music as part of mathematics, as the most esteemed of the arts of antiquity, and how I Kings had told the story of David appeasing the fury of Saul.[54]

But it is perhaps more likely that the manner of performance did engage with rhythm as a major component of the "effectiveness," associating it with the measured music of antiquity, especially since Reims had been at the forefront of humanist-inspired chant reforms ever since Cardinal de Lorraine, archbishop of Reims, had instigated changes to the liturgical books on his return from the Council of Trent.[55] At court, too, *fauxbourdon* seems to have been an essentially rhythmic, "measured" practice: Le

---

[51] Archon, *Histoire ecclésiastique*, II, pp. 660 and 708.
[52] Nicolas Formé, *Musica simplex* (Paris, Pierre Ballard, 1638). See also Chapter 6.
[53] For other, later, examples of *fauxbourdons*, see Deborah Kauffman, 'Fauxbourdon in the seventeenth and eighteenth centuries: "le secours d'une douce harmonie"', *Music & Letters*, 90/1 (2008), 68–93; and Xavier Bisaro, *Guide historique et pratique du plain-chant et du fauxbourdon. France XVIIe–XVIIIe siècles* (Collection numérique du CMBV, 2017), pp. 115–16.
[54] Jean Macé, *Instructions pour apprendre à chanter à quatre parties, selon le Plain chant, les Pseaumes, & Cantiques* (Caen, Jean Macé, 1582).
[55] See Chapter 6 for the role of the Lorraine/Guise family in chant reform.

Roy and Ballard's 1584 semi-official collection *Octo cantica Divae Mariae virginis* provided a set of *fauxbourdon* settings of the Magnificat in the eight tones and various other standard liturgical items that would have been commonly used in the liturgy – the Sunday vespers psalms, the *O salutaris* verse for the elevation, the psalms *De profundis* and *In exitu Israel*, and the Te Deum.[56] In both volumes, all the *fauxbourdons* are through-composed, notated in unequal note values, paying close attention to the text declamation, and complex enough that, reading from part-books, the singers would need to obey all the notated rhythms strictly. The volume's colophon describes how these texts are *simplici, prepequae syllabico concentu contexta* ("fitted to a simple and almost syllabic harmony") and *pari syllabici concentus modulatione confecta* ("completed with a well-matched rhythmic measure of syllabic harmony"), and while the editors make no overt claims that such declamation is modeled on that of antiquity, the settings would, if performed strictly, at some level be barely distinguishable from *musique mesurée*, although obviously the repeated larger metrical patterns that *musique mesurée* relies on would not be present. In the same way, another source, even closer in time and place to the coronation, points to a highly structured performance of the text – the bass part of settings of the psalms *Lauda Jerusalem* and *Dixit Dominus* included in the fragments that survive of Abraham Blondet's *Officii Divae Ceciliae virgo et martyr Musicorum patronae musici concentibus expressi*, published in 1611 and presumably performed at the cathedral of Notre-Dame.[57] Carefully notated in just two note values (semibreve and minim), with a c time-signature (i.e. a sign that specifies the ratio between note values, a sign that is not found in music that is to be performed "freely," such as chant) (see Figure 2.1), this setting, too, has enough "musical" content (particularly harmonic motion) that it must surely have been performed metrically. If we accept, then, that such a technique was used by the canons of the cathedral, we can imagine the powerful effect of this "measured" music (in its most general sense) elevating the psalm text just as Mauduit's settings of Baïf's paraphrases had done some thirty years earlier.

---

[56] *Octo cantica divae Mariae Virginis, quae vulgo Magnificat appellantur* (Paris, Le Roy and Ballard, 1584, reissued 1599). The later edition includes two additional psalms – the *Exaudiat te Dominus* and the *Laudate Dominum*. See also Lauren Guillo, *Pierre I Ballard et Robert III Ballard: Imprimeurs du roy pour la musique (1599–1673)* (Sprimont, Mardaga, 2003).

[57] Abraham Blondet, *Officii Divae Ceciliae virgo et martyr Musicorum patronae musici concentibus expressi* (Paris, Pierre I Ballard, 1611). Fragments of this publication – settings of the *Dixit Dominus*, the *Laudate Dominum*, and an *Agnus Dei* in ten parts, together with a motet to Saint Cecilia, a setting of the *Domine salvum fac regem*, and the measured music – are bound into the F-Pn copy of Orlando de Lassus, *Moduli duarum, vel trium vocum* (Paris, Robert and Pierre Ballard, 1601). Only one voice part is preserved. See also Guillo, *Pierre Ballard*, pp. 100–1.

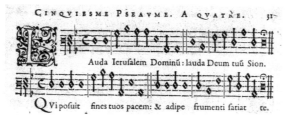

Figure 2.1 Abraham Blondet, *Lauda Jerusalem*, fragment, bass part.
Abraham Blondet, *Officii Divae Ceciliae virgo et martyr Musicorum patronae musici concentibus expressi* (Paris, Pierre Ballard, 1611). Bibliothèque nationale de France

Following this ceremonial entrance and more prayers, a cleric fetched the holy oil, during which the responsory *Inveni servum meum* was sung. Also sung on the Feast of Saint Remi, and based on Psalm 88:20, the text of this responsory establishes a covenant between the anointed one, David, and God – promising that David will crush his enemies:

20 I have found David my servant: with my holy oil I have anointed him.

...

29 And I will make him my firstborn, high above the kings of the earth.

The Archbishop then approached the altar and prepared the chalice of Saint Remi and the Holy Ampoule, before saying another prayer and beginning the Litany. With the litany and Agnus Dei completed, the crux of the ceremony began – the anointing – in which Cardinal de Joyeuse applied the holy oil to various parts of Louis's body while the Antiphon *Unxerunt Salamonem* was sung.[58] In an echo of the rites of both baptism and confirmation, the first application was to the head, a moment shown in Figure 2.2, where we see Cardinal de Joyeuse placing the oil on a kneeling Louis, with Marie de Médicis looking on from under the Baldachino, the caption announcing the role of the Holy Spirit:

Qu'ainsi le Sainct Esprit tousiours dedans ton Cœur	That thus the Holy Spirit always within your Heart,
Comme de divin Huille en toy montre sa gloire:	Like the divine Oil, in you shows its glory:
Confirme son amour d'un amour si vaincueur	Confirms its love of a love so conquering
Que jusqu'au plus haut Ciel en lui se la victoire.	That up to the high Heavens in him will be the victory

[58] Godefroy, I, p. 65

Figure 2.2 Coronation of Louis XIII. Anointing of the head, with Marie de Médicis and musicians in the background.
Engraving, Thomas de Leu, c. 1610. Bibliothèque nationale de France

Godefroy's 1649 account reports that the *chantre* and *sous-chantre* sang the antiphon, but his 1618 account of Henri IV's coronation has the *musique de la chapelle* singing at this point, and this seems more likely to have been the case here.[59]

The anointing process culminated with Louis's right hand (the eighth anointing) and his left (the ninth). At the same time the archbishop proclaimed:[60]

Ungantur manus istae de oleo sanctificato, unde uncti fuerunt Reges et Prophetae, & sicut unxit Samuel David in Regem …

These hands are anointed with holy oil, where the Kings and Prophets were anointed, and as Samuel anointed David king …

---

[59] Godefroy, I, p. 66; Thédore Godefroy, *Le Cérémonial de France* (Paris, Abraham Pacard, 1619), p. 655.
[60] Godefroy, I, p. 67.

After the blessing and presentation of the gloves, the ring, and the scepter, Cardinal de Joyeuse then blessed and took the crown in his left hand, placing it on Louis's head with the assistance of the twelve peers who joined their hands with his. That done, and after several blessings, the king was accompanied to his throne in the nave, which faced the altar. Cardinal de Joyeuse then kissed the king with great reverence before proclaiming in a loud voice, *Vivat rex in aeternum*. The other peers did the same, before the whole cathedral began to resound to the cry of *Vivat rex in aeternum* and the sound of "trompettes, haut-bois, & tous instruments." The longest "musical" item – the Te Deum – was then performed, intoned by Joyeuse and then continued by the singers "accompagné d'orgues, & autre Musique."[61]

The history of the musical performance of the Te Deum at the coronation, and of its broader meaning, remains unclear. In the seventeenth century, it was widely considered that the hymn itself had been dictated by God to Saint Augustine and Saint Ambrose at the former's baptism, although much of the text is drawn either directly or indirectly from the psalms.[62] Generally regarded as a hymn to the Trinity and originally, in the early church, part of the celebration of the Mass, the Te Deum was later incorporated into the Office of Matins, where it replaced the concluding lesson and response to the Holy Trinity on Sundays.[63] It is in this liturgical role that it would have been most commonly heard (sixteenth- and seventeenth-century liturgical treatises focus almost exclusively on this aspect of its significance), although, because of the tradition that Ambrose and Augustine had composed the hymn "in a state of joy and in thanksgiving for the favor which God had shown to Saint Augustine by the infusion of grace of the baptism," it subsequently became a hymn of praise and thanksgiving more generally, often appended to para- or extra-liturgical events such as processions, celebrations, and acts of thanksgiving.[64] For the typical urban resident of the early seventeenth century

---

[61] Godefroy, I, p. 72.
[62] See, for example, Simplician Saint Martin, *Histoire de la vie du glorieux père S. Augustin religieux, docteur de l'église* (Toulouse, Adrien Colomiez, 1641), p. 30. For a detailed discussion of the history and structure of the Te Deum, and its derivation from the psalms, see John Julian, *A Dictionary of Hymnology* (New York: Dover, 1906/R 1957), p. 1125; and John Wordsworth, *The Te Deum: Its Structure and Meaning and Its Musical Setting and Rendering* (Oxford, John Hart, 1903), pp. 11–16.
[63] Arnaud Peyronnet, *Manuel du Bréviaire Romain* (Toulouse, Jean Boude, 1667), pp. 161–2.
[64] Peyronnet, *Manuel du Bréviaire*, pp. 165–6. The liturgy of such processions of thanksgiving can be found in, for example, *Rituale Romanum Pauli V. Pont. Max. iussu editum* (Rome, Typographia Reverendae Camerae Apostolicae, 1615), p. 196.

who lived, for example, in the vicinity of a cathedral, a collegiate church, or a religious house, the Te Deum might have been heard as part of a procession to give thanks for a good harvest, or the resident might have had to enter the cathedral to hear it sung at the end of the procession – but in either case it was one relatively minor component of a long liturgy consisting of psalms, hymns (including alternatives to the Te Deum such as the *Canticum trium puerorum* or the *Canticum Zachariae*), litanies, and prayers, and there is no reason to suppose that it was typically sung in polyphony. Fogel's important study on the Te Deum ceremony (discussed more fully in Chapter 5) points to a contrasting practice that developed early in the hymn's history by which it became associated with earthly power, but we should not necessarily equate "earthly power" simply with the coronation:[65] after all, as Giesey has pointed out, coronations, as once-in-a-lifetime events, actually had much less impact than other ceremonies celebrating and legitimating royal power that were repeated more frequently – most notably the *entrée*, during which the Te Deum was also performed.[66] For the reign of Louis XIV, Montagnier has shown, based on Bossuet's translation, that most lines can be read as commentary on either the king or his political situation, and a paraphrase he quotes from the 1670s certainly replaces the opening line – *Te Deum laudamus* – with *Te Regem laudamus*, among many other parallels.[67] Likewise, in a similar but possibly less extreme analogy, a paraphrase and commentary from around 1616, *Le Te Deum de la Paix*, avoids equating Louis with God himself, but does render *Tu rex gloriae, Christe* as *Tu rex gloriae, Ludovice*, a reasonable substitution if we read *Christe* in its literal sense of "anointed." But neither of these examples – non-liturgical, encomiastic paraphrases – while certainly implying that the hymn was associated with royalty, establishes any kind of primacy of the coronation Te Deum over other performances of the hymn (given that they were not written with the coronation in mind), an important consideration when we approach other ceremonies that feature this hymn.

Seen from the perspective of a liturgical act, contemporaries in the early and later seventeenth century certainly did not prioritize either coronation or indeed any royal associations in their descriptions of the Te Deum. Villette's *Les Raisons de l'Offices*, a comprehensive study of all the liturgies

---

[65] Michèle Fogel, *Les Cérémonies d'information dans la France du XVI au XVIII siècle* (Paris, Fayard, 1989), p. 157. See also Sabine Zak, 'Das Tedeum als Huldigungsgesang', *Historisches Jahrbuch*, 102 (1982), 1–32.

[66] Giesey, 'The King imagined', p. 53.   [67] Montagnier, 'Le Te Deum en France', 207–9.

of the church, including coronations, published in 1611, does not mention the coronation at all in the discussion of the Te Deum, even though a full chapter is devoted to the coronation itself (where it is mentioned just in passing). Instead, Villette considers the hymn only in the context of Matins, where he reads the Te Deum, uniquely, as the work of the Holy Spirit:[68]

It is a profession of faith, the adoration due to the very holy Trinity, that the Angels offered to it as a Hymn, and to the church as a Cantique. It is the first and most excellent Hymn that we possess. It is the only Cantique in which the Holy Spirit made itself apparent to the Church since it completed and sealed the Holy Scriptures through the Apostles, and the first orthodox and ecumenical Council of Nicea.

Others later than Villette began to acknowledge the broader role in celebrations and in the earthly realm, but still saw it primarily as an act of thanksgiving. Simplician's account of the life of Saint Augustine of 1641 describes it being sung:[69]

on the Feasts of Jesus Christ, of the Virgin and of the Saints, but at the coronation of Popes, of Kings, and in many other situations, where one bears testimony to the recognition of blessings received, and of graces bestowed, by the public and solemn singing of Te Deum laudamus.

But even an author as late as Peyronnet, after describing at length its use in Matins (1671), remarks simply that:[70]

Otherwise it was an ancient practice of the Church to sing the Te Deum in thanksgiving as it is sung at this time to thank God for all kinds of happy success. The examples are frequent in the Authors who have treated the Ceremonies observed on these occasions.

And while by the turn of the seventeenth century other texts were beginning to become "officially" associated with the king – the psalms *Exaudiat*

---

[68] Villette, *Les Raisons de l'Office*, p. 412: "C'est la profession de foy, & l'adoration deuë à la très-saincte Trinité, que les Anges luy offrent pour Hymne, & l'Église pour Cantique. C'est le premier & plus excellent Hymne que nous ayons. C'est le seul Cantique dont le sainct Esprit ait fait présent à l'Église depuis qu'il a clos & seellé les sainctes Escritures par les Apostres, & premier Concile de Nice Orthodoxe œcuménique."
[69] Saint Martin, *Histoire de la vie du glorieux père*, p. 30: "aux festes de Iesus-Christ, de la Vierge & des Saincts, mais au sacre des Papes, des Roys, & en plusieurs autres rencontres, où l'on témoigne la reconnoissance des bien-faits receus, & des grâces concédées, par le chant public, & solennel du *Te Deum laudamus*."
[70] Peyronnet, *Manuel*, p. 165: "Au reste c'a esté une ancienne pratique de l'Église de chanter le Te Deum en action de grâces ainsi qu'on le chante en ce temps pour remercier Dieu de toutes sortes d'heureux succez. Les exemples en sont fréquents dans les Auteurs, qui ont traité des Cérémonies observées en ces occasions."

te Dominus (Psalm 19) and *Laudate Dominum omnes gentes* (Psalm 116) were added to the 1599 reprint of Ballard's *Octo Cantica*, the title proclaiming *quod communiter gratias Regis vocant* (which are commonly called prayers for the king) – no such designation was ever attached to the Te Deum, even where it appeared in the same context.[71] At the beginning of the seventeenth century, then, we should probably hear the Te Deum not as a hymn whose character was defined by the coronation, but rather as a common, shared component of the liturgy, associated equally with solemn thanksgiving, with Matins, with a procession for a successful harvest, with welcoming a king to a grateful city, and (most rarely) with the coronation.

In its role in Matins, the Te Deum was supposedly never sung with music of any kind (polyphony or instruments), but in ceremonies such as the Te Deum, the *entrée*, and the coronation, it was probably liberated from the strict liturgical constraints described by Villette:[72] many descriptions of its performance on royal occasions (not just coronations, but also *entrées*) mention the organ or other instruments, and of course iconographical evidence from Louis XIII's coronation shows a variety of instruments as well as singers. An early account of the coronation of Charles VIII, in 1484, describes how the Te Deum was performed by the organ, in plain chant, and in polyphony, because it was so long,[73] but closer to 1610, for the coronation of Henri IV in 1594: "The Bishop of Chartres descended from the pulpit by the stairway to the left, and positioned by the Eagle of the choir began the Te Deum 'à haute voix', which was followed and finished 'en musique' by the King's Chapel."[74] The account of Louis XIII is more specific: "my lord of Rheims beginning the Te Deum, accompanied by organs and 'autre musique,'" and on other occasions the accounts went into even more detail.[75]

---

[71] *Octo cantica*, 1584 and 1599. The Te Deum also receives no royal ascription in the 1623 *Airs sur les hymnes sacrées* (where, by contrast, the *Exaudiat* is described as a *Prière pour le Roy*).

[72] Villette argues that, since the Te Deum is a profession of faith, it is never accompanied with organ, or set to music, because it is the mouth that should utter these words, not the organ (the same applies to the Credo of the Mass): see Villette, *Les Raisons de l'Office*, pp. 413–14. Bauldry, however, writing in 1646, assumes that at Matins the Te Deum will be performed alternatim with organ, although in processions of thanksgiving it should be performed "in qua Musicorum chori cum citharis, fistulis & aliis instrumentis musicis laetitiae signa": see Michel Bauldry, *Manuale sacrarum caeremoniarum iuxta ritum S. Romanae ecclesiae* (Paris, Ioannem Billaine, 1646) pp. 38 and 195.

[73] Godefroy, I, p. 204

[74] Godefroy, 1619, p. 676: "l'Évesque de Chartres descendit du pulpitre par l'escalier gauche, & à l'endroit de l'Aigle du Chœur commença à haute voix Te Deum laudamus, qui fut suivy & achevé en musique par la Chapelle du Roy."

[75] Godefroy, I, p. 72: "mondit sieur de Rheims commençant le Te Deum laudamus, accompagné d'orgues, & autre musique."

For example, a Te Deum ceremony at Notre-Dame in 1622 featured instrumentalists and singers grouped together around a lectern, in alternatim with the organ: "then the Te Deum was sung 'en musique' by the singers and musicians who were at a lectern, the organ taking the alternate verses."[76]

The use of the terms "en musique" or "autre musique" imply at least some level of composition beyond simple performance of the chant (and certainly including instruments), but surviving composed settings of the Te Deum are rare, suggesting that on many festive occasions the Te Deum was performed only in semi-improvised polyphony or in chant with alternatim improvised organ versets, or with composed organ versets such as those provided by Attaingnant in his 1530 organ book.[77] It is certainly possible that this was the case in 1610, although perhaps more likely that a composed setting was performed. Again, the actual setting is unknown to us, but it is worth exploring the implications of the possible candidates that do survive – perhaps Le Blanc's setting from the *Octo cantica* of 1584/99 or one of Eustache Du Caurroy's four alternatim settings in imitative polyphony from the two volumes of 1609 *Preces ecclesiasticae*.

Le Blanc's through-composed homophonic and syllabic setting, while part of what appears to be a semi-official court publication, seems a less promising candidate, since it barely qualifies as "musique," though on the other hand, it would be a straightforward matter for instruments and singers to collaborate in this simple, text-driven homophonic piece, and for it to have the same effect as the earlier *fauxbourdon* (see Example 2.1). Like the Le Blanc, the four Du Caurroy settings all present the chant of Te Deum in the tenor, although the chant itself is not the standard, traditional melody, but one that may be associated with the Congregation of the Penitents of our Lady (see Chapter 3). Two of these settings are scored for four voices, c1, c3, c4, and f4, with the tenor presenting the chant almost literally, untransposed. A third setting, scored for five voices, c1, c3, c4, c4, and f4, likewise presents the chant almost literally, untransposed, this time shared between the two c4 voices (tenor and quinta). Based on the descriptions of the performances by the *chapelle royale* that refer to them singing "low and full" (this evidence will be elaborated on in Chapter 7), such a scoring and its relatively low tessitura, coupled with the subdued nature of the settings and the literal presentation of the

---

[76] F-Pn MS nouv. acq. fr. 23474: "ensuite s'en chanté se Te Deum en musique par les chantres et musiciens qui étoient au lutrin, l'orgue faisans les intermèdes des Versets."

[77] *Magnificat sur les huit tons avec Te Deum laudamus et deux Préludes* (Paris, Pierre Attaingnant, 1530).

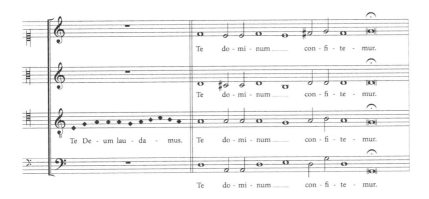

Example 2.1 Didier Le Blanc, *Te Deum*, opening.
Octo cantica divae Mariae Virginis (Paris, Adrian Le Roy and Robert Ballard, 1584).

chant, suggests that Du Caurroy composed these two settings to be performed by the *musique de la chapelle*, alone and without any instruments, as liturgical settings for regular performance in the liturgy of the Penitents and probably the occasional performances in the *chapelle* itself, during the 1580s.[78] On the other hand, the fourth setting, for six voices scored g1, c1, c2, c3, c4, and f4, with the chant transposed up a fourth and presented in the c3 voice (tenor), appears more likely to have invited performance by the combined forces of the *chambre* and the *chapelle* in the manner alluded to by Contarini (see Chapter 7) – the high sweet voices of the *chambre* (with their soft plucked instruments) combined with the low voices of the *chapelle* (accompanied by their louder wind instruments) (see Example 2.2). Given that we know the two ensembles, *chambre* and *chapelle*, were present and that Figure 2.3 shows both wind instruments and a lute (in the front row to the right), such a manner of performance, both for this work in particular, and any others, seems entirely plausible. Since the tessitura of the chant would now be higher, it is also likely (since Godefroy mentions the participation of the organ) that the organ played the alternatim versets (as described in the 1622 ceremony) not provided by Du Caurroy, since they would now have sat uncomfortably high for vocal performance by the clergy or *chantre*.

Of course, given the description of the performance, during which the people acclaimed the king, doves were released and "the trumpets, *hautsbois* and drums sounded pell-mell, with such a great noise that nobody could hear themselves speak," it is possible that very little musical effort was expended at this point.[79] But whatever the exact musical dimension to the Te Deum, the performance by organs, the *musique*, and the singers clearly articulated a significant moment of the ceremony, but it was by no means the conclusion, since the ceremony continued with Cardinal de Joyeuse celebrating High Mass. At the coronation of Henri IV in Chartres, Godefroy reports that "La Messe fut dicte du iour, qui estoit le premier Dimanche de Quaresme" (Mass was said for the day, which was the first Sunday in Lent), but for Louis XIII the account mentions, halfway through, that the Mass then continued according to the ordinary of the day (the double yet still relatively minor Feast of Saint Luke the Evangelist) – suggesting that, up until that point, the Mass had been celebrated according to some other feast.[80] The accounts of the Mass are brief, and only one clue survives: at the offertory, Monsieur de Rhodes, the *grand maître de cérémonies*, led four Knights of the Holy Spirit up to the altar to make the offertory gifts of Wine (in a heavily decorated golden vessel), a silver

---

[78] See Colin, 'Eustache Du Caurroy', p. 216.
[79] Godefroy, I, p. 432: "les trompettes, hauts-bois & tambours sonnoient pesle mesle, avec un si grand bruit, que personne ne s'escoutoit parler."
[80] Godefroy, 1619, p. 677; Godefroy, I, p. 415.

Example 2.2 Eustache Du Caurroy, *Te Deum*, opening.
Preces ecclesiasticae (Paris, Pierre Ballard, 1609).

Figure 2.3 Musicians with shawm and *cornet* (the *écurie*) and a lute and flute (the *chambre*) at the coronation of Louis XIII.
Engraving, Pierre I Firens, 1610. Bibliothèque nationale de France

loaf, a gold loaf, and a gift of golden coins, imprinted with images of the king.[81] The king, carrying his scepter and the *main de justice*, then joined the procession to the altar, where (after giving the symbols of kingship to the Duc de Roannois and Monsieur de Crequy) he placed the gifts on the altar with much ceremony before returning in procession to his throne.

In itself this detail may not seem significant, but it resonates strongly with another liturgy celebrated in the king's presence – the Mass celebrated at the investiture of the Knights of the Holy Spirit. In the accounts of this Mass that survive (described in more detail below), it is this same part of the liturgy that is the only moment described in any detail, and in it, too, the Knights of the Holy Spirit (including the king) were to process together up to the altar to make their offering. And why was this detail added by Godefroy and the author of the Statutes of the Order? Because if – as we must assume – both Masses were celebrated in honor of the Holy Spirit, the Offertory chant which accompanied this act would have had the following text:[82]

Confirma hoc Deus, quod operatus est in nobis, a templo tuo quod est in Jerusalem, tibi offerent Reges munera. Alleluia.

Confirm, O God, what thou hast wrought in us. From thy temple in Jerusalem, Kings shall offer gifts to thee. Alleluia.

---

[81] Godefroy, I, p. 432, or 72–3. For the role of the *grand maître de cérémonies*, see Marie-Lan Nguyen, *Les Grands maîtres des cérémonies et le service des Cérémonies à l'époque modern 1585–1792* (Mémoire de maîtrise, University of Paris IV-Sorbonne, 1999).

[82] For the order of Mass for the Holy Spirit, see, for example, *Missale Romanum ex decreto sacrosancti Concilii Tridentini restitutum* (Paris, Societatem Typographicam, 1627), pp. lv–lvii.

At the Mass of the Holy Spirit, then, in the presence of the king, this moment of the liturgy was not just a metaphor, but a literal description of an act made real, an account of Louis offering gifts in Reims cathedral just as Solomon brought gold and silver gifts and utensils to the Temple of Jerusalem.[83]

After more prayers, the king took communion in both species representing his now priestly status, before the assembled company departed for lunch in the Archbishop's Palace, led by the trumpeters and heralds, marching in rank order, with Knights of the Holy Spirit together, and the sword, *main de justice*, and the crown of Charlemagne carried by Monsieur de Montbazon.[84] The *Mercure* report of the dinner records that each course was accompanied by "des trompettes, clairons & hautbois," while between the courses "la Musique chanta très mélodieusement."[85] Chapter 3 will explore further the tradition of singing at dinner, but the duties of both the *chambre* and *chapelle* required them to be present and singing "graces" (i.e. psalms or motets) at mealtimes anyway, and it is here that the assembled company could have heard any number of appropriate non-liturgical works. Du Caurroy's *Christus vincit*, a setting based on the famous Carolingian coronation acclamation and presumably composed for similar circumstances at the coronation of Henri IV in 1594, could have been repurposed (with Henrico replaced by Ludovico),[86] or, depending on how far back or how contemporary the repertoire was, they could even have performed Maillard's *Domine salvum fac regem*, which, though opening with Psalm 19, continues with Psalm 20, taking part of the liturgy of the coronation and framing it as a non-liturgical celebration.

A New Pentecost: Louis XIII and the Knights of the Holy Spirit

The day after the coronation, following the statutes established by Henri III in 1578 (in what we might actually consider the climax of this complex of ceremonies), Louis was inducted as Chief and Grand Master of the Order

---

[83] II Chronicles, 5:1.   [84] Godefroy, I, p. 501, 433.
[85] *Le Mercure françois*, 1 (1606–10), p. 542v.
[86] Colin, 'Eustache Du Caurroy', p. 215. For the significance of these acclamations, see Ernst Kantorowicz, *Laudes Regiae: A Study in Liturgical Acclamations and Medieval Ruler Worship* (Berkeley, University of California Press, 1946).

of the Holy Spirit (Ordre du Saint-Esprit) at the hands of Cardinal de Joyeuse, who had the day before performed the *sacre*. After attending Mass at Saint Remi in the morning, Louis returned to the cathedral at 3.00 p.m., accompanied by the officers, prelates, cardinals, commanders, and knights of the Order, all dressed in their appropriate regalia, where he heard Vespers of the Holy Spirit, after which the ceremony of investiture took place. In doing this, he took his place alongside his predecessors Henri III and IV, confirmed his role as a conduit for the Holy Spirit, and reinforced the centrality of the regular liturgy to the Holy Spirit celebrated at the *chapelle royale*. At the same time, by their presence and participation, the clerics and nobles gave their assent to this reading of kingship, and were, in turn, seen to do so by the broader populace of Reims and France.

The Order of the Holy Spirit had been founded in 1578 by Henri III, the first of several religious/chivalric orders he would establish over the following eleven years.[87] Born on the Feast of Pentecost 1550, Henri had succeeded to the Polish throne on Pentecost 1573 and (on the death of his brother Charles IX) to the French throne on Pentecost 1574. Passing through Venice in that year on his way back to Paris to take up the French crown, Henri had been received with great ceremony by the Doge and presented with a manuscript of the statutes of the Ordre du Saint-Esprit au Droit Désir, founded by Louis d'Anjou at his own coronation on Pentecost 1352.[88] By 1578, as the nascent Catholic League was beginning to threaten the king's power, Henri determined to found his own Order, taking the ancient Order as a model and supplementing, but not replacing,

---

[87] For the history of the Order, see André Favin, *Le Théâtre d'honneur et de chevalerie, ou L'Histoire des ordres militaires des Roys* (Paris, Robert Foüet, 1620), pp. 643–96; *Histoire des ordres monastiques, religieux et militaires, et les congrégations séculières* (Paris, Jean-Baptiste Coignard, 1719), pp. 397–415; *Les Cérémonies royales qui se doivent faire à la réception de Messieurs les Chevaliers de l'Ordre du S. Esprit* (Paris, Isaac Mesnier, 1619); for a more general history, see Jacques-Auguste de Thou, *Histoire universelle, depuis 1543 jusqu'en 1607* (London, 1734), Vol. 8, pp. 73–4; Archon, *Histoire ecclésiastique*, II, p. 620. For the statutes, see *Le Livre des Statuts et ordonnances de l'Ordre du benoist Sainct Esprit, estably par le très-chrestien Roy de France & de Pologne Henry Troisiesme de ce nom* (1578); and Favin, *Le Théâtre d'Honneur*. For an excellent overview of the order into the later seventeenth century, see Thomas Leconte, 'Entre religion et pouvoir à la cour de France: les cérémonies de l'ordre du Saint-Esprit (1578–1661)', in Peter Bennett and Bernard Dompnier (eds.), *Cérémonial politique et cérémonial religieux dans l'Europe modern: échanges et métissages* (Paris, Garnier, 2020). Leconte reproduces the full text of the ceremony of foundation in 1578/9, found in AN KK 1431.

[88] For Henri's reception in Venice, see Iain Fenlon, *The Ceremonial City: History, Memory and Myth in Renaissance Venice* (New Haven and London, Yale University Press, 2007), pp. 193–216. This manuscript still exists and is preserved at F-Pn MS fonds fr. 4274.

the already important Ordre de Saint Michel that Louis XI had created in 1469.

By emphasizing his Catholic credentials, reminding his enemies (especially the Guises, who saw themselves as true heirs to the throne) of his relationship with the Holy Spirit, and by requiring them to join him in the Order and swear allegiance, Henri was putting into place the beginnings of his resistance against the League.[89] More broadly, though, the Order was an attempt to create a new Pentecostal age, an age in which, like the final days before the last judgment, the Holy Spirit would reign supreme. Much of the reign of Henri III certainly had an air of the end of times about it: Denis Crouzet describes how astrological predictions in the 1570s and a conjunction in 1583 were taken to mark the Second Coming, and how the prophets had predicted only 1,600 years for the life of the world.[90] Such predictions also aligned with broader contemporary conceptions of the history of the world. According to Joachim de Flore's commentary on the eighth chapter of the Book of the Apocalypse in his *Concordia novi et veteris testamenti* (a synthesis of the Old and New Testaments), the history of the world could be divided into seven days or ages. In the sixth age (the present):[91]

a violent tribulation will disrupt the Church of God so that in the seventh Age, the creator of all things will rest ... And just as on the sixth day Christ suffered, so in the sixth Age, a passion will unfold, preceding the sabbath of peace.

On the other hand, the forthcoming seventh age, the Sabbath, was "the Time of the Spirit, the hour of spiritual understanding and the manifest vision of God."[92] In other words, the Order reflected a millenarist conception of the world in which the kingdom of Henri III, the "Time of the [Holy] Spirit," would precede the last judgment. Obviously, the seventh age did not come to pass during these years (quite the opposite), but followers of Flore reformulated the same arguments in later years. Thus, Claude

---

[89] For the early manifestations of the League and its religious and dynastic aims see Jervis, *The Gallican Church*, p. 172 ff.

[90] Denis Crouzet, 'La Représentation du temps à l'époque de la Ligue', *Revue Historique*, 270/2 (1983), 297–388, esp. p. 313; and Denis Crouzet, *Les Guerriers de Dieu* (Paris, Champ Vallon, 1990), pp. 142–3. See also Ann Ramsey, *Liturgy, Politics, and Salvation: The Catholic League in Paris and the Nature of Catholic Reform, 1540–1630* (Rochester, NY, University of Rochester Press), pp. 160–1.

[91] Quoted in Jean Delumeau, *Une histoire du paradis; le jardin des délices* (Paris, Fayard, 1992), p. 48: "une tribulation violente remuera l'Église de Dieu afin que dans le septième Temps, le Créateur de toutes choses se repose réellement ... Et comme le sixième jour le Christ a souffert, ainsi dans le sixième Temps, une passion se déroulera, précédant le sabbat de la paix."

[92] Ibid.: "Le Temps de l'Esprit, l'heure de la compréhension spirituelle et de la manifeste vision de Dieu."

Villette's *Extraits des Prophéties et révélations des Saincts Pères* (1617) also pointed to "la Paix du Saint-Esprit," which would now be established under the reign of Louis XIII.[93] To those who subscribed to this "over-enchanted" view of the world, the Order of the Holy Spirit prepared them for the afterlife, an age of peace free from the turmoil of religious conflict and earthly pain.

The founding session of the Order was held on the New Year's Eve and New Year's Day of 1579 at the Church of the Augustines in Paris, and the published statutes describe how those attending were divided into various classes of membership. The king himself was the *souverain chef et grand maître*, assuming this office (for Henri's successors) only after swearing to uphold the statutes of the Order as part of the *sacre* and receiving the habit and collar of the Order in a ceremony the following day. (The vow he took was to be included in the *Livre du Sacre* alongside all the other vows that the king took.) The rank beneath the king was to be the commanders, four cardinals and four archbishops, bishops, or prelates chosen from the most virtuous clergy of the kingdom, alongside the king's personal almoner. (The exact number and role of the commanders was somewhat fluid.) These clerics were required to wear their collars and regalia as part of their usual clerical functions back in the diocese. The officers consisted of the *chancelier* (responsible for administrative affairs), the *prévost*, the *maître de cérémonies*, *grand thrésorier*, and *greffier*.[94] The number of members, excluding the king, was to be 100, so the remaining members were the *chevaliers*, chosen from the nobility (which had to be proved by a complicated process). All took vows to uphold both the authority of the king and the teachings of the church (to be enforced by the commanders), and to receive communion on New Year's Day, at the annual meeting (typically in Paris) and on the Feast of Pentecost. All members of the Order were also required to attend Mass on Feast days, to recite the *Heures du Saint-Esprit* daily from a book of hours that they were issued with when they were inducted (or to recite the seven penitential psalms) and to say "un Chappelet d'un Dizain," the *Pater noster*, ten Ave Marias, and the *Credo*.[95]

The annual services and chapter took place around New Year's Day, usually, but not always, at the Church of the Augustines in Paris. At some

---

[93] See Alexandre Haran, *Le Lys et le globe: messianisme dynastique et rêve impérial en France aux xvie et xviie siècles* (Seyssel, Champ Vallon, 2000), pp. 231, 128–9.
[94] Favin, *Le Théâtre d'Honneur*, pp. 660–5.
[95] A later edition of this Office survives as *L'Office des chevaliers de l'Ordre du St. Esprit* (Paris, Imprimerie Royale, 1703), but the rubrics suggest that the Office had not changed since 1578.

of these meetings new members were inducted, while on other occasions no new members joined. But the published lists of inductees, and the frequency with which these inductions took place, offers a window into the changing fortunes of the king (be it Henri III, IV, or Louis XIII) and which of the nobility were either in or out of favor. In the early years of the Order, the members included many Leaguers, individuals who would shortly betray the king: at the first ceremony in 1578/9, for example, Charles de Bourbon, Archbishop of Rouen, was inducted as a *prélat commandeur* – though it was he who would later be put forward as Henri's successor by the League. Likewise, at the same ceremony, other leading league figures such as Charles de Lorraine became a *chevalier*, as did, in 1582, Henri, duc de Joyeuse, who as Père Ange de Joyeuse famously led a League procession through Paris dressed as Jesus and carrying a cross.[96] For the 1610 ceremony in Reims, the seventeenth "creation," only Louis and his half-brother Henry de Bourbon were inducted.[97] Obviously, as an eight-year-old boy, the decision as to whom to induct was not his, but by the next creations, in 1618/19 and 1619/20, Louis had recently deposed both Concini and his mother, and the list of new members reflects his growing assertiveness: just, then, as Henri III had held members of the Guise family close by admitting them as members, so too did Louis, admitting Charles de Lorraine, Henri de Lorraine, and Claude de Lorraine, at the same time as elevating Charles d'Albert, his new ally.[98]

Apart from at coronations, when the new *grand maître* was inducted, the ceremonies followed a standard pattern: Vespers and Compline of the Holy Spirit on New Year's Eve (during which the new members were typically inducted); Mass of the Holy Spirit on New Year's Day, followed by the Office of the Dead to commemorate departed members; and on the following day, a Requiem Mass, again for the departed members.[99] The members of the Order would process from the Louvre to the Church of the Augustines, dressed in black velvet capes ornamented with gold flames, a reminder of the tongues of fire imagery of Pentecost, but also of the Oriflamme, the legendary standard carried by kings of France into battle that had supposedly been given to the Abbey of Saint-Denis by Dagobert. The statutes provide no details of the liturgy or music that was to feature at

---

[96] The procession is described in Abbé Fleury, *Histoire ecclésiastique pour server de continuation à celle de Monsieur l'Abbé Fleury* (Paris, Pierre-Jean Mariette, 1738), Vol. 36, p. 192.
[97] *Recherches historiques de l'Ordre du Saint Esprit* (Paris, Claude Jombert, 1710), pp. 198–201.
[98] For lists of the membership, see *Recherches historiques*, pp. 203–81. For an account of the 1619/20 ceremony, see *Les Cérémonies royales qui se doivent faire*.
[99] Favin, *Le Théâtre d'Honneur*, pp. 667–9.

Vespers, focusing instead on the regalia that the various officers and other participants were to wear, but we can assume that it was Vespers for the Holy Spirit. The same is true for the Mass the following day: almost nothing is specified in the statutes (although again we can assume Mass for the Holy Spirit), but they do highlight just one moment – the Offertory, when the *chevaliers* were to process in rank and order up to the altar to make their offerings of gold coins which were to benefit the novice Augustinians (see the account above).[100] That said, an account of the Mass celebrated by the Order on Christmas Day 1605 highlights the unique role of the king, reporting that "à l'offertoire il n'y vint personne que le Roy qui se mist à deux genoux & baiser la paix, et offrit une pièce d'or que Mr le Comte de Soissons luy portois"(at the Offertory nobody came [to the altar] except the king, who got down on two knees and kissed the peace [a vessel], and offered a piece of gold that Mr the Count of Soissons brought to him).[101]

After lunch the *chevaliers* returned to the Church of the Augustines to hear Vespers for the Dead, where the next day they also heard Mass for the Dead, at the offertory of which a *De profundis* was sung, and after lunch the chapter meeting of the Order. For these later services, the church was transformed and decorated with black and a *chapelle ardente* erected in the center. At this event, the *chevaliers* were also all to wear black, except the king.

The focus on the Holy Spirit exemplified in the Order did not remain just a semiannual event for long. As part of the revisions to the *chapelle royale* liturgy of 1587, a weekly Mass for the Holy Spirit was instituted to be celebrated on Mondays (during which *Veni creator* was to be sung), this practice continuing into the reign of Louis XIII.[102] And at the Church of the Augustines, a side chapel was dedicated to the Holy Spirit and in regular use by the time of Louis XIII for the celebration of the "King's Masse." Favin (in the English translation of 1623) described the altar as follows:[103]

High Masse is daily celebrated at nine of the clocke in the morning, at the high Altar, wholly new made and enriched with foure Colombs of black marble, and size goodly Angels of Brasse: the Table hanging thereon, containeth the adoration of the three Kings. This high Altar is adorned on the day of Pentecoste, and solemne Festivals of the Order, with a Cloth of State, Coapes, Chasubles & Tuniques of

---

[100] Ibid., p. 668.
[101] Carpentras, Bibliothèque Inguimbertine, MS 1794, p. 439 (notes by Pieresc).
[102] *Règlement* for the *chapelle royale* MS fonds fr. 7008, ff. 4v–5r.
[103] Andrew Favin, *The Theater of Honour and Knighthood* (London, William Laggard, 1623), p. 415.

Figure 2.4 Arms of Henri III with the *collier* of the Knights of the Holy Spirit.
André Favin, *Le Théâtre d'Honneur* (Paris, Robert Foüet, 1620), p. 643. Bibliothèque nationale de France

Cloth of Silver, the ground green, powdered with flames of Gold in embroyderie, hardly any place wanting or voyd, with divers Figures, expressing the misteries of our Redemption, and the Armes of the King that was the Founder, in the most excellent imbroderie, not to be equalled. The said Ornaments, Coapes, Chasubles, and Tuniques are lined with Orange colour Taffata; and the Chappell beautified with vessles of Gold and Silver, of most inestimable value, and truely worth the Greatnesse of a King of France, especially King Henry, Third of the name, Great in all his actions and the most bountiful Prince of his time.

The altar cloth described by Favin still exists, and we can see on it the "misteries of our redemption" represented in the symbols around the two images (Pentecost and the Annunciation), the same symbols that adorned the collar of the Order pictured in Favin's volume (see Figure 2.4), and which also appeared in Renaud de Beaune's translation of the psalms, a volume presumably published with the Order in mind in some way (Renaud de Beaune was inducted into the Order in 1591 by virtue of his status as almoner to Henri III).[104] In her study of imagery associated with Henri III, Haquet has explored these symbols, proposing that they indicate "Henri," "Logos," and "David," but Favin has a simpler, if less complete explanation:[105]

---

[104] Claude de Luz, *Retable de l'autel*, 1585–1587. Broderie, Paris, Musée du Louvre, CL 18550.

[105] See Isabelle Haquet, *L'Énigme Henri III: ce que nous révèlent les images* (Nanterre, Presses Universitaires de Paris Nanterre, 2012), p. 364. Favin, *Le Théâtre d'Honneur*, p. 645: "Le premier Chiffre est d'un H & d'un Lamba [sic], Λ & le tout double, qui se peut lire haut & bas: ce sont les premières lettres des noms dudict Roy Fondateur, & Instituteur de l'Ordre, HENRY, & de la Royne sa Femme LOUISE DE LORRAINE. Les deux autres sont Chiffres réservés en l'Esprit du Roy Fondateur de personnes favorites."

Figure 2.5 Celebration of Mass for the Holy Spirit, 1703.
L'Office des chevaliers de l'Ordre du St. Esprit (Paris, Imprimerie Royale, 1703), p. 3. Bibliothèque nationale de France

The first figure is of an H, and of a Lambda Λ, the whole doubled, which can be read from top to bottom: these are the two letters of the name of the said King, the founder and instituter of the Order, Henry, and of the Queen his Wife Louise de Lorraine. The two others are Figures reserved in the Spirit of the King the Founder for his favourites.

At Reims in 1610, the ceremonies reflected the standard pattern of events. The choir of the cathedral had been decorated with all the ornaments of the Order: the fabric that decorated much of the altar, the platforms, and the king's dais was decorated with embroidered golden flames and "chiffres," with each panel featuring a dove representing the Holy Spirit,[106] while the central panel was the altarpiece from the Church of the Augustines itself, showing the descent of the Holy Spirit to the Apostles.[107] The newly crowned king entered the cathedral dressed in silver with silver embroidery, accompanied by Cardinal de Gondi (who was not wearing his Cardinal's robes) and Monsieur de Langres (who was dressed in a long gown and wearing the Cross of the Order), and took his place beside the chancellor, Monsieur du Châteauneuf, who was seated on a throne of blue satin decorated with *fleurs de lys*. Cardinal de Joyeuse then began Pontifical Vespers, "which was continued by the Musique du Roy" "in very beautiful and good Music, composed of voices and instruments."[108] Unlike the coronation ceremony itself, in which nothing was

---

[106] Godefroy, I, p. 434.   [107] Godefroy, I, p. 454.
[108] Godefroy, I, p. 455: "qui furent continues par la Musique du Roy"; p. 435: "en très-belle & bonne Musique, composée de voix & d'instruments."

specified "en musique," here we are told that much of the liturgy was sung to polyphony, making it probably the most "musical" moment of the whole weekend's events.

The Office of Vespers for the Holy Spirit (Pentecost) features the psalms *Dixit Dominus* 109, *Confitebor* 110, *Beatus vir* 111, *Laudate pueri* 112, and *In exitu Israel* 113 (i.e. all the standard psalms for Sunday Vespers). Just as for the other events of the weekend, we might expect to hear the music of the recently deceased Eustache Du Caurroy, especially when we consider that Du Caurroy joined the court of Henri III in 1578 just as the Order was founded, that he would have spent his entire career providing whatever music was required for its meetings, and that the one surviving liturgical psalm setting by Du Caurroy (i.e. one that provides the doxology) is of *In exitu Israel*, the final psalm of the sequence:[109]

1 In exitu Israhel de Aegypto, domus Iacob de populo barbaro:	When Israel went out of Egypt, the house of Jacob from a barbarous people:
2 Facta est Iudaea sanctificatio eius: Israhel potestas eius.	Judea made his sanctuary, Israel his dominion.
3 Mare vidit, et fugit: Iordanis conversus est retrorsum.	The sea saw and fled: Jordan was turned back.
4 Montes exultaverunt ut arietes: et colles sicut agni ovium.	The mountains skipped like rams, and the hills like the lambs of the flock.
5 Quid est tibi mare quod fugisti? Et tu Iordanis, quia conversus es retrorsum?	What ailed thee, O thou sea, that thou didst flee: and thou, O Jordan, that thou wast turned back?
6 Montes exultastis sicut arietes, et colles sicut agni ovium?	Ye mountains, that ye skipped like rams, and ye hills, like lambs of the flock?
7 A facie Domini mota est terra, a facie Dei Iacob.	At the presence of the Lord the earth was moved, at the presence of the God of Jacob.

That Du Caurroy chose to prioritize *In exitu Israel* (either by only composing it or only publishing it) is probably no accident. The psalm itself, which describes the wanderings of the Jewish people and their escape from Egypt appealed to a number of composers associated with the French court in the earlier sixteenth century – Mouton, Certon, Sermisy, and Josquin – all of whom seem to have seen the vivid imagery of the psalm and the fact that it was traditionally intoned to the so-called *tonus peregrinus* – the "wandering" psalm tone that stands outside the standard eight- or twelve-mode framework of the time and features different reciting notes for each half of the verse – as a spur to composition, all of them

---

[109] Colin, 'Eustache Du Caurroy'.

incorporating the psalm tone into their polyphonic compositions.[110] Patrick Macey has pointed out that on the death of René of Anjou in 1480, his title as king of Jerusalem would have passed to Louis XI, possibly stimulating a renewed interest in the Israel/France connection which had a history stretching back to the eighth century, when the Pope had named Pepin a *novus David*.[111] Charles VIII, Louis XI's son, was also addressed in these terms, as were both Louis XII and Francis I. These facts alone do not uniquely account for a heightened interest in the concept of a new David leading Israel to peace and prosperity, but clearly this psalm became newly significant in some way to the French crown, and apparently the tradition persisted. At the abjuration of Henri IV at Saint-Denis in 1593, Félibien reports that at the Office of Vespers following the ceremony, the four psalms specified by the Benedictine Breviary were supplemented with *In exitu Israel*, "qui convenoit si bien au Roy dans cette célèbre journée" (which suited the king so well on this celebrated day).[112] Lamothe has also identified Claude Le Jeune's *musique mesurée* setting of Baïf's 1570 translation of *In exitu Israel*, published much later in 1606 and also based on the *tonus peregrinus*, as part of some kind of "academic vespers" or royal liturgy performed at the Sunday night meetings of the Académie de poésie et de musique.[113] This would make sense given that the other *musique mesurée* psalm in Le Jeune's 1606 collection, Psalm 3 (this time in a translation by Agrippa d'Aubigné), features the so-called Ton Royal or royal psalm tone, another tone that stands outside the conventional modal framework and that also uses two different reciting notes. The origins of this tone are not clear, and the term "Ton Royal" does not appear alongside its earliest notated appearances, but it does seem to have been associated with the psalm *Laudate Dominum* (already identified as a prayer for the king), and Gastoué even claimed that it was written by Louis XIII himself.[114] A similar "wandering" chant is found in Mersenne's

---

[110] Mattias Lundberg, *Tonus Peregrinus: The History of a Psalm-Tone and Its Use in Polyphonic Music* (Farnham, Ashgate, 2011), pp. 59–74.

[111] Patrick Macy, 'Josquin's *Misericordias Domini* and Louis XI', *Early Music*, 19/1 (1992), 163–77.

[112] Michel Félibien, *Histoire de l'Abbaye Royale de Saint-Denis en France* (Paris, Frederic Leonard, 1706), p. 422.

[113] Donat Lamothe, *Claude Le Jeune, le Psautier huguenot et la musique religieuse à la Cour, pendant les règnes de Charles IX, Henri III et Henri IV* (PhD dissertation, University of Strasbourg, 1980), pp. 105–20. See Henri Expert, ed., 'Claude Le Jeune, Pseaumes mesurés', *Monuments de la Musique Renaissance Française*, 22, pp. 15–16.

[114] Amadé Gastoué, 'Le Chant des Oratoriens: Louis XIII maître de chapelle', *La Tribune de Saint-Gervais*, 19/5 (1913) 121–6; 19/6 (1913), 149–54; Amadé Gastoué, *Cours théorique et pratique de chant Grégorien* (Paris, Schola Cantorum, 1917), p. 91.

Figure 2.6 Recitation of *Laudate Dominum* accompanied by the Lyre.
Marin Mersenne, *Harmonie universelle* (Paris, Sebastien Cramoisy, 1636), *Livre quatrième des instruments*, p. 207. Bibliothèque nationale de France

Harmonie universelle of 1636, where it is again associated with *Laudate Dominum*. (See Figure 2.6). Mersenne's example is particularly striking in that the tone is used as an example of how to accompany solo song/psalm recitation with the lyre.[115] *In exitu Israel* thus seems to be connected to royal liturgies through several paths: its own text describing the wanderings of the people of Israel; its appearance alongside psalm tones with different reciting notes that seem to be associated with the Académie or with Louis XIII; and the concept of recitation to the lyre/harp.

Unlike the settings from the early sixteenth century, Du Caurroy's version of *In exitu Israel* does not integrate the antiphon *Nos qui vivimus* and its chant into the composition (see Example 2.3). And unlike the earlier versions, its sectional nature is not based on contrasting compositional techniques. Instead, over six long sections, the text unfolds undramatically, with the psalm tone clearly present in the tenor voice (especially near the beginning) or outlined (later in the piece), with sections of reduced voices expanding to full scoring at the conclusion of the work. Recognizable to those who heard it (as it was to Félibien) as part of a tradition reaching back to the sixteenth century, highlighted by polyphony, this performance brought the Vespers psalm *cursus* to a fitting conclusion.

After the psalms, and framed by an antiphon that recounted the dramatic appearance of the Holy Spirit to the disciples recorded in Acts 2:1–2, the Magnificat would have been sung. We have no record of this being "en

---

[115] Marin Mersenne, *Harmonie universelle* (Paris, Sebastien Cramoisy, 1636), *Livre quatrième des instruments*, p. 207.

Example 2.3 Eustache Du Caurroy, *In exitu Israel*, opening, showing psalm tone in tenor (c3).
Preces ecclesiasticae (Paris, Pierre Ballard, 1609)

musique," nor do we have any obvious surviving musical candidates, although Nicolas Formé's Magnificats, preserved in a manuscript copy in 1638 but originating much earlier, would be in exactly the same stylistic universe as the Du Caurroy (see Chapter 7). Following this, the brief swearing-in ceremony began, with trumpets accompanying the procession of the king, led by the Chancellor to a chair beside the altar, after which Monsieur de Rhodes, the *maître de cérémonies* took his place behind the king, the Chancellor on his right and Sceaux and Pisieux on his left.[116] Cardinal de Joyeuse approached the king and read the vow to him, before presenting it to him to sign. After swearing on a Bible held by the Chancellor, M. de Rhodes presented the king with his robes, after which the Cardinal gave him his collar. Louis then stood up, at which point the trumpets began to sound to symbolize that the king was now a *chevalier*.

[116] Godefroy, I, p. 456.

Godefroy's account does not mention any music at this point, but two accounts of the later ceremonies (1619, 1620) suggest that the Office hymn *Veni creator spiritus* was reserved for this point in the ceremony – either sung by the king's musicians, or in chant by the clerics themselves:[117]

The trumpets sounded after the reception of each Knight. When all the ordinary Knights had been inducted, the Ecclesiastics sang a hymn to the Holy Spirit, which was the hymn *Veni creator spiritus*, and all the onlookers fell deep into prayers for the protection of the King, and the new Knights. Then, in a demonstration of rejoicing, the trumpets sounded a pleasing fanfare.

In either case, such accounts suggest that in this, its final appearance in the events of the weekend, *Veni creator spiritus* was yet another musical high point of the ceremony, a hymn that testified to the joy of those present, prompting prayers for the king and for the other knights of the Order, and a festive trumpet fanfare. In Reims, the assembled company then displayed their great reverence before the king took his place on his throne, after which the brief Office of Compline was sung when all the knights came to pay their respects to their new *grand maître*.

With this final performance of Charlemagne's hymn to the Holy Spirit, the "coronation" came to an end. In the immediate aftermath of these events, the emphasis accorded to the Holy Spirit here does not seem to have manifested itself in any particularly overt way (other than the weekly Mass at the Church of the Augustines and the *chapelle royale*), and for the next eight years the Order of the Holy Spirit does not even seem to have met, despite the requirements of the statutes for it to do so: Jean Héroard reports that on a typical New Year's Day the king would attend Mass at Notre-Dame, the church of the Cordeliers, or some other church in Paris, but makes no mention of the Order.[118] But in 1618, in the aftermath of the

---

[117] Pierre Boitel, *Histoire générale de tout ce qui s'est passé de plus remarquable tant en France qu'aux Païs estrangers les années 1618, 1619, 1620, ensemble un relation historique des Pompes & magnifiques cérémonies observées à la réception de Chevaliers de l'Ordre du S. Esprit, faits par LOUYS XIII du nom, surnommé IUSTE, Roy de France & Navarre* (Paris, Pierre Billaine, 1620), p. 31: "Les trompettes sonnoient après la réception de chasque Chevalier. Quand tous les généreux Chevaliers eurent esté faits, les Ecclésiastiques chantèrent un cantique au S. Esprit, qui est l'hymne, *Veni Creator Spiritus*, & tous les spectateurs se mirent en prières pour la conservation du Roy, & des nouveaux Chevaliers. Puis pour une démonstration de resiouyssance les trompettes sonnèrent une plaisante fanfare." See also p. 61.

[118] On January 1, 1611, for example, he attended Vespers at the Jesuit church of Saint-Louis, while on the same day in 1612 he heard Mass in the chapel of the Petit-Bourbon: see *Journal de Jean Héroard*, ed. Eudore Soulié and Édouard de Barthélemy (Paris, Firmin Dido frères, 1868), Vol. 2 (1610–28), p. 48.

Concini affair – in which Marie's favorite, Concino Concini, the Maréchal d'Ancre, had been assassinated at Louis's behest and after which Louis began to assert his authority over the *dévot* faction at court – the Order was reinvigorated (alongside a devotion to Saint Louis, discussed in Chapter 3), with new inductions (though no ceremony) in 1618/19 (when François de La Rochefoucauld was inducted to replace Cardinal du Perron as prelate) and a major induction in 1619/20, when the full set of ceremonies specified in the statutes was again followed and in which essentially the whole Order – officers, commanders, and knights – was created afresh with all the nobility and power players of the day becoming members. Ceremonies followed in 1622, 1625, 1632, and finally on May 14, 1633, at Fontainebleau, when again some fifty knights were inducted, the new generation of nobility who had successfully seen off the end of the Wars of Religion, but who were about to face the threat of Spanish invasion outlined in Chapter 6.[119]

But a constant reference to the Holy Spirit ran through Louis's reign as a common thread uniting his own kingship with that of David, and underpinning the fire imagery that accompanied him more broadly. Louis appeared as a Fire spirit in *La Délivrance de Renaud*, the 1617 *balet de cour* generally recognized as an expression of his new power after the assassination of Concini.[120] And in a famous engraving of 1637, he appears as *Sidus Borbonicum*, the Bourbon sun, an image of the French monarchy that would obviously persist into the later part of the century.[121] But it is in the context of the accession of Louis to the throne that the imagery of a fiery rebirth through the Holy Spirit was most potent. Favin's account describes how it had been suggested to Henri III that he found an Order of the Phoenix, to which the king is reported as replying that he had no need of such an Order because the Holy Spirit was his Phoenix.[122] But in nevertheless adopting Phoenix imagery (the phoenix appears on the king's arms; see Figure 2.4), Henri was aligning himself with a rich and centuries-old vein of thought. Kantorowicz, for example, describes how the mythical bird became an important symbol of the royal succession in

---

[119] This 1633 creation was recorded, with lavish illustrations, in Pierre d'Hozier, *Les Noms surnoms qualitez, armes et blazons de l'ordre du Sainct Esprit* (Paris, Melchior Tavernier, 1634).

[120] For the significance of the Fire demon in the 1617 *balet du roi*, see Margaret McGowan, *L'Art du ballet de cour en France, 1581–1643* (Paris, CNRS, 1963) and Mark Franko, 'Jouer avec le feu: la subjectivité du roi dans La Délivrance de Renaux', in Giovannni Careri (ed.), *Jérusalem délivrée du Tasse. Poésie, musique, ballet* (Paris, Klincksieck, 1999), pp. 159–77.

[121] For sun imagery at the *lit de justice*, see Hanley, *Lit de justice*, pp. 248–66.

[122] Favin, *The Theater of Honour*, p. 416.

the Middle Ages:[123] as a bird that never died (mortal yet immortal), it represented the maxim *dignitas non moritur* or "le roi meurt jamais" (the king never dies); as a creature that only existed as a single unique exemplar, heir to itself, it represented the continuity between father and son on which royal succession depended; as a creature that rose from the dead, it symbolized the resurrection of Jesus; and as a creature who was "self-begotten," it reenacted the Virgin birth. Such ways of thinking had, however, by no means fallen out of favor: Favin, too, recounts the powers of the Phoenix, quoting the authors of antiquity and Church Fathers, and finally reproducing a long extract of du Bartas's *Première semaine* in which the Phoenix is essentially framed as a model for mankind's redemption in Christ himself.[124] For Louis XIII, then, being reborn by the fiery power of the Holy Spirit at the coronation (as, in fact, he had also been at his *lit de justice*, sitting on the *lit* just as the Phoenix rises from its nest), was the defining feature of his succession, an infusion of God's spirit (the Spiritus Domini) that he shared with his predecessor and model, David.

---

[123] See Kantorowicz, *The King's Two Bodies*, pp. 385–401 and 414.
[124] Favin, *Le Théâtre d'Honneur*, pp. 694–5.

3 | The Sword of David and the Battle against Heresy

The coronation of Louis XIII, following an *Ordo* that his forebears had used for centuries – albeit with the addition of framing liturgies that explicitly highlighted the role of the Holy Spirit and looked forward to a new Pentecostal age – remained, in many ways, relatively neutral in tone. In its narrow sense it did not directly address the specific and pressing political and religious concerns of the day, nor could its influence – as a single event – last much beyond that immediate moment, although obviously the identification of Louis as an agent of the Holy Spirit, with its connotations of both fiery power and Phoenix-like continuity, would endure as part of the legitimizing framework.[1] Yet, for the first twenty years of his reign, such concerns were a constant threat, not just to Louis, but to the idea of kingship itself: from the moment of his accession as an eight-year-old boy until the early 1630s, Louis was almost constantly subject to attacks of one kind or another, rarely receiving the cooperation of all of France's competing factions as they jostled for advantage in the complex political, geopolitical, and confessional circumstances of the early seventeenth century.[2] Things began inauspiciously when, as Louis's regent, Marie de Médicis aligned herself with an Italian faction at court that included Leonora Dori (one of her ladies-in-waiting, known as "Galagai") and her husband, the adventurer Concino Concini, the Mareschal d'Ancre, subsequently gathering around herself a group of individuals who would come to be known as the *dévots*, individuals whose members typically had familial ties to the Catholic League of the sixteenth century and who espoused pro-papal, ultramontane policies, sometimes at the expense of

---

[1] Giesey makes the point that ceremonies such as the *lit de justice* and the *entrée* were more effective in reinforcing the essential ideas of kingship (what du Chesne calls *Majesté*) because, unlike the coronation, they could be repeated: see Ralph Giesey, 'The King imagined', in K. Baker (ed.), *The French Revolution and the Creation of Modern Political Culture, Vol. 1: The Political Culture of the Old Regime* (Oxford, Pergamon Press, 1987), pp. 41–59.

[2] For a general characterization of Louis's early reign, see A. Lloyd Moote, *Louis XIII, The Just* (Berkeley, Los Angeles, and London, University of California Press, 1989), pp. 79–96; and Victor Tapié, *France in the Age of Louis XIII and Richelieu* (New York, Praeger, 1974); the first part of Tapié's study is subtitled "France in decline and a prey to factions (1610–24)."

the French crown.[3] Subsequent major events such as Louis's appearance at the *États Généraux* (Estates General) in 1614–15 and his marriage to the Spanish *infanta* Anne of Austria in 1615 also took place against a backdrop of widespread discontent and unrest (Louis and his sister needed the protection of the army on their journey to Bordeaux, where the double wedding was celebrated),[4] and by 1617 Concini himself had gained so much power – becoming first minister in Marie's regency – that Louis had to act. Under the influence of his *confidant*, Charles d'Albert, duc de Luynes, Louis ordered Concini's assassination, an act of violence that spoke to one of the fundamental attributes of kingship (military aggression) and asserted his power in a manner frequently adopted by kings at the beginning of their reign.[5] Exiling his mother to Blois shortly afterwards, Louis assumed the reins of power under the guidance of Luynes as first minister, but on Luynes's death in 1621, an ascendant Richelieu became his primary advisor and would remain so until his death in 1642.[6] A temporary reconciliation between Louis and Marie took place in the early 1620s, but by that time his brother, Gaston d'Orléans, was also fomenting rebellion. Louis's campaigns against the Huguenots in the early 1620s brought him some success and credibility with his *dévot* critics, and the 1628 capture of the Huguenot stronghold of La Rochelle certainly silenced other opponents. But it was only in 1630 – after twenty years on the throne – that Louis could finally be said to be master of his own kingdom when, on the famous Day of the Dupes, he chose to follow the guidance and policies of Richelieu rather than those of his mother, stripping her of her power and influence.[7]

As the coronation receded into a distant memory, then, how did those responsible for music and liturgy – as it intersected with the received and evolving concepts of kingship – respond to these new and difficult circumstances? Who were they, what ideological stances did they adopt, and in

---

[3] For more on the concept of the *dévot*, see the discussions in Chapters 6 and 7, and Joseph Bergin, *The Politics of Religion in Early Modern France* (New Haven and London, Yale University Press, 2014), pp. 86–104. See also Barbara Diefendorf, 'Henri IV, the Dévots and the making of a French Catholic Reformation', in Alison Forrestal and Eric Nelson (eds.), *Politics and Religion in Early Bourbon France* (Basingstoke, Palgrave Macmillan, 2009), pp. 157–79.

[4] A *Mandement de Monseigneur l'Évesque de Paris pour le voyage du Roy* (Paris, François Julliot, 1615) required the churches of Paris to pray daily for the king's safety on the journey. See also Chapter 5.

[5] See Kate van Orden, *Music, Discipline, and Arms in Early Modern France* (Chicago, Chicago University Press, 2005), p. 65.

[6] See Sharon Kettering, *Power and Reputation at the Court of Louis XIII: The Career of Charles d'Albert, duc de Luynes (1578–1621)* (Manchester and New York, Manchester University Press, 2008).

[7] Lloyd Moote, *Louis XIII, the Just*, pp. 199–219.

what ways did music or liturgy shape, participate in, or simply reflect the wider political, military, or confessional circumstances of the first decades of Louis's reign? This chapter focuses on the role that the liturgy and the psalms played as a bulwark against his enemies, emphasizing his victories, and reinforcing the perception of the king as a warrior who conquered all his adversaries, be they a foreign nation abroad or the Huguenots at home. During the reign of Louis XIV, this aim would become familiar – if somewhat abstracted – through the repertoire of *grand motets* performed at the *chapelle royale* from the early 1660s onward. Whole psalm texts being adopted and set to music complete, the king and his courtiers/congregation were certainly invited to hear such texts as "representations" of the king's power, his special relationship with God, or of his latest military victory. By contrast, the liturgy of the *chapelle royale* under Louis XIII did not participate in this process, the liturgy following a simple cycle established by Henri III: to the extent that psalms were performed, they were specified by the Roman Breviary and performed in chant or *fauxbourdon* like any other religious institution. There were therefore few opportunities for musical and textual innovation, and while the absence of an important surviving repertoire of polyphony from Louis XIII's *chapelle* does not necessarily indicate that music was not important, it does reinforce the probability that the liturgy of the *chapelle* itself was not a site in which the kinds of strategies used later were employed.

That is not to say, however, that the musician, warrior king, and notional forebear David was not invoked through music as a way to help the people understand the role of Louis himself, nor that another figure also later conscripted by Louis XIV – the Saint King, Louis IX, crusader, namesake, and literal forebear of Louis XIII – did not also play a role. On the contrary, along with the theories of monarchy that underpinned Louis XIII's absolute status, both David and Saint Louis were central to the legitimizing framework that sustained the king in the early days of his reign. The psalms of David featured widely in various ways – set to elaborate and complex music in their "original" Latin and probably performed by the *musique de la chapelle royale* or the *musique de la chambre* at the king's mealtimes, during which an extensive grace (*Benedictio mensae*) was performed: in the well-known paraphrases by Philippe Desportes and others, set to simple strophic music for small ensemble or solo voice and performed at court or in noble households; or paraphrased into specially written "cantiques" commemorating a particular person (Richelieu, the king, the queen mother) or event (the victory at La Rochelle) that were either musical in the abstract sense (because they were structured as lyric verse) or were literally provided with music (at all levels of complexity). Since Saint Louis neither left behind a corpus of appropriate lyric poetry nor was known as a musician, the adoption of Louis's ancestor was a less seamless process (and ultimately less musically influential), but he too was nevertheless central to the means by which the country at large came to know the young king, with the feast of Saint Louis being upgraded to a Holiday of Obligation in 1618 and with the development of a new liturgy that aimed to unite the country behind the king's forebear and to remind the people of his pious yet warrior-like heritage.

Louis IX, Warrior King

After the king's induction as the commander of the Order of the Knights of the Holy Spirit at his coronation, the Order remained – as Chapter 2 related – relatively dormant until 1618/19, when, after the dramatic events of 1617 and the beginning of Louis's more assertive reign, the focus moved back toward institutions that consolidated the king's power, and when – as at its foundation – the Order became a body that constrained the behavior of those nobility and clergy who might otherwise be a threat to the fledgling king by requiring them to publicly swear an oath of loyalty to the crown and the church. It was the same circumstances and a similar impulse that led those around Louis (in particular his confessor, Father Arnoux) to bring to fruition a long-held wish to elevate and reinvigorate the celebration of the feast of Saint Louis, August 25, in order to recognize the sanctity of Louis IX and to clarify to the faithful his status as the ancestor and model for Louis XIII. Saint Louis was already an important figure for the French community in Rome, where, on October 8, 1589, Cardinal de Joyeuse had dedicated the French national church to the saint (together with the Virgin Mary and Saint Denis/Dionysius), and where an active musical tradition testified to the esteem in which he was held;[8] and more broadly, the feast of

---

[8] See Galliano Ciliberti, 'Qu'une plus belle nüit ne pouvoit précéder le beau jour': Musica e cerimonie nelle istituzioni religiose francesi a Roma nel Seicento (Perugia, Aguaplano, 2016); Jean Lionnet, La Musique à Saint-Louis des Français de Rome au xviie siècle (2 vols., Venice, Edizioni Fondazione Levi, 1985); and the essays in Music and the Identity Process: The National Churches of Rome and Their Network in the Early Modern Period, ed. Michela Berti and Émilie Corswarem (Turnhout, Brepols, 2019); For the later period, see also Michela Berti, 'La Musique pour les "Messe di Francia" à Rome au regard des dispositions pontificales', in Sophie Hache and Thierry Favier (eds.), Réalités et fictions de la musique religieuse à l'époque moderne. Essais d'analyse des discours (Rennes, Presses Universitaires de Rennes, 2018), pp. 253–72.

Figure 3.1 Louis IX (top left) portrayed as the root of a dynastic tree. Engraving of unknown origin. Bibliothèque nationale de France

Saint Louis was already celebrated by the universal church as an Ordinary (or Simplex) Feast, a Common of Confessors. But by the early years of the seventeenth century, court clerics around Henri IV and then Louis worked to elevate this celebration not just to a Double Feast (or Duplex) but also a *Fête de commandement* (i.e. a Holiday of Obligation, a feast which all Catholics, both lay and clergy, were required to observe), as a means of highlighting the saint's significance across the whole of Christendom. At the same time, the original liturgy, created shortly after Louis's canonization in 1297, which emphasized his saintly status and his sympathy to the ideals of the mendicant orders, was replaced with a newly revised rite that now cast the saint more as a king and warrior, emphasizing his descent, too, from the model of all kings, David.

As Louis XIII's namesake, root of the newly restored Bourbon dynasty and therefore a direct ancestor of the king, and as a saint, Saint Louis was of course in many ways an excellent model for the kind of king that Louis wished to be identified with.[9] (See Figure 3.1 for a contemporary illustration highlighting the direct lineage between the saint, Henri IV, and Louis XIII.)

---

[9] For the ways in which Saint Louis was held up as a model, a "mirror of princes," during the Middle Ages, see Jaques le Goff, *Saint Louis*, trans. Gareth Evan Gollrad (Notre Dame, IN, University of Notre Dame Press, 2009), pp. 315–40: Colette Beaune, *The Birth of an Ideology: Myths and Symbols of Nation in Late-Medieval France* (Berkeley, University of California Press, 1991); Alain Boureau, 'Les Enseignements absolutistes de Saint Louis 1610–30', in Chantal Grell and François Laplanche (eds.), *La Monarchie absolutiste et l'histoire en France* (Paris, Presses de l'Université de Paris-Sorbonne, 1987), pp. 79–97; Jean Richard, *Saint Louis, Crusader King of France*. ed. Simon Lloyd, trans. Jean Birrell (Cambridge, New York, Cambridge University Press, 1992).

As the best known of the thirteenth-century kings of France, a crusader who had fought heresy in the Holy Land, Louis was widely recognized for his personalized approach to power, his sanctity and humility, and for his affinity for the mendicant orders such as the Franciscans, Carmelites, and Dominicans. It was these same mendicant orders that Louis placed in charge of the Sainte-Chapelle to protect the sacred relics that he had brought back from the Holy Land, and it was the Franciscans who pressed for his canonization in 1297 and who originally created the liturgies that were celebrated in his honor once his feast was established.[10]

The mendicant orders also commemorated Louis's life in a number of histories, most of which likewise focused on his piety and spirituality: in addition to accounts by Geoffroy de Beaulieu (Louis's Dominican confessor) and Guillaume de Chartres (also a Dominican), Guillaume de Pathus's *Vita* (written around 1303) famously highlighted his three theological virtues (piety, love, and compassion) and his virtues as a king (justice, honesty, and clemency).[11] But alongside Louis's own *Enseignements* (instructions in the art of kingship) addressed to his son Philippe, an early history by Jean de Joinville, commissioned by Blanche of Navarre for the future Louis X, also focused more exclusively on the concept of kingship itself, and it was this history that came to renewed prominence in the early reign of Louis XIII.[12] Prompted by criticism of the king for aiding the heretical Germans in the Thirty Years' War, and as part of a series of broader contributions on the merits of Louis's recent policy choices, the 1625 *Parallèles du Roy S. Louys, & du Roy Louys XIII* (derived from Joinville's work) explains how Saint Louis made peace between "plusieurs Roys & grands Princes de son temps" (several kings and great princes of his time) and how, just as Saint Louis enjoyed hunting, Louis XIII too would chase out those who occupied the countries of his allies.[13] The same report also looks back to 1621, when the king (clearly alluding to his crusading forebear) sent one Sieur Des Hayes to Jerusalem via Constantinople to ensure that the community of Cordeliers at the Church of the Holy

---

[10] See M. Cecilia Gaposchkin, *The Making of Saint Louis: Kingship, Sanctity, and Crusade in the Later Middle Ages* (Ithaca and London, Cornell University Press, 2008).

[11] Le Goff, *Saint Louis*, p. 262.

[12] For the *Enseignements*, see Boureau, 'Enseignements absolutistes'; Jean de Joinville, *Histoire de S. Loys IX du nom, Roy de France ... avec diverses pièces du mesme temps non encore imprimées, & quelques observations historiques par Me Claude Menard, Conseiller du Roy, & Lieutenant en la Prévosté d'Angers* (Paris, Sebastien Cramoisy, 1617). For Joinville's history, see Gaposchkin, *Making of Saint Louis*, pp. 181–96.

[13] *Le Mercure françois*, 11 (1625), pp. 96 ff.

Sepulchre were safe from the Armenians, and to found a chapel in his honor. Such renewed attention to Joinville's history followed on the heels of other, more recent and extensive contributions to the hagiography, such as Pierre Matthieu's *Histoire de saint Louys, roi de France* (1618) and Étienne Molinier's *Panégyrique du Roy-Sainct Louys* (1618), both of which, while ostensibly produced to commemorate the elevation of the Feast, were thinly disguised references to the circumstances of Louis XIII's reign, in particular his decisive and violent action against Concini.[14] Matthieu's long work focused less on the parallels and more on the virtues of the saint, although in 1617 he had also published *La Merveille royale de Louis XIII*, in which the case for Louis XIII's greatness had already been made.[15] Molinier, on the other hand, having pointed out that Saint Louis came to the throne at the age of twelve, but that he had nevertheless exhibited exceptional valor even at that young age, reminded the reader of the king's divine status and humility:[16]

This holy King, perfect imitator of Jesus Christ, and who prefers the title of Christian to the title of King, often saying that he had never received such as great honour as on the day of his baptism, practiced so perfectly Christian humility.

Although the decisive events connected with the changes to the liturgy – the request for the feast to be elevated, its "first" celebration, and the publication of Mathieu's and Joinville's histories – were undoubtedly prompted by the Concini assassination, the desire to see the feast of Saint Louis elevated had in fact begun much earlier: as Bernard Dompnier has convincingly shown, Henri IV clearly saw the advantages of invoking his own ancestor and naming his son after him, the first King Louis since Louis XII, who had died a century earlier.[17] In November 1607, Henri had written to the Pope, both directly and through his ambassador Charles d'Alincourt, to request the elevation of the feast, which was celebrated as a

---

[14] Pierre Matthieu, *Histoire de saint Louys, roi de France, IX du nom, XLIIII du nombre* (Paris, Bertrand Martin, 1618); Étienne Molinier, *Panégyrique du Roy-Sainct Louys, sur le subject de la célébration de sa feste* (Paris, René Giffart, 1618).

[15] Pierre Matthieu, *La Merveille royale de Louis XIII* (Paris, Joseph Guerreau, 1617). In a similar vein was the anonymous *Les Triomphes du très-Chrestien Roy ... Louis le Juste, digne héritier & successeur du Roy Sainct Louis* (Paris, Nicolas Alexandre, 1618).

[16] Molinier, *Panégyrique*, pp. 23, 32: "Ce sainct Roy parfaict imitateur de Iésus-Christ, & qui préfère le titre de Chrestien au titre de Roy, disant souven qu'il n'a iamais reçue si grand honneur que le iour de son baptesme, pratique si parfaitement l'humilité Chrestienne."

[17] Bernard Dompnier, 'La Saint-Louis sous le règne de Louis XIII. Fête liturgique, fête nationale?', in Peter Bennett and Bernard Dompnier (eds.), *Cérémonial politique et cérémonial religieux dans l'Europe modern: Échanges et métissages* (Paris, Garnier, 2020), pp. 39–66.

Simplex, to a Duplex across not just France but the whole of Christendom. The Congregation of Rites had debated the request in 1608 and again in 1609, ultimately agreeing that the feast could be elevated in France, but declining to impose it outside that country. Finally, the papal brief authorizing the elevation was sent via the archbishop of Lyon in July 1610, but in the confusion surrounding the assassination of the king just two months earlier, the impact of the elevation was minimal, and no great changes to the liturgy were instigated. Nevertheless, over the following years, 1611, 1614, and 1616, the day was celebrated with many festivities, with an engraving from 1613 showing a firework display on the Seine in front of the Louvre on the day of the feast itself, and another on its octave, September 2, at the Quai des Célestins, close to the island now known as Île-Saint-Louis, which was subsequently created by Louis XIII and on which the Église Saint-Louis was constructed in 1622–75 (see Figure 3.2).[18]

Following the events of 1617, however, a new request was submitted to Rome, a request that on this occasion was finally granted. The Congregation of Rites approved the elevation of the feast to a Semi-Duplex across the universal church and a *Fête de commandement* in France, and on August 8, Archbishop Gondi notified the diocese of the news, reminding his flock "how it is useful and necessary in this State, in such dangerous times, to seek out more than ever the assistance and protection of the beloved and favorite saints of his divine Majesty."[19] The account of the first celebration on August 25, 1618, in the *Mercure françois* does not record the details of what Louis himself did, but a manuscript note at the end of the surviving copy of Gondi's *Mandement* records that the king and his queen attended Mass at the Jesuit Church of Saint-Louis on rue Saint-Antoine in the presence of the king's confessor, Father Arnoux, followed later by Vespers.[20] (At this stage, the dedication of the Jesuit church to Saint Louis was less significant than it would become later, the land on which the church was built having been given in 1585 by Cardinal de Bourbon, who wished to commemorate his own descent from Saint

---

[18] The events were also recorded in *Discours sur les triomphes que esté faicts le 25, 26, 27 aoust 1613 dans la ville de Paris a l'honneur & loüange de la feste S. Louys, & de Louys XIII* (Lyon, Jean Poyet, 1613).

[19] *Bref de nostres père la Pape Paul V pour la célébration de la feste de Sainct Louys iadis Roy de France, par tout ce Royaume, Avec le Mandement de Monseigneur l'Illustrissime & Reverendissime Cardinal de Retz, Évêque de Paris* (Paris, François Julliot, 1617), p. 9: "combien il est utile & nécessaire à cest Estat, en temps si dangereux, de rechercher plus que jamais l'assistance & protection des saincts amis & favoris de sa divine Majesté . . ."

[20] Manuscript note in *Bref*, p. 13 and unpaginated.

Figure 3.2 Fireworks on the Seine for the octave of the feast of Saint Louis.
Matthias Mérian, *La Représentation des artifices de feu, & autres triomphes faits à Paris sur le gué des Célestins & en l'isle Louviers, le lundy deuxiesme septembre 1613 en l'honneur de la fest de S. Louys* (Paris, Nicolas de Mathonière, 1613). Bibliothèque de l'INHA

Louis. The 1627 rebuilding of the church was more directly influenced by Louis himself.)[21]

At this first celebration of the newly elevated feast, the Office of Saint Louis would have followed the rite prescribed in the Paris Breviary, the 1617 edition of which already incorporated some changes from the previous 1584 edition prompted by the burgeoning interest in the saint in the intervening years.[22]

---

[21] For the commissioning of this important church, see Julianne Sandlin, *Asserting Royal Power in Early Seventeenth-Century Paris: Louis XIII, Maria de' Medici, and the Art and Architecture of Reformed Religious Orders* (PhD dissertation, Florida State University, 2009).

[22] The lessons in the third nocturne of Matins had been changed. See *Breviarium insignis Ecclesiae parisiensis restitutum ac emendatum* (Paris, Jean Charron, 1584), pp. 91v–95v; *Breviarium parisiense ad formam Sacrosancti Concilii Tridentini restitutum* (Paris, Rolin Thierry et Eustache Foucault, 1617), pp. 632–9. For a survey of some of the other changes (in the context of the liturgy of the French national church of San Luigi in Rome), see Ciliberti, 'Musica e liturgia'; and Ciliberti, '*Qu'une plus belle nüit*', pp. 176–206. Unfortunately, the surviving 1650 noted antiphoner from San Luigi does not preserve any of the liturgy or chant from the feast of Saint Louis itself: see *Antiphonae quae in solemnitatibus totius anni cum organo*

But the 1584 liturgy already differed from the Roman celebration, which treated the feast as a Common of Confessors, with Vespers featuring the Sunday Psalms (but finishing with *Laudate Dominum*) and the Office hymn *Iste confessor*. In Paris, by contrast, the Office hymns provided in both the 1584 and 1617 editions were those specially composed for the feast by Arnauld du Pré – *Gaude mater Ecclesia, Nova regis praeconia*, and *Hymnum novae laetitiae* – probably originating in the liturgies of the early fourteenth century.[23] But after requests submitted to Cardinal Bellarmine and the Congregation of Rites in 1619, a number of substantial modifications to the liturgy were made. While no breviaries were published in (or at least survive from) the immediate aftermath of this change, the 1636 Paris edition testifies to the substantial changes that had been made in the intervening years, transforming the rite from a mendicant-inspired celebration of the godliness of the saint into a celebration of kingship itself.[24]

The most publicly visible Office, Vespers, saw the most dramatic changes. The opening Capitulum was now based on I Ezra, 7:27:[25]

V. Benedictus Dominus Deus patrum nostrorum, qui dedit hanc voluntatem in cor regis, clarificare domum suam quae est in Hierusalem. R. Deo gratias.

Blessed be the Lord God of our fathers, who hath put this in the king's heart to glorify the house of the Lord, which is in Jerusalem: R. Thanks be to God.

Although obviously intended to allude to Saint Louis, the biblical account itself refers to Cyrus, king of Persia, another model biblical king: responsible for the refounding of Judea and the rebuilding of the temple (i.e. a protector of the true religion) in the fifth century BCE, it was Cyrus who, as the subject of the *Cyropédie* (one of the best known "mirrors of princes"), became a model for Francis I.[26] The opening responses then featured the account in I Samuel 16, in which Samuel finds David for the first time and anoints him in preference to his brothers, the moment when the *Spiritus Domini* first entered David:

---

solemniter decantari solent in ecclesia S. Ludovici, F-Pn Département de musique, MS Rés. 2299c.

[23] Dompnier, 'La Saint-Louis', p. 53.

[24] *Breviarium parisiense ad formam sacrosancti Concilii Tridentini restitutum* (Paris: Sebastien and Gabriel Cramoisy, Stéphane Richer and Antoine Vitray, 1636); also *Breviarium parisiense ad formam sacrosancti Concilii Tridentini restitutum* (Paris, Sebastien and Gabriel Cramoisy, Stéphane Richer and Antoine Vitray, 1640).

[25] Ibid., p. 662.

[26] Emmanuel le Roy Ladurie, *The French Royal State, 1460–1610*, trans. Juliet Vale (Oxford, Blackwell, 1994), p. 110.

V. Tulit Samuel cornu olei & unxit David in medio fratrum suorum. R. Et directus est spiritus Domini a die illa in David.

Then Samuel took the horn of oil, and anointed him in the midst of his brethren: and the Spirit of the Lord came upon David from that day forward.

This text was then followed by a versicle taken from the account in Psalm 88:21 (and which featured prominently in the coronation) in which God declares his support for David:

V. Inveni David servum meum, oleo sancto meo unxi eum, manus enim mea auxiliabitur ei et brachium meum confirmabit eum.

I have found David my servant; with my holy oil have I anointed him. For my hand shall help him; and my arm shall strengthen him.

Subsequent antiphons and prayers were now infused with references to David as the archetypal king, but two other major changes were also made. The first, to the Matins lessons, replaced the existing first three readings of the first Nocturne with readings from 3 Kings 3, an account that features Samuel's dream in which he is persuaded to grant Solomon the wisdom to dispense justice and judgment.[27] But the most substantial change, in musical terms, was to the hymns. Superseding the early fourteenth-century texts were two new hymns by Isaac Habert, *Rege summe Regum* and *Te sancta rursus Ludovice praelia*.

The phenomenon of neo-Latin sacred poetry in liturgical or paraliturgical contexts is more associated with the rise of neo-Gallicanism, in particular the works of Pierre Perrin (*Cantica pro Capella Regis*, 1665) and Jean Santeul (*Hymni sacri et novi*, 1689), and with the Paris *Breviarium* of 1680, than with the early seventeenth century, and so we have little context to guide us in considering these early hymns.[28] But we should remember that the 1620s also saw the humanist impulses of Pope Urban VIII expressed in his revisions to the Roman hymnal, "correcting" the barbarisms of the medieval hymn repertory and modifying their scansion to reflect more closely the practices of classical Latin.[29] The old

---

[27] Ibid., p. 663.
[28] See Jean Duron, 'Les "Paroles de musique" sous le règne de Louis XIV', in Jean Duron (ed.), *Plainchant et Liturgie en France au XVIIe siècle* (Versailles, Fondation Royaumont, Éditions du CMBV, Klincksieck, 1997), pp. 125–84; Jean Duron, '"Ces Mrs ne sont pas trop chargés de Latin": la langue d'église dans les nouvelles forms musicales du XVIIe siècle', in Cécile Davy-Rigaux (ed.), *La Musique d'Église et se cadres de creation dans la France d'Ancien Régime*, (Florence, Olschki, 2014), pp. 175–93; Louis Auld, *The Lyric Art of Pierre Perrin, Founder of French Opera* (Henryville, Institute of Medieval Music, 1986), Vol. 1, pp. 11–24.
[29] *Hymni Breviarii Romani S^{mi} D.N. Urbani VIII* (Rome, Typis Vaticanis, 1629). For a detailed study of Urban's revisions, see George Warren McGrath, *The Revision of the Hymns of the Roman Breviary under Urban VIII* (MA thesis, Loyola University, 1939).

hymns to Saint Louis, *Gaude mater Ecclesia, Nova regis praeconia,* and *Hymnum novae laetitiae* were certainly ripe for modification or complete replacement, since they, too, adopted the accentual procedures of medieval hymnody, a feature noted by Guyet in his slightly later survey, in which he described them as *hymni rhythmici*.[30] Habert, however followed Urban's lead. Son of a *valet de chambre* of the same name to Henri IV and Louis XIII, and future bishop of Vavres, Habert was already well established as an author of encomiastic and religious poetry.[31] His *Pietas regia Ludovici Iusti, Pii, Triumphantis* of 1622, dedicated to Cardinal de Richelieu, set out to celebrate the king's piety and strength through Latin verse paraphrases of a number of psalms, while his *Votum regium, Davidici carminis paraphrasi conceptum* of 1637 contained the same Latin paraphrases as the 1622 publication together with the two new hymns and a poem in praise of Saint Louis, *Ignis solemnit. Sancti Ludovici*.[32]

For the new hymns, then, Habert adopted an overtly "classical" approach, setting each line to a ——^——^——^— quantitative pattern and aligning his poetry with the humanist tradition not just of Ronsard and the Pléiade but of Baïf himself. *Rex summe Regum* immediately alludes to the concept of kingship as a divinely ordained creation, with kingdoms distributed according to God's will. The narrator also notes that both kings came to the throne at a young age, that both their mothers acted as regents (Blanche de Castille for Louis IX), and that both learned to serve Christ from an early age:

Rex summe Regum, qui poténti númine	Highest King of Kings, you who by the mighty divine power
Quo sunt creáta regna, nutu dívidis	By which are created kingdoms, distribute them according to your will,
Dum thure fumant templa, voce pérsonant,	While incense burns in your churches and voices resound,
Audi profúsas regis in laudem preces.	Hear the abundant prayers in praise of the King.
Nascens in ipsa Ludovícus púrpura,	Louis, beginning life in that purple itself,

---

[30] Charles Guyet, *Heortologia, sive de festis propriis locorum & ecclesiarum* (Paris, Sebastien and Gabriel Cramoisy, 1657), p. 379. I am grateful to Dr. Darren Keefe for his help with the Latin scansion.

[31] See Sabine Lardon, 'Inspiration biblique et forms poétiques dans les *Œuvres chrestiennes* d'Isaac Habert', in Pascale Blum and Anne Mantero (eds.), *Poésie et Bible de la Renaissance à l'Âge Classique, 1550–1680* (Paris, Champion, 1999), pp. 49–64.

[32] The two hymns are attributed to Habert in Ulysse Chevalier, *Repertorium hymnologicum* (Louvain, Polleunis & Ceuterick, 1894) and appear in Habert's *Votum regium: Davidici carminis paraphrasi conceptum* (Paris, Petrum Blasum, 1637), pp. 27, 41.

Sceptris avítis parvus ádmovet manus;	Though young, he reaches for the ancestral scepter;
Piǽque ductu matris, ignárus mali,	With his dutiful and pious mother's guidance, knowing no evil,
Servíre Christo discit ántequam ímperet.	He learns to serve Christ before he would reign.

Te sancta rursus Ludovice, on the other hand, alludes to the immediate predicament faced by Louis – "divine battles call" – but reassures the listener that Saint Louis will intercede as a soldier of Christ, whose relics he bears:

Te Sancte rursus Ludovice, praelia	Once again divine battles call, Holy Louis:
Divina poscunt: tu crucis clavum tenens,	Bearing a nail of the Cross,
Speique sacras anchora fundans rates,	And as an anchor of hope steadying the sacred vessels,
Moves tyrannis bella, Christo militas.	You declare war on tyrants, you serve as a soldier for Christ.

Although the feast of Saint Louis was celebrated with more fervor in the years following 1618, the phenomenon was mainly restricted to Paris, and the focus on the saint as a king certainly quickly dissipated. By 1643, when the book of hours *Parva christianae pietatis Officina per christiannissium regem Ludovicum XIII ordinata* (Little Offices of Christian Piety for the Most Christian King Louis XIII) was published (a testament to Louis's devotion, commissioned by him and compiled by the chancellor and two doctors of the Sorbonne in 1640), texts for even more hymns to Saint Louis had been composed: but in the context in which this volume was produced, a *dévot*, more Christocentric conception of kingship was now the norm (see Chapter 7), and these hymns – indeed the whole Office – reverted to a more saintly conception of Louis's forebear.[33] The one lesson provided, excerpted from the full office of Matins, was now the account of Saint Louis's birth, life, and canonization, not the lesson from Samuel that began the contemporary Breviary version. And at the same time, the responses, prayers, and capitula lost their reference to the anointing of David. Yet, in other ways, the elevated feast of Saint Louis was and would become even more central to France's national identity, or at least to the identity of the Bourbon dynasty: the construction of the new Jesuit church of Saint Louis on rue Saint-Antoine, the reinvigoration of the church of San Luigi dei Francesi in Rome, and the construction of the Île Saint-Louis and its

---

[33] *Parva Christianae pietatis Officina per christiannissium Regem Ludovicum XIII ordinata* (Paris, Typographia regis, 1643).

church were all followed (during the reign of Louis XIV) by the dedication of the Chapel of the Invalides to Saint Louis, and the foundation of the Maison royale de Saint-Louis at Saint-Cyr, home to an important musical tradition under the direction of Guillaume-Gabriel Nivers.[34] Later in the century, and into the eighteenth, the Office of Saint Louis took pride of place in several elaborately ornamented manuscripts copied for the Invalides and the Church of Saint Louis in Versailles (manuscripts which preserve the earliest known chants for the hymns), while as late as 1760 a new edition of the Office was published specifically for the *chapelle royale* at Versailles itself.[35] And so, while Louis IX never quite lived up to his potential to be a national focus of devotion (Saint Denis always remained a more potent figure), the steps taken early in the reign of Louis XIII certainly laid the foundation for an enduring liturgical interest in the Saint.

The Sword and Keys of David

As a non-musician, Saint Louis's influence on music itself was relatively minor, even if, as a figure, he became central to distinctively French conceptions of the nation of France and if his liturgy was clearly highly valued into the eighteenth century.[36] The influence of David, on the other hand, spans the entire gamut of musical practices – from those in which music remains simply an abstract concept, reflected in strophic, songlike paraphrases of his psalms that might simply be recited in a heightened declamatory style, to elaborate conservative polyphonic settings that would require the most substantial and expert choral ensembles to perform. All such musical settings, however, need to be considered in the even broader

---

[34] For the *Maison royale*, see the recent study by Deborah Kauffman, *Music at the Maison Royale de Saint-Louis at Saint-Cyr* (Abingdon and New York, Routledge, 2019).

[35] See, for example, the elaborately decorated manuscripts produced for the chapel of the Invalides, *Officium S. Ludovici regis Franciae ac missae festorum annualium ad usum domus regiae Invalidorum* (1719) (F-Pn MS lat. 8831) and for the church of Saint Louis in Versailles, *Graduale et antiphonale ad usum S. Ludovici domus regiae Versaliensis* (1684–6)(F-Pn MS lat. 8828). See also *L'Office de saint Louis roy de France, à l'usage de la chapelle du roy à Versailles. Avec des Méditations pour l'Octave & pour les autres Fêtes que l'Église célèbre à l'honneur du S. Roy* (Paris, G. Desprez, 1760).

[36] Only one motet for the feast of Saint Louis, Nivers's *O sancti regis Luvdovici*, is listed in the *Catalogue du motet imprimé en France (1647–1789)*, ed. Nathali Berton-Blivet (Paris, Société française de musicologie, 2011). Dumont's *Pulsate, pulsate tympana* is a rare example of a *grand motet* for the feast: see Epilogue.

context in which the biblical king served as a model not just for Louis himself (and for specific actions he took) but for the entire concept of the monarchy, the church, and its relationship with the state. While the theoretical treatises of du Chesne and others only broadly alluded to the divine nature of kingship, pamphlets and paraphrases produced by those around Louis engaged with the biblical king directly and extensively, interpreting his actions toward his immediate enemies, and toward the broader challenge from the Huguenots, through the lens of David.

In the months and years that followed Concini's assassination, Louis's decisive action became a touchstone of his new image and was celebrated in many publications, among them *Le Combat de David contre Goliath au Roy très chrestien Louys* (The Combat of David against Goliath, to the Very Christian King Louis). In this short pamphlet, an anonymous author celebrates in coded terms (and sometimes not so coded terms) the victory of the young king over Concini (here played by the lion), noting Louis's important relationship with the Holy Spirit:[37]

So he [David] engaged in combat, little child, and little shepherd that he was, against a wolf, then later against a lion, then later against this great and fierce giant who wished to destroy his people. In this combat David demonstrated such strength and courage that he strangled the wolf, disemboweled the lion, and cut off the head of the fierce giant with his own sword, and then later, David easily exterminated the enemies of the people of God. In the same way, Sire, among all the men who are now on the earth, and particularly among all the Kings, Princes and great Lords living under the Christian law, it is the general opinion of noble people that you are found the most agreeable to the Holy Spirit.

On the other hand, the later *Glaive de David et de Louis XIII roy de France* (The Sword of David and of Louis XIII King of France), by the Avignon cleric Gilles Chaissy, focuses on David/Louis's central role as defender of the church and state in a remarkable (if somewhat opaque) synthesis of the

---

[37] *Le Combat de David contre Goliath, au Roy très Chrestien Louys* (n.p., 1618), p. 3: "Il employa doncques au Combat, petit enfant, & petit Berger qu'il estoit, contre un Loup, puis après contre un Lyon, puis après contre ce grand & fier Géant, qui vouloit exterminer tout son peuple. Auquel Combat David tesmoigna tant de force & de courage, qu'il estouffa le Loup, esgorga le Lyon, & coupa la teste au fier Géant de sa propre espée, & puis après David extermina facilement les ennemies du peuple de Dieu. De mesme, SIRE, entre, tous les hommes qui sont maintenant sur la terre, & particulièrement entre tous les Roys, Princes & grands Seigneurs vivant sous la loy Chrestienne, c'est la commune opinion des gens de bien que vous estes trouvé le plus agréable au sainct Esprit." For a full discussion of the political context and ramifications of this event, see Lloyd Moote, *Louis XIII*, pp. 79–96. For a more focused account of the assassination, see Kettering, *Power and Reputation*, pp. 63–88. See also the articles in the special edition '1617: Louis XIII's coup d'état', *Dix-septième siècle*, no. 276 (2017/3).

ideas relating to military might, divine power, and biblical antecedents.[38] Chaissy begins by addressing the reader and explaining that the "désobeïssance des hérétiques" has prompted him to pen this work in defense of the church. In this light, he begins the first chapter ("How in the Church of God There is a Sword for the Defence of the Same") by explaining the origins of the church in the Holy Spirit:[39]

The Holy Spirit which, by the mouth of the Prophets and by the pen of the Sages, like a most excellent painter, has drafted on the paper of the scriptures his most-loved church.

Having then shown how the church will defend itself with the Sword of David, a sword referenced throughout the psalms and prophesied in the remainder of the Bible,[40] Chaissy quotes Psalm 128:2 to demonstrate how both Louis and David were threatened by rebellion from an early age. Yet it is the uniquely humble and peaceful quality of David, who initially went into battle armed only with his sling, that the reader is invited to see in Louis:[41]

David was served by the sword against those who wished to trouble the temporal and spiritual state of Israel, and when victory had been assured he lay his sword in the Temple, though when the need arose he retrieved it: in the same way, the King in times of peace occupies himself in the service of God, but when the time is right knows to retrieve his sword, similar and like the one of David, forged by the enemy.

If the *Glaive de David* focused primarily on David/Louis's response to the threat of heresy, by 1628 the psalm paraphrases being produced as pamphlets were adopting a more positive tone, celebrating the recent victory at La Rochelle and making claims that the psalmist had in fact predicted it. And in this new atmosphere, the musical dimension to the king was more able to flourish, becoming a key identifier of kingship itself. Thus, in the *Description prophétique du Roy David de la prise de la Rochelle* of 1629, the author, François Véron, one of the king's preachers, recounts:[42]

---

[38] Gilles Chaissy, *Glaive de David et de Louis XIII roy de France et de Navarre* (Avignon, Jean Bramereau, 1623).
[39] Ibid., p. 1.   [40] Ibid., p. 6. Deuteronomy 32:25, 32:42; Genesis 3:24; Psalms 149:6.
[41] Chaissy, *Glaive*, p. 10.
[42] François Véron, *Description prophétique du Roy David de la prise de La Rochelle* (Paris, Jean Mestais, 1629), p. 3: "Vostre grande pieté vous fera volontiers, parmy les acclamations de la terre [,] prester l'oreille au Prophète Roy David, qui en esprit de Prophète prédit & chante sur sa Harpe divine, plus mélodieuse que tous nos luts, violes, & hautbois, vostre glorieuse victoire en

Sire, Your great piety makes you willing, among the acclamations of the earth, to lend your ear to the Prophet King David, who in the spirit of a Prophet predicts and sings on his divine Harp, more melodious than all our lutes, viols and *hautbois*, your glorious victory of taking La Rochelle, describing the quality of this rebel town, refuge of heresy, its situation, its canal, the coming of the English with their great warships, but to make mockery of itself, the royal virtues of your Majesty themselves besiege this place of rebellion, the town returned to your discretion, your entry into the same, the demolition of its walls, gates and forts, your glorious return to your capital city of Paris, your entry into the same with such public acclamation, the *Te Deum* sung, and the good benefitting the Church and the State in this victory. You will hear it also, because it merits this respect, giving you some advice of consequence on what it would be good to do, La Rochelle having been taken, for the complete repose of the Church, and of your subjects, and for the eternal salvation of those over whom you are now absolutely King.

While framing David as a musician who was able to predict the famous victory, and Louis as "absolute" king, Véron also takes the opportunity to draw the parallel between the king and Christ:[43]

You enter full of glory with your nobles and your army, into this Rock and there re-establish political and ecclesiastical authority, of religion, and of the state, before you had those gates demolished, which had been principal gates of a state set up in France against your authority ... You here [are] absolute King of all of France; David does not forget it. Psalm 117:22 *The stone which the builders rejected has become the cornerstone.* If this text applies to the Messiah, as he himself interpreted it [Matthew 21:42], then it also applies to your Majesty, our Christ visible on earth.

---

la prise de la Rochelle descrivant la qualité de ceste ville rebelle, refuge de l'hérésie, la situation d'icelle, son Canal, la venue des Anglois avec leurs grandes Ramberges, mais pour se faire mocquer, les royales vertus de vostre Maiesté assiégeant elle mesme ce lieu de rébellion, la ville rendue à vostre discrétion, vostre entrée en icelle, les démolitions de ses murailles, portes & bastions, vostre retour glorieux en vostre ville capital de Paris, vostre entrée en icelle avec tant d'acclamations publiques, le Te Deum chanté, & le bien provenant à l'Église & à l'Estat de ceste victoire. Vous l'escouterez aussi, car il mérite ce respect, vous donnant quelque advis de conséquence de ce qu'il vous convient faire, la Rochelle prise, pour le repos entier de l'Église, & de vos subiets, & pour le salut éternel de ceux desquels vous estes maintenant absolument Roy."

[43] Véron, *Description prophétique*, pp. 8–9: "vous entres plain de gloire avec vostre Nobles & vostre Armée, dans ceste Rochelle & y restablissez l'authorité Ecclésiastique & Politique, de la Religion, & de l'Estat, Puis que vous faictes abatre & demolir ces portes, qui avoient esté portes principales d'un Estat souslevé dans la France contre vostre authorité, & faictes combler les fossez & ietter par terre les bastions d'Evangile ou plustost d'hérésie, que s'ensuit-il? Vous voilà Roy absolu de toute la France; David ne l'oublie pas: [Pseaume 117, vers 22] *Lapidem quem reprobaverunt aedificantes hic factus est in caput anguli; La Pierre laquelle les édifiants ont reprouvé, a esté faite la maistresse pierre du coin.* Si ce texte s'entend du Messie, comme luy mesme l'interprète [Matth. 21 vers 42], aussi faict-il de vostre Maiesté, nostre Christ visible en terre."

Even for Louis's *entrée* back into Paris on his return from La Rochelle, the ceremony in Notre-Dame and the singing of Te Deum was explained by reference to David, who sang the king's praises on his Harp:[44]

David does not forget your return and *entrée* into your capital, and the acclamations of the Parisians, and the *Te Deum* sung in the great church with the crowd of innumerable people filling the church right up to the altar. [Psalm 117:24] *This is the day which the Lord has made; let us rejoice and be glad in it*, you say to your people. [v.26] *Save us, we beseech thee O Lord. O Lord, we beseech thee, give us success. Blessed is he who come in the name of the Lord*. To the thanksgiving is joined the blessing of the Church. [v.27] *We bless you from the house of the Lord*, says the prelate of it, *because the Lord is God and he has given us light*, in the presence of an innumerable presence of people according to the law of David, *Bind the festal procession with branches, up to the horns of the altar!* Thus, Sire, David sings melodiously on his harp of your admirable victories.

But much more common than the prolix texts of Véron and Chaissy were the innumerable psalm paraphrases produced to commemorate Louis's military accomplishments and other events worthy of celebration, typically dedicated either to the king himself or to Richelieu, Marie de Médicis, or some other powerful patron.[45] Such paraphrases, only very loosely adhering to the sense of the original, tended to make the voice of David more real, his singing more an actual part of the rationale for the poetry. Thus, another publication to celebrate the capture of La Rochelle, Honorat de Meynier's *Cantique Royale sur la réduction de la Rochelle*, claimed that these paraphrases, celebrating the victory at La Rochelle and describing everything that occurred there, were made "in imitation of those which King David made when God gave him victory against his

---

[44] Véron, *Description prophétique*, pp. 10–11: "David n'oublie pas vostre retour & entrée en vostre capital, & les acclamations de vos Parisiens, & le Te Deum chanté en la grande Église avec la foulle d'un Peuple innombrable iusques aux cornes de l'Autel. [v.22] *Haec est dies quam fecit Dominus exultemus & laetemur in ea*, Ce est la iournée que le Seigneur a fait, esiouyssons nous & prenons liesse en icelle, O Domine, Seigneur, vous dict vostre peuple, *Salvum me fac*, [v.26] sauvez nous, maintenez nous pour tousiours hors de troubles: *O Domine bene prosperare*, Vive le Roy: *Benedictus qui venit in nomine Domini*, Benist soy celuy qui vient au nom du Seigneur. A l'action de grâces s'est ioincte la bénédiction de l'Église [v.27] *Benediximus vobis de domo Domini*, Nous vous avons beny de la maison du Seigneur, dist le Prelat d'icelle, car *Deus Dominus & illuxit nobis*, Le Seigneur est Dieu & nous a donné sa lumière en l'assistance d'un peuple innombrable selon l'ordonnance de David, *Constituiste diem solemnem in condensis usque ad cornu altaris*, Solennisez ce iour en grande foule iusques aux cornes de l'autel. Ainsi, Sire, David chante sur sa Harpe mélodieusement vos admirables victoires."

[45] See, for example, *Votum regium Davidici carminis paraphrasi conceptum*, dedicated to chancellor Seguier: *Pseaumes pour le Roy* (Paris, 1637).

Table 3.1 Text and translation of Psalm 128, *Qu'Israel maintenant*, and *Leandre estant dessus le bord de l'Elespont* (verse 1)

Qu'Israël dise maintenant	Leandre estant dessus le bord
Dès ma plus débile jeunesse,	De l'Elespont enflé d'orages,
Ils m'ont pressé, me surprenant	Consultant l'amour & la mort
Par leur descevante finesse,	Dont il contemploit les images,
Volontiers ils m'eussent perdu,	Tandis que ses desirs passoyent
Mais l'Eternel m'a deffendu.	Les ondes qui le menassoyent.
Let Israel now say	Leandre, being on the banks
From my most feeble youth	Of the Hellespont swollen by storms,
They have pressed me, surprising me	Consulting love and death
By their deception,	Whose images he contemplated,
Gladly they would have lost me,	While his desires passed
But the Eternal one defended me.	The waves which menaced him.

enemies."[46] Presenting paraphrases of Psalms 18, 17, 126, and 128, the verses were intended to be sung to the popular melodies found in Gabriel Bataille's collections of *airs de cour* published during the 1610s and 1620s, songs such as *Lorsque Leandre* (by Pierre Guédron), *Il s'en va l'infidel*, *La Reyne d'angleterre*, *Ne veuillez pas o Sire me reprendre*, or *Adorable Princesse*. De Meynier's paraphrase of Psalm 128 – which again makes reference to David and Louis's youth – was specified to be sung to the anonymous *Leandre estoit dessus le bord de l'Elespont* (from Bataille's second book of *Airs de cour* 1609/1611), an air that became a popular vehicle for many other *contrafacta*.[47] (See Table 3.1 and Example 3.1.)

Even though music featured as a concept in such publications, none of the psalm paraphrases or lengthier tracts such as Chaissy's *Glaive* or Véron's *Description prophétique* engaged with music other than as a generic vehicle for text. But more specifically musical sources, part of a wider and better documented tradition of devotional psalm singing, can also tell us about the role David played at court and in the country more widely.[48] Closest to the

---

[46] Honorat De Meynier, *Cantique Royale sur la réduction de la Rochelle* (Paris, Nicolas Alexandre, 1628).

[47] *Airs de différents auteurs mis en tablature de luth par Gabriel Bataille* (Paris, Pierre Ballard, 1609/1614).

[48] The practice of devotional psalm singing was, of course, widespread in both Catholic and Huguenot communities. For an overview of the practice in the early seventeenth century, see Denise Launay, *La Musique religieuse en France du Concile de Trente à 1804* (Paris, Société de musicology, Klincksieck, 1993), pp. 167–80. See also Marc Desmet, 'Introduction: Quelle

Example 3.1 *Qu'Israel die maintenant*, set to the melody of *Leandre estant dessus le bort de l'Elespont*.
From *Airs de différent auteurs mis en tablature de luth par Gabriel Bataille* (Paris, Pierre Ballard, 1609/1614)

contrafacta sung to popular *airs* (in addition to the numerous individual appearances of settings of Desportes's psalm paraphrases in the Bataille *airs de cour* volumes) were publications such as those of Denis Caignet, a musician associated with the court from 1600 and a viol player in the *musique de la chambre* from 1614 until his death in 1625.[49] Arguing in his dedication to the king that "These divine songs would finally, in this French translation, lose the power of the name which their Author, the King Prophet, gave to them, if they were to be left without being sung," Caignet provided the means for bourgeois, noble, and even royal households to sing French paraphrases of the psalms, publishing simple monophonic settings of Desportes's paraphrases without accompaniment (the 1624 publication), with lute accompaniment (1625), or, if resources allowed, in up to eight voices (the 1607 publication).[50] By the 1620s, Desportes's paraphrases had achieved "classic" status: produced while under the influence of Jean-Antoine de Baïf, the paraphrases (or more accurately metrical translations) first appeared in 1592 (sixty psalms) followed by an expanded collection of 100 in 1598, and finally the complete set of 150 in 1603, an edition that was subsequently republished countless times over the next several decades.[51] Caignet's later melody-only settings evoked both the Genevan psalm

---

musique pour les psaumes en vers français?' in Marc Desmet (ed.), *La Monodie du psautier en vers français au XVIIe siècle* (Lyon, Symétrie, 2015), pp. 1–12.

[49] See Marc Desmet, 'Les Psaumes en vers français de Philippe Desportes, mis en musique par Denis Caignet (1624), in Desmet (ed.), *La Monodie du psautier*, pp. 17–18.

[50] Denis Caignet, *Cinquante pseaumes de David mis en vers François par Philippes Desportes, Abbé de Thiron, et mis en musique à 3.4.5.6.7. & 8 parties* (Paris, Pierre Ballard, 1607); Denis Caignet, *Cinquante pseaumes de David mis en vers François par Ph. Desportes, Abbé de Thiron, et les chants en musique* (Paris, Pierre Ballard, 1624); Denis Caignet, *Cinquante pseaumes de David mis en vers François par Philippes Desportes, Abbé de Thiron, et en musique, et sur le luth* (Paris, Pierre Ballard, 1625).

[51] For an overview of Desportes in relation to music, see André Verchaly, 'Desportes et la musique', *Annales musicologiques*, 2 (1954), 271–345.

melodies and Baïf's measured music, and for Psalms 126 and 133 (which Desportes had set in *vers mesurés*) he even adopted a *musique mesurée* approach, although in practice such settings were not that different from the other psalms (which also used a very limited range of note values).(See Figure 3.3 for Caignet's setting of Desportes's "vers mesurez Sapphiques" translation of Psalm 126.)

But although Caignet's 1624 edition was dedicated to the king, and the 1625 edition to Cardinal de Richelieu, in setting all 150 of the psalms to music and using a by now almost canonical version of the text, Caignet did make any choices that might reveal the significance of any particular psalm over another. Another collection, Charles de Courbes's *Cantiques Spirituels* of 1622 selected just six of Desportes's translations – psalms 150, 6, 116, 4, 129, and 50 – but although De Courbes was familiar with members of the court, he was not a member of the musical household, and the choice of these psalms seems arbitrary.[52] Du Caurroy, on the other hand, was a central figure at court for three decades, and his *Meslanges* of 1610 contains several settings of paraphrases by Desportes (French, in rhymed verse and *vers mesurés*), Durant de la Bergerie (French, in rhymed verse), and Louis Servin (Latin, in *vers mesurés*).[53] Although, as its name suggests, the *Meslanges* contains a variety of genres, the psalms are prioritized, occupying the first four places in the volume and concluding the whole collection. The volume opens with Durant de la Bergerie's paraphrase of Psalm 136, "Le Long des eaux," the famous psalm that recounts the travails of the people of Israel as they weep by the waters of Babylon and ask how they may sing in a strange land.[54] The next three works, setting paraphrases by Desportes of Psalms 45 (*Le Seigneur, dès qu'on nous offence* [Deus noster refugium]), 25 (*Juge ma cause* [Judica me, Domine]), and 129 (*Du profound des maux de mon âme* [De profundis clamavi]), continue this theme and occupy a variety of emotional registers. In the middle of the collection we find *musique mesurée* settings of psalm 133 and 126 (both by Desportes, also both set in *musique mesurée* in Caignet's collection), 87 (Agrippa d'Aubigné), and 5 (Jean-Antoine de de Baïf), but the collection concludes with Louis Servin's remarkable Latin paraphrase of Psalm 1, *O quam*

---

[52] Marc Desmet, *Charles de Courbes: Cantiques Spirituels* (Saint-Étienne, Lyon, Publications de l'Université de Saint-Étienne, Symétrie, 2005)

[53] See Marie-Alexis Colin, *Eustache Du Caurroy: Meslanges* (Turnhout, Brepols, 2010).

[54] This psalm became especially popular in the seventeenth century: see Christian Belin, 'Comment se tenir sur un fleuve? Paraphrase et exégèse du Super flumina Babylonis au xviie siècle', in Véronique Ferrer and Anne Mantero (eds.), *Les Paraphrases bibliques au xvie et xviie siècles* (Geneva, Droz, 2006), pp. 343–57.

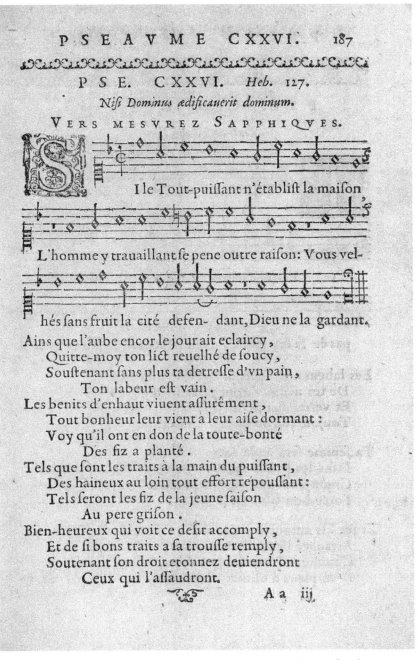

Figure 3.3 Caignet's monophonic setting of Desportes's translation of Psalm 126 in vers mesurez.
Denis Caignet, *Cinquante psaumes de David mis en vers François par Ph. Desportes, Abbé de Thiron, et les chants en musique* (Paris, Pierre Ballard, 1625), p. 187. Bibliothèque municipale Bourges

beatus ille vir. Louis Servin, Avocat general to Henri IV and Louis XIII, was an ardent supporter of the monarchy in the face of the attacks described in Chapter 4, and this paraphrase, published separately in 1610 shortly after the assassination of Henri IV (though clearly written before this date), takes the general sentiment of the psalm – a brief six verses that contrast the blessed man with the wicked – and embroiders and expands it into a poem of epic proportions, a celebration of a man who is now coheir of the highest kings, distant offspring of Jesus himself, a king who will bloom from a noble strain of the *fleur de lys*, here likened to the long hair of the Merovingian dynasty, the famous *reges criniti*:[55]

Titulis superbis stemma clarius feret,	By his glorious titles his lineage will become more renowned,
Regis cohoeres optimi.	He coheir of the best King,
Quem Nazaretha separatum surculum,	The tender shoot, separated from Nazareth,
Sinu fovebit florido,	Which he will nurture in his flourishing bosom,
Palmasque puras efferens ad sydera,	Bearing its pure topmost leaves to the stars,
Densis virescet frondibus,	Will become verdant with dense foliage,
Bonumque regis nomen, inscriptus boni,	And the good name of the King, inscribed with the name of the good,
Vigebit almo germine,	Will bloom from the nourishing sprig,
Ut sena blando crine surgunt Lilia,	Just as six-petalled lilies of pleasing hair rise up,
Floresve Regum nomina,	Also named Fleurs des Rois.
Vir ille quicquid cogitat, dicit, facit,	Whatever that man thinks, says, does,
Ubique prosperum cadet.	Everywhere he will prosper.

The *Chapelle Royale*

Unlike the psalm paraphrases or the musical publications that provided settings of the complete psalter for a non-musical or semi-musical public, the elaborate and sophisticated compositions of court composer Eustache Du Caurroy, setting the Latin texts of the psalms, can only have originally been intended for performance at court itself.[56] But while we would certainly expect the musical/textual strategy of alluding to the model kingship of David to naturally find a home at court, it is somewhat

---

[55] For the classic description, see Marc Bloch, trans. J.E. Anderson, *The Royal Touch: Sacred Monarchy and Scrofula in England and France* (London, Routledge and Kegan Paul, 1973), p. 33.

[56] Colin argues that the publication was intended for domestic performance: see Marie-Alexis Colin, *Eustache Du Caurroy: Preces ecclesiasticae* (Paris, Klincksieck, 2000), p. xvii. See, however, Colin, 'Eustache Du Caurroy', pp. 218–23 for a survey of the psalms.

surprising that this trend did not continue into the main and most obvious venue of sacred music there, the liturgies celebrated in the *chapelle royale*. But as far as we can tell, this is the case, the *chapelle* simply following the Roman rite and singing psalms as specified for the Offices in *fauxbourdon*.[57] After Henri III's reforms to the practices of the *chapelle royale* in 1587 (the term *chapelle* referring to the body of singers, clerics, and musicians charged with celebrating the liturgy rather than to any specific venue), both Henri IV and Louis XIII stressed the continuity of their reigns by making no major changes to the liturgy or personnel, or indeed the musical practices: according to Archon, after his coronation Henri IV recalled all the singers who had worked under Henri III and Charles IX and wished for the Offices to be celebrated in the same way they always had; likewise, after the accession of Louis XIII, no changes were made at all.[58] Thus, according to the *règlement*, the "Grande Messe" was to be celebrated at 9.00 a.m., although if the king needed to leave early in the morning to travel, two Low Masses could be said in his presence at 5.30 a.m. instead. On the other hand, if the king was unexpectedly absent at 9.00 a.m., the *chapelle* was to postpone Mass until he arrived, although by 11.15 a.m. they were permitted to celebrate it without him. Likewise, a clause specifies that Vespers (followed immediately by Compline) was to be sung at 4.00 p.m., but that, again, if the king was not present by that time, the *chapelle* was to wait until 6.00 p.m. before continuing.[59]

The *règlement* also indicates that the clerics of the *chapelle* followed the Roman Rite using the Roman Breviary and Missal, although rather than obeying the Roman Calendar, the liturgical theme of the daily High Mass generally followed a specified regular pattern.[60] On Mondays, the *chapelle*, following the tradition initiated at the Church of the Augustines on behalf of the Ordre du Saint-Esprit, sang a Mass of the Holy Spirit preceded by the hymn *Veni creator spiritus*.[61] On Tuesdays, they celebrated a Mass of the Angels preceded by the hymn *Christe sanctorum*. On Wednesdays, they sang a Mass for Sinners, after which the Passion according to Saint John was to be recited "à voix basse." On Thursdays, a Mass of the Blessed Sacrament was followed by the hymn *Pange lingua*, whilst on Fridays it was a Mass of the Holy Cross preceded by the hymn *Vexilla regis* and again followed by the Passion according to Saint John. On Saturdays, a Mass of

---

[57] F-Pn MS fonds fr. 7008.
[58] Jean-Louis Archon, *Histoire ecclésiastique de la chapelle des rois de France*, 2 vols. (Paris, Pierre-Augustine Le Mercier, 1711), pp. 660, 708.
[59] MS fonds fr. 7008.   [60] Ibid., ff. 4v–5v.   [61] See Chapter 2.

Our Lady was celebrated with the hymn *Ave maris stella*, and Sundays were to follow the feast specified in the Roman Calendar, although if any one of these days was designated as a double feast, it too was celebrated according to the rubrics of the Roman Breviary and Missal, and during High Mass two other Low Masses were to be celebrated in the king's oratory, one for the Trinity and one for All Souls. (It was probably for these occasions, rather than the Offices themselves, that Du Caurroy and the anonymous composers of the Paris manuscript composed their polyphonic hymn settings.)[62] Although there were several small chapels in the Louvre, and although one of them was remodeled by Jacques Lemercier in 1629, Mass on Sunday and feast days was typically celebrated in the chapel of the Hôtel de Petit-Bourbon, across the street from the Louvre and immediately in front of the church of Saint-Germain-l'Auxerrois.[63] Figure 3.4 shows the chapel as illustrated on the 1615 map by Mérian, while Figure 3.5 shows the internal arrangement of the chapel on Sundays and feast days as represented in another *règlement* from 1585. Unfortunately, the plan does not indicate where the musicians and clerics of the *chapelle* itself stood, but from other descriptions of such events we can assume that the singers were probably grouped around a lectern for any polyphony that was sung, and on either side for chant.

One significant exception to the Roman rite was made, however. After every Mass, Psalm 19, *Exaudiat te Dominus*, was to be sung, although by the time of Louis XIII it is likely that this was beginning to be abbreviated to just the final verse, *Domine salvum fac regem*. And on certain occasions, Psalm 129, *De profundis*, was to be substituted for the *Exaudiat* (when a Messe de Trespasses had been celebrated) or Psalm 78, *Deus venerunt gentes* (on Wednesdays "during these wars of religion"). (See Chapter 4 for a discussion of these psalms). The Mass then concluded with three prayers – *Deus refugium nostrum, Ineffabilem misericordiam tuam*, and

---

[62] See Peter Bennett, *Sacred Repertories in Paris under Louis XIII: Paris, Bibliothèque nationale de France, MS V^{ma} rés. 571* (Farnham, Ashgate, 2009), pp. 121–6.

[63] The list of courtiers and dignitaries who attended, and the order in which they processed to the Petit-Bourbon, is preserved in F-Pn MS nouv. acq. fr. 9740 of 1585. Sauval describes the fourteenth-century decorations of the chapel in the Louvre, but these must have been removed when the chapel was remodeled by Jacques Lemercier in 1629: see also Alexandre Gady and Marc Fumaroli, *Jacques Lemercier, architecte et ingénieur du Roi* (Paris, Éditions de la Maison des sciences de l'homme, 2005), p. 238. A new chapel by Le Vau was dedicated on February 18, 1659. That same year, the chapel of the Petit-Bourbon was also renovated, although the whole Petit-Bourbon complex was demolished shortly afterward: see Henri Sauval, *Histoire et Recherches des Antiquités de la ville de Paris* (Paris, Charles Moette and Jacques Chardon, 1724), p. 22; Abbé Oroux, *Histoire ecclésiastique de la cour de France* (Paris, Imprimerie Royale, 1776–7), Vol. 2, p. 477.

The Chapelle Royale 113

Figure 3.4 The Hôtel de Bourbon (between the Louvre and the church of Saint-Germain-l'Auxerrois) and its chapel.

As seen in the map by Matthias Mérian (Paris, Nicolas de Mathonière, 1615). Bibliothèque nationale de France

Rex Regum Deus. As far as the Offices were concerned, the *règlement* specifies a full cycle beginning with Matins at 5.00 a.m., followed by Lauds, Prime, Terce, and Sext, with Vespers at 4.00 p.m. Finally, the *règlement* specifies that all the Offices were to be sung in chant "according

114 *The Sword of David and the Battle against Heresy*

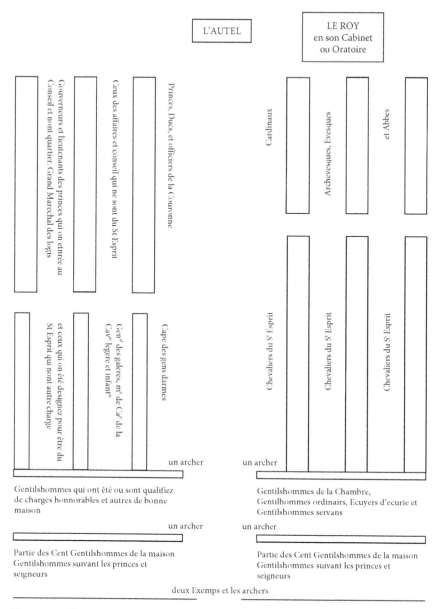

Figure 3.5 Illustration of the internal arrangement of the chapel of the Petit-Bourbon.
After F-Pn MS nouv. acq. fr. 9740

to the Roman usage," although "the chants and tones in fauxbourdon and in music [i.e. polyphony] which his Majesty found the most *dévotieux* and most agreeable were to be sung more often than the others."[64] Archon reports that Louis XIII was an enthusiastic participant from an early age, following the readings in a small Missal that he had been given; even though this Missal provided French translations, Louis was able to follow the Latin, and in addition to daily Mass, he attended Vespers every Sunday and Feast Day.[65] Later in his life we can assume that the king, at a minimum, heard Mass every day, though probably Vespers too. Certainly, a 1653 *Ordre et règlement* records exactly the same kind of routine at the chapel of the young Louis XIV – daily Mass with the addition of devotional hymns before or afterward, although now the only Offices mentioned are Vespers and Compline.[66]

The *Benedictio Mensae*

If the liturgy and music of the Chapelle Royale remained relatively conventional, essentially following Roman usage and not prompting (we assume) the composition of a significant new polyphonic repertory – certainly not a body of psalm-based music comparable to the later works at the chapel of Louis XIV – another venue of performance at court seems to have been much more important musically. We know that in November and December 1586 a paraphrase of Psalm 136 by Cardinal Jacques Davy du Perron (*Quand loin de Palestin*) was sung every day after lunch, and Jacqueline Boucher has suggested that this was part of regular cycle of psalm paraphrases that were performed at the king's mealtimes.[67] Psalm 136 is, of course, the same psalm that opens Du Caurroy's *Meslanges* (in the Durant de la Bergier paraphrase), and so it is possible – in fact more than likely – that this psalm recounting Israel's grief in exile, just like Psalm

---

[64] MS fonds fr. 7008, f. 9v: "les chants et les tons en fauxbourdon et musique que sa Majesté trouve les plus dévotieux et les plus agréables pour les chanter plus souvent que les autres."

[65] Archon, *Histoire ecclésiastique*, pp. 707–8.

[66] *Ordre et règlement qui doit estre tenu et observe en la maison du Roy* (Paris, Marin le Che, 1651), pp. 21–6. By this date, Mass is specified to be celebrated at 6.00 a.m.

[67] "... se chantoit en musique devant le Roy tous les jours après son repas, 1586, mois de No. et Dec.": F-Pn MS Dupuy 844, ff. 430r–431r, quoted in Jacqueline Boucher, *Société et mentalités autour de Henri III* (Paris, Garnier, 2007), p. 1031. Du Perron's version is one of a handful of psalm paraphrases that he wrote and which were later published in his *Poésies*: *Domine ne in furore* (Psalm 6), *Benedic anima mea Domino* (Psalm 103), and *Exaudiat te Dominus* (Psalm 19).

113, *In exitu Israel*, discussed in Chapter 2, had acquired particular resonance at that time.

A musical setting of Du Perron's paraphrase survives in a manuscript compiled by Charles Tessier, a composer who was known to be active at the court in the 1590s. Preserved here as a lute song, it is nevertheless entirely possible that it also existed in a parallel polyphonic arrangement now lost.[68] And while the mournful text of this work suggests that it should more appropriately be considered in Chapter 4, its existence nevertheless points squarely to the practice of singing such psalms at mealtimes, especially when we consider other, archival evidence. A 1578 *règlement* and an *Ordre* of 1651, both specify (in exactly the same words) that:[69]

> The musicians of his majesty's *chapelle* are present at his lunch on Sundays when he eats in public to sing in that place during lunch, and until the table rises the musicians place themselves in such a position close to him so that his Majesty can hear better.

At such an occasion (shown in Figure 3.6), they could certainly either have performed the paraphrases mentioned above or they could also have been involved – alongside the *musique de la chambre* – in the daily performance of Grace that the later 1587 *règlement* also describes:[70]

> the almoner ... putting himself at the same end of the table as the singers of his Majesty's *chambre* will begin the graces ordained by the Roman Breviary ...; then the singers will respond alternately. The said almoner will afterward begin the first verse of the psalm of graces, which must be said according to the season and the

---

[68] See Frank Dobbins, *Charles Tessier, Œuvres complètes* (Turnhout, Brepols, 2006). For a discussion of the fluid boundary between polyphonic originals and lute-song arrangements from around this time, see Jeanice Brooks, '"O quelle armonye": Dialogue singing in late Renaissance France', *Early Music History*, 22 (2003), 1–65.

[69] *L'Ordre que le Roy veut estre tenu par son grand ausmosnier*, F-Pn MS nouv. acq. fr. 32, f. 131r–131v: "Se trouvera la musique de la chapelle de sa maiesté au disner dicelle tous les jours de Dimanche en lieu de sejour quand Elle mangera en publicq pour chanter audit lieu Durant le disner et jusques à ce que la table se lève, laquelle musique se trouvera en tel endroit qui se trouvera le plus à propos pour estre mieux entendue de sa Maiesté.'" See also *Ordre et règlement*, p. 25.

[70] F-Pn MS fonds fr. 7008, ff. 14v–17r: "ledit aumosnier ... se mettant au mesme bout de la tables avec les Chantres de la Chambre de sa Majesté commancera lors les grâces ordonnées par le bréviaire Romain ...; puis les Chantres respondront alternativement. Le susdit Aumosnier après commencera le premier verset du psalme des grâces qui se doit dire selon la saison et selon les Rubriques dudit Bréviaire puis les Chantres aussy respondront lautre verset en chantant et ainsy ledit aumosnier dira tousjours un verset et lesdict Chantres diront lautre alternativement en fauxbourdon et le psalme achevé ledit aumosnier dira le paster noster, et au temps que l'on dira les versets qui commencet Dispersit dedit pauperibus le premier sera dit par laumosnier et respondu en musique ou fauxbourdon par lesdicts Chantres aussy alternativement ..."

Figure 3.6 Henri III dining "en public" in 1584.
Richard Cooke, *La Première partie du compte de Richarde Cooke de Kent pour son voyage et temps employé en France,* Folger Shakespeare Library, MS V.a.146, f.62

according to the rubrics of the said Breviary, then the singers will also respond the other verse singing, and then the said almoner will always say a verse and the said singers will say the other alternately in *fauxbourdon*, and, the psalm completed, the said almoner will say the *Pater noster*, and at the time when one will say the verses which begin *Dispersit dedit pauperibus*, the first will be said by the almoner and replied in music or fauxbourdon by the said singers also alternately ...

The so-called *Benedictio mensae* that the *règlement* describes is a long and complex ceremony, performed before and after both lunch and dinner, modified according to the season, and set out in the Breviary. While the 1587 *règlement* emphasizes lunch, the 1651 *Ordre*, while not nearly so detailed, does treat both lunch and dinner equally, and so the additional complexity of the Order at dinner may well have been reflected musically in the years following 1587.[71] At lunch, the serving of the food was preceded by versicles and responses, the *Kyrie*, the *Pater noster*, and a blessing, while afterward another set of responses and prayers was recited to give thanks for the meal, followed by Psalm 50, *Miserere mei*, and Psalm

---

[71] *L'Ordre*, p. 24, specifies Graces "tous les iours au disners & souper de sadite Majesté."

114, *Laudate Dominum omnes gentes*. At dinner, a similar ceremony occurred, this time with only Psalm 114 during ordinary time; during Nativity Psalm, 96 *Cantate Domino* was sung in addition; during Epiphany, Psalm 76, *Deus judicium*; on Good Friday, Psalm 50, *Miserere*; on Holy Saturday, Psalm 114; at Easter and its octave, Psalm 21, *Confitemini Domino*; on Ascension, Psalm 60, *Omnes gentes plaudite manibus* and 114; and at the feast of Pentecost and its octave, Psalm 47, *Magnus Dominus*.[72]

Whether at lunch or dinner, as part of the complex Grace liturgy, or simply for entertainment, music and the psalms were clearly a part of the mealtime ritual, and it seems entirely likely that many of the surviving psalm-based works for a large group of singers would have been performed in this context by the expert musicians of the *chapelle* or *chambre*.[73] Of all Du Caurroy's psalm "motets" preserved in the *Preces ecclesiasticae*, for example, only *In exitu Israel* is provided with the Doxology that would make it appropriate for liturgical performance. But given the regular nature of psalm performance at mealtimes, the others, without doxology, must surely have been destined for this occasion or at least composed with this possibility in mind.[74] In the same way, the psalms in Du Caurroy's *Meslanges*, too, may well have been performed in this context, and even a lost work such as Nicolas Formé's motet *Nonne Deo subjecta erit anima mea* (Psalm 61).[75]

But perhaps the music that we can most closely associate with this performance venue (or at the very least, non-liturgical performances by court ensembles) during the reign of Louis XIII is Artus Auxcousteaux's 1631 collection of psalms, *Psalmi aliquot ad numeros musices IIII–V et sex vocum redacti*, presumably published as a response to Louis's success at La Rochelle and strikingly reflecting the focus on David that this chapter has

---

[72] See, for example, *Breviarium Romanum ex decreto sacrosancti Concilii tridentini restitutum* (Rome, Typographia Vaticana, 1633), supplementary p. clvii. The observation in F-Pn MS Dupuy 844 highlighted by Boucher can probably be interpreted as an approximation of the seasonal shift in psalm.

[73] In suggesting this, I am merely following Anthony Cumming's important but brief observations on the "motet" at mealtimes at the Papal court in the sixteenth century: see Anthony Cummings, 'Toward an interpretation of the sixteenth-century motet', *Journal of the American Musicological Society*, 34/4 (1981), 43–59. For the motet in France, see John Brobeck, 'Some "liturgical motets" for the French Royal Court: A reconsideration of genre in the sixteenth-century motet', *Musica Disciplina*, 47 (1993), 123–57.

[74] See listing in Colin, 'Eustache Du Caurroy', pp. 208–12.

[75] Mentioned in Louis Aubinau, 'Fragments des mémoires de Dubois', *Bibliothèque de l'Ecole des Chartes*, 9 (1858), 1–48. Quoted in Formé, *Œuvres*, p. xxxii.

sketched out.[76] As the only composer (apart from Formé) associated with Louis's *chapelle* for whom any musical works survive, Auxcousteaux is an important witness to the musical practices at court. Serving as a singer under Nicolas Formé and Eustache Picot, probably between 1614 and 1627, he was appointed *maître de musique* at Saint Quentin in 1627, publishing his psalms while employed there, though dedicating the collection to the king.[77] After a period in Amiens, Auxcousteaux returned to Paris, being appointed to the Sainte Chapelle in 1634 and becoming its director in 1643.

Only three of the original six part-books of Auxcousteaux's volume survive (the superius, quinta, and contra), and the quinta book is itself incomplete, but enough remains to show that the volume preserves twenty-one psalms in Latin, set to elaborate and complex polyphony, though without doxologies – in other words, these were not psalms for the Offices but psalm "motets." In his prefatory letter to the king, Auxcousteaux explains why he had compiled the collection:[78]

After such victories achieved by your virtue, among the praises and vows of affection and benediction of your people, I come with all humility to offer at the feet of Your Majesty these truly royal songs. These are the sacred verses of the Holy-King-prophet set according to measured notes and harmonies. My Music, not daring to stand alone before Your Majesty, borrows from such a worthy subject of which to present in a more suitable state: to which it can serve for private delight to ease your military and political cares, and as a means of praising God publicly.

For Auxcousteaux, the sacred verses of the prophet king, set to music ("measured," but only in the most general sense), thus had two functions – to assuage the pain and troubles of the king in private (a theme which I will continue in Chapter 4) and to celebrate his successes and to praise God in public – presumably as a non-liturgical adornment to public events (processions, *entrées*, etc.) and in other places where celebratory music might be

---

[76] Artus Auxcousteaux, *Psalmi aliquot ad numeros musices IIII–V et sex vocum redacti* (Paris, Pierre Ballard, 1631).

[77] Auxcousteaux claims that these works were written while at Saint Quentin; nevertheless, we can be fairly certain that at some stage they were performed at court, since in his note "aux amateurs de la musique," he hopes that they will cause the king to think of him: Auxcousteaux, *Psalmi*, p. 3.

[78] Auxcousteaux, *Psalmi*, pp. 2r–2v: "Apres tant de victoires acquises par vostre vertu, parmy les louanges & les vœux d'affection & bénédiction de vos peuples, je viens avec toute humilité offrir aux pieds de V.M. *des chants vrayement royaux*. Ce sont les sacrez vers du *Sainct-Roy-prophète* accommodées aux reigles des *tons & accords mesurez*. Ma Musique n'osant paroistre seule devant V.M. emprunte d'un si digne sujet dequoy se présenter en estat plus convenable: auquel elle pourra servir & de délectation privément pour tremper vos soings guerriers & politiques, & de moyen pour louer Dieu publiquement."

Example 3.2 Artus Auxcousteaux, reconstruction of Psalm 80, *Exultate Deo adjutori nostro*.
Psalmi aliquot ad numeros musices IIII, V et sex vocum redacti (Paris, Pierre Ballard, 1631)

appropriate, such as at mealtimes (which the illustration in Figure 3.6 describes as "en public"). Leaving behind (like the Du Caurroy collections) any liturgical utility (i.e. the collection contained no standard vespers

Example 3.2 (*cont.*)

psalms, no *Miserere*, no *De profundis*, and no *Exaudiat te Dominus*), but also clearly beyond the capabilities of typical domestic performers, Auxcousteaux's collection surveys the psalter, extracting psalms that would have clearly resonated with Louis's situation and the requirements of the court, leading the listener through despair and anguish to ultimate victory.

The collection begins with Psalm 2, *Quare fremuerunt gentes*, God's promise to his anointed, which opens with the lines "Why have the Gentiles raged, and the people devised vain things? The kings of the earth stood up, and the princes met together, against the Lord and against his Christ [i.e. the anointed one: *christum* in the Vulgate]." The anointed one then replies in verses 6–9 that God has appointed him king, declaring in verse 9 that "Thou shalt rule them with a rod of iron, and shalt break them in pieces like a potter's vessel."

Among the many other psalms included, Psalm 17 was well known as a song of thanksgiving for royal victories, while others in the collection either reinforced this message or presented an alternative perspective, using the language of despair that was picked up in the compositions for the *musique de la chambre* discussed in Chapter 4. But, perhaps most fittingly, the collection ends with a setting of Psalm 146, a celebration of psalmody itself: "Praise ye the Lord, because [to sing] psalm[s] is good: to our God be joyful and comely praise." The source for this final work is too corrupted to recreate, but Example 3.2 shows a reconstruction of another psalm of celebration, the first seven verses of Psalm 80, Exultate Deo adjutori nostro ("Rejoice unto God our helper: sing aloud to the God of Jacob"). In this piece, we get a first glimpse of the capabilities of the musicians of the chapelle royale during the seventeenth century and the composers who provided music for it, an essay in close six-voice counterpoint and a fitting accompaniment to a celebratory feast.

4 | The Penitent King

By the time that Auxcousteaux's psalms settings had been published and dedicated to the king in 1631, partly as a "moyen pour louer Dieu publiquement" (a means of praising God publicly), Louis's status as monarch was relatively secure: the Pope, Urban VIII, had publicly and effusively praised his contribution as savior of the church after the recapture of La Rochelle in 1628, and in 1630 his mother, Marie de Médicis, had been successfully outmaneuvred on the so-called Day of the Dupes.[1] Yet in the first years of his reign, particularly in the late 1610s and early 1620s, this successful future was by no means guaranteed. The repercussions of Henri IV's assassination had continued to play out in the following years, with the anti-monarchial sentiment of both Protestant Monarchomachs and pro-papal Jesuits (who were blamed for the assassination) only intensifying.[2] In particular, Robert Bellarmine's 1610 *Tractatus de potestate summi pontificis* (Treatise on the Power of the Supreme Pontiff), a tract that set out the case that Temporal power should be subordinate to Ecclesiastical power, directly challenged Louis's authority and status as the "most Christian king."[3]

In response, jurists associated with the court continued to push back against these Jesuit, pro-papal policies, clarifying the basis of the king's absolute power and his relationship to the Pope. Thus, in 1611 Bedé de la Gormandière's *Droit des rois contre le cardinal Bellarmine et autres jesuites* explicitly argued against Bellarmine by name, and in 1615 Jerome Bignon's *La Grandeur de nos rois et leur souveraine puissance* even took on the Pope, laying out twenty arguments against "Le Glaive temporal du Pape"

---

[1] Artus Auxcousteaux, *Psalmi aliquot ad numeros musices III, V et sex vocum redacti* (Paris, Pierre Ballard, 1631), n.p. A. Lloyd Moote, *Louis XIII, the Just* (Berkeley, Los Angeles, and London, University of California Press, 1989), pp. 199–219.

[2] Francis Ravaillac, Henri IV's assassin, was thought to have taken his inspiration from the Jesuit Juan de Mariana's 1599 treatise *De rege et regis institute* (On the King and the Institution of Kingship): see Roland Mousnier, trans. Joan Spencer, *The Assassination of Henri IV; The Tyrannicide Problem and the Consolidation of the French Absolute Monarchy in the Early Seventeenth Century* (New York, Scribner, 1973), pp. 251–80.

[3] William Jervis, *The Gallican Church: The History of the Church of France from the Concordat of Bologna to the Revolution* (London, John Murray, 1872), p. 260: Mousnier, *Assassination*, p. 252.

(The Temporal Sword of the Pope).[4] But Jean Savaron's *Traité de la souveraineté du Roi et de son Royaume* of the same year opened with the clearest defense yet of the French king, making the case that in Temporal matters, the king was God's true representative on earth. Addressing the king directly, Savaron begins the treatise:[5]

Sire,
God made you to be born sovereign and absolute King, recognizing only God alone as higher Temporal [authority] of your Kingdom, and none other. It is why you are honored with the titles of Vicar of JESUS CHRIST in Temporal [matters].

But despite the constructions of these jurists and many others, and despite Louis's military achievements in Béarn (1618–19) and the signing of the Peace of Montpellier in 1622, the Jesuits again began to take exception to the king's more tolerant attitude toward heresy (the Peace of Montpellier in 1622, after all, did not mark the end of Huguenot worship), an attitude encouraged by his new mentor Cardinal Richelieu. Keller's 1625 *Admonitio ad Regem Christianissimum Ludovicum XIII* (Warning to the Most Christian King Louis XIII) argued that the king should be excommunicated for his tolerant attitude, while in the same year Antonio Santarelli's *Tractatus de haeresi* (Treatise on Heresy), another extremist ultramontane tract, restated the same arguments as the *Admonitio* and Bellarmine's *De potestate* – that the Pope enjoyed not only Ecclesiastical and spiritual but also Temporal authority over the monarchy. Beyond that, however, Santarelli also claimed that the Pope had the power and duty to punish temporal princes for dereliction of their duties (i.e. tolerating heresy), and even to take away their earthly dominions.[6]

This chapter explores the musical and liturgical response to these deeply troubled years, the first two decades of Louis's reign, focusing not on the attempts to understand the the nation, the king, and kingship itself through the model of David the military leader who, against all the odds, defeated the heretic Philistines, but as a nation in mourning, an Israel in metaphorical exile, with a leader in personal distress, crying out to God in penitence

---

[4] Jean Bignon, *La Grandeur de nos Roys et de leur souveraine puissance. Au Roy* (Paris, n.p., 1615), pp. 36–62: Mousnier, *Assassination*, pp. 240–42.

[5] Jean Savaron, Second *Traicté de la souveraineté du Roy. Au Roy Très-Chrestien Louis XIII* (Paris, Pierre Chevalier, 1615), p. 3: "Dieu vous a fait naistre Roy souverain & absolu, ne recognoissant supérieur au Temporel de vostre Royaume que Dieu seul, & non autre. C'est pourqoye vous estes honoré des titres de Vicaire de JESUS-CHRIST au Temporel."

[6] For an extensive discussion of these events and of Keller's and Santarelli's tracts, see Jervis, *History of the Church*, pp. 303–11.

and humility for his sins.[7] As we might expect, some responses were relatively "private" – music composed for performance in the *chambre* for Louis and his closest courtiers, music that might, in Auxcousteaux's words, "détremper vos soings guerriers & politiques" (ease your military and political cares). But much of it was public: following the initiatives of Henri III, who had experienced much the same kind of threats to his own rule and whose identity – pious and devoted to the Virgin Mary – Louis shared, France redoubled its public prayers for the king in the words of the psalmist *Exaudiat te Dominus in die tribulationis ... Domine salvum fac regem* (May the Lord hear thee in in the day of tribulation ... O Lord, save the king.)

A Penitent Court

The troubled and turbulent nature of the early years of Louis's reign is acknowledged in Chaissy's *Glaive de David et de Louys XIII Roy de France* (Sword of David and of Louis XIII, King of France) of 1624, which (as Chapter 3 showed) set out the parallels between David's and Louis's early struggles.[8] Other psalm paraphrases also framed the king's military prowess as a response to the dangers he faced at that time, but numerous sources also testify specifically to the penitential and introspective atmosphere at court during those years. In *Les Pseaumes des courtisans* (The Psalms of the Courtiers) of 1620, an anonymous author chronicles daily conversational interactions at court, framing many of these in terms of the psalms.[9] The book opens with an observation that courtiers no longer study their "grands livres de Devotion," preferring to carry about their person just small books that contained the most important devotional texts, most notably the Penitential Psalms, which – the author goes on to show – serve as shorthand or code through which they can petition the king to deliver them from their discomforts: many of these courtiers were *dévot* figures whose status in the aftermath of Marie's fall in 1617 was distinctly problematic, and so most of these petitions involved asking the king for forgiveness. Thus, for example:[10]

---

[7] Early versions of some of this material first appeared in Peter Bennett, 'Hearing King David in early modern France: Politics, prayer, and Louis XIII's *Musique de la Chambre*', *Journal of the American Musicological Society*, 69/1 (2016), 47–109.

[8] See Chapter 3, note 38.

[9] *Les Pseaumes des courtisans dédiés aux braves esprits qui entendent le jars de la Cour* (Paris, n. p., 1620).

[10] *Les Pseaumes des courtisans*, p. 14: "Monsieur de Guyse fermant le Psaultier, & le mettant sur le buffet ... a protesté devant le Roy de sa fidelité pour l'avenir, disant humblement, *Domine, ne reminiscaris delicta nostra, vel parentum nostrorum, neque vindictam sumas de peccatis nostris.*"

Monsieur de Guise, closing his psalter and placing it on a side table ... protested before the king his future fidelity, saying humbly, "Lord, remember not our offenses, nor those of our forefathers, nor take revenge on them" [Antiphon to Psalm 6].

("Monsieur de Guise" was Charles de Lorraine, duc de Guise, son of Henri de Guise, one of the leaders of the League, assassinated by Henri III in 1588, and a leading *dévot* with ultramontane, pro-Jesuit sympathies, while his wife, Henriette-Catherine de Joyeuse, was the daughter of the Leaguer and mystic Ange de Joyeuse, and a leading patron of the Abbey of Montmartre; see Chapter 6). In another case the author simply framed the internal reflections of a courtier in terms of a psalm verse:[11]

Monsieur de Vendosme, realizing the impossibility of his vain schemes, noticed the source of his faults, because he found them in his Penitential Psalm: "For behold, I was conceived in iniquities, and my mother conceived in sin" [Psalm 50:7].

("Monsieur de Vendosme" was César de Vendosme, illegitimate son of Henri IV, half brother of Louis XIII, later expelled for his support of the ultra-Catholic *dévot* faction at court.) Most strikingly, a final example refers to the use of a "motet" for addressing the king:[12]

Monsieur le Général des Galères, to demonstrate that he was a gentleman, clean, neat, and well disposed toward the king, before he presented himself questioned the king using this motet from his abridged psalter: "You will sprinkle me with hyssop, and I will be made clean: you will wash me, and I will be made whiter than snow" [Psalm 50:9].

(Philippe-Emmanuel de Gondi was commander of the royal fleet and brother of the Bishop of Paris, Henri de Gondi.)

The accounts of the conversations (presumably fictitious, but nonetheless indicative of a real phenomenon) in Les Pseaumes des courtisans point to a particular practice in which psalm texts had become so familiar and so much a part of the shared cultural and religious heritage of the court (reminiscent of the court of Henri II discussed in Chapter 1) that they were able to serve as a set of shared references that courtiers could employ

---

[11] Ibid., p. 11: "Monsieur de Vendosme cognoissant l'impossibilité de ses vains desseins, à remarqué le lieu d'ou vient le deffaut, parce qu'il l'a trouvé dans son Psalme Poenitentiel: *Ecce in iniquitatibus conceptus sum, & in peccatis concepit me mater mea.*"
[12] Ibid., pp. 11–12: "Monsieur le Général des Galères, pour se monstrer galant homme, propre, net, & bien accomodé aupres du Roy, avant que s'y présenter demande au Roy par ce motet de son Psaultier abregé. *Asperges me, Domine hyssopo, & mundabor, lavabis me, & super nivem de albabor.*"

to convey and frame their regrets and supplications to the king. And the fact that these phrases might be identified as "motets" also suggests some common ground with musical practices, even if *Les Pseaumes des courtisans* did not invoke music at all. In other words, just as in this context we can read the term "motet" as a phrase or verse, selected from a larger whole that can be used to express a particular meaning, so too can we read the musical term "motet" as a musical setting of a similarly consciously selected text.[13]

As was the case for the works discussed in Chapter 3, we find the musical equivalent of these textual "motets" not in the liturgy of the *chapelle royale*, but in a variety of other contexts, performed either by the *musique de la chapelle royale* or the *musique de la chambre*. Just as, for example, Auxcousteaux's 1631 collection provides musical settings of psalms that celebrated David's/Louis's military successes and strength, it also provides settings of psalms (and occasionally excerpts of psalms) that focus on exactly the opposite – David's despair, his prayers expressing hope that the nation will turn to God, and his own personal doubts – at the same time providing comfort to the king.

The second work in Auxcousteaux's collection, for example, a setting of all nine verses of Psalm 3 *Domine, multiplicati sunt*, begins by asking "Why, O Lord, are they multiplied that afflict me? Many are those who rise up against me." In response, the remainder of the psalm provides comfort, however, expressing faith that God will deliver David from his adversaries, and that "Salvation is of the Lord: and thy blessing is upon they people." By contrast, Auxcousteaux's setting of Psalm 21 (*Deus, Deus meus, respice in me*) offers no such consolation. Generally acknowledged to be a prefiguration of Christs's passion, and, according to its opening verse, set in the morning hours, the time that tradition holds Christ to have been crucified, the psalm opens with the cry that the crucified Jesus would later utter, "My God [my God] why hast thou forsaken me," and continues through a series of statements of personal anguish. At v. 20, however, the tone changes entirely, now looking forward to the resurrection through a series of supplications and assertions ("The Kingdom is the Lord's," etc.).

---

[13] The use of the word "motet" here mirrors, for example, the *Motets pour la chapelle royale, mis en musique par Monsieur Dumont* (Paris, Christophe Ballard, 1686) in which the word "motet" itself does not seem to connote music. Jean Nicot's *Thresor de la langue françoyse* (1606) defines "motet" in both ways, as "Un Motet de musique, Versus." See, however John Brobeck, 'Some "liturgical" motets for the French royal court: A reconsideration of genre in the sixteenth-century motet', *Musica Disciplina*, 47 (1993), 123–576. Brobeck considers the term "motet" as indicative of the more complex musical style that was associated with non-liturgical works.

But by concluding his setting at v. 19 as he does, Auxcousteaux's motet remains a bleak commentary on a time of utmost despair. And while the musical setting is perhaps not as expressive as similarly themed motets from the sixteenth century, it is nonetheless hauntingly recitational, in some ways reminiscent of Josquin's *Miserere* with its psalm-tone-like contra (c3) voice. (See the reconstruction in Music Example 4.1.)

We can imagine such works being performed in the relative "privacy" of lunch or dinner by the musicians of the *chapelle royale* (though the royal meal was actually considered "public"), but an even more intimate performance venue was the king's chamber itself, the musical domain of the *musique de la chambre*. We know from the 1587 *règlement* (see Chapter 3) and from the 1665 (and subsequent editions) of the *État de la France*, that the *musique de la chambre* were present at lunch, where they performed grace, but a 1578 *règlement* also required them to be available to sing in Louis's chamber before the daily 9.00 a.m. Mass.[14] We would certainly expect the *musique de la chambre* to be performing secular music – *airs de cour* – at the regular evening attendance (as specificied in the same *règlement* as 7.00–8.00 p.m.) in the king's chamber, but even there the devotional and introspective atmosphere of the court might intrude. Publications such as the *Odes chrestiennes* of 1625, a collection of sacred contrafacta of *airs* by *chambre* composers Antoine Boësset and Pierre Guédron could easily have been performed, and a group of three of these contrafacta explore various facets of David's life under the titles of "David, pasteur," "David disgracié," and "David remis en grâce."[15] In the early morning, though, it is much easier to imagine the *chambre* performing sacred, paraliturgical, or devotional works in preparation for the Mass, which, according to the *règlement*, was celebrated "with the honor and regard which is fitting in this holy place."[16]

---

[14] F-Pn MS nouv. acq. fr. 32, f. 36r–36v: "Les chantres et autres de la musique de la chambre se trouveront tous les matins en l'antichambre de sadicte Maiesté pour entrer dans la Chambre quand ils seront appelez." By the time of the *Ordre* of 1651, Mass seems to have been celebrated at 7.00 rather than 9.00; see *Ordre et règlement qui doit estre tenu et observé en la maison du Roy* (Paris, Marin le Che, 1651), pp. 21–6. According to the 1669 edition of *L'État de la France*, p. 107, "La Musique de la Chambre ... Qui s'y trouve lorsque le Roy le Commande, comme les soirs à son coucher & au diner du Roy les jours des bonnes Fêtes, pour chanter les Grâces" (The Musique de la Chambre ... goes where the king commands, such as in the evenings at his *coucher* and at the king's dinner on feast days, to sing graces).

[15] *Odes chrestiennes accommodés aux plus beaux Airs à quatre & cinq parties de Guédron et de Boësset* (Paris, Pierre Ballard, 1625). For the contents of this collection, see Denise Launay, *La Musique religieuse en France du Concile de Trente à 1804* (Paris, Klincksieck, 1993), pp. 217–20.

[16] F-Pn MS nouv. acq. fr. 32, f. 36v: "avec l'honneur et veuë qui est deue a ce sainct lieu."

Music Example 4.1. Artus Auxcousteaux, reconstruction of *Deus, Deus meus, respice in me*.
Psalmi aliquot ad numeros musices IIII, V et sex vocum redacti (Paris, Pierre Ballard, 1631).

As befits its more private status, the sacred repertoire of the *chambre* was never published, being preserved in a single section of the Paris manuscript copied in the mid 1620s.[17] Consisting of about fifty works for voices and continuo, most of it preserved anonymously (but presumably composed by figures associated with the *chambre* such as Antoine Boësset, Henri Le

---

[17] The *chambre* music, distinguished most clearly from the other contents of the Paris manuscript by its use of *basse-continue*, is found in a section copied before 1632, ff. 128r–177v; see Peter Bennett, *Sacred Repertories in Paris under Louis XIII: Paris, Bibliothèque nationale de France, MS V^{ma} rés. 571* (Farnham, Ashgate, 2009), pp. 71–106 and Appendix 2.

Table 4.1 Psalm-texted and Songs-texted "motets" from the repertoire of the *musique de la chambre* preserved in the Paris manuscript

Location in the Paris manuscript	Text incipit	Text source
128v–129r	Deus intende mihi	Psalm 54:3
129v–131r	Domine Deus noster	Psalm 8 complete
142v–143v	Domine multiplicati sunt	Based on Psalms 3:2, 69:6
148v–149r	Adiuva nos	Psalm 78:9, Exodus 32:11, 131:1
131v–132v	Veni sponsa mea	Song of Solomon 4:8, 1, 3, 7:5, 5:6, 2:5
132v–133v	Egredimini filiae Sion	Song of Solomon 3:11, 6
141v–142r	Flores apparuerunt	Song of Solomon 2:12, 1, 5:8

Bailly, François Richard, and others), some of this *chambre* repertoire has conventional and identifiable liturgical functions – Mass Ordinary settings, Marian antiphons, Magnificats, *fauxbourdons* for the recitation of Vespers psalms, and so on, which were presumably performed in liturgical or paraliturgical ceremonies outside the regular musical and liturgical framework of the *chapelle royale* (but about which we have no information). But the remaining works set texts either from the Book of Psalms or from the Song of Solomon (see Table 4.1). With the exception of *Domine Deus noster*, which uses the text of a complete psalm (although without Doxology), all the other works employ a patchwork or centonization of single verses. In the context I have just outlined, in which single "motet" psalm verses had become the conversational currency of the court, and in which composers such as Auxcousteaux would engage in a certain amount of text editing (or at least selection), we can probably see the way the texts were manipulated in these settings as even closer to the practices of the courtiers in *Les Pseaumes des courtisans* than Auxcousteaux's psalms, although the much more radical textual choices must have been officially sanctioned by clerics whose interests were closely allied with those of the king.[18] But how did these more "official" works reflect the way in which the young king was understood?

Much more so than the Auxcousteaux settings, which set substantial sections or complete psalms, the clerics or composers who made the textual choices here actively manipulated psalm and other scriptural verses to produce a rich mosaic of meaning. In *Domine multiplicati sunt*, for

---

[18] Abbé Oroux provides a listing of the most important clerics at court: presumably the numerous *aumôniers* and *maîtres de l'oratoire* are the kinds of people who might compile such texts; see Oroux, *Histoire ecclésiastique*, p. 440.

Table 4.2 Text, translation, and source of *Domine multiplicati sunt*

Domine multiplicati sunt inimici mei, et gloriantur in virtute tua.	Based on Psalm 3:2 and/or Matins Responsory	Lord, how increased are my enemies, and they glorify themselves in your virtue.
[Domine quid multiplicati sunt qui tribulant me multi insurgunt adversum me.]	[Psalm 3:2]	[Lord, how are they increased that trouble me! Many are they that rise up against me.]
[Congregati sunt inimici nostri, et gloriantur in virtute sua.]	[Responsory III, Matins, first Sunday in October]	[Our enemies are gathered together, and boast of their strength.]
Ego vero egenus et pauper sum. Deus adiuva me, Deus libera me, adiutor meus et liberator meus. Domine ne moreris.	Psalm 69:6	But I am afflicted and needy. O God save me, O God free me, my help and my deliverer; O Lord, do not delay.

Table 4.3 Text, translation, and source of *Adiuva nos Deus salutaris*

Adiuva nos Deus salutaris noster: et propter gloriam nominis tui, libera nos Domine.	Psalm 78:9	Save us. God of our salvation: and by the glory of your name, save us. Lord.
Cur Domine irascitur furor tuus contra populum tuum quem eduxisti de terra Aegypti?	Exodus 32:11	Why, Lord, are you angry with your people, whom I led out of the land of Egypt?
Memento Domine regni tui Gallii: et per merita divi Ludovico exaudi nos.	Based on Psalm 131:1	Remember, Lord, your King of France: and by the merit of holy Louis, hear us.
[Memento Domine David, et omnis mansuetudinis.]	[Psalm 131:1]	[Remember, Lord, David, and all his meekness.]

example, the psalmist beseeches God for help in the face of numerous enemies (see Table 4.2). Unlike Auxcousteaux, who set this text directly from the psalter, the compiler of the text here has paraphrased the opening verse, borrowed text from a Matins responsory, and selected a verse from another psalm, an even more direct appeal to God, to serve as the peroration.

Adiuva nos Deus salutaris noster casts its textual net even wider, combining direct psalm quotation, psalm parody or paraphrase, and a verse from Exodus (see Table 4.3). By substituting "your king of France" for "David" in the final section paraphrasing the Sunday Vespers psalm *Memento Domine David* (Psalm 131), the compiler of the text makes the connection between the two kings unambiguous. At the same time it establishes a close connection with the final strophe of the contrafacta "David disgracié" from the 1625 *Odes chrestiennes*.

Souvenez-vous, Seigneur,	Remember, Lord,
De vostre petit coeur,	From your little heart,
De cet homme d'eslite:	This remarkable man:
Pensez à vostre amour, & non à son mérite.	Think of your love, and not of his merit.
C'est David, o grand Dieu,	It is David, O great God,
Qui dans vos bras se jette	Who throws himself into your arms
N'ayant point de retraitte	Having no surer refuge
Plus seure en aucun lieu.	Anywhere else.

Just as the psalm text asks God to remember David, so too does the anonymous text here ("Souvenez-vous, Seigneur"), also alluding to the "merits" of the king (either Louis or David), and concluding with an allusion to the strong and sure refuge of Psalm 46. The verse from Exodus, on the other hand, strikingly plays into the narrative of France as the new Israel most notably exemplified in the setting of *In exitu Israel*, discussed in Chapter 2. But here, the leader of Israel (God's chosen people), who has already led his nation from captivity to freedom, asks why God is still angry with his people, just as – it would seem to all contemporaries – he was in the 1620s. In a striking twist, the final verse, a paraphrase of a psalm in which David prays for himself by name, is modified to invoke the prayers of Saint Louis – another divinely ordained model of kingship – on behalf, now, of the King of France (see Chapter 3). The text of *Adiuva nos* thus calls upon the two royal predecessors most associated with the ideals of kingship during a period in which the very notion itself was under threat.

Of the three settings of texts from the Song of Solomon, two seem to be functioning as Assumption or Marian motets, the anonymous *Veni sponsa mea* and Étienne Moulinié's *Flores apparuerunt* (see Chapter 7 for further discussion of Song's texts and the Assumption). A third example, however, *Egredmini filiae Sion*, does not necessarily express the same feelings of despair and dejection found in the previous works, but it is nonetheless undoubtedly a response to contemporary events (see the text in Table 4.4). On one level, we might justifiably read this celebration of the mystical and springlike virtues of an unnamed queen as an allusion to Mary, Queen of Heaven (by virtue of the Marian symbolism of roses and lilies), to Marie de Médicis (associated with the *fleur de lys*), or to Louis XIII's queen, Anne of Austria, for whom a comparison with Mary, born in the line of David and mother of the anointed "monarch" Jesus, would have been a fitting compliment.

But at a deeper level, the text reflects more closely the reality at court. Shortly after Concini's assassination, Louis's brother Gaston began to test

Table 4.4 Text, translation, and source of *Egredimini filiae Sion*

Egredimini filiae Sion	Songs 3:11	Go forth, ye daughters of Sion,
Et videte Reginam sicut columbam ascendentam ex aromatibus mirrhae et thuris.	Based on Songs 3:6	And see the Queen ascending like a dove from the cloud of myrrh and incense.
Et sicut dies verni circumdabant eam flores rosarum et lilum convallium.	Based on Songs 2:1	And like a spring day there were around her roses and lilies of the valley.

the bounds of loyalty, making clear his own ambition to be king. That same year, several publications featuring David's son and successor, King Solomon, appeared, most notably *Le Salomon de la France, ou le rapport de nostre Roy à Salomon, en sa sagesse par la iustice, & la clémence* (The Solomon of France, or the Relationship of Our King to Solomon, in His Wisdom by Justice and Clemency).[19] Although, of all the biblical kings, it is Solomon who is featured during the central act of the coronation ceremony (the anointing by Zadok the priest), his image was nevertheless not widely adopted as a model for kingship itself or as a mirror of princes.[20] David had sinned in his private life, but God forgave him after he begged for forgiveness through the prophet Nathan; Solomon, on the other hand, never repented of his own personal sins, and even though he was credited with finally building the temple in Jerusalem (a highly appropriate metaphor for Louis given his ultimate victory over heresy), the Kingdom of Israel was nevertheless as a result split into two on his death (I Kings 11).

References to Solomon were therefore problematic, but he did share several useful features with Louis: as 2 Samuel recounts, Solomon's half brother Adonijah (born of Haggith) attempted to usurp the throne, ultimately being thwarted by the actions of Solomon's own mother.[21] And the decisive moment at which Solomon succeeded to the kingdom came when he commanded Benaiah to assassinate Shimei for his disloyalty (1 Kings 2:46). In this light, the account in *Le Salomon de la France* is unambiguous:

---

[19] *Le Salomon de la France, ou le rapport de nostre Roy à Salomon, en sa sagesse par la iustice, & la clémence* (Paris, Pierre Chevalier, 1617).

[20] Le Goff, *Saint Louis*, pp. 306–8.

[21] Chaissy's *Glaive* makes reference to this event in his broader characterization of the difficulties of Louis's early reign: "comme un enfant de David a levé la main pour se saisir du throne de son père": Gilles Chaissy, *Glaive de David et de Louis XIII roy de France et de Navarre* (Avignon, Jean Bramereau, 1623), p. 10.

guided by the Spiritus Domini, and acting against both his brother and his mother,[22]

He [Solomon/Louis] thus began his reign by justice, as the Scripture says, that the kingdom be confirmed to Solomon by the power of his hand [assassination of Concini].

When considered in the context of the complete verse from which it is taken, the text of *Egredimini* reflects this reality:

Egredimini et videte filiae Sion [regem Salomonem in diademate quo coronavit eum mater sua in die disponsionis illius et in die laetitiae cordis eius]. (Songs 3:11, complete verse)

Go forth and see, ye daughters of Sion, [King Solomon in the diadem, wherewith his mother crowned him in the day of his espousal and in the day of the joy of his heart].

Undoubtedly a verse familiar to all those present, its unspoken/unsung continuation would have been clearly understood, reminding the highly biblically literate listeners of Louis's coronation (under Marie's regency), his wedding, but most significantly his shared experience with Solomon, threatened by his own brother but ultimately securing power through violence.

The *Prière pour le Roy*: Psalm 19, *Exaudiat te Dominus*

It is in the context of these supplicatory "motets" for the *chambre* and *chapelle* that we should consider the eight settings of the psalm verse *Domine salvum fac regem* (O Lord, save the King, the final verse of Psalm 19, *Exaudiat te Dominus in die tribulationis* [May the Lord hear thee in the day of tribulation]) that appear alongside the works just discussed in the *chambre* repertoire of the Paris manuscript, and the broader genre itself. Becoming the most widely set single psalm verse through the seventeenth and eighteenth centuriues, and best known from

---

[22] *Le Salomon de la France*, p. 9: "Il vint à la couronne d'Israël presque en mesme âge que vous, & rencontra un Adonias qui pratiquant les faveurs de la mère du Roy, se vouloit préparer un chemin pour monter à la Royauté! Mais le Prince conduit de l'esprit de Dieu, arma le bras d'un valeureux Capitaine, pour se deffaire du rebelle, & des complices de sa pernicieuse ambition: il estoit le frère du Roy, toutesfois ceste proximité de sang ne le sauva pas; tant il est dangereux de tomber au crime de lèse-Majesté. Il commença ainsi son regne par la justice, que dit là dessus Escriture, que le Royaume fut confirmé à Salomon par la puissance de sa main."

the reign of Louis XIV (during which a composed version acted as a conclusion to the daily Low Mass in the *chapelle royale*), the *Domine salvum fac regem* text acquired almost mythical status as an emblem of royalty, eventually featuring prominently at the coronation of Charles X and, in other circumstances, appearing in musical settings by Berlioz, Gounod, and others.[23] As the earliest extant settings of this single psalm verse set to music, these eight examples testify to the practice of heightening the effect of a psalm (and making it more affective) by selecting from it a single verse. More than that, however, when considered in the context I have set out, they also suggest that, far from musical settings of this verse being reflections of royal strength and power, they actually form part of the sixteenth-century practice of performing the complete *Exaudiat* – now becoming known as the *Prière pour le Roy* – in moments of profound national or personal despair.[24] (See Music Example 4.2 for one of these anonymous works.)

In Chapter 3, we saw that the three sixteenth-century settings that begin *Domine salvum fac regem* were unlikely to have had any liturgical connection to the coronation (in its narrow sense), although they might have been performed at dinner after the ceremony. Instead, what is clear is that a completely separate tradition of performing the complete psalm began to emerge in royal circles during the 1580s, a moment in history with striking parallels to the religious turbulence of the 1620s, and that as a means of combating the ultramontane Catholic League (which began to threaten his reign from the mid 1570s), Henri III had begun to give the psalms prominence at court and in the liturgy more widely as part of a broader religious strategy.[25] In particular, Henri seems to have focused on those psalms that could be heard as expressions of despair at both the wretched state of the country and his own circumstances, adding such psalms to the liturgy of the wider church (not just his own chapel) and to a number of

---

[23] See Nathalie Berton, *Catalogue du motet imprimé en France, 1647–1789* (Lyon, Société française de musicologie, 2011). Berton lists some sixty-two settings of the *Domine salvum*, making it by far the most frequently set text in the whole motet repertory. See also the *avant-propos* to Pierre Perrin, *Cantica pro Capella Regis* (Paris, Robert Ballard, 1665), n.p.

[24] It is important to distinguish between settings of the complete psalm and those of the final verse only. Apart from these eight works in the Paris manuscript, and the three examples published by Nicolas Formé in 1638 (see Chapter 7), the wider tradition only began with the settings that appeared in Henri Dumont's *Cantica sacra* (Paris, Pierre Ballard, 1652).

[25] For an overview of Henri III's religious strategy, see Édouard Frémy, *Henri III pénitent: étude sur les rapports de ce prince avec diverses confrères et communautés Parisiennes* (Paris, Féchoz, 1885); and Jacqueline Boucher, *Société et mentalités autour de Henri III* (Paris, Garnier, 2007), chapters 5–6.

Music Example 4.2 Anonymous, *Domine salvum fac regem*.
Paris manuscript, f. 168r–168v.

religious orders and confraternities that he founded, to enable the people to participate in appropriate exhortations to God for the kingdom. Indeed, the dedication to the king in Renaud de Beaune's translation of the psalter, originally published in 1563 but reissued in 1587, makes the point that even in the hands of a great king such as David, the psalms are primarily cries for divine assistance:[26]

---

[26] Renaud de Beaune, *Pseaumes de David* (Paris, Gilles Beys, 1587): "Son principal discours en ces Pseaumes, est des afflictions & travaux: puis des faicts & actes des anciens Patriarches, & de tout le peuple d'Israel ... Ce livre (SIRE) fournit remèdes & médecines convenables à toutes passions, à tous maux & travaux, consolation & assurance en adversitez, ioye modeste selon

Music Example 4.2 (*cont.*)

His principal discourse in these Psalms is of afflictions and travails: then the deeds and acts of the ancient Patriarchs, and of all the people of Israel ... This book (Sir) provides remedies and medicines suited to all passions, and all evils and travails, consolation and reassurance in adversity, modest joy according to God in prosperity, the means to govern the peoples and Kingdoms well, and to conquer and reign happily.

In 1581, for example, an edict entitled *Litanies et prières pour le Roy, et nécessité du Royaume* (Litanies and Prayers for the King, and for the Needs of the Kingdom) called for the peformance of a number of psalms after

Dieu en prospérité, les moyens de bien gouverner les peuples & Royaumes, de vaincre & régner heureusement."

Music Example 4.2 (*cont.*)

Mass, including the earliest documented instance of the *Exaudiat*.[27] The prayers it prescribed were to be said across the whole of France in the hope that the collective piety of the nation would result in the birth of an heir to the still childless king and his queen, Louise de Lorraine-Vaudémont, with the litany sung at the end of the specified weekly procession concluding with the recitation of Psalm 127, *Beati omnes*, and Psalm 19, *Exaudiat te Dominus*. Psalm 127 was clearly intended to be heard as a prayer for a dauphin, the text of the psalm addressing the king directly: "Thy wife as a

---

[27] *Litanies et prières pour le Roy, et nécessité du Royaume* (Rouen, Matthais l'Allement, 1581). The word "nécessité" had connotations beyond "need": Nicot's *Thresor* equates it with the Latin *necessitas*, indicating an "urgent and compelling" requirement.

fruitful vine" (verse 3) and "Mayest thou see thy children's children, peace upon Israel" (verse 6). Psalm 19, *Exaudiat te Dominus*, on the other hand, seems to reflect wider concerns, a cry by the people of France for divine assistance (see text in Table 4.6): the first verse, in particular, in which the people entreat God to hear "thee" (Henri) in this "day of tribulation," sets the scene for the whole of the psalm as a prayer in times of adversity.

Génébrard's almost exactly contemporary translation and commentary on the psalm reports that it is[28]

a prayer that Israël made for the happy success in war which David undertook against his enemies. *May the Lord hear you*, that is to say, that he will save you *on the day of affliction* & of combat . . .

And a few decades later, this sense of both affliction and personal danger was reinforced and dramatized in paraphrases by Philippe Desportes and Jacques Davy du Perron, two of the most influential poets and clerics of the late sixteenth century.[29] Du Perron translated the opening of the psalm as "au jour que le tempeste de mille flots armez menacera ta teste" (the day in which the storm of a thousand waves threatens your head) and Desportes as "En ces jours si troublez, qu'une guerre effroyable tasche à tout reverser" (In these troubled days in which a terrible war will reverse everything).[30]

As the political and religious situation continued to decline, however, Henri intensified his religious devotion, founding several new confraternities over the following years. Just two years after the prayers for the kingdom were issued, and five years after he had founded the Congregation of the Knights of the Holy Spirit, under the influence of the Jesuit Edmond Auger he founded the Congregation of the Penitents of the Annunciation of Our Lady, a confraternity whose primary purpose,

---

[28] Originally published in 1577. Quotation taken from 1640 edition, Gilbert Génébrard, *Les Pseaumes de David traduits en François avec une explication tirée des Saints Pères, & des Auteurs Ecclésiastiques* (Paris, Guillaume Desprez, 1640), p. 178: "une prière que fait Israël pour l'heureux succès du guerre que David entreprenoit contre ses ennemies. Que le Seigneur vous exauce, c'est-à-dire, qu'il vous sauve dans le jour de l'affliction & du combat"; Génébrard was Archbishop of Aix.

[29] Philippe Desportes, *Cent pseaumes de David mis en vers françois* (Rouen, Raphaël du Petit Val, 1600), pp. 35–7; 'Recueil de toute la poésies', pp. 15–17, in Jacques Davy du Perron, *Les Diverses œuvres de l'illustrissime Cardinal du Perron* (Paris, Antoine Estiene, 1622)

[30] Jacqueline Boucher makes reference to testimony that Louise de Lorraine heard the *Exaudiat* after Henri's assassination and was upset by being reminded of better days. The original text does not imply, though, that the psalm itself had positive associations: see Hilarion de Coste, *Les Éloges et vies de reynes, princesses, dames et damoiselles illustres* (Paris, Sebastien Cramoisy, 1630) p. 373; and Boucher, *Société*, pp. 1030–1.

Table 4.5 Text and translation of Psalm 19, *Exaudiat te Dominus*

1. Exaudiat te Dominus in die tribulationis; protegat te nomen Dei Jacob.	May the Lord hear thee in the day of tribulation: may the name of the God of Jacob protect thee.
2. Mittat tibi auxilium de sancto, et de Sion tueatur te.	May he send thee help from the sanctuary: and defend thee out of Sion
3. Memor sit omnis sacrificii tui, et holocaustum tuum pingue fiat.	May he be mindful of all thy sacrifices: and may thy whole burnt offering be made fat.
4. Tribuat tibi secundum cor tuum, et omne consilium tuum confirmet.	May he give thee according to thy own heart; and confirm all thy counsels.
5. Laetabimur in salutari tuo; et in nomine Dei nostri magnificabimur.	We will rejoice in thy salvation; and in the name of our God we shall be exalted.
6. Impleat Dominus omnes petitiones tuas; nunc cognovi quoniam salvum fecit Dominus christum suum. Exaudiet illum de caelo sancto suo, in potentatibus salus dexterae ejus.	The Lord fulfill all thy petitions: now have I known that the Lord hath saved his anointed. He will hear him from his holy heaven: the salvation of his right hand is in his powers
7. Hi in curribus, et hi in equis; nos autem in nomine Domini Dei nostri invocabimus.	Some trust in chariots, and some in horses: but we will call upon the name of the Lord our God.
8. Ipsi obligati sunt, et ceciderunt; nos autem surreximus, et erecti sumus.	They are bound, and have fallen; but we are risen, and are set upright.
9. Domine, salvum fac regem, et exaudi nos in die qua invocaverimus te.	O Lord, save the king: and hear us in the day that we shall call upon thee.

while not explicitly stated in its statutes was, again, to pray for the birth of an heir (hence the Feast of the Annunciation).[31]

The congregation met for the first time on March 10, 1583. According to the preface of the *Heures de nostre-Dame*, the volume produced that same year which contained details of the complex liturgical cycle that the confraternity celebrated, the burdens that God gave to kings (described in the words of their fellow king in the psalms) were great, but Henri – through the "faveur secrette" of the Holy Spirit and the guidance of his mother – had developed a religious zeal that enabled him to act always in accordance with God's wishes. Through this zeal, and by the means of holy ceremonies, he wished to move the whole kingdom to devotion by founding a congregation that would perform good works, celebrate the liturgy like the early Christians (dressed in such a way as to avoid any

---

[31] Boucher, *Société*, pp. 1037–42; Frémy, *Henri III*, pp. 10–16. For the classic account of the Congregation's penitential processions, see Frances A. Yates, 'Dramatic religious processions in Paris in the late sixteenth century', *Annales musicologiques*, 2 (1954), 215–70. See also Kate van Orden, *Music, Discipline, and Arms in Early Modern France* (Chicago, Chicago University Press, 2005), pp. 125–31 and 170–1. The procession on March 25, 1583, is described in detail by Pierre de l'Estoile, quoted in Frémy, *Henri III*, pp. 11–12.

possibility of vanity), and whose members would lead an exemplary and virtuous life.[32]

At the first meeting, the roll call of members was essentially the same as that of the Order of the Holy Spirit: the king as its head, Cardinal de Bourbon as rector, Guillaume Du Peyrat (the king's almoner) as *sous-rector*, then Cardinal de Guise, Charles de Lorraine, Anne de Joyeuse, and many others associated with the League.[33] (There are some hundred names listed for the first meeting, with an additional twenty joining at the second meeting, the Feast of the Annunciation itself.) At that first meeting too, eight *chantres* were also listed as members, described in the statutes as singers from the *musique de la chambre*: M. de Beaulieu (the famous bass singer Girard de Beaulieu), M. de St Laurens (the famous castrato Étienne le Roy, Abbé de St Laurent), M. Mainguon, M. Salmon (creative force behind the Balet comique de la Reine of 1581), M. de Laurigni, M. de Mesme, M. Baliffre (Claude Baliffre), and M. Busserat.[34] According to the statutes, "their duties will be only to sing the *fauxbourdons* in the chapels of the Congregation, and other music if it is commanded," to which end they were joined by two "enfants de la musicque de ladicte chambre."[35] In addition to these singers, the statutes also specified that there were to be four *choristes* to lead and intone the psalm singing, two of whom were "perpetuelz," and two of whom were "annuelz." In the early years of the Congregation, the king himself occupied the position of *choriste*, presumably therefore singing and leading the musicians of his *chambre* in the same way that Louis XIII would some forty-five years later.[36]

The liturgy to be followed, led by the clergy of the Church of the Augustines when the penitents themselves were not present, and sung only in chant, was spelled out in great detail in the *Heures de nostre-Dame*.[37] Each day four low masses were to be sung, at 7.00, 8.00, 9.00, and 11.00 a.m.

---

[32] *Heures de nostre-Dame, à l'usage de Rome ... pour la Congrégation Roiale des Pénitens de l'Annonciation de nostre Dame* (Paris, Jamet Mettayer, 1583), n.p. The preface refers the reader to Psalm 2, 'Why do the nations rage'.

[33] The lists of membership are preserved in F-Pn MS nouv. acq. fr. 7549. The king's address to the penitents, together with a much more extensive justification for the congregation, is recorded in Edmond Auger, *Métanoeolegioe sur le suget de l'Archicongrégation des Pénitens de l'Annonciation de nostre Dame, & de toutes tells autres dévotieuses assemblées, en l'Église sainte* (Paris, Jamet Mettayer, 1584), n.p.

[34] F-Pn MS nouv. acq. fr. 7549, f. 2r.

[35] *Les Statuts de la congrégation des Pénitens de l'Annonciation de Nostre Dame* (Paris, Jamet Mettayer, 1583), p. 59. The process of alternatim psalm singing with the *chambre* is described in *Les Statuts*, pp. 69–70.

[36] F-Pn MS nouv. acq. fr. 7549, f. 16v.

[37] *Heures de nostre-Dame*, pp. 366–9.

In addition, on Mondays the clergy were to celebrate Matins and Lauds of Our Lady, followed by the recitation of the *Miserere*, then a Low Mass followed by the *Exaudiat*, and in the afternoon Vespers and Compline, again followed by the *Miserere*. Wednesdays, the most important day of the week, on which the Penitents themselves were expected to attend, followed a similar pattern, although the singers were required to be in attendance too, and Matins – the *Ave Maria*, the *Venite*, the hymns, the antiphons, psalms, the Te Deum, and the Benedictus – was "sung," presumably much of it in *fauxbourdon*.[38] Friday was similar to Monday, and Saturday was again a more "musical" day, repeating the practices of Wednesday. No services were held on Sundays because the members were to attend church in their own parishes. Beyond the weekly cycle there was also a monthly cycle and an annual cycle in which the six Marian feasts of the year were to be celebrated with a full round of offices (still followed by the *Exaudiat*) and a procession, with the Feast of the Annunciation itself requiring the members to take communion before holding their annual meeting at 1.00 p.m.

In recording that the *Exaudiat* was performed after the daily Mass (the position in the liturgy that it would retain), the *Heures de nostre-Dame* confirms that the psalm was still heard as a response to current religious, political, and dynastic turmoil. The *Exaudiat*, described as a "prayer for the king, which is said every morning, after Mass, kneeling," was sung by the *choristes* taking the first verse, and the *chœur* (i.e., the rest of the Congregation) continuing with the remainder.[39] After the Doxology, two Penitents were to come forward to the altar, and on their knees sing "That you, in your piety, will deign to give a son and heir to the king of France, your servant, our most Christian king Henri." Two choirboys then sang the verset, "Your wife as it were abundant with life," the Penitents replying, "In the bricks of your house." Finally, the three collects that completed this prayer again made specific reference to the need for an heir.

After the death of Henri's younger brother, François, Duc d'Alençon, in 1584, Henri, the Huguenot king of Navarre, now stood next in line to the throne. Without an heir, the Valois dynasty would come to an end and France would have to endure the ignominy of a Huguenot monarch, and so Henri's penitential behavior was redoubled. The statutes of the Oratoire et

---

[38] *Les Statuts*, p. 59: "Et leur charge sera seulement de chanter les fauxbourdons és chapelles de la Congrégation, & autre musique s'il est arresté" (And their duties will be only to sing the *fauxbourdons* in the chapels of the Congregation, and other music if it is commanded).

[39] *Heures de nostre-Dame*, 351–3: "Prière pour le Roy, qui se dit tous les matins, apres la Messe commune, à genoux."

Compagnie du benoist Sainct François (founded by the king in 1586) also specified the singing of the *Exaudiat* as a "prayer for the king" after Mass by two *choristes* on their knees in front of the altar,[40] while the statutes of the Oratoire nostre-Dame de Vie-Saine (founded by the king in 1585) also required the performance of the *Exaudiat* and a prayer after Mass "for the king, who instituted them, to pray to God for him": in this case, the *Exaudiat* was to be followed by the Penitential Psalm *De profundis* (Psalm 129) and the *Inclina Domine*, a prayer from the Office of the Dead.[41] The psalm also made its first documented appearance as a regular feature in the *chapelle royale* around this time, statutes from 1585 calling for it to be performed after the daily Mass together with unspecified prayers.[42] Shortly afterward, in 1587, Henri III reorganized the *chapelle royale* and reformed the liturgy, the final significant act that he was able to accomplish before his assassination in 1589; the new regulations again specified the singing of the complete *Exaudiat* or the *De profundis* after Mass every day, and included the same collects praying for an heir as the 1581 *Litanies et prières pour le Roy* and the statutes of the Congregation of the Penitents.[43] They also introduced the singing of Psalm 78, *Deus venerunt gentes*, every Wednesday "during these wars in the kingdom,"[44] another psalm that reflected the anguish of the people at this time: "O God, the heathens have come into they inheritance: they have defiled they holy temple." By contrast – and most significantly – the statutes also specify that the *Exaudiat* was *not* to be recited on the four annual feasts of Christmas, Easter, Pentecost, and All Saints. Clearly, for these occasions of liturgical solemnity a prayer with such negative associations, focusing only on the king's well-being, was not considered appropriate.[45]

The wider context in which the *Exaudiat* became part of the official liturgy of Henri III's confraternities and *chapelle royale*, together with

---

[40] *Les Statuts de la reigle de l'oratoire et compagnie de benoist Sainct François* (Paris, Jamet Mettayer, 1586), p. 48.

[41] *Les Statuts de l'oratoire Nostre-Dame de Vie-Saine* (Paris, Jamet Mettayer, 1585), p. 27: "pour le Roy, qui les a instituez pour prier Dieu pour luy."

[42] *Règlement pour la Chambre*, F-Pn MS nouv. acq. fr. 32, f. 124v.

[43] See Chapter 3 and and *L'Ordre que la Roy veut estre suivy et observé desormais pour le service Divin*, F-Pn MS fonds fr. 7008. The new statutes specified a range of additional services and refinements to the liturgy, calling for the *Exaudiat* to be sung at the end of each daily Mass, although it was also listed as to be performed on Wednesdays (when Mass was to be said "Pro Peccatis") and Fridays ("de la Croix," followed by the reading of the Passion according to St. John): ibid., f. 5r–5v.

[44] Ibid., f. 7v.   [45] Ibid., f. 7r–7v.

contemporary interpretations from psalm commentaries and paraphrases, all point to the psalm itself being heard as a desperate plea for God's assistance.[46] But after Henri's assassination in 1589, France saw a period of relative stability under Henri IV, a strong and politically astute monarch who succeeded in uniting the country and introducing a measure of religious tolerance, although until his abjuration in 1593 and coronation in 1594, civil war still reigned in France. While Henri was not particulary known for his adoption of the psalter, it was during his reign that the earliest known musical setting of the *Exaudiat* was published, in the second edition of Pierre Ballard's *Octo cantica divae Mariae Virginis* of 1599. While the first, 1584, edition contained eight Magnificats and a selection of other useful liturgical items (including the psalms *In exitu Israel* and *De Profundis*) the 1599 revised edition added in settings of the *Laudate Dominum* and the complete *Exaudiat*, both in very simple *fauxbourdon* settings, and both described on the colophon as "quod communiter gratias Regis vocant" (which are commonly called prayers for the king), presumably reflecting the fact that the *Exaudiat* had only become a common liturgical item between the publication of the two editions (which were otherwise identical).[47] Nevertheless, the *Exaudiat* does not seem to have been generally more widely performed outside the *chapelle royale* at that time: Nicolas de Thou's *Bref receuil et explication de la Messe* of 1598, a detailed study of the liturgy of the Mass, features prayers and collects for the king but no mention of the *Exaudiat*.[48] By 1602 the Paris edition of the *Missale Romanum* did now include the *Exaudiat* as part of a short set of verses and responses, but it took its place in a separate section of prayers

---

[46] See Chapter 5 for more liturgical evidence.

[47] *Octo cantica divae Mariae virgins* (Paris, Robert and Pierre Ballard, 1599). No settings survive by Eustache Du Caurroy, who served in the *chapelle royale* from the mid 1670s until 1609 (although he did provide four versions of the Te Deum), nor do any settings by other *sous-maîtres*. A *fauxbourdon* setting of verses from the *Exaudiat* appeared in the non-liturgical *Airs sur les hymnes sacrez* (1623), although the collection on which the *Airs* was based, Michel Coyssard's *Paraphrase des hymnes et cantiques spirituelz* (1592), did not contain this particular psalm; see Launay, *La Musique religieuse*, pp. 119–36, and van Orden, *Music, Discipline, and Arms*, p. 165, for a discussion of the significance of Coyssard. Settings of the complete *Exaudiat* appear elsewhere in the Deslauriers collection (i.e. were not intended for the Chambre), as do other, "transitional" versions probably representing an earlier stage in the development of the genre: a version on ff. 67v–69r, for example, sets the psalm complete, but with a refrain of the final *Domine salvum* verse between each of the other verses; see Bennett, *Sacred Repertories*, p. 98 and Appendix 2.

[48] Nicolas de Thou, *Bref recueil et explication de la messe et du divin service y faict* (Paris, Jacobum Kerver, 1598).

for various purposes rather than at the end of Mass, and there was no indication that it was to be sung.[49]

In 1610 the eight-year-old Louis XIII became king, his two predecessors – his father Henri IV and his distant relative Henri III – having both been assassinated. The tensions that had lain dormant for twenty years again rose to the surface, and Louis (as we have seen) became the object of religious and political attacks from all sides. In the first decade or so of his reign, then, the *Exaudiat* would have taken on renewed significance: while Louis was too young for concerns about his succession to have yet emerged, the stability of the country was nonetheless under threat from Huguenot and other rebels. Thus, the author of the 1622 *Prière et oraisons très-dévotes aux Catholiques françois, pour la conservation & prosperite du Roy, avec un paraphrase & brève explication du psalme Exaudiat, &c.* (Very Devout Prayer and Intercession to the French Catholics, for the Conservation and Prosperity of the King, with a Paraphrase and Brief Explanation of the Psalm *Exaudiat*) announced that he had produced a "Paraphrase and brief explanation of the psalm *Exaudiat*, with an exhortation to pray to God for the king." According to an "Exposition morale" addressed to the king that prefaces the short volume:[50]

When this psalm is recited, in either high or low voice, it is a prayer mixed with many types of prayer, which the Holy Spirit through his organ the king and prophet David has revealed to his church, to be said sacredly and devotedly for the protection and prosperity of the king, *principally when he goes to war, and is in danger for his person, as you are often and too often*. It is for this reason that your faithful subjects and servants say it for you gladly, *that which was said in his time by the nobility of Israel to their well-loved king David* [my emphasis].

But a paraphrase from 1621 makes clear the growing interest in the final verse for expressing the sentiment of the whole psalm, just as the courtiers in the *Psaumes de Courtisans* highlighted only the particular verse they wanted to use. *Les Vœus des bons Français sur les victoires de nostre Roy,*

---

[49] *Missale insignis ecclesiae Parisiensis restitutum et emendatum* (Paris, Stephanum Valletum, 1602), p. 138.

[50] *Prière et oraisons très-dévotes aux Catholiques françois, pour la conservation & prosperité du Roy, avec un paraphrase & brève explication du psalme Exaudiat* (Paris, Houdenc, 1622), p. 10: "Quand ce Psalme est recité, soit à haute ou à basse voix, cest une prière meslangée de plusieurs sortes de prières, laquelle le S. Esprit par son organe le Roy & Prophète David à revelée à son Église, pour le dire sainctement & devotement pour la protection & pour la prosperité du Roy, lors principalement qu'il va à la guerre, & est en danger de sa personne, comme vous este souvent & trop souvent. C'est pourquoy vos plus fidèles subjets & serviteurs vous diroient volontiers, ce que dist en son temps la noblesse d'Israel à leur Roy bien aymé David."

très-chrestien & très-auguste Louys XIII, ou paraphrase sur l'Exaudiat au subiect des guerres de la presente année 1621 (The Vows of the Good French People on the Victories of Our King, the Very Christian and Very August Louis XIII, or Paraphrase on the *Exaudiat* on the Subject of the Wars of the Present Year 1621) paraphrases the whole psalm in *sizains*, with verse 1 rendered as "Le Grand Dieu te protège au milieu des batailles" (The great God protect you in the midst of battles), a clear reference to personal danger and a formulation that also references the final verse, "O Lord, save the king."[51] But the paraphrase includes three alternative versions of the final verse, "Domine salvum fac regem," each of which begins "Seigneur, sauve le Roy!" (Lord, save the king!) and each of which goes on to lament the current circumstances – "ce siècle malheureux" (this unfortunate century), "tout funeste danger" (all disastrous danger), and "ton courroux" (your wrath).[52]

If the technique of highlighting a single verse of a psalm reached its musical conclusion in the *Domine salvum fac regem* settings of the *musique de la chambre* with which this discussion began, the same practice soon spread outward across the wider church, the final verse gradually supplanting the complete psalm in liturgical contexts, effectively creating a new liturgical phenomenon. Already in 1610, the single verse *Domine salvum fac regem* was being performed in chant, without music, at Angers Cathedral, a practice that had been instituted on October 13 of that year, presumably as a response to the recent assassination of Henri IV and the iminent accession of Louis XIII (later that week).[53] And at almost the same time a *fauxbourdon* setting appeared in Abraham Blondet's *Officii Divae Ceciliae* of 1611, undoubtedly for the same reasons.[54] Evidence for more "musical" settings does not appear until later, however. Both the 1612 and 1625 editions of Jean de Bournonville's *Octo cantica divae Mariae* (which includes liturgical items such as vespers psalms, a simple Mass, elevation motets, almost all in syllabic, *fauxbourdon*-like settings) feature the *Exaudiat*, complete, and provided with a doxology. But Charles d'Ambleville's later volumes of *Harmonia sacra* in four and six voices

---

[51] Pierre Le Comte, *Les Vœus des bons François sur les victoires de nostre Roy Très-Chrestien & Très-Auguste Louis XIII* (Paris, Pierre Ramier, 1621), n.p.

[52] Génébrard's commentary also explains how in this verse the mouths of the faithful pray for King David as he is about to do battle with the enemies of Israel; see Génébrard, *Les Pseaumes*, p. 182.

[53] See the manuscript notes of René Lehoreau, a canon at Angers cathedral, from c. 1680–1700 in Archives départementales de Maine-et-Loire, 5 G 1-3. This taken from Vol. 1, p. 173.

[54] See Chapter 5.

(1636, similar in function and scope to the Bournonville volumes) show the increasing interest in the final verse. The four-voice setting begins with the *Domine salvum* verse, returns to verse 1, *Exaudiat* ... 4., *Tribuat* ..., 8. *Ipsi obligati* ..., before indicating a reprise of the *Domine salvum* verse and omitting the Doxology. (See Figure 4.1.) In this case, the musical interest is also clearly concentrated in the *Domine salvum* verse (with its dramatic pause and active voice part), the others being much more simply recited.

By contrast the six-voice version is even more curtailed, beginning with *Domine salvum* ..., and now featuring only verse 4 *Tribuat* ... before returning to the *Domine salvum* (again without a Doxology.) We hear of the final verse alone being performed in music in an account of Mass at le Mans in 1633 during the famous Puy du Mans in which the *Domine salvum* was sung straight after the *O salutaris* at the elevation (with instruments, then voices, then with organ), but it is only in Nicolas Formé's publications of 1638 (the subject of Chapter 7) that we find the first surviving published setting that adopts the format that would subsequently become standard.[55]

By 1633 François Véron records that the *Domine salvum* was "sounded daily in all our churches, and sung each day in the presence of his Majesty" and confirms that the *Domine salvum* still retained its original associations, for "la conservation de cette personne Royale."[56] And by the middle of the century a musical setting seems to have been norm, if Martin Sonnet's later *Directorium chori* (1656), a set of liturgical and musical instructions compiled for the clergy of the Cathedral of Notre-Dame, is anything to go by. According to Sonnet,

In the cathedral on duplex feasts, Postcommunion having been sung, *Domine salvum fac regem* is sung in composed music, for the most Christian king, which practice was begun around the year 1614, in the time of the minority of Louis XIII, on account of the civil war following the death of Henri IV, who had reigned before him and who had had the psalm *Exaudiat* with its verse *Quaesumus* sung every day after High Mass by the clergy *on their knees*.[57]

---

[55] See Prosper-Auguste Anjubault, *La Sainte-Cécile au Mans depuis 1633* (Le Mans, Monnoyer frères, 1862).

[56] François Véron, *Plainte et accusation troisiesme contre tous les ministres* (Paris, Claude Morlot, 1633), pp. 50–1: "retentit iournellement en toutes nos Églises, & qui se chanté chacque iour en la presence de sa Majesté."

[57] Martin Sonnet, *Directorium chori* (Paris, Sebastien Cramoisy, 1656), pp. 220–1: "In Ecclesia Metropolitana in duplicibus, cantata Postcommunione, Musicè cantatur Domine salvum fac Regem, pro Rege Christianissimo, quod institutum fuit circa annum 1614. tempore minoritatis Ludovici XIII. propter bellum civile, post obitum Henrici IV. paulò ante enim regnante eodem

148 The Penitent King

Figure 4.1 *Dessus* part of *Domine salvum fac regem*.
Charles d'Ambleville, *Harmonia sacra . . . cum quatuor vocum* (Paris, Pierre Ballard, 1636).

As late as the 1650s, then, the *Exaudiat* and its later derivation the *Domine salvum fac regem*, gave voice to the people of France as they prayed

Henrico IV. quotidie post maiorem Missam cantabatur a Clero flexis genibus, Psal. Exaudiat, cum Versu & Oratione Quaesumus."

for the King's deliverance in the face of overwhelming personal danger. Far from being an evocation of the splendor of the coronation, the *Domine salvum* thus continued to recall the febrile religious atmosphere of the late sixteenth and early seventeenth century and the vulnerability of not just the king, but the Temporal monarchy itself. Of course, musical performances of the *Exaudiat* and *Domine salvum fac regem* appeared in other circumstances – most notably as part of Te Deum and *entrée* ceremonies – throughout this period. But as the next chapter shows, even in such public displays, accompanied by the Te Deum and all the civic pomp that Paris or any other city could muster, the psalm seems to have retained the same meaning.[58] While eventually it is possible that the psalm may have been heard as an expression of strength (perhaps in the eighteenth century?) we should be prepared to understand such ceremonies, as much as the daily recitation after Mass, as being rooted in the dangers and dilemmas of France's bitter religious wars.

---

[58] The works using the text of Psalm 19 found elsewhere in the Paris manuscript will be considered in the next chapter.

5 | Pillars of Justice and Piety

The Entrée, the Te Deum, and the Exaudiat te Dominus

The previous chapters explored the various ways in which biblical imagery identified Louis XIII as a successor to King David. At his confirmation, coronation and induction into the Knights of the Order of the Holy Spirit, the multitudes present would be reminded that both David and Louis were anointed through the Holy Spirit and acted as God's agent on earth; on the streets of Paris, those who purchased psalm paraphrases and pamphlets, and who possibly sang them to popular tunes at home, would be reminded of David's military prowess, the power of his sword, and his victory over Goliath. At the same time, a more select few, those present at the king's lunch or dinner, might hear straightforward psalm motets in which David's exploits were recounted; while in even more intimate circumstances, in the king's chamber, a very few people – close courtiers, clerics, confessors, and the king himself – would have heard the devotional and supplicatory works in the voice of David the penitent and David the defeated warrior, asking for God's forgiveness and protection. Since the regular *chapelle royale* liturgy was only modified to the extent that individual days of the week were designated for particular celebrations (see Chapter 3), there are relatively few other types of situations in which the liturgy and music played a central role in an "official" court ceremony. One remaining case, though, is one of the most important – the *entrée royale* and its corollary ceremony, the "Te Deum."

A tradition and practice dating back centuries by which a monarch was welcomed into a loyal city by its dignitaries, clerics, and citizenry, the typical *entrée* in the hands of the last Valois kings was a spectacular festival, calling on all the creative resources of a city – artists, poets, architects, set designers, composers, and musicians – to produce a visual and aural feast that is generally considered to have given expression to the king's power.[1]

---

[1] To the extent that the literature on the *entrée* and other court festival engages with the creative/artistic dimension of these events, the focus is almost exclusively on the visual, architectural, and literary rather than the musical. For McGowan, for example, the intention of Catherine de Médicis's *entrées* was to create a triumphal form that could "give visual expression to her conceptions of power and accomplishments"; see Margaret McGowan, *Ideal Forms in the Age of Ronsard* (Berkeley, University of California Press, 1985), p. 126. See also many of the essays in

Yet these events – archetypally "Renaissance" in conception – also survived into the seventeenth century, and while they were later celebrated with less pomp and extravagance (although several were entirely comparable to their sixteenth-century models), they were nonetheless mounted throughout Louis XIII's reign.[2] In particular, the years 1617–1623 were especially rich in *entrées* as, in an attempt to assert his authority after the assassination of Concini, Louis embarked on a decade-long quest to subjugate the Huguenots, marching throughout the west, southwest, and south of France, and making his *entrée* into both long-loyal cities and recently conquered rebel strongholds.[3] These *entrées*, like their sixteenth-century forebears, were usually documented in some kind of printed pamphlet or book (sometimes running to several hundred pages) in which the details of the procession into the city were typically described in great detail. But the accounts are almost invariably silent on the conclusion and culmination of the ceremony, the king's entry into the city cathedral where a liturgy of some kind, including the performance of the Te Deum, was celebrated. Over the same period another ceremony was also developed – the "Te Deum" (I will used inverted commas to denote the ceremony as opposed to the hymn) – the most important and well-documented manifestations of

---

Jean Jacquot et al. (eds.), *Les Fêtes de la Renaissance*, 3 vols. (Paris, CNRS, 1956–75); Frances A. Yates, *The Valois Tapestries*, Studies of the Warburg Institute, 23 (London, Warburg Institute, 1959); Roy Strong, *Art and Power: Renaissance Festivals, 1450–1650* (Berkeley, University of California Press, 1984); J. R. Mulryne, Helen Watanabe-O'Kelly, and Margaret Shewring (eds.), *Europa Triumphans: Court and Civic Festivals in Early Modern Europe* (Aldershot, Ashgate, 2004); and Yves Pauwels, 'La Thème de l'arc de triomphe dans l'architecture urbaine à la Renaissance: entre pouvoir politique et pouvoir religieux', in Patrick Boucheron and Jean-Philippe Genet (eds.), *Marquer la ville, Signes, traces, empreintes du pouvoir (xiiie–xvie siecle)* (Paris and Rome, Publications de la Sorbonne, École française de Rome, 2013), pp. 181–91. For case studies on the musical dimension to the *entrée* in the seventeenth century, see Alexander Robinson, 'Music and politics in the entry of Maria de' Médicis into Avignon (19 November, 1600)', in Rudolf Rasch (ed.), *Music and Power in the Baroque Era* (Turnhout, Brepols, 2018), pp. 179–202; Iain Fenlon, 'Competition and emulation: Music and dance for the celebrations in Paris, 1612–1615', in Margaret McGowan (ed.), *Dynastic Marriages 1612/1615: A Celebration of Habsburg and Bourbon Unions* (Farnham, Ashgate, 2013); Kate van Orden, *Music, Discipline, and Arms in Early Modern France* (Chicago, Chicago University Press, 2005); and Stephen Bonime, 'Music for the royal entrée into Paris, 1483–1517', in Mary-Beth Winn (ed.), *Le Moyen français V. Musique naturelle et musique artificielle: In memoriam Gustave Reese* (Montreal, Gros, 1980), pp. 115–29.

[2] For the *entrée* in seventeenth century, see the important dissertation by Fiona Czerniawska, *A Study of the Printed Accounts of French Entrées, 1610–60* (PhD dissertation, London University, 1993), and the articles by Marie-Claude Canova-Green, Daniel Vaillancourt, Marie-France Wagner, Hélène Visentin, Dominique Moncond'huy, and Jean-Marie Apostolides in *Dix-septième siècle*, 212 (2001/3).

[3] See A. Lloyd Moote, *Louis XIII, the Just* (Berkeley, Los Angeles, and London, University of California Press, 1989), pp. 116–36.

which took place at the cathedral of Notre-Dame, Paris.[4] Each celebration instigated by the king himself in a letter from the campaign trail, the "Te Deum" ceremony, as we understand it, was called to allow the people of Paris the same opportunity to give thanks for the military or other successes that the king celebrated in the *entrée*. Although we do not know the details of the liturgy, the ceremony mirrored the *entrée* in that the Te Deum was also performed, though without the king present.

Seen from the perspective of the so-called American "ceremonialists," or through the studies of subsequent generations of francophone scholars, the *entrée* occupies a central position as one of the key juridico-political rites of Western kingship itself.[5] Yet despite its significance, and the fact that both it and the "Te Deum" culminate in the celebration of some kind of liturgy,

---

[4] The standard work on the Te Deum ceremony remains Michèle Fogel, *Les Cérémonies de l'information dans la France du XVIe au XVIIIe siècle* (Paris, Fayard, 1989).

[5] For the work of the "ceremonialists" (a term coined by Alain Boureau, see below), see, for example, Ralph Giesey, 'The King imagined', in Keith Michael Baker (ed.), *The French Revolution and the Creation of Modern Political Culture, Vol. 1: The Political Culture of the Old Regime* (Oxford, Pergamon Press, 1987), pp. 41–59; Ralph Giesey, 'Models of rulership in French royal ceremonial', in Sean Willentz (ed.), *Rites of Power: Symbolism, Ritual, and Politics since the Middle Ages* (Philadelphia, University of Pennsylvania Press, 1985), pp. 41–64; Ralph Giesey, *Cérémonial et puissance souveraine: France, xve–xviie siècle* (Paris, Colin, 1987); Lawrence Bryant, *The King and the City in the Parisian Royal Entry Ceremony: Politics, Ritual and Art in the Renaissance* (Geneva, Droz, 1986); Sarah Hanley, *The Lit de Justice of the Kings of France: Constitutional Ideology in Legend, Ritual, and Discourse* (Princeton, Princeton University Press, 1983). For the early Francophone scholarship, see Bernard Guenée and Françoise Lehoux, *Les Entrées royales françaises de 1328 à 1515* (Paris, CNRS, 1968); Pierre Bourdieu, 'Les Rites comme actes d'institution', *Actes de la recherche en sciences sociales*, 43 (1982), 58–63; Michèle Fogel, *Les Cérémonies de l'information*; Roger Chartier, 'A desacralized King', in *The Cultural Origins of the French Revolution*, tr. Lydia Cochrane (Durham, Duke University Press, 1991), pp. 111–35; Alain Boureau, 'Ritualité politique et modernité monarchique', in Neithard Bulst, Robert Descimon, and Alain Guerreau (eds.) *L'Etat ou le Roi. Les Fondations de la modernité monarchique en France (XlV–XVIe siecles)* (Paris, Éditions de la Maison des sciences de l'homme, 1996); Alain Boureau, 'Les Cérémonies royales françaises entre performance juridique et compétence liturgique', *Annales. Économies, Sociétés, Civilisations*, 46/6 (1991), 1253–64; and the many important contributions in Alain Boureau and Claudio-Sergio Ingerflom (eds.), *La Royauté sacrée dans le monde chrétien* (Paris, EHESS, 1992). More recent scholarship has moved beyond this simple US/European divide; see, for example, Christian Desplat and Paul Mironneau (eds.), *Les Entrées. Gloire et déclin d'un cérémonial* (Biarritz, Société Henri IV, 1997); Robert Descimon, 'Le Corps de ville et le système cérémonial parisien au début de l'âge modern', in Marc Boone and Maarten Prak (eds.), *Individual, Corporate and Judicial Status in European Cities (Late Middle Ages and Early Modern Period)* (Leuven, Apeldorn, Garant, 1996), pp. 73–128; Joël Blanchard, 'Le Spectacle du rite: les entrées royales', *Revue historique*, 305/3 (2003), 475–519; Fanny Cosandey, 'Entrer dans le rang', in Marie-France Wagner, L. Frappier, and C. Latraverse (eds.), *Les Jeux de l'échange: entrées solennelles et divertissements du xve au xviie siècle* (Paris, Honoré Champion, 2007), pp. 17–46; and the essays in Marie-Claude Canova-Green, Jean Andrews, and Marie-France Wagner (eds.), *Writing Royal Entries in Early Modern Europe* (Turnhout, Brepols, 2013).

details of this liturgy and what it might mean (from either a music-historical or a more broadly political perspective) have remained either obscure or of little interest to scholars, with the event's significance and role in defining power structures thus seen as belonging exclusively to the procession. Giesey, for example, overlooked the ceremony in the cathedral entirely, seeing the event as essentially a theatrical performance in which the king was displayed in the procession as a successor to the kings of antiquity.[6] Bryant's study from around the same time also saw the *entrée* (i.e. the procession) as "one of the principal ceremonial ways to dramatize political concepts," a "dramatic and symbolic mediation of social, legal, and power relations." While acknowledging the existence of final liturgy, Bryant nonetheless argued that the culminating event in the cathedral had lost all significance by the time of Henri IV and Louis XIII, and was ignored in the printed accounts of the events because it existed merely to "demonstrate the king's piety."[7] Guenée and Lehoux's foundational study, by contrast, certainly acknowledged a religious undercurrent to the whole event, seeing in it a recreation of a Corpus Christi procession, with the king, venerated under a *baldachino* from the end of the fourteenth century, standing in for the body of Christ itself; but although some of the *entrées* they considered featured religious dramas at stations along the procession, they did not explore the concluding events in the cathedral.[8] For the "Te Deum," too, scholars have seen the public display (rather than the liturgy itself) as the essential component, with Fogel and, following her, Chartier characterizing the "Te Deum" as a "ceremony of thanksgiving – ordained by royal letter and celebrating the triumphs of the monarch, who bent religious ritual to

---

[6] Giesey, 'Models of rulership', pp. 51–3; Giesey, 'The King imagined', p. 44. Giesey saw the public law dimension to the *entrée* as being frequently overshadowed by the artistic production that accompanied the procession, but did not acknowledge any role for the concluding church ceremony.

[7] Bryant does fleetingly acknowledge the debt owed to the Corpus Christi procession identified by Guenée and Lehoux; see Bryant, *King and the City*, pp. 17–18, 60, 69–73, 102. Jean Jacquot, in his contribution to *Les Fêtes de la Renaissance*, one of the seminal articles of the field, saw the key to the *entrée* as essentially a meeting of two processions at the city gates – one royal (as the king approached the city) and one civic (the local dignitaries who had come out to meet him.) In his construction, the joint processions back through the city then displayed the royal power; see Jean Jacquot, 'Joyeuse et triomphante entrée', in Jacquot, *Les Fêtes de la Renaissance I*, p. 11.

[8] For Guenée and Lehoux, the event was a transformation of the *Fête-Dieu* ceremony to a *Fête-Roi*; see Guenée and Lehoux, *Les Entrées royales*, p. 18. For another discussion of the religious perspective during the reign of Louis XIII, see Marie-Claude Canova Green, 'De Dieu et du roi dans l'entrée solennelle de Louis XIII', in Peter Bennett and Bernard Dompnier (eds.), *Cérémonial politique et cérémonial religieux dans l'Europe modern: échanges et métissages* (Paris, Garnier, 2020), pp. 87–104.

his glory."[9] Kate van Orden's recent reexamination of the "Te Deum" ceremony (an important study I will consider later in this chapter) comes the closest to engaging directly with liturgy (in her case also through the means of music), but for an age in which all scholars agree that royal ceremonial played a vital role in the functioning of the polity, it is striking how little is known about the ceremony in the church and the role it played in the wider significance of both the *entrée* and the "Te Deum."[10]

Based on a study of liturgical sources and printed and manuscript accounts of *entrées* and "Te Deums," and previously overlooked musical fragments, this chapter reevaluates our understanding of these ceremonies and explores how the liturgy and music performed might have participated in the legitimizing framework of monarchical power. Although we might assume, for example, that both the liturgy and its musical manifestations would prioritize the king's strength and military success, "representing" the king as a successful warrior in the mold of King David, both the *entrée* and the "Te Deum" were in fact much more ambiguous in tone than is generally recognized – not just celebrations of victory or kingship itself (which to a limited extent they were), but acts of supplication, prayer, and genuinely humble thanksgiving. As the king approached the cathedral, then, the tone of the procession changed, and by the time he knelt in front of the bishop at the cathedral door, his transformation into a humble pilgrim or a member of the chapter itself was complete. Inside the cathedral, too, in what contemporaries actually considered the climax of the event, the liturgy reinforced this theme of supplication, and the final musical item – typically the performance of Psalm 19, *Exaudiat te Dominus* – asked for God, just as it did in the relative privacy of the *chapelle* and the *chambre*, to save and safeguard the vulnerable king himself, reaffirming his reliance on God and his descent from the model of all kings.

The *Entrée* as Procession

Most *entrées* followed a standard pattern, consisting of what I call a "processional phase" (the arrival of the king at the city walls, the greeting

---

[9] Chartier, 'Desacralized King', p. 127, quoting Fogel. Fogel does briefly consider the psalm performed during the ceremony; see Fogel, *Cérémonies de l'information*, p. 167.

[10] Van Orden, *Music, Discipline, and Arms*, pp. 136–73; for another music-centered approach covering this period, see Robinson, 'Music and politics'.

Figure 5.1 The *entrée* of Louis XIII into Paris in 1614 (Paris?, 1614?).
Bibliothèque nationale de France

by the city dignitaries, and the procession through the city through a number of triumphal arches or past other significant sites) and a "liturgical phase" (the culminating ceremony in the city cathedral at which the accounts describe a Te Deum being sung). The processional phase, a sumptuous display of classical architecture, symbols, emblems, and texts (inscriptions of Latin sonnets and odes) certainly reflected the humanistic model of kingship that Francis I, Henri II, Henri IV, and, to a lesser extent, Henri III embraced (discussed in Chapter 1). For Louis XIII, too, the processional phase was typically modeled on the Roman triumph (especially those of Numa Pompilius and Alexander Severus), the implication being that the king and all his forebears followed in the lines of the great military leaders of antiquity (see Figure 5.1).[11] More generally, though, the *entrée* would often have an overarching allegorical basis taken from, for example, the Trojan Wars (Paris, 1614), or feature characters from myth and legend such as Perseus (Arles, 1622) or Glaucus and Scilla (Dijon, 1629).[12] On the other hand, increasingly popular from around 1610, the theme might reflect not the kings of Rome or the myths of antiquity, but the ancient kings of France. So, among many other examples, in Montélimar in 1622 the king is described as surpassing the excellence of

---

[11] See Czerniawska, *Printed Accounts*, pp. 96–8.
[12] C. Jourdan, *L'Ordre, entrée, et cérémonies observées par les habitans de Paris à l'heureux retour de Louys XIII* (Lyon, Claude Cayne, 1614); Pierre Saxi, *Entrée de Loys XIII Roy de France et de Navarre dans sa ville d'Arles, le XXIX Octobre MDCXXII* (Avignon, Jean Bramereau, 1623); *Les Arcs triomphaux érigez à l'honneur du Roy dans sa ville de Dijon* (Paris, Jacques Dugast, 1629 [Dijon, 1629]).

Clovis, the grandeur of Clotaire, the justice of Childebert, and the holiness of Saint Louis, while in Dijon in 1629, Louis was "Sainct, à l'exemple des Clovis et Charlemagne."[13]

Whatever the overall conception, the *entrée* would begin at or near the city walls, where typically a procession of dignitaries (and sometimes clergy) from the city would meet the king (who might be seated in some kind of elaborate temporary structure), would present him with the keys of the city, and make a number of speeches or *harangues* expressing both the city's devotion and admiration, and its acknowledgment (in the same kind of terms that we saw in previous chapters) of the king as divinely ordained. At the *entrée* to Dijon in 1629, for example, the Premier Président de Parlement addressed the king on behalf of the people, who were there to[14]

prostrate themselves at the feet of your Royal Majesty, and there, to rise from him as the only power that they recognize on earth, and the first after that of God.

In Lyon, the *Prévost des Marchands* came forward "in order to express most energetically the entire submission and devotion of their hearts," took up six gilded keys (one for each of the gates of the city), kissed them, and presented them to the king as a sign of their vows of "obeisance and fidelity."[15]

After this initial greeting, which might also be framed within a network of allegorical or mythical allusions, the king's and the civic processions would begin their progress into the city, the king either on horseback (sometimes in armor) or in a chariot, as in the *entrée* to Paris in 1628 when, following the model of Emperor Camillus, the chariot was drawn by four white horses.[16] Music often featured in the processional phase,

---

[13] *Le Mercure françois*, 1622, p. 883; *Dijon, 1629*. See also Czerniawska, *Printed Accounts*, pp. 93–132 for this change of emphasis.

[14] *Dijon, 1629*: "se prosterner aux pieds de vostre Royale Majesté, & là, relever d'elle comme de la seule puissance qu'ils recognoissent en terre & la première après celle de Dieu."

[15] *Le Soleil au signe du Lion, d'où quelques parallèles sont tirés avec le très-chrétien, ... monarque Louis XIII, roi de France et de Navarre, en son entrée triomphante dans sa ville de Lyon; ensemble un sommaire récit de tout ce qui s'est passé de remarquable en ladite entrée de Sa Majesté, et de là*. 1623 (Paris, Jean Julliéron), p. 148. Bryant, *King and the City*, p. 100.

[16] For the distinction between a "victorious" *entrée* (in which military might was on display), and a "triumphal" *entrée* (in which victory was already assumed), see Marie-Claude Canova-Green, 'Warrior King or King of War? Louis XIII's entries into his *bonnes villes* (1620–1629)', in J. R. Mulryne, Maria Ines Aliverti, and Anna Maria Testaverde (eds.), *Ceremonial Entries in Early Modern Europe: The Iconography of Power* (Farnham, Ashgate, 2015), pp. 77–98. The Romans considered the four-horse chariot to be sacred, "set apart for the king and the father of the gods" [Plutarch]; see *Éloges et discours sur la triomphante réception du roi en sa ville de Paris, après la réduction de La Rochelle* (Paris, Pierre Rocolet, 1629), p. 22.

typically in the form of singers and instruments placed on platforms (*échaffeaux*). Thus, at Orléans in 1614,[17]

Entering the town, there was heard music, mixed from voice and instruments, like the *hautboy*, *cornets à bouquin*, trumpet, and clarion, which gave the most sweet and melodious harmony in the world, to the great contentment of the entering king.

At Orléans, the implication is that this music was secular, though at Poitiers in 1619 the description seems to refer to sacred music, the king being met at the gates by the singers and choirboys of the Royal Church of Saint-Hilaire, who "sang very beautiful and devout motets, his Majesty taking very great pleasure to hear such good and sweet music."[18]

As befits the primarily classical theme of the processional phase, one of the few fragmentary surviving sources of music likewise adopts the guise of antiquity. The *Mercure françois* account of the *entrée* into Paris of 1614 preserves the text of a "Choriambique tetrametric catalectique" Ode, *Peuple accourez hastivement voir nostre Roy qui s'en vient Victorieux* (People, Hurry to See Our King Who Comes Victorious).[19] No music is provided in the *Mercure*, but the identification there of the composer as Jacques Mauduit (who provided the *musique mesurée* settings of Baïf's psalms that are preserved in Mersenne's 1623 Quaestiones celeberrimae in Genesim; see Chapter 1) leads to a related musical setting by the same composer in Bataille's fifth book of *airs* of 1615. We can assume that this "Ode à la Reyne" (*Soit que l'œil pourveu de nouvelle clairté*) is a companion piece to the Ode (presumably "au Roy") mentioned in the *Mercure*, especially as it too uses the technique of *musique mesurée*. Set for one voice and lute in the Bataille version, the surviving score represents a version of a piece probably originally intended, just like the *Ode au Roy*, to be performed in many

---

[17] Claude Malingre, *Entrée magnifique du Roy, faicte en sa ville d'Orléans, le mardy huictiesme juillet 1614, avec l'ordre et cérémonies observées en icelle* (Paris, Melchiore Mondière, 1619): "Entrant en la Ville fut oüye une musique, meslangée de voix & d'instruments, comme de hautsbois, Cornets à bouquin, Trompettes, & Clerons qui rendoient une harmonie la plus douce & mélodieuse du monde au grand contentement du ROY entrant ..."

[18] *Entrée royale faite en la ville de Poictiers, au très-chrestien roy de France & de Navarre, Louys XIII. & à la Royne sa mère* (Paris, Charles Pignon, 1619), p. 4: "lesdits chantres & enfans de chœur chantèrent de très-beaux & dévotieux motets, sa Majesté prenant un très-grand plaisir d'ouyr une si bonne & si douce musique."

[19] *Le Mercure françois*, 1614, p. 489: "Peuple accourez hastivement voir nostre Roy qui s'en vient Victorieux, & courageux plein de nouvelle grandeur." Mersenne specifies the metrical feet used in the *Choriambique tetrametric catalectique* meter in Marin Mersenne, *Quaestiones celeberrimae in Genesim* (Paris, Sebastien Cramoisy, 1623), column 1596.

Music Example 5.1 Jacques Mauduit, "Ode à la Reyne," *Soit que l'œil pourveu de nouvelle clairté*, in reconstructed version for four voices.
Airs de différents auteurs mis en tablature de luth par Gabriel Bataille. Cinquiesme livre (Paris, Pierre Ballard, 1614), ff. 52v–53r. Reconstruction based on melody and lute tablature.

voices.[20] (See Music Example 5.1 for a reconstruction of this work as it might have been performed that day.)

Another similar example, surviving in a format possibly closer to the reality on the street, is a setting by Nicolas Métru of verses by Guillaume de Baïf, Jean-Antoine de Baïf's son, which was definitely performed at the *entrée* into Paris of 1628.[21] In this simple piece, which was probably sold on the streets as single sheets for each voice part (since the extant source provides only the *cinquiesme* voice part; see Music Example 5.2), the

---

[20] *Airs de différents auteurs mes en tablature de luth par Gabriel Bataille. Cinquiesme livre* (Paris, Pierre Ballard, 1614), ff. 52v–53r. For a discussion of the fluid boundary between polyphonic originals and lute-song arrangements from around this time, see Jeanice Brooks, '"O quelle armonye": Dialogue singing in late Renaissance France', *Early Music History*, 22 (2003), 1–65.

[21] *Recueil de vers du Sr. G. de Baïf, mis en Musique par N. Métru, chantez en allégresse de l'heureux retour du Roy* (Paris, Pierre Ballard, 1628), n.p.

Music Example 5.2 Extant *cinquiesme* voice part of Nicolas Métru, *Vive le Roy*. *Recueil de vers du Sr. G. de Baïf, mis en musique par N. Métru, chantez en allégresse de l'heureux retour du Roy* (Paris, Pierre Ballard, 1628).

"chœur de la ville" in five voices sings a refrain concluding with "Vive le Roy," while a smaller group in four voices sings the praises of the king, whose deeds surpass those of "all the Caesars" (see Table 5.1).

The third and final extant piece that can be linked to the processional phase of an *entrée* – an anonymous setting of the text "Vivat Rex in aeternum" ("May the king live for ever," or "Long live the king," equivalent to *Vive le Roy*) – appears in the Newberry/Avignon manuscript, a source whose provenance is important for the discussion of both this and another work later in the chapter. The single *superius* part-book in which it survives (MS 5123) is preserved alongside a group of five other part-books (collectively MS 5136) now in the Newberry Library Chicago, but a number of

Table 5.1 Text and translation of *Recueil de vers du Sr. G. de Baïf, mis en musique par N. Métru, chantez en allégresse de l'heureux retour du Roy* (Paris, Pierre Ballard, 1628)

À cinq	A 5
Vive le Roy. etc.	[Long] live the king, etc.
C'est le plus valeureux en guerre	He is the most valorous in war
Qui soit aujourd'huy sur la Terre	Who is today on the Earth
Pour la défenses de la foy.	For the defense of the faith.
Vive le Roy.	[Long] live the king.
À quatre	A 4
v. 1	v. 1
Toutes les puissances célestes,	All the celestial powers,
Pour ses vertus si manifestes,	For his virtues so apparent
Destinent à jamais	Forever destine
Ses peuples uni plains d'allégresse & de paix.	His peoples [to be] united full of happiness and peace.
v. 2	v. 2
O Roy! triomfant des armées,	O King! Triumphant of armies,
Combien faut-il de renommées	How renowned you are,
Pour dire à haute voix	To say in a loud voice.
Tes gestes passer tous les Caesars à la fois.	Your deeds to surpass those of all the Caesars together.
Vive le Roy.	[Long] live the king.

connections place all these books at a major church or cathedral in Avignon in the early 1620s. Originally part of a larger set (the others of which are now lost), these part-books contain repertoire in up to twelve voices for the canonization of Saints Ignatius of Loyola in 1622 and Saint Francis Xavier in 1624, events which were celebrated with great solemnity in Avignon, together with other works dated from 1622 and 1623; but most persuasively, they also contain many works attributed to the composer Sauvaire Intermet, long active in Avignon and closely involved in the music for both the canonization ceremonies and Louis XIII's *entrée* of 1622.[22]

The *entrée* into Avignon was both one of the most well documented and one of the most splendid of Louis's reign, described in astonishing detail over several hundred pages by Thomas Berton in his *La Voye de*

---

[22] For biographical information on Intermet and an overview of the Newberry/Avignon sources, see Lauren Guillo, 'Un recueil de motets de Sauvaire Intermet (Avignon, *c.* 1620–1625): Chicago, Newberry Library, Case MS 5136', *Dix-septième siècle*, 232 (2006/3), 453–75; and Jean Robert, 'La Maîtrise Saint-Agricol d'Avignon au XVIIe siècle', *Actes du quatre-vingt-dixième*

Music Example 5.3 Anonymous, opening of *Vivat Rex in aeternum*, superius voice. Newberry/Avignon manuscript (MS 5123), pp. 34–5.

laict. Berton reports that during the procession the king stopped to hear a group of 120 musicians directed by Intermet, "one of the Orpheuses of our time," and that when it came time for the King to move on,[23]

all the people sounded so loudly their "Vive le Roy," that one did not know if this was a new whirlwind of music, or a new group of voices which had just joined with the first, for the glory and praise of His Majesty.

Given the provenance of the Newberry/Avignon source, the setting of *Vivat rex in aeternum* – a piece surely intended to be performed at some kind of royal event – seems most likely to have been connected with the *entrée* of 1622. While not necessarily the piece (or at least musical phenomenon) that the account describes, both it and the Métru (to which it is very similar and which actually specifies participation by the "ville") could easily have been sung by the people themselves in the street, their homophonic, repetitive, and declamatory settings evoking the spontaneous cries of the crowds (see Music Example 5.3).

To whatever musical accompaniment was provided, the procession would make its way through the city, past arches, obelisks, and *tableaux vivants* that either followed a specific overall theme or were simply

---

congrès national des sociétés savantes, Nice, 1965: section d'histoire moderne et contemporaine, vol. 3 *De la restauration à nos jours, histoire de l'art* (Paris, Bibliothèque nationale, 1966), p. 624. For an inventory of the contents of Case MS 5123, see Peter Bennett, 'The *entrée royale* and the *Exaudiat te Dominus* in early seventeenth-century France: Evidence from Chicago, Newberry Library, Case MS 5123', in Bernard Dompnier, Catherine Massip, and Solveig Serre (eds.), *Musique en liberté. Entre la cour et les provinces au temps des Bourbons* (Paris, École nationale des chartes, 2018), pp. 113–26. See also Alexander Robinson, 'Music and politics'.

[23] Thomas de Berton, *La Voye de laict, ou Le Chemin des héros au palais de la gloire* (Avignon, Jean Bramereau, 1623)[*Avignon, 1622*], p. 226: "tout le peuple fit retentir si haut son Vive le Roy, qu'on ne sçavoit si cestoit un nouveau tourbillon de musique, ou un renfort de voix qui vint concerter avec les premières, pour la gloire & loüanges de S. M."

self-contained, referencing either figures from antiquity or mythology, or the great French kings of the past. (The overwhelming majority of the contents of all the accounts of *entrées* is dedicated to recording the details of these creations.) Thus, at Aix in 1622, the second arch was decorated with statues of Sextus, Marius, and the two Caesars, while the account of the event, by local intellectual Louis de Galaup de Chasteuil, explained how Louis surpassed all their conquests, and documented the inscriptions by both Malherbe and César de Nostrodame, son of the famous astrologer Michel de Nostrodame.[24]

Despite the secular tone of the procession, the subtext of many *entrées* was religious, and it is frequently possible to see the encroachment of religious symbolism, especially toward the end of the route through the city as the procession neared the cathedral. At its most superficial, of course, many of the *entrées* were held in response to military victories against heretical Huguenot towns. Thus, the king as defender of the faith was an obvious theme. At Arles, for example, in 1622, fresh from signing the Treaty of Montpellier, the overall conception of the *entrée* was based on Perseus (Louis) rescuing Andromeda (France) from the sea monster (heresy).[25]

The first arch in Arles presents this theme in stark simplicity (see Figure 5.2). As the account explains, the arch of the Tuscan order is without ornament because the word that the king gives to France, under the guise of Perseus, has no need for other adornment, being predicated on his goodness and his "royal force."[26] Indeed, the account reminds the reader that while the mythological analogy is useful for effect, Perseus will only ascend to an "*imaginary* place in the sky" when he dies. On the other hand, the king,[27]

by a Holy Apotheosis, will be gloriously transported to heaven, for which he went into battle, and to the honor of which he gave his victories.

---

[24] *Discours sur les arcs triomphaux dressés en la ville d'Aix à l'heureuse arrivée de très-chrétien, très-grand et très-juste monarque Louis XIII, roi de France et de Navarre* (Aix, J. Tholosan 1624), pp. 5–12.

[25] *Entrée de Loys XIII, Roy de France et de Navarre dans sa ville d'Arles, le XXIX. octobre M. DC. XXII* (Avignon, Jean Bramereau, 1623)[*Arles, 1622*], p. 3. A manuscript account of the same event recalls, "Tout le subiect de ceste Entrée estoit le Roy habille en Persée"; see Carpentras, Bibliothèque Inguimbertine, MS 1794, p. 186.

[26] *Arles, 1622*, p. 17.

[27] *Arles, 1622*, p. 3: "par un saincte apothéose, estre glorieusement transporté au Ciel, pour lequel il combat, & à l'honneur duquel il donne ses victoires."

The Entrée *as Procession* 163

Figure 5.2 First arch at Arles, 1622.
Entrée de Loys XIII, Roy de France et de Navarre dans sa ville d'Arles, le XXIX. octobre M. DC. XXII (Avignon, Jean Bramereau, 1623), p. 9. Bibliothèque nationale de France.

The final progression of arches at Arles completed a sequence of increasingly religious references: the penultimate arch showed Perseus being pulled in a triumphal chariot while being crowned by an angel; while the final arch, dedicated to the king's clemency and Christian qualities, now showed Louis himself, no longer in the guise of Perseus, praying before an altar, his royal regalia at his feet, appearing simply as a humble man (see Figure 5.3).The account also explains how this final arch is the gateway to the culmination or "anacéphalose" of the triumph:[28]

The king did not wish to burn the spoils, but he wished to throw the offenses of the rebel subjects into the fire of his love and clemency, and, by this sacrifice agreeable to God, to acquit himself of a vow so holy and sacred that he owed to heaven for his victory.

This sense that the religious dimension was the climax or peroration of the *entrée*, in which the king demonstrated his clemency and piety in a way that superseded the mythological explanations and celebrations of victory that had preceded it, is a prominent theme. In Lyon in 1622, the clergy of the cathedral had built an arch outside the cathedral based on the theme of the return of the Golden Age. In their account of the event, the clergy considered this arch to be "la Couronne de l'œuvre" (i.e. of the *entrée*), and they reminded the reader that they did not need to resort to the "fables of the ancients."[29] The Archbishop, too, made this point directly to the king: having passed through this final arch, with the choir singing the antiphon to for the Feast of Saint John the Baptist *Inter natos* (the cathedral is dedicated to the saint), the Archbishop welcomed the king, reminding him that his final destination was not the city's Roman Capitol, where "the ancient idolatrous triumphers gave their sacrifices to the false Jupiter, but at this ancient church, capital of your kingdoms."[30] At Chartres, too, in 1619, the portal of the cathedral itself was converted into a "sacred arch" in order to encroach upon the procession, and at Avignon in 1622, an arch was constructed on the front of the church of Notre-Dame des Doms for the same purpose.[31]

But perhaps one of the most striking moments of the procession was an incident recorded in Toulouse in 1622, during which the king was

---

[28] *Arles, 1622*, p. 64: "Le Roy ne vouloit pas brusler les despouilles, mais il vouloit ietter dans le feu de son amour & de sa clémence, les offenses de ses subiects rebelles, & par ce sacrifice agréable à Dieu s'acquitter d'un vœu si sainct & sacré, que celuy qu'il devoit au ciel pour sa Victoire."

[29] *Réception de ... Louis XIII, Roy de France par MM. les Doyen, Chanoines, & Comtes de Lyon ...* (Lyon, Jacques Roussin, 1623)[*Lyon, 1623*], p. 3.

[30] *Lyon, 1623*, p. 20: "les anciens Triomphateurs idolatres alloyant faire leurs offrandes à leur faux Iupiter; mais à ceste ancienne Église, capitale de vos Royaumes ..." The Archbishop of Lyon is also "Primate of the Gauls" and holds the most high-ranking bishopric in France.

[31] *Les Magnificences préparées en l'église Notre-Dame de Chartres, pour les dévotes actions de grâce du roi et de la reine sa mère, de leur heureuse entrevue et de leur aimable réconciliation* (Paris, S. Benoist, 1619); *Avignon, 1622*, p. 252.

Figure 5.3 Final arch at Arles, 1622.
Entrée de Loys XIII, Roy de France et de Navarre dans sa ville d'Arles, le XXIX. octobre M. DC. XXII (Avignon, Jean Bramereau, 1623), p. 61. Bibliothèque nationale de France.

presented with a *Te igitur* and a cross to touch, in turn promising to guard and conserve the rights of the church.[32] In the revised Roman Missal of 1570, the Canon of the Mass (the *Te igitur*, the prayers said by the priest as he prepares the Eucharist) had contained a prayer for the Pope but made no reference to the king. In 1580 the *parlement* of Paris (as self-styled guardian of Gallican liberties) had taken objection to this omission, that same year passing an *arrêt* (driven by Advocat Servin, who was intensely hostile to Rome) requiring all missals published in France to insert the king's name at that point – "una cum famulo tuo Papa nostro N. & Antistite nostro N. & Rege nostro N."(together with your servant our Pope N., our Bishop N., and our King N.).[33] But the addition of the prayer for the king at this most sacred moment of the Mass subsequently became a point of contention as the religious wars played out. In the days that followed the assassination of Henri and Louis de Guise in December 1588, and in which League sentiment had reached fever pitch, the sixty-six doctors of the Sorbonne met on January 7, 1589 and, having celebrated a Mass of the Holy Spirit, deliberated on how to react to the king's murderous acts.[34] As a first step, they released the people of France from their vows of obedience to the king, but at a later meeting in April, they followed this up with an *arrêt* removing the prayer for the king from the canon. Presumably this prayer was reinstated after the accession of Henri IV in 1594, because by 1598 a published guide to the Mass featured a lengthy exposition on the merits of praying for the king at this point.[35] Indeed, the section on the *Et Rege nostro* prayer is effectively a treatise on absolutism, reminding the reader that both the Pope and the king are God's lieutenants on earth, and that the king's first duty is to advance God's glory

---

[32] Jean d'Alard, *Entrée du roy à Tolose* (Toulouse, R. Colomiés, 1622), p. 51: "Le Roy ayant osté le gand, toucha de sa Royale main *où reside la valeur & la foy, à un Te igitur & Croix apporté à cet usage*, promit de garder & conserver iceux droicts, privilèges, & libertés."

[33] Prosper Guéranger, *Institutions liturgiques*, 3 vols. (Paris, Victor Palmé, 1878), Vol. 1, p. 451. Jean Grancolas, *Commentaire historique sur le bréviaire Romain* (Paris, Philippe Lottin, 1727), p. 30.

[34] William Jervis, *The Gallican Church: The History of the Church of France from the Concordat of Bologna to the Revolution* (London, John Murray, 1872), p. 187; Jean-Claude Fabre, *Histoire ecclésiastique pour servir à celle de Monsieur l'Abbé Fleury* (Paris, Gabriel Martin, etc., 1743), p. 236.

[35] *Bref recueil et explication de la messe et du divin service y faict* (Paris, Jacobum Kerver, 1598), p. 97. Significantly for our understanding of the *Exaudiat*, in a section on prayers for the king (p. 100), the *Exaudiat* is not mentioned. Guéranger, *Institutions*, pp. 502–3 describes how at the 1605–6 Assemblée de clergé it was officially resolved to reintroduce the *pro rege nostro* prayer, but it seems that this had, in practice, already occurred, the 1602 Paris *Missale*, for example, already including this text.

and to protect the church. In this brief moment of the procession at Toulouse, then, we can see not just a sign of the king's piety, but the acknowledgment of a contract between the Gallican church and the monarchy itself, and the church's willing participation in the absolutist project.

After passing through all the arches, what we might call the "transitional" ceremony began, and it is at this point that the liturgical dimension comes sharply into focus. Having typically been led through the city by the combined local dignitaries, the king would be met at the doors of the cathedral by the Bishop and the cathedral clergy in a sacred counterpart to his greeting at the city gates. But where the first ceremony consisted of displays of obedience by the civic authorities to the king, the encounter with the clergy was intended to express his own devotion to the church and his humility, while nonetheless giving the opportunity to the clergy to praise his piety and devotion. Thus, rather than welcoming the king as a Roman warrior, in Grenoble in 1622, for example, the Bishop quoted the Book of Kings, in which God denies David (the father, in this case Henri IV) the opportunity to build the Temple of Jerusalem (i.e. religious unity in France), reserving the honor for his son Solomon (i.e. Louis).[36] And at Montélimar, a series of clerics quoted the same scripture, comparing him to Saint Louis (for his fight against heresy) and Solomon (for his wisdom at such a young age).[37]

After such harangues, the king would typically kneel before the bishop on a tapestry rug provided for the purpose, be blessed with holy water, and be presented with a crucifix, which he was reported to have kissed and revered. At Le Mans in 1614, this act was taken as a sign of submission to the cross, typical of other acts of subdued piety that occurred at this point;[38] at Le Mans again, the king's humility was likened to that of David, who danced in front of the Ark of the Covenant as it returned to Jerusalem, not in his royal regalia but in the clothes of a commoner;[39] while at Chartres in 1619 and Troyes in 1629, the king is reported to have entered the cathedral as a pilgrim, intent on seeing and touching the relics.[40] Such

---

[36] *Harangue au roy, prononcée à Grenoble, le 29 novembre 1622 au nom du clergé* (Paris, N. Rousset, 1622), p. 5.

[37] *Le Mercure françois*, 1622, p. 890.

[38] *Entrée solennelle du roi Louis XIII et de Marie de Médicis en la ville du Mans, le 5 septembre 1614* (Le Mans, G. and F. Les Oliviers, 1614)[*Le Mans, 1614*], p. 64. The same things is described in *La Ioyeuse entrée du Roy en sa ville de Troyes ... Le Ieudy vingt cinquiesme iour de Ianvier, 1629* (Troyes, Jean Jacquard, 1629)[*Troyes, 1629*] and *Arles, 1622*.

[39] *Le Mans, 1614*, p. 64

[40] *La Royale entrée du Roy, et de la Royne en la ville de Chartres, avec les Magnificences & Cérémonies qui s'y sont observées le Ieudy le 26 Septembre* (Paris, Iozue Chemin, 1619), p. 9:

humility was also on display at Lyon, Poitiers, Le Mans, Angers, and Saint Martin of Tours, where the king enjoyed a special status as "first canon" of these cathedrals.[41] Accordingly, whenever he made his *entrée* there he was presented with the *aumusse* and *surpelis* (hood and surplice) that the canons wore before entering the cathedral. In these places, then, the transformation from Roman emperor to cleric and *Roi-prêtre* was not just notional, but literal and complete.

The *Entrée* as Liturgy

At this point, the published narratives and descriptions lose their utility, typically providing only the most generic information about the entrance into the cathedral, the music (a Te Deum sung "most excellently" or other such commonplaces), and prayers (the "usual prayers"), before reporting that the king retired to the bishop's palace. But at Arles in 1622, uniquely, we are told that, after the performance of the Te Deum, "Monsieur the Archbishop, having recited the Prayers that are found in the Roman Pontifical, for the *entrée* and reception of kings, gave the blessing," an observation that points us to the Roman *Pontificale*, a manual that provides instructions and texts for ceremonies that are to be celebrated by a bishop, in much the same way that a *Rituale* provides instruction for ceremonies celebrated by a priest.[42] Several other brief mentions referring to the prayers being said "in the usual manner" (in other words, the ceremony was standardized in some way) support that idea that the ceremony was conducted according to the rubrics of the *Pontificale*, a fact that should come as no surprise.[43] The rite was included in French editions of the *Pontificale* throughout the sixteenth century (Lyon, 1511 and 1543), and

---

Troyes, 1629. The *registres* of the cathedral also tell us that a special temporary chapel was built in the cathedral, inside which was the King's *oratoire*, richly decorated with fabric; see Troyes, Archives départementales de l'Aube, G-1613.

[41] According to René Lehoreau, Canon at Angers Cathedral, "Le Roy de France est premier Chanoine de Lyon, de Poitier, d'Angers, Du Mans, et de St Martin de Tours: et quand le Roy fait son entrée en ces églises on luy présenterai la porter l'aumusse & le surpelis," Angers, Archives départementales de Maine-et-Loire, 5-G-1, p. 51.

[42] *Arles, 1622*, p. 67: "Monsieur l'Archevesque après avoir recité les Oraisons qui se trouvent dans le Pontifical Romain, à l'entrée & réception des Roys, donna la bénédiction."

[43] *Le Mans, 1614*, p. 70: "les oraisons ordinaires"; *Aix, 1622*, p. 40: "On sçait assés l'ordre & les Cérémonies qui sont observées en ces lieux sacrés aux réceptions des Roys." (One knows well enough the order and the ceremonies which are observed in these sacred places for the reception of kings.)

although the French valued their liturgical independence (the so-called Gallican liberties), the texts of the Lyon, Rome (1596 and 1611), and Paris (1615) editions are all identical.[44] So while the push to update the liturgical books across France and the beginning of Louis's military campaigns both coincided with the publication of the "new" *Pontificale* in 1615, in reality there was nothing novel about the ceremony itself; on the contrary, the *Pontificale* preserved an ancient and unchanging liturgy, successive editions testifying to a continuous tradition linking the famous *entrées* of Francis, I, Henri II, and Charles IX (who almost certainly used this rite) with those of the young king Louis.[45]

The *Ordo ad recipiendum processionaliter regem* (the "order for receiving kings in procession") confirms the details of the "transitional" greeting ceremony noted in some the printed accounts – the kissing of the cross, the kneeling on a rug, and the blessing with holy water, although in the *Pontificale*, which must have regarded the liturgy as a freestanding event rather than as part of a joint civic and ecclesiastical *entrée*, this ceremony takes place as the king enters the city rather than at the church door, and is followed by an ecclesiastical procession under a *baldachino* rather than the militaristic or civic procession of the *entrée*.[46]

The *Pontificale* then specifies that the Responsory *Elegit eum Dominus* should be sung, providing the only notated chant we have from the ceremony, a chant unique to this liturgy that takes its inspiration from the prophet Samuel's account of David's anointing:[47]

The Lord chose him and made him high over the Kings of the earth. He glorified him in the sight of Kings, and he was not confounded. And ... Glory ... And.

In the *Pontificale* rubrics, this chant was to be sung during the procession through the city to the church, although none of the printed accounts of the *entrée* mentions it. But in Aix in 1622, the *Actes de Chapitre* tell us that it was indeed sung in the cathedral with organs and instruments, presumably in some kind of improvised polyphony, confirming that the *Pontificale* ceremony was probably simply "compressed" into the cathedral for the

---

[44] The order is preserved in *Pontificale Romanum Clementis VIII, Pont Max* (Paris, Rolinum Thierry and Eustachium Foucualt, 1615), pp. 382–3. Bauldry provides an abbreviated version of the rite but does not offer any performance information; see Michel Bauldry, *Manuale sacrarum caeremoniarum iuxta ritum S. Romanae ecclesiae* (Paris, Ioannem Billaine, 1646), pp. 104–5.
[45] See Chapter 6 for the adoption of the revised books after the Council of Trent.
[46] *Pontificale*, 1615, p. 382.
[47] Ibid.: "Elegit eum Dominus, et excelsum fecit illum prae Regibus terrae. Glorificavit eum in conspectu Regum, & non confundetur. Et ex ... Gloria ... Et excelsum."

entrée.[48] The *Elegit* Responsory was then followed by the singing of "hymni, vel alia cantica magis placentia." Given that almost every printed account mentions the performance of the Te Deum, we can assume that the first of these "hymni" refers to the hymn or canticle *Te Deum laudamus*.[49]

As I argued in Chapter 2, although the Te Deum certainly featured in the coronation, the coronation itself probably did not define the way in which the Te Deum was heard more generally, nor was it the most important musical or liturgical item of the ceremony taken as a whole. Instead, contemporaries described it primarily as a Hymn to the Trinity, inspired by the Holy Spirit, that functioned most frequently as a Doxology to Sunday Matins, but that also acted as the conclusion to numerous general rites and processions of thanksgiving. A subset of such processions or rites of thanksgiving were, of course, those that celebrated victory in the wars of religion, rites which could form part of the "official" royal *entrée* ceremony or could also simply be celebrated by the church authorities on their own initiative. Thus, Simplician Saint Martin, in his history of Saint Augustine, suggests one of the appropriate times to sing the Te Deum by asking:[50]

Have we seen reestablished the exercise of [the true] Religion, and the raising of the standard of the Holy Cross in our towns from where the insolence of the Heretics had without dignity rejected it? Have we purged our Temples of the abomination with which they soiled them: and returned to our Savior and Redeemer Jesus Christ on the holy altars the censing, the honors and adoration which they had sacrilegiously ravaged? These are the obligations for which God does not require the blood of his victims: he is content with the sacrifice of praise which we offer him by the public singing of the *Te Deum laudamus*.

---

[48] *Livre de cérémonies de l'église métropolitaine de S. Sauveur*, Aix, Bibliothèque Méjanes, MS 272, p. 138: "Les Orgues & Musique Chantoient *Elegit eum Dominus, &c.*"

[49] The meaning and connotations of terms such as *canticum* and *hymnum* were widely debated by theologians and the church fathers, debates that continued into the seventeenth century. See note 56 below.

[50] Simplician Saint Martin, *Histoire de la vie du Glorieux père S. Augustin religieuse, docteur de l'église* (Toulouse, Colomiez, 1641), p. 31: "Avons-nous veu restablir exercice de la Religion, & arborer l'étandart de la saincte Croix dans nos villes d'où l'insolence des Hérétiques armée de force l'avoit indignement reieté? Avons-nous purgé nos Temples de l'abomination dont ils les avoient soüillez: & faict rendre à nostre Sauveur & Redempteur Iesus-Christ sur les saincts Autels les encesemens, les honneurs & adorations qu'ils luy avoient sacrilégement ravy? Ce sont des obligations pour lesquelles Dieu ne requiert point de nous le sang des victimes: il se contente d'un sacrifice de loüange que nous luy offrons par le chant public du *Te Deum laudamus*."

Outside the confines of the liturgy, the imagery and text of the Te Deum did, of course, lend itself to reinterpretation as a means of emphasizing the divine nature of kingship. A poem/*cantique* published in 1623, *Le Te Deum contre les athéistes libertins*, glosses each important line of the hymn with French verses, although the approach the author takes is relatively neutral in tone.[51] But a version in the account of the *entrée* into Montpellier in 1622 is, however more pointed, this time paraphrasing the text directly and enabling those who later read the account to appreciate the king's role in doing God's work – subjugating the Huguenots (although, of course, we assume this text was never performed or used in a liturgical context).[52] Going even further than the 1616 *Te Deum de la paix*, here the king stands in not just for Christ, but for God himself, the repeated supplications at the end of the hymn ("O Lord") being modified to, for example "In te **Rex** speravimus" from "In te **Domine** speravit." Yet the text is also remarkably conciliatory to both the Huguenots and simultaneously the Pope, clearly informed by the Treaty of Montpellier (just recently signed), which allowed the Huguenots to continue to worship, even if their military and defensive forces were to be dismantled. Thus (modifications in bold):

When you took it upon yourself to deliver the **Catholic Faith**, you did not abhor the **Huguenot faith of your father** [i.e. Henri IV, a Huguenot].
. . .

When you had overcome the sharpness of heresy, you opened the **kingdom of France** to all believers [i.e. you allowed freedom of worship]
. . .

You sit at the right hand of the **Pope**, in the glory of **your ancestors**.

Just as for the coronation, we do not know exactly how the Te Deum was performed, very few accounts going beyond generalities involving the organ, instruments, and singers. So at Angers in 1619, "la musique & les orgues remplirent les voultes du *Te Deum*, que l'on chanta," while in Orléans in 1614, the Te Deum was sung "en musique, avec orgues & hautbois."[53] We know nothing of the composers of these works, but at Avignon in 1622 a Te Deum by "Monsieur de la Tour" from Flanders was

---

[51] Garnier, *Le Te Deum, contre les athéistes libertins* (Paris, Daniel Guillemot, 1623).
[52] *Actions de Grâces de la France, sur la prise, réduction, & capitulation des Villes de Montpellier, Nismes, Castres, Millaud, Uzès, & autres places Rebelles. Avec le Te Deum de resiouyssance des fidèles François, pour l'heureux succès des armes du Roy* (Bordeaux, 1622), p. 8.
[53] *Le Mercure françois*, 1619, p. 329. *Entrée magnifique du Roy, faicte en sa ville d'Orléans, le mardy huictiesme juillet 1614, avec l'ordre et cérémonies observées en icelle, par Claude Malingre* (Paris, Melchiore Mondière, 1619), p. 11.

sung "superbly to the organ, along with several other motets."[54] Such organized music was probably not typical. The *entrée* at Avignon was relatively well planned, and the cathedral had a skillful *maîtrise* for whom a composed Te Deum and motets would present no problem. But in other cities, at short notice, the Te Deum may well have simply been chanted, with the organ playing the alternatim versets, either improvised or to a setting such as that by Attaingnant (see Chapter 2 for other performance options).[55]

If the Te Deum corresponds to the "hymni" specified by the *Pontificale*, what about the *cantica magis placentia* (songs of more pleasingness)? In addition to its association with vocal music in general, the term *canticum* is used as a superscription in the Vulgate psalter and generally indicates a psalm of rejoicing or celebration that, according to Church Fathers such as Hilaire of Poitiers (on whom authors such as Duranti and Peyronet were heavily dependent), derives its effect directly from the Holy Spirit.[56] Certainly, in the *Rituale Romanum*, the Te Deum sung as part of a procession of thanksgiving is followed by one or more psalms.[57] Given that in Avignon the Te Deum was followed by "quelques motets," and that in Paris in 1622,[58]

arriving at the said Church [Notre-Dame] they sang many Hymns, and many motets in Music in honor of God, and to rejoice in the victories and triumphs of the King

we can probably read *cantica* as some kind of psalm motet, in this case celebrating the success of the king. While musical settings of the Te Deum remain elusive and the message of the text ambivalent, seemingly

---

[54] *Avignon, 1622*, p. 259: "superbement sur l'orgue avec quelques autres motets."

[55] At the Te Deum celebrated in Paris for the Peace of Montpellier in 1622, "on a sonné une Clochette qui servoit de signal aux orgues par où on a Commencé ensuite s'en chanté se Te Deum en musique par les chantres et musiciens qui étoient au lutrin, l'orgue faisans les intermèdes des Versets ..."; F-Pn MS nouv. acq. fr. 23474, p. 331.

[56] Based on Hilaire, subsequent authors discussed extensively the qualities of *psalmi, cantica,* and *hymni*; see Patrick Descourtieux (trans and ed.), Hilaire de Poitiers, *Commentaires sur les pseaumes* (Paris, Le Cerf, 2008), p. 159; Jean-Étienne Duranti, *De ritibus ecclesiae Catholicae libri tres* (Lyon, Landry, 1606), p. 623. For Peyronet, *Manuel du Bréviaire Romain* (Toulouse, Jean Boude, 1667), pp. 104–6, a *canticum* "est un chant de ioye spirituelle conceuë sur l'espérance de la béatitude éternelle." The Te Deum was thus both a hymn and a *canticum*.

[57] *Rituale Romanum*, 1615, p. 196.

[58] *Les Préparatifs ordonnés pour l'entrée et réception du roi, suivant les commandements de MM. les prévôts des marchands et les échevins de la ville de Paris* (Paris, N. Alexandre, 1622), p. 11: "arrivé en ladite Église, l'on chantera forces Hymnes [= Te Deum], & forces motets en Musique [= *cantica*] en l'honneur de Dieu, & en resiouyssances des victoires & des triomphes du Roy."

appropriate psalm-based motets are not hard to find. A work such as *Omnes gentes plaudite manibus*, from the Tours manuscript, seems particularly fitting. Like the *Te Deum* with modified text from Montpellier described above (although in this case actually set to music and performed, rather than intended as a commentary), this setting of a modified version of Psalm 46, attributed to Guillaume Bouzignac by Launay and others, takes the framework of the original psalm but heightens its effect, spelling out the metaphor rather than leaving it to the imagination (France, Louis, etc.), with the people of France singing to their king as Israel sang to David, and God choosing ("elegit") the "pride of the Bourbons," just as he did in the Responsory as the king entered the cathedral (see Music Example 5.4. and Table 5.2).[59]

Likewise, a fragment of a longer piece based on Psalms 95 and 23 preserved in both the Tours and Paris manuscripts (and also sometimes attributed to Bouzignac) is equally apposite. Described in the Vulgate as a "Song of David himself, when the house was built after the captivity" and recalling the joy of receiving the Ark in Jerusalem, we hear the voice of David/Louis exhorting the French to praise God, with the people of France in turn inviting the king to literally enter the city of La Rochelle, crying "vive le roy/Vivat rex" as they did in Avignon, Paris, and many other cities (see Table 5.3).[60]

While psalm-based motets such as these reflect one particular celebratory approach to the *canticum* – they could certainly be described as "cantica magis placentia" – it is perhaps more likely that they were performed in the processional phase rather than in the cathedral (following the accounts above), especially since in the very few instances where we have direct and unequivocal evidence of what was performed, it was not works such as these. Instead, evidence from all three *entrées* where the psalm is specified – Troyes in 1629, and Lyon in 1622 and 1642 – while complex and requiring careful reading, indicates that Psalm 19, *Exaudiat te Dominus*, or verses from it, was frequently performed.

---

[59] This piece is preserved in the Tours manuscript, ff. 125v–127r. For the biography of Bouzignac and the conventional attribution of anonymous works in the Tours manuscript, see Henri Quittard, 'Un musicien oublié du xviiie siècle: G. Bouzignac', *Sammelbände der Internationalen Musik-Gesellschaft*, 6 (1904–5), 356–417; and Martial Leroux, *Guillaume Bouzignac vers 1587– vers 1643: l'énigme musicale du XVIIe siècle français*, (Montpellier, Presses du Languedoc, 2002). For an alternative view see Peter Bennett, *Sacred Repertories in Paris, 1630–43: Paris, Bibliothèque nationale de France, V^{ma} rés. 571* (DPhil dissertation, Oxford University, 2004).

[60] Tours manuscript ff. 127r–128v; fragment in the Paris manuscript at f. 125r. For the relationship between the Paris and Tours manuscripts, see Bennett, *Sacred Repertories*, 2004.

Music Example 5.4 Guillaume Bouzignac (attrib.), opening of *Omnes gentes plaudite manibus*.
Tours manuscript, ff. 125v–127r.

At Troyes in 1629 the published account tells us unambiguously that:[61]

> the musicians of the said two Churches together [the cathedral and Saint-Étienne] began to sing on the *jubé* [the screen] with the organs the Te Deum, with the psalm *Exaudiat*, at the end of which the Sieur Bishop said the Antiphons and Collects customary for the King, and finished this act with his blessing.

---

[61] *Troyes, 1629*, p. 43: "la musique desdites deux Églises jointes ensemble commença à chanter au jubé avec les Orgues le *Te Deum*, avec le Psalme *Exaudiat*, à la fin duquel ledit Sieur Évesque dist les Antiennes & Collectes accoustumés pour le Roy, & termina ceste action par sa bénédiction."

Music Example 5.4 (*cont.*)

At Lyon in 1622, a much more detailed manuscript account from the cathedral archives reports that:[62]

> The *sous-maître* intoned *Domine salvum fac regem* in the tone on which one sings the psalm *Exaudiat* at the Benediction, which verse was repeated three times by the Choir, after which Monsieur the Dean said the verset *Domine in virtute tua laetabitur* ...

---

[62] Lyon, AD 10 G 442, n.f.: "Le soumaître entonna *Domine salvum fac regem* au ton qu'on le chante au pseaume *Exaudiat* a la Benediction, lequel verset fut répété trois fois par le Chœur, après lequel Mr le Doyen dit le verset *Domine in virtute tua laetabitur* ..."

Music Example 5.4 (*cont.*)

The 1622 Lyon description is not all that it seems, however, since the liturgical details of the 1642 account are identical, word for word, except that in the 1642 account the event is not described as an *entrée* but as a "Te Deum solemnel chanté, le roy present" (solemn Te Deum, sung, the king present). (Given that the manuscript is a later copy of the cathedral *actes*, it seems likely that the account originally described the 1642 event, but was miscopied into the 1624 record.) This description strongly suggests that the *entrée* and the "Te Deum" (to which I will turn below) were considered essentially the same apart from the presence of the king, especially when we remember that by far the most commonly performed psalm in the "Te Deum" ceremony (which was, by contrast to the *entrée*, frequently identified by Godefroy and others) was also the *Exaudiat* or the *Domine salvum*. But what exactly was the "Te Deum" ceremony, why was it important, and how might considering it alongside the *entrée* be productive?

By the time the second edition of Théodore Godefroy's *Le Cérémonial français* was published in 1649 with the help of his son Denys (described as "Historiographe du Roy"), the "Te Deum" had assumed an important role in the ceremonial life of the monarchy, and would continue to do so for the remainder of the century.[63] The culmination of a process instigated by Henri II in 1548 (in which the details of ceremonies were to be recorded and documented), given impetus by Henri III's creation of a *maître de*

---

[63] Théodore Godefroy, *Le Cérémonial de France* (Paris, Abraham Pacard, 1619); Théodore and Denys Godefroy, *Le Cérémonial français*, 2 vols. (Paris, Sebastien Cramoisy, 1649).

Table 5.2 Text and translation of Guillaume Bouzignac (attrib.), *Omnes gentes plaudite manibus*, Tours manuscript, ff. 125v–127r

2. Omnes gentes plaudite manibus. Jubilate Deo in voce exultationis. Alleluia.	O clap your hands, all ye nations: shout unto God with the voice of joy. Alleluia
4. Subjecit **Galliam nobis** et **rebelles** sub pedibus nostris. Jubilate Deo in voce exultationis.	He hath subdued **our France**; and **the rebels** under our feet. Shout unto God with the voice of joy.
5. Elegit nobis haereditatem suam speciem **Borbonii** quem dilexit. Alleluia.	He hath chosen for us his inheritance the beauty of the **Bourbons** which he hath loved. Alleluia.
7. Psallite Deo nostro, psallite **Jesu Christo**, psallite **Regi nostro**, psallite **Ludovico**, psallite Alleluia.	Sing praises to our God, sing ye: sing praises to **Jesus Christ**, sing praises to **our king**, sing praises to **Louis**, sing ye. Alleluia.
8. Quoniam Rex omnis terrae Deus, psallite sapienter. Jubilate Deo in voce exultationis.	For God is King of all the earth: sing ye wisely. Shout unto God with the voice of joy.

Modifications to Psalm 46 in bold.

Table 5.3 Text and translation of Guillaume Bouzignac (attrib.), *Cantate Domino, omnis Francia*, Tours manuscript, ff. 127r–128v

95: 2. Cantate Domino, **omnis Francia**, canticum novum. Alleluia. **Vivat, vivat, Rex Ludovicus.**	Sing ye to the Lord, **all France**, a new canticle. Alleluia. **Long live King Louis.**
23:7. Atollite portas **Rupellenses** et introibit **Rex Franciae**. **Quis est iste Rex Franciae? Ludovicus ipse est Rex Franciae.** **Vivat, vivat Rex Ludovicus.**	Lift up the gates of **La Rochelle**: and the **King of France** shall enter in. **Who is the King of France? Louis himself is King of France.** **Long live King Louis.**
95:2. Cantate Domino, **omnis Francia**, canticum novum. Alleluia.	Sing ye to the Lord, **all France**, a new canticle. Alleluia.

Modifications to psalm texts in bold.

cérémonies in 1585, brought to partial fruition by Louis XIII in Théodore's first edition of 1619 (which features coronations, baptisms, funerals, and one or two *entrées*), and completed by those around Louis XIV, Godefroy's second edition essentially provided a means of memorializing ceremonies (now including the "Te Deum") that, by their very nature, were temporary, but which contributed to the *grandeur* and *majesté* of the king described by

Duchesne and now so essential to the absolute conception of the monarchy.[64] Based on extensive archival research, the Godefroys reproduced accounts of not all, but certainly some of the most important ceremonies of the late sixteenth and early seventeenth century.

From these numerous accounts we can indeed clearly see the connection between the *entrée* and the "Te Deum." After the 1615 marriage of Louis to Anne of Austria in Bordeaux, for example, on October 18, Godefroy's volume briefly records the letters written by the king, the action this letter prompted, and the resulting organization of the ceremony.[65] The king initially wrote to the Prévost des Marchands et Eschevins (Head of the Merchants and Aldermen) in Paris commanding them to celebrate the happy news of the wedding in the same way that the king himself had in Bordeaux shortly before.[66] The Prévost then wrote to the various constituent *corps* of the city, commanding them in turn to be present at the Hôtel de Ville at 9.00 the following morning, and specifying what livery they were to wear. Just as they would in an *entrée*, these *corps* then marched to the cathedral of Notre-Dame in rank order, though unlike the *entrée*, without the king. The City Archers led, followed by the Maistre des œuvres de la ville on horseback, ten *sergents* of the city; the Greffier de la ville, the Prévost des Marchands et Eschevins, the Procureur du Roy, the Receveur de la ville, and finally the *conseillers*, *quarteniers*, and *bourgeois*. They entered the cathedral, where the Duc d'Anjou (Gaston, the king's brother), the Count of Soissons, and other princes of the blood were waiting, before the Cour des Aydes, the Cour de Parlement, and the Cour des Comptes arrived. At that point the Te Deum was sung, followed by the *Exaudiat*, after which all present returned to the Hôtel de Ville in the same order.

Michèle Fogel has described the development of this ceremony through a centuries-old tradition of processions and Masses that finished with the performance of the Te Deum at Notre-Dame, and which had gradually evolved during the sixteenth century, ultimately being refashioned under Henri III and combined with elements of the *entrée*, though stripped of its processional phase.[67] Fogel was unaware of the presence of a psalm in the

---

[64] For the creation and role of the *maître de cérémonies* see Godefroy, I, unnumbered pages; see also Marie-Lan Nguyen, *Les Grands maîtres des cérémonies et le service des Cérémonies* (MA thesis, University of Paris, Sorbonne, 1998.)

[65] Godefroy, II, pp. 88–91.

[66] There was a series of *entrées* into Bordeaux in 1615, but they followed the same pattern as many others. No liturgical or musical details of the wedding itself survive, but see McGowan (ed.), *Dynastic Marriages 1612/1615*.

[67] Fogel, *Cérémonies de l'information*, esp. pp. 163–7.

Table 5.4 Psalms identified in the *entrée* ceremony

Date	Event	Description	Source
1629	*Entrée* into Troyes	Ce faict la musique desdites deux Églises jointes ensemble commença à chanter au jubé avec les Orgues le *Te Deum*, avec le Psalme *Exaudiat*.	*La Ioyeuse entrée du Roy en sa ville de Troyes* (Troyes, Jean Jacquard, 1629), 43.

An undated manuscript, a French translation of some kind of *Rituale*, contains an order "De l'entrée du roy, de la reine, et des enfants de France," which specifies "on pourra chanter le ps. 71 ou le ps. 19." By offering the choice between the *Exaudiat* and *Deus judicium*, this source reflects in general terms the argument I am putting forward, but in the absence of any dating information (it may be a copy of a 1712 ritual) it is not conclusive; see Bibliothèque municipale de Tours, MS 180, p. 162.

entrée liturgy (indeed of any liturgical dimension to the *entrée* at all beyond the Te Deum), and thus saw the first time that a psalm was recorded as being performed after the Te Deum (December 23, 1587, for the victory over the Reîtres) as the decisive moment in its history: for Fogel, the addition of the psalm was a significant liturgical modification, a masterstroke by Henri III to make the liturgy serve his own ceremonial agenda. As Fogel puts it, "A rejection of the *entrée*, the performance of the hymn, of a psalm and prayers for the king, accompanied by organ, the *coup* by Henri III was a stroke of genius."[68] While the distinction between this "first" "Te Deum" and the *entrée* is more complex than it may initially seem (Fogel's account of the genesis involves many other questions), nevertheless in liturgical terms, as Fogel unknowingly acknowledged, the two appear to be identical in many respects.

At the "first" "Te Deum" in 1587, the psalm performed was Psalm 116, *Laudate Dominum omnes gentes* – a celebratory psalm similar in tone to those mentioned above.[69] But thereafter, Psalm 19, *Exaudiat te Dominus*, or, later, its final verse, *Domine salvum fac regem*, became the most common, apart from at the ceremonies celebrating the birth of both Henri IV's and Louis XIII's sons, when Psalm 20, *Domine in virtute tua* (as sung at the coronation) was performed (see Tables 5.4, 5.5, and 5.6). Kate van Orden's important study of both the Te Deum and the "Te Deum" has painted a vivid picture of the complex array of associations between the "Te Deum" and the coronation (and, to a lesser extent, the

---

[68] Ibid., p. 167: "Refus de l'Entrée, articulation de l'hymne, d'un psaume et des prières pour le roi, accompagnement des orgues, le coup de force de Henri III est un coup de génie."
[69] Fogel, *Cérémonies de l'information*, p. 167.

Table 5.5 Psalms identified in the "Te Deum" ceremony

Date	Event	Description	Source
1587	Defeat of the Reîtres	Le *Te Deum chanté*, avec le Psalme, *Laudate Dominum omnes gentes*, en Musique, ...	Godefroy, II, 989
1601	Wedding of Henri IV and Marie de Médicis	& ayans pareillement pris leurs places, fut chanté en Musique à haute voix, & en grande dévotion, *Te Deum laudamus*, & après l'*Exaudiat*.	Godefroy, II, 55
1601	Birth of Louis XIII	... & aussit tost fut chanté en Musique le *Te Deum laudamus*, avec le Pseaume, *Domine in virtute tua*, &c.	Godefroy, II, 163
1601	Peace treaty with Savoy	... les Gens d'Église chantèrent en Musique le Cantique de *Te Deum laudamus*, & après le Pseaume *Exaudiat*, &c.	Godefroy, II, 912
1607	Birth of the Duc d'Orléans	... & aussit tost fut chanté en Musique ledit *Te Deum laudamus*, avec le Pseaume, *Domine in virtute tua*.	Godefroy, II, 194
1608	Birth of the Duc d'Anjou	... & aussit tost fut chanté en Musique le *Te Deum laudamus*, avec le Pseaume, *Domine in virtute tua*.	Godefroy, II, 198
1615	Marriage of Louis XIII	Le *Te Deum* a esté chanté en Musique, & à la fin l'*Exaudiat* & les *Oremus*, dits par Monsieur l'Évesque de Paris.	Godefroy, II, 90; MS 18531, 59v
1620	Subjugation of the Château of Caen	Et aussitôt le Chœur d'Église ont chanté en musique le *Te Deum laudamus* avec d'orgues. Et à la fin l'*Exaudiat*.	MS fonds fr. 18531, 149v
1620	Peace between Louis XIII and Marie de Médicis	Aussi tost l'on commença à chanter en Musique le *Te Deum laudamus*, & à la fin *Domine salvum fac Regem*.	Godefroy II, 919; MS fonds fr. 18531, 151v
1621	Subjugation of Saint Jean d'Angély	... où est chanté le *Te Deum Laudamus* et à la fin l'*Exaudiat*.	MS fonds fr. 18531, 168v
1622	No stated purpose	Ci tost après a esté chanté le *Te Deum Laudamus* et à la fin du Pseaulme l'*Exaudiat*.	MS fonds fr.18531, 200r
1622	Peace of Montpellier	... on a sonné une Clochette qui servoit de signal aux orgues par où on a Commencé ensuite s'en chanté se *Te Deum* en musique par les chantres et musiciens qui étoient au lutrin, l'orgue faisans les intermèdes des Versets ... On après chanté l'*Exaudiat* en musique excellente sans intermède en forme de motet ...	MS nouv. acq. Fr 23474, 331-2
1627	Victory over the English	Aussi tost les Orgues commencèrent à sonner, & fut dit en Musique le *Te Deum laudamus*, & en suite le Pseaume *Exaudiat*.	Godefroy, II, 993

Table 5.5 (*cont.*)

Date	Event	Description	Source
1628	Subjugation of La Rochelle	... le Te Deum commença d'estre chanté en Musique, & après par trois fois *Domine salvum fac Regem*.	Godefroy, II, 999
1635	Victory in the Battle of Avain	... qui fit commencer à chanter le *Te Deum* en musique, & après *Domine salvum fac Regem*, répété trois fois.	Godefroy, II, 1002
1638	Birth of Louis XIV	... le *Te Deum* sera chanté, après le Psalme *Domine in virtute tua*, & *l'Exaudiat*.	Godefroy, II, 217
1640	Subjugation of Arras	... le *Te Deum* commença d'estre chanté à deux chœurs ... à la fin de laquelle on commença le *Domine salvum fac Regem*.	Godefroy, II, 1021

The extensive list in Fogel, *Cérémonies de l'information* (Appendices I and II) does not indicate the psalm performed, nor in general do the sources on which it is based.

Table 5.6 Psalms identified in the "Te Deum"/*entrée* ceremony

Date	Event	Description	Source
1624	*Entrée* into Lyon	As below	Lyon, Archives municipales, 10 G 442, n.f.
1642	*Entrée* into Lyon	Monsieur le Doyen entonna le Te Deum lequel fini il alla au milieu du chœur où il dit le verset *Benedicamus patrem et filium cum Sancto Spiritu*, et le chœur ayant répondu *Laudemus* Il dit l'oraison *Dominus Deus pater omnipotens et famulos tuos* etc. qui est dans le Bréviaire pour la procession de la Trinité. Ensuite Mr le sous-maître entonna *Domine salvum fac regem* au ton qu'on chante au psaume *Exaudiat* à la Benediction lequel verset fut répété trois fois par le chœur après lequel Mr le Doyen dit le verset *Domine in virtute tua laetabitur Rex* etc. et l'oraison *Quaesumus omnipotens Deus ut famulus tuum Ludovicus*.	Lyon, Archives municipales, 10 G 442, n.f.[a]

[a] Another account at 10 G 58 pp. 241–6.

entrée), seeing the pairing of the Te Deum hymn with the two psalms that were so central to royal ceremonial as a unifying feature of the coronation and the "Te Deum," a common thread that reminded the listener that "praise to God was synonymous with thanksgiving for the Holy Balm received by the French kings."[70] And yet, given the associations and history of Psalm 19 outlined in Chapter 4 and below, it seems that, alongside the *entrée*, we should probably reconsider at least those "Te Deum" ceremonies that featured the *Exaudiat*, especially when we remember that the complete psalm itself belongs to an entirely different tradition to the so-called coronation motets (the centonized motets that begin with the *Domine salvum* text) identified by Lowinsky and discussed in Chapter 2. Yet while we might be surprised to now find the *Exaudiat* in the context of both the *entrée* and "Te Deum," there is nothing in its broader liturgical or public use to suggest that it had different connotations here. Indeed, as I will argue in the remainder of this chapter, musical and historical evidence suggests that the *Exaudiat* remained a cry for help deep into the seventeenth century in all ceremonies in which it was performed, in both public and private contexts.

In addition to the non-liturgical evidence (primarily psalm translations and commentaries) presented in Chapter 4, all the evidence from more official liturgical sources points the same way. Roman liturgical books featuring processions, prayers, and other ceremonies for the safety of the king, or for peace or the resolution of war, all feature the common denominator of the *Exaudiat*. Thus, in the 1615 *Rituale Romanum*, the liturgy for processions in times of trouble, "Quacumque tribulatione," is entirely built around the psalm, featuring as it does the Major Litany, the Lord's Prayer, the *Exaudiat* itself, and then some closing versicles, responses, and collects.[71] A fifteenth-century processional from Angers, clearly conceived and used in time of war (since it contains short prayers added in a later hand in 1582 and 1614 for the protection of the king and his army when they are in danger) also contains psalms and prayers for the sins of the king and the people, a set of collects for peace, and specifies the *Exaudiat* for the protection of the king and the *Laetatus sum* as a prayer for peace.[72] The newly revised Paris *Processionale* of 1588, published at the height of the Wars of Religion, also calls for *Laetatus sum* (prayer for peace) and the *Exaudiat* (prayer for the protection of the king) in its rubric for a procession around the church, "Pro quacumque tribulatione," while the Paris *Missale* of 1602 specifies the *Exaudiat* as prayer for the king in a section of "Preces pro sancta & pro rege."[73]

---

[70] Van Orden, *Music, Discipline, and Arms*, p. 167.   [71] *Rituale Romanum*, 1615, p. 195.
[72] Bibliothèque municipale d'Angers, MS 2103, f. 19v.
[73] *Processionale noviter emendatum et auctum iuxta ritum insignis ecclesie & dicocesis Parisiensis. Quod quidem complectitur et continet ea que in Processionibus per totum anni curriculum sunt*

Outside the liturgy, but in other "public" (i.e. not under court control) or ceremonial circumstances, we know that the *Exaudiat* was sung when the king was in personal danger. For Louis XIII's journey to Bordeaux in 1615 in preparation for his marriage to Anne of Austria, the Bishop of Paris decreed to all churches in the diocese that they sing the *Exaudiat* after daily Mass, "that it might please the divine bounty to assist in his holy protection, to preserve him from all dangers and inconveniences."[74] And on May 20, 1628, during the siege of La Rochelle, a procession for the safety of the king was held at the Sainte-Chapelle, during which monks sang the *Miserere* and the *Exaudiat* "en musique."[75] Even as late as 1636, prayers ordained for the "succez des armes de sa Majestie contre tous les ennemies de son Estat," to be said as part of a Forty Hours' devotion, began with the Pentecost sequence *Veni sancte Spiritus* to invoke the grace of the Holy Spirit, continued with prayers for the church and the Pope, and then featured the *Exaudiat* itself as the *Prière pour le Roy*, a prayer which was immediately followed by an *oraison* "pour son armée."[76]

If all the evidence – liturgical sources, accounts of *entrées* and "Te Deums," psalm translations, paraphrases, and commentaries – suggests the widespread conception of the *Exaudiat* as a prayer for the king when he was in danger, a supplication to God to keep him safe on the battlefield or on a dangerous journey, what about musical settings for public performance? How might such settings support – or not – such a reading? No settings of the psalm survive from the sixteenth century before Ballard's 1599 publication (see Chapter 4), implying that the text itself was not the focus of compositional attention. (Du Caurroy, for example, did not provide, or at least publish, a setting in his 1609 *Preces ecclesiastices*.) The later published versions, such as those in the widely circulated collection by Bournonville (1612/25), were probably intended for the kinds of situations

---

cantanda (Paris, Societatem Typographicam, 1588); *Missale insignis ecclesiae Parisiensis restitutum et emendatum* (Paris, Stephanum Vallaetum, 1602), p. 138.

[74] *Mandement de Monseigneur l'Évesque de Paris pour le voyage du Roy* (Paris, François Julliot, 1615), p. 4: "afin qu'il plaise à la divine bonté d'assister de sa saincte protection, le préserver de tous dangers & inconvéniens..." Any number of other published and archival records attest to the same kind of practice. In Aix, for example, in 1616 the *actes de chapitre* record that the *Exaudiat* was sung as part of the prayers, processions, and expositions of the Blessed Sacrament for the health of the king; see Aix, Bibliothèque de Méjanes, MS 276, p. 145.

[75] Archives nationales de France, LL. 602, ff. 12r–14v, in Michel Brenet, *Les Musiciens de la Sainte-Chapelle du Palais* (Paris, Picard, 1910), p. 169.

[76] *Prières ordonnées par Monseigneur l'Archevesque de Paris pour dire aux Églises où sont les Prières de Quarante-heures. Pour le bon succez des armes de sa Majesté, contre tous les ennemies de son Estat* (Paris, Pierre Targa, 1636), p. 4. See Chapter 7 for the circumstances in 1636 that necessitated such prayers.

outlined above, where the *Exaudiat* was performed after Mass or where it featured in a procession or other extraordinary liturgy.[77] But these functional settings – frequently little more than *fauxbourdons* setting all verses and the doxology – do not really provide a "reading" of the psalm in the way that the Tours manuscript motets, with their interpolated and modified text, do for their psalms, nor do they seem appropriate for a major event such as a "Te Deum" or *entrée*.

There are, however, a number of settings that do shed light on the way in which the psalm was performed, and what it meant in such contexts. A setting in the Paris source from a section containing repertoire assembled in the 1630s features the *Domine salvum fac regem* verse sung three times in ABA musical form, just as the 1628 and 1642 accounts of the "Te Deum" describe (see Music Example 5.5).

In the same source, we also find a setting of four verses of the psalm, beginning with *Domine salvum* and ending with *Exaudiat*,[78] and another setting with a refrain in six voices (the *Domine salvum* verse) to be performed between four-voice settings of the remainder of the verses.[79] With their sumptuous scoring for large ensemble (sometimes in "two choirs"), it is entirely reasonable to assume that these very pieces were performed in a Te Deum ceremony at Notre-Dame in the later 1630s or early 1640s, especially given the association of the source with both the court and the cathedral.[80] A setting of the *Domine salvum* by Nicolas le Vavasseur (*maître des enfants* at the cathedral of Saint-Pierre in Lisieux), concluding his second book of *airs* of 1630, though surviving in only two voices, also seems appropriate for some kind of ceremony, adopting (as far as it is possible to tell) the same kind of homophonic declamatory style, pitting blocks of voices against each other.[81] Perhaps most strikingly, a fragment of the *dessus* voice of Abraham Blondet's 1611 *Officii Divae Ceciliae* preserves a setting of the *Domine salvum* verse in *fauxbourdon* to be performed in conjunction with the text "Exaltate Regem regum, &

---

[77] Jean Bournonville, *Octo cantica virginis matris* (Paris, Pierre Ballard, 1612/25).
[78] Ibid., f. 90r.   [79] Ibid., ff. 67v–69r.
[80] One other work in the Paris manuscript, f. 47r, features the *Domine salvum fac regem* verse prominently within a much longer and unrelated text, but is very likely to have been composed after 1638, when the sense in which the psalm was heard does indeed seem to be changing. We should also note the existence of an elaborate setting for nine voices and organ in the repertoire of San Luigi de Francesi, Rome, in which the final verse is modified to "Domine salvum fac regem nostrum Ludovicum"; see Galliano Ciliberti, *"Qu'une plus belle nüit ne pouvoit preceder le beau jour": Musica e cerimonie nelle istituzioni religiose francesi a Roma nel Seicento* (Perugia, Aguaplano, 2016), pp. 183–8.
[81] Nicolas le Vavasseur, *Second livre d'airs a IIII. et V. parties* (Paris, Pierre Ballard, 1629/30).

Music Example 5.5 Anonymous, *Domine salvum fac regem*.
Paris manuscript, f. 95r.

hymnum dicite Deo in aeternum," followed by a "Vivat rex" adopting the same repetitive formula as the Newberry/Avignon setting discussed above.[82] (For this juxtaposition, see below.)

[82] Abraham Blondet, *Officii Divae Ceciliae virgo et martyr Musicorum patronae musici concentibus expressi* (Paris, Pierre Ballard, 1611), p. 28.

Music Example 5.5 (*cont.*)

But what about the *entrée*, and what about musical settings of the *Exaudiat* (rather than the *Domine salvum*), the complete text that was called for earlier in the century in both the *entrée* and the "Te Deum"? An alternatim setting, again by Le Vavasseur (from his 1626 volume) may well have been performed as Louis XIII traveled through Lisieux in 1626, although there was no formal *entrée* made on that occasion, nor does the

Music Example 5.6 Nicolas Le Vavasseur, *Exaudiat te Dominus* (vv. 1–2). *Airs a III. IIII. et V. parties* (Paris, Pierre Ballard, 1626).

Music Example 5.6 (*cont.*)

setting in itself affect our understanding of the text (other than to confirm that it now merited performance *en musique* rather than in *fauxbourdon*) (see Music Example 5.5.) That said, a dedicatory Ode to the composer reports that "Déjà tes doctes Motets / Chantez devant nos authels / Ont contre-quarré la Peste" (Already your learned motets / Sung before our altars / Have fought the Plague), probably confirming the role of the *Exaudiat* in ceremonies "in quacumque tribulatione."[83]

But one setting in the Newberry/Avignon source confirms the liturgical evidence that characterizes the *Exaudiat* as a prayer in times of great troubles. As with all the other works in Case MS 5123, this setting of the *Exaudiat*, preserved just a few pages away from the *Vivat rex* (which helped to place the source at the 1622 *entrée*) survives in just one, *superius* voice part, but its companion sources (Case 5136) testify to the presence of a twelve-voice choir in Avignon at this time. So, although we have no direct evidence for the scope of the ensemble that performed it, it is entirely possible that this *Exaudiat* setting was scored for six, eight, or even twelve voices; certainly, from the surviving *superius* part we can infer that the setting was a far cry from all other extent versions of the psalm, a dynamic and complex piece of polyphony (see Music Example 5.7.) And again, even if we have no irrefutable evidence to place this work conclusively in the *entrée* liturgy itself (the published account is almost silent on the liturgical phase), this work was clearly performed in Avignon, around the same time,

---

[83] See Nicolas le Vavasseur, *Airs a III. IIII. et v. parties* (Paris, Pierre Ballard, 1626). See also note 78.

Music Example 5.7 Anonymous, *Exaudiat te in die dolentis animae tua*, surviving superius part.
Newberry/Avignon Manuscript (MS 5123), pp. 19–20.

by the same forces – a substantial and expert cathedral choir – and in the same kind of context – the liturgy, or at least a major public liturgical or paraliturgical celebration – as the 1622 *entrée*. The reading of the psalm that this work provides is therefore unlikely to be an outlier.

Unlike the few other surviving settings from the early part of Louis's reign, such as the *Domine salvum* and *Exaudiat* settings mentioned above, this version modifies the text of the psalm (see Table 5.7) to emphasize the supplicatory nature of the text. Rather than "in the day of tribulation," the text offers the alternative "in the day of the suffering of your soul." And rather than sending help from the sanctuary, the psalmist begs for God's Angel to come. But most significantly, rather than God saving the king in the generic sense of the standard *Exaudiat* text, the psalmist here asks, "O Lord God, save King Louis in the day on which we call upon you." Not only that, but, calling on text from Psalm 17, the psalmist provides a reason – "For you deliver a humble people, but the haughty eyes you bring down"; in other words, Louis and/or the French people are sufficiently humble for God to save. This setting of the *Exaudiat*, then, confirms that the psalm itself, even when performed in the most public of contexts and in the most elaborate musical settings, was still understood as a supplication, a cry to God for help in extreme adversity or battle, just as it was in the private chamber of Louis XIII or ceremonies of the Congregation of the Penitents of Notre-Dame for Henri III.[84]

---

[84] It is interesting to compare this *Exaudiat* with a setting of psalm verses in Newberry Case MS 5136, part-books 1 and 2, pp. 2–3. Between repeated statements of Psalm 95:1 used as a refrain ('Sing to the Lord a new song'), the text presents Psalm 54:2 ('Hear my prayer, O God, despise not

Table 5.7 Text and translation of *Exaudiat te Dominus*, Newberry/Avignon manuscript

19:2. Exaudiat te **in die dolentis animae tuae:** protegat te et nomen Dei Jacob.	May [the Lord] hear you **in the day of the suffering of your soul**; may the name of the God of Jacob protect thee.
19:3. Mittat tibi **Deus Angelus suum** de Sion.	May **God** send thee **his Angel** out of Sion.
19:10. Domine **Deus salva Regem Ludovicum** in die qua invocaverimus te.	O Lord **God save King Louis** in the day in which we call upon thee.
17:28. **Quoniam populum humilem salvum facies quod oculos superborum humiliabis.**	**For you deliver a humble people, but the haughty eyes you bring down.**

Modifications to psalm text in bold.

How, then, might we explain the choice of this text for the *entrée* into Avignon in 1622 (or in comparable circumstances), and particularly the unmodified *Exaudiat* (we assume) in Troyes in 1629, given our assumption that such events were typically celebrations of victory? And how might such a revised understanding account for the appearance of Psalm 19 in the *entrée*, the "Te Deum," and in other "public" liturgies more generally?

We can begin to explain this apparent paradox by considering a comment by the author of the Troyes account. Addressing the king in the prefatory material, the author reminds him of a traditional commonplace, that "to thank God for a benefit received, it is to ask him for another which he will unfailingly grant us."[85] This observation in turn leads the author to report that the inhabitants of Troyes considered the *entrée* itself to consist of two corresponding parts:[86]

> These are the sacrifices [i.e. the *entrée*] which we divide into two parts: that is to say into thanksgiving, which represents Justice, and into vows/requests and prayers, which represent Piety.

---

my petition'), 54:3 ('Attend to me and hear me'), 54:17 ('But I have cried to God, and our Lord will save me.'), 54:19 (Douai–Reims translation unclear; New International Version, 'He rescues me unharmed from the battle waged against me, even though many oppose me'). While we can only place this work in the general context of early 1620s Avignon, the choice of texts seems to express exactly the same sentiment as the *Exaudiat*, a supplication and thanksgiving for safety in battle.

[85] *Troyes, 1629*, n.p.: "un antien Père de l'Église nous asseure que remercier Dieu d'un bénéfice receu, c'est luy en demander un autre qu'il nous accorde infailliblement."

[86] Ibid., n.p.: "Ce sont les sacrifices que nous diviserons en deux parties: sçavoir en actions de grâces, qui représentent la Iustice, & en vœux & prières, qui signifient la Pieté."

It is relatively straightforward to see the first part, the "actions de grâces" which signified "Justice," as represented not just by the "processional phase" of the event and the triumphal arches, but also by the *Te Deum*, as well as by the first of the concluding responses (all based on psalms) specified by the *Pontificale*: Psalm 71:2 "V. Give the King your justice, O God; R. And your righteousness to a king's son."[87]

But as a result of this thanksgiving, "un autre bénéfice" could be granted through the second part of the ceremony, the "Vœux et prières, qui signifient la Piété"; and it is this part, the *Exaudiat*, that reflects the other dimension to the entrée at Troyes and, we assume, others – not just a celebration of victory, but a supplication to God for assistance in adversity. Thus, the people of Troyes, in describing their "vœux et prières," declared:[88]

> we ask him with heart and mouth, that he will long preserve you in France, that he will always be present with you, that his Holy Angels will accompany you, that his Holy Spirit will preside in your councils, that these high mountains that nearly reach the Heavens, and seem to oppose your glorious plan, will humbly abase themselves before you, that the sea which you have already catpured and enslaved will be calm, and that the great rivers will halt the impetuousity of their flow at the approach your Majesty.

This call for help against the mountains, seas, and rivers is, of course, generic metaphor, but in this case also closely mirrors the imagery used in the royal psalm *In exitu Israel* (Psalm 113; see Chapter 3), a psalm that recounts the trust the nation of Israel placed in God to deliver them from adversity.

> [3] The sea saw and fled: [the River] Jordan was turned back.
> [4] The mountains skipped like rams, and the hills like the lambs of the flock.

And perhaps even more importantly, such imagery also reflected the reality of the king's imminent and dangerous journey. Having recently conquered the seas (the English fleet at La Rochelle), Louis was about to embark on one of the most heroic exploits of his reign, crossing the river Rhône and literally scaling mountains, leading (at great personal danger) his army across the Alps to liberate the city of Casale in one of the most famous

---

[87] *Pontificale*, 1615, p. 382.
[88] *Troyes, 1629*, n.p.: "nous luy demanderons de coeur & de bouche, qu'il vous conserve longuement à la France, qu'il vous assiste tousiours, que ses Saincts Anges vous accompagnent, que son S. Esprit préside en vos conseils, que ces hautes montagnes qui voisinent les Cieux, & semblent *s'opposer à vostre glorieux dessin*, s'humilient & s'abaissent devant vous, que la mer que vous avez désia captivée & enchaisnée, se calme, & ces grands fleuves arrestent l'impétuosité de leurs courses à l'abord de vostre Majesté."

battles of the War of the Mantuan Succession.[89] And we know that at Troyes a special wooden chapel or oratory had been constructed in the nave in which Louis spent the whole ceremony, the account telling us that while the Te Deum and *Exaudiat* were being sung, he prayed and looked attentively at the many relics placed on the high altar.[90]

The *Exaudiat*, then, with its long association with the darkest moments of the sixteenth-century Wars of Religion, and its supplicatory tone, was an entirely appropriate component of the liturgy – the king was in personal danger, the country in a state of disarray, and the army barely able to cope. Thus, while the author of the account at Troyes acknowledged that the state of the nation was now much improved, the recent context for this *entrée* was nonetheless chaotic:[91]

What confusion? Good God: what disorder! Rebellion, felony, factions, divisions, libertinage, troubles, fire, blood, sacrilege, and in one word, the war visited but ravaged the most beautiful Provinces of your Kingdom . . .

This supplicatory dimension that the *Exaudiat* brings to the liturgy is reinforced by the remainder of the responses specified in the Pontifical, which again take verses of psalms (including the *Exaudiat*, and in one case modified to include "the king") to ask for God's assistance and succor, the final versicle and response ("Lord, hear my prayer") taken from the Penitential Psalm 101, described in the as "Prayer to the Eternal King for Help: A prayer of one afflicted, when faint and pleading before the Lord."[92] And we should not forget that the final section of the Te Deum itself, taken

---

[89] Moote, *Louis XIII*, pp. 201–2.

[90] *Troyes, 1629*, p. 43: "Pendant laquelle musique sa Majesté faisant ses prières regarda attentivement plusieurs fois les précieux reliquaires en grand nombre de ladite Église, que l'on avoit mis sur le Maistre Autel, & à main droicte le chef St. Loup, jadis Évesque de Troys, & à gauche la Chasse d'argent de St. Savinien Disciple de S. Pierre, & Apostre de Champagne." The precise construction of the chapel is described in Troyes, AD, G 1613.

[91] *Troyes, 1629*, n.p.: "Quelle confusion! bon Dieu; quel désordre! La rébellion, la félonie, les factions, les divisions, le libertinage, les troubles, le feu, le sang, le sacrilège, & en un mot, la guerre cantonnoit, mais ravageoit les plus belles Provinces de vostre Royaume . . ." This sense of complete desolation is confirmed by many sources, but see for example *Actions de grâces et allégresses de la France sur la Reduction de la Rochelle à l'obeysance du Roy* (Paris, Julien Jacquin, 1628), pp. 7, 13, which frames the celebrations within France "comme saizie de la crainte d'une totale désolation, qu'après la tourmente qui s'estoit eslevée en ce Royaume . . . S'en est faict, tous ces broüillars sont dissipez, le deül que la France portoit en son Coeur, est changé en rejiouyssance, & tel paroissoit demy mort, attaint qu'il estoit d'affliction, qu'à present il paroist estre ressuscite."

[92] *Pontificale*, p. 383. The responses include Psalm 85:2, modified ('O Lord, save our King, who puts his trust in you'); 19:3 ('May he send thee help from the sanctuary: and defend thee out of Sion'); and 101:2 ('Lord, hear my prayer, and let my cry come to thee').

from the psalms and also in verse and response form, expresses entirely similar supplicatory sentiments: indeed, the psalms used are those categorized by Gunkel as "Psalms of personal complaint," psalms that were written in life-threatening situations and make prominent use of words such as "distress," "danger," and "fear."[93]

Thus at Troyes and elsewhere, the concluding moments of the ceremony – the performance of the *Exaudiat* highlighted by the account, and the final responses – were characterized by supplication, with the voice of the psalmist (speaking as either King David or the people of Israel) crying out to God for his help.

The danger at Troyes for which the people prayed was, of course, not unique to this situation. France was a nation continuously at war, both internally – the religious wars until 1628 – and externally – the Thirty Years' War (1618–48) and the Franco-Spanish War (1635–49), not to mention spin-offs such as the War of the Mantuan Succession – and the king or his army were in almost constant danger. It would therefore have been appropriate at almost every *entrée* to give thanks for the most recent success while looking forward to the inevitable future danger. For the "Te Deum," too, the thanksgiving celebrated at the king's command – his letters asked for the singing of the Te Deum, but did not specify the psalm – would be matched by the same kind of prayers that we saw for the protection of the king when he was in danger, chosen by the clergy. Even in the "Te Deums" that Godefroy associates with, for example, the marriage of Henri IV or the birth of Louis XIV, events where we might think the *Exaudiat* as I have framed it would be out of place, these events took place in the context of dangerous military campaigns. For the birth of Louis XIV, the appropriately celebratory Te Deum and *Domine in virtute* were performed by "trois chœurs de musique excellente."[94] But since June, the French had been besieging the Spanish border city of Fuenterrabía, the army led by Henri de Bourbon, Prince de Condé, second in line to the French throne, and Henri d'Escoubleau de Sourdis. On September 7, the siege was lifted by Spanish troops in a major defeat for France, something that those in Paris were probably anticipating. At the same time, the French Navy had been in action against the Spanish Navy since

---

[93] Hermann Gunkel, *Introduction to the Psalms: The Genres of the Religious Lyric of Israel* (Macon, Mercer University Press, 1998), p. 130. The final lines of the Te Deum include Psalm 122:3 ('Have mercy on us, O Lord, have mercy on us'); and 33:22 ('Let they mercy, O Lord, be on us, as we have hoped in thee').

[94] *Le Mercure françois*, 1638, p. 307.

the middle of August in an important battle described at great length in the *Mercure françois*.[95] Thus, at the same time as celebrating the birth of the Dauphin, the *Exaudiat* was an important public acknowledgment of the continued danger the nation faced. For that reason, as Charles Bernard reports, the response to the birth of the Dauphin was as much pious as festive:[96]

> all the other towns of France [i.e. outside Paris] in turn, did not miss the opportunity to demonstrate their joy, not just with fireworks, *comédies*, *balets*, and other diversions, but by prayers, processions, and all other acts of piety.

Likewise, for the marriage of Henri IV and Marie de Médicis in Lyon on December 17, 1600, the "Te Deum" was "celebrated" with the *Exaudiat* in Paris on January 9, 1601. But his wedding was only held in Lyon because of its proximity to the battlefield: Henri had personally been leading the French army for six months in the Franco-Savoyard War of 1600–1, a war which was not ultimately resolved until the Treaty of Lyon on January 17, 1601, a week after the Paris ceremony.

Given the congruence of the "Te Deum" and the *entrée*, then, the liturgy and music tell us that both events seem to be about two things – an act of thanksgiving for a recent success, followed by a prayer for the safety of the king, his army, and the nation as it was "seized by the fear of total desolation."[97] In these circumstances the Te Deum and *Exaudiat* – either in the *entrée* or the "Te Deum" ceremony – were not exclusively (or even primarily) celebrations, but simple acts that resonated with many other liturgies of thanksgiving (the Te Deum) or supplication (the *Exaudiat*). After the immediate danger to the kingdom gradually subsided – though this would not be until well into the reign of Louis XIV – the direct supplicatory quality does seem to have been downplayed, and by the time the *Domine salvum fac regem* became part of the revised liturgy of the Chapelle Royale in 1660 it no longer had the urgent quality it had when the *Exaudiat* formed part of Henri III's chapel liturgy. Nevertheless, the designation "prière pour le roy" that accompanied the text (and accompanied it in its musical journey into the nineteenth century and settings by Berlioz, Gounod, and others) undoubtedly concealed a dark subtext rooted in the millenarian days of the Wars of Religion, a subtext that Louis XIII was not afraid to embrace and share with his people.

---

[95] *Le Mercure françois*, 1638, pp. 67–101.
[96] Charles Bernard, *Histoire du Roy Louis XIII* (Paris, Nicolas de Sercy, 1646), p. 429: "tous les autre villes de la France à leur tour, ne manquèrent pas de tesmoigner leur allégresse, non seulement par des feux, des Comédies, des balets, & autres recréations, mais par des prières, des processions, & toutes autres actions de piété."
[97] *Actions de grâces et allégresses.*

6 | Plainchant and the Politics of Rhythm

The Royal Abbey of Montmartre and the Royal Congregation of the Oratory of Jesus Christ

We should not lose sight of the fact that in the majority of circumstances throughout the late sixteenth and into the seventeenth century – be it in a parish church, cathedral, monastic house, or even a royal chapel – the performance of composed sacred "music" as part of the regular liturgy was a relative rarity. On a Sunday or Feast Day, singers recruited and paid for their musical ability might perform a polyphonic Magnificat or psalm setting at Vespers, or a polyphonic ordinary setting at Mass, but through the daily cycle of the Offices and Masses that occupied clerics at relatively high-status institutions (a cathedral for instance, would probably celebrate a full round of offices and several votive masses each day), the vast majority of the liturgy was performed in what we would generically call "Gregorian" chant, albeit possibly embellished with improvised performance practices such as *fauxbourdon* or *chant sur livre*, or performed in alternatim with composed or improvised organ music.[1]

During the sixteenth century, such chant had increasingly been seen through the lens of humanist teachings, with more and more attention being paid to the appropriate relationship between text and melody, and with the rhetorical, affective, and speechlike dimension coming more and more into focus.[2] But the Council of Trent gave renewed impulse to such efforts (many of its doctrinal aims coinciding with the literary aims of the humanists), and so by the end of the century, in both Italy and France, the

---

[1] For an overview of chant and liturgy in France and its relation to polyphony and organ music, see Denise Launay, *La Musique religieuse en France du Concile de Trente à 1804* (Paris, Klincksieck, Sociéte française de musicologie, 1994). For an overview of these improvised practices, see Philippe Canguilhem, 'Pratique et context du faux-bourdon et du chant sur le livre en France (xvie–xixe siècles)', *Études grégoriennes*, 38 (2011), 181–99; Deborah Kauffman, 'Fauxbourdon in the seventeenth and eighteenth centuries: "Le Secours d'une douce harmonie"', *Music and Letters*, 90/1 (2009), 68–93. For the participation of the organ in the liturgy (though focusing on a later period), see Edward Higginbottom, 'French classical organ music and the liturgy', *Proceedings of the Royal Musical Association*, 103 (1977), 19–40.

[2] For the rhetorical aspects of chant in the late sixteenth century, see Barbara Swanson, *Speaking in Tones: Plainchant, Monody, and the Rhetoric of Antiquity in Early Modern Italy* (PhD dissertation, Case Western Reserve University, 2013), especially pp. 1–59; see also Don Harran, *Word–Tone Relations in Musical Thought: From Antiquity to the Seventeenth Century* (Neuhausen-Stuttgart, American Institute of Musicology, 1986).

chant repertoire began to be subjected to wide ranging yet somewhat fragmented humanist-inspired revisions that attempted to match syllable length more closely to a classical ideal of speech declamation.[3]

In Italy, this process was formalized in 1577 when, following the decrees of the Council of Trent, Gregory XIII commissioned Palestrina and Zoilo "to purge, correct, and reform, Gregorian chant."[4] But since the two composers abandoned their task shortly afterward, it fell to Giovanni Guidetti to produce the first published response to the Pope's call, issuing his *Directorium Chori* in 1582, a volume that used a variety of notational innovations to specify exact syllable length, all to be performed in simple harmonic ratios according to Pythagorean principles.[5] (Guidetti focused on so-called *accentus* chants, speechlike recitational chants, rather than song-like *concentus* chants.) Later editions of Guidetti's books dispensed with the precise notation, and by the time that the so-called Medicean edition of the Gradual under the direction of Soriano and Anerio appeared in 1614–15, note length had clearly become less of a priority.[6] In France the overall picture is less clear. While the famous reformed chant repertories of Guillaume-Gabriel Nivers, together with his and others' associated theoretical works from the 1650s–80s, have been the focus of studies by Cécile Davy-Rigaux, Patricia Ranum, and others, the earlier part of the century remains relatively unexplored.[7] In the late sixteenth century, too, there was

---

[3] Edith Weber, 'L'Intelligibilité du texte dans la crise religieuse et musicale du XVIe siècle: incidences du Concile de Trente', *Études Grégoriennes*, 24 (1992), 195–202.

[4] Robert Hayburn, *Papal Legislation on Sacred Music, 95 AD to 1977 AD* (Collegeville, Liturgical Press, 1979), p. 27.

[5] Giovanni Guidetti, *Directorium chori* (Rome, Granjon, 1582). See Swanson, *Speaking in Tones*, for a bibliography of his other works.

[6] The classic study is Raphael Molitor, *Die nachtridentinische Choral-reform zu Rom* (Leipzig, F. E. C. Leuckart, 1901–2); see also Joshua Joel Veltman, *Prosody and Rhythm in the Post-Tridentine Reform of Plainchant* (PhD dissertation, Ohio State University, 2004).

[7] Cécile Davy-Rigaux, *Guillaume-Gabriel Nivers: un art de chant grégorien sous le règne de Louis XIV* (Paris, CNRS, 2004); Patricia Ranum, '"Le Chant doit perfectionner la prononciation, & non pas la corrompre": L'Accentuation du chant grégorien d'après les traités de Dom Jacques Le Clerc et dans le chant de Guillaume-Gabriel Nivers', in Jean Duron (ed.), *Plain-chant et liturgie en France au XVIIe siècle* (Versailles, Centre de musique baroque de Versailles, 1997), pp. 59–83; Cécile Davy-Rigaux, 'Le Clerc et Jumilhac et la question de la "durée ou mesure des sons" dans le plain-chant', *Études Grégoriennes*, 31 (2003), 105–31; see also the other studies in Duron (ed.), *Plain-chant et liturgie*, in particular Jean-Yves Hameline, 'Le Plain-chant dans la pratique ecclésiastique aux lendemains du Concile de Trente et des reformes post-conciliaires'. The most specific, though brief, account of the reforms to the chant itself in France during the late sixteenth and early seventeenth centuries remains Amédée Gastoué, 'Les Livres de plain-chant en France, 1583–1630', *La Tribune de Saint-Gervais*, 20 (1914–15), 1–4, 29–33; see also the same author's *Le Graduel et l'Antiphonaire Romains* (Lyon, Janin frères, 1913) and Xavier Bisaro, *Guide historique et pratique du plain-chant et du faux-bourdon. France XVIIe–XVIIIe siècles*

certainly a parallel if much less dramatic move (and much less centralized) to revise the chant of the wider Gallican church, with each province being charged with "correcting" their own chant books to incorporate liturgical changes mandated by the Council of Trent and, at the same time, minor revisions to the chant. But in the early seventeenth century we also find two important instances of chant revisions that were as thoroughgoing as those of Nivers, both of which originated in religious houses that made chant and music central to their identity, and both of which had close connections to the court of Louis XIII.

The way in which these two religious houses approached their chant in the context of the wider religious and political circumstances of early seventeenth-century France is the subject of this chapter. The Royal Benedictine Abbey of Montmartre reformed its chant during the period c. 1610–30, partly during the tenure of its music director, court composer Antoine Boësset, although those associated with the Abbey published its revised *Antiphonier* after his death, in 1646. A stronghold of the vestiges of League sentiment, the Abbey was effectively under Guise patronage, a spiritual home of numerous *dévots*, a center for the celebration of the Eucharist, and a bastion of ultramontane and thus potentially antiroyal sentiment.[8] The Royal Congregation of the Oratory of Jesus Christ, created its repertory of chant over much the same period, some of it being published in the *Brevis psalmodiae ratio* of 1634. Located next to the Louvre, its church gradually coming to supplant the chapels of both the Louvre and Petit-Bourbon, the Congregation was founded by similarly *dévot* figures, although, in contrast to Montmartre, the Oratorians ultimately aligned themselves closely with the king.[9] As we might expect, then, the way in which these two houses approached the process of chant reform

---

(Collection Numérique du CMBV, 2017). The broader history of the reception of reformed liturgical and chant books in France is very thoroughly explored in Prosper Guéranger, *Institutions liturgiques*, 2nd ed., 4 vols. (Paris, Victor Palmé, 1878–85), pp. 408–536.

[8] For the music-historical literature on this chant repertory, see Peter Bennett, 'Antoine Boësset's sacred music for the Royal Abbey of Montmartre: Newly identified polyphony and *plain-chant musical* from the "Deslauriers" manuscript (F-Pn V^{ma} rés. 571)', *Revue de Musicologie*, 91/2 (2005), 322–67; and Peter Bennett, 'Chant reform at the Royal Benedictine Abbey of Montmartre, 1607–46: The evidence of Antoine Boësset', in William Renwick (ed.) *Chant Old and New* (Ottawa, Institute of Medieval Music, 2012), pp. 189–213. For Boësset's polyphonic compositions, many of which interact with the chant, see Peter Bennett (ed.), 'Antoine Boësset: Sacred Works', *Recent Researches in the Music of the Baroque Era*, 164–5, 2 parts (Middleton, A-R Editions, 2010).

[9] See Philippe Vendrix, 'Pour les grands et les autres: la réforme oratorienne du plain-chant', in Duron (ed.), *Plain-chant et liturgie*; and Amédée Gastoué, 'Le Chant des Oratoriens: Louis XIII maître de chapelle', *La Tribune de Saint-Gervais*, 19 (1913–14), 121–6 and 150–4.

(or more accurately chant reinvention) differed dramatically: set in the wider context of chant reform with which I will begin, we can see in these approaches competing visions not just of the relationship between music and text, but of the influence of the key *dévot* figures behind these monastic houses, who worked either reluctantly to legitimate the king's power or to subtly undermine it.

Chant Reform in France to *c.* 1610

Given the interest in uniting biblical and classical approaches to text and its declamation outlined in Chapter 1, it should come as no surprise that chant reformers in France were as, if not more, enthusiastic than those in Italy about new ways of setting text to chant, and even more eager to put into effect the textual reforms agreed at the Council of Trent.[10] The leader of the French delegation to Trent, for example, Charles, Cardinal de Lorraine (d. 1574), Archbishop of Reims, was among the first to do so. A member of the Guise family, Charles aligned himself with Rome in many ways, a fact that may have increased his appetite for externally mandated chant reform. At the Council of Reims in 1564, called by Charles shortly after his return from Trent, the record of proceedings declared that:[11]

As for the lengthy prolongation of chant on the last syllable of each antiphon [often used to mean chant in general], a prolongation commonly called a "neume," since one sees that it wastes much time for no purpose, and that, for another thing, this neume is still sung at the end of the last antiphons of Vespers, the Nocturns [of Matins], the Magnificat and the Benedictus, it is appropriate to remove it. In the same way one will shorten the chant, as far as one can, when one finds on a single syllable or word more notes than are appropriate. One will take care to preserve in the chant the declamation suitable for the letters and the words, and, as much as one can, that the quantity is observed.

Such attention to prosody is entirely in keeping with what we know about Charles. Around 1558, while in the Cardinal's employment, Jacques Arcadelt had composed a setting of verses from Virgil's *Aeneid*, *At trepida et coeptis*, a work that – while resorting to occasional moments of

---

[10] The French church did not officially adopt the decrees of the Council of Trent for many decades. Their influence instead was gradual; see below and Jervis, *The Gallican Church*.
[11] Latin text in Philippe Labbé and Gabriel Coassartii, *Sacrosancta Concilia ad regiam editionem* (Venice, Sebastianum Coleti), Vol. 20, column *1314 (French translation in Gastoué, 'Les Livres de plain-chant', 2; translation of Gastoué my own).*

counterpoint – essentially sets the text in homophonic style that respects syllable quantity in a manner reminiscent of (although actually anticipating) *musique mesurée*.[12] Ronsard's 1559 *Hymne de tresillustre prince Charles cardinal de Lorraine* describes a performance of this piece by the Ferrabosco brothers (in Charles's presence) in which they played the lower voices on the lute, with a solo singer declaiming the top line, and we can see in this mode of performance the seeds of later humanist experiments in monody.[13] Boucher's famous 1579 biography of Charles and his brother Francis, *La Conjunction des lettres et des armes*, confirms this interest in classical declamation, the author making a strikingly precise diagnosis of the problems that were considered to beset chant at this time:[14]

He [Charles] reforms the chant of the church. And because the prolongation of liturgical chant is for the most part on the short syllables of the words, so that frequently short syllables are made long, and long are made short, he specifically commanded that the chant correspond to the quantity of the syllable, and not the syllable to that length and variation of the chant.

Charles was not alone in his desire to see a more humanist text declamation. In 1565 the Council of Cambrai had reaffirmed the need to avoid "prolixity" in chant (i.e. melismas on short syllables),[15] but it was the later Councils, those held in the 1580s, that reinforced the need to adopt changes

---

[12] See also Kate van Orden, 'Les Vers lascifs d'Horace: Arcadelts Latin Chansons', *Journal of Musicology*, 14/3 (1996), 338–69.

[13] See Jeanice Brooks, 'Italy, the ancient world and the French musical inheritance in the sixteenth century: Arcadelt and Clereau in the service of the Guises', *Journal of the Royal Musical Association*, 121/2 (1996), 188. The musicians of the Académie had ultimately settled on a multi-voiced homophonic technique to recreate the music of the ancients, although Pontus de Tyard had argued for monody. See Chapter 2, note 40 for a discussion of lute-song vs. polyphonic performance.

[14] "Il reforme le chant de l'église. Et pour autant que la prolongation du chant ecclésiastique est pour la plus-part sur les syllabes brèves des dictions, de façon que le plus souvent on fait longue celle qui est brève, & brève celle qui est longue: il a ordonné expressément, que le chant respondit a la quantité de la syllabe, & non la syllabe a ceste longueur & diurnité de chant. Car voicy qu'il allégoit: Si en une harangue civile, qui se fera touchant les affaires & négoces d'une République, l'orateur se destourne tant soit peu hors de la mesure: S'il commet quelque faute à prolonger les longues syllabes, & abréger les brèves, il est moqué, il est mesprise: en l'Église, qui requiert un geste plus modéré en ceux qui chantent au Seigneur Dieu, laquelle comme est la maistresse des meurs, aussi est-elle la mère & nourrice des bonnes arts & sciences, si tu faux, n'estimes tu la faute non plus, que celle qui est commise en un plaidoyer, ou en quelque chanson rustique?" Nicolas Boucher, *La Conjunction des lettres et des armes* (Reims, Jean de Foigny, 1579), pp. 20–1. Translation taken from Brooks, *Italy*, p. 164. Brooks translates "chant" as "song," but in this case I believe the English "chant" is a closer rendering.

[15] "Tollatur illa prolixitas quae ad rem non pertinet, quam solent in fine antiphonarum in cathedralibus ecclesiis maxime prolixius abuli"; Gastoué, 'Les Livres de plain-chant', 3.

to the liturgy called for by Trent (although not receiving Trent as official policy) while continuing to amend and modify the chant. Thus, at the Council of Rouen in 1581, it was decreed that the revised books should be printed after the models published by Pius V (the Breviary and the Missal) and used in all religious houses, both secular and monastic.[16] Likewise, at the Council of Reims in 1583, the bishops were exhorted to inspect their liturgical books and, if they found any problems, to reprint them according to the Roman usage, while also making sure that the chant reflected the text.[17] It is especially significant that it was these two Councils, the first of a total of eight held across France in the 1580s, that took the lead in closely following a Roman model when we consider that the new Archbishop of Reims was Louis, Cardinal de Guise, brother of Henri, Duc de Guise, the leader of the League at war with Henri III, who had succeeded his uncle Charles, Cardinal de Lorraine, on his death in 1574.[18] In one of the most bloody episodes of the Wars of Religion, both brothers, Louis and Henri, would be assassinated by the king in 1588, resulting not long thereafter in the assassination of the king himself in 1589. Likewise, the leader of the Council of Rouen, Archbishop Charles de Bourbon, was aligned with Guises and the League, having been proclaimed the rightful heir to Henri III and anointed king in a secret ceremony in 1584. On Henri III's assassination in 1589, Charles was proclaimed king of France by the League, only ceding to Henri IV when it became clear that the League's aims would be satisfied by the new king.

The association of the Roman liturgy (as a symbol for Papal authority) with something potentially hostile to the Gallican Church and its identity (and through it the French king) was long-standing. France had for many years enjoyed "Gallican liberties," an independence from Rome not shared by others in the Catholic world in which the Pope had much less authority (in particular to appoint Bishops) and in which the king, the Parlement, and the Council of Bishops instead vied for power against each other in matters ecclesiastical.[19] The adoption of reforms, then, were controversial;

---

[16] Labbé, *Sacrosancto Concilium* (Venice, Coleti and Hieron, 1733), Vol. 21, column 620; see also Guéranger, *Institutions liturgiques*, p. 440.

[17] Labbé, *Sacrosancto Concilium*, Vol. 21, column 693: "sed integra canticorum ecclesiasticorum verba, sensumque referens."

[18] For a full discussion of the way the eight Councils (the others were Bordeaux, Tours, Aix, Toulouse, and Narbonne) adopted Trent, see Guéranger, *Institutions liturgiques*, Vol. 1, pp. 440–9.

[19] Jervis, *The Gallican Church*, pp. 12–13: "that a national Church, while following the broad track of Latin tradition as to the primacy of the 'Cathedra Petri' may witness at the same time to the co-ordinate power of government which resides by Divine right in the whole Episcopal

after all, one of the central demands of the League had been to receive the decrees of Council of Trent, to secure the sovereignty of the Pope, and to abrogate the liberties of the Gallican Church, which they saw simply as a justification for heresy.[20] The adoption of the details of Tridentine liturgy (modifications to the calendar such as replacing local French feasts with Roman feasts, removal of sequences, reform to chant, etc.,) thus followed a tortuous path, being received piecemeal and always associated with controversy. Nevertheless, in 1580 Henri III allowed the printing of the Roman Breviary in France (at the instigation of the Jesuits), and in 1583 he even allowed the revised Roman liturgy to be adopted by the *chapelle royale*, presumably as an act of appeasement to League forces; the 1583 statutes of the *chapelle royale* record the introduction of this revised liturgy, and the attention that those celebrating it were to pay to text declamation in the performance of chant [my emphasis]:[21]

All the Divine Service which is said or sung in the said Chapel when in plain chant will be according to the usage of Rome ...

... his Majesty ordains that all the people of the church who serve in the said chapel should study to pronounce well to say or sing devotedly, *making well the points and accents* in the Mass as well as the hours and all other divine serves which are said or sung by them having regard for the psalmody in not beginning one verse before the other is finished, ...

As the century turned, the Roman books gradually began to gain wider acceptance.[22] The Assemblée de Clergé of 1605–6 agreed to receive the new

---

college; that the Canon Law, not the will of a personally infallible Pontiff is the standard of the Church's jurisprudence; that it is possible to hold the doctrinal creed committed to the Church from the beginning without acquiescing in the Roman usurpation in other departments of the ecclesiastical economy; – in short that in order to be Catholic it is not absolutely necessary to be Ultramontane."

[20] Jervis, *The Gallican Church*, p. 175.
[21] Guéranger, *Institutions liturgiques*, Vol. 1, p. 450 and Grancolas, *Commentaire historique sur le Bréviaire Romain* (Paris, Lottin, 1727), Vol. 1, p. 28. The revised statutes of the Chapelle Royale of 1583, F-Pn MS fonds fr. 7008, f. 7v: "Tout le service Divin qui se dira ou chantera en la susdite Chapelle de sa Majesté quand au plain chant sera à l'usage de Rome"; f. 9r: "sadicte Maiesté l'ordonnera tous les gens d'Église qui serviront en ladicte Chapelle se studieront de bien prononcer dire ou chanter dévotement faisans bien les points et les accends tant au service de la messe que es heures canonicales et tout autre service Divin qui se dira ou chanter par Eux en icelle ayant pour le regard de la psalmodie la considération de ne commencer un verset que l'autre ne soit achevé ..."
[22] Guéranger describes this process in great detail; see Guéranger, *Institutions liturgiques*, pp. 437 ff. For a brief checklist of published French liturgical books, see Jean-Yves Hameline, 'Le Plain-chant dans la pratique ecclésiastique aux lendemains du Concile de Trente et des réformes pontconciliaires', in Duron (ed.), *Plainchant et liturgie*, p. 29.

liturgy throughout church (although it was several more years before action was taken), the Assemblée finally deciding to distribute the reformed books to all dioceses who requested them.[23] But despite the early efforts of Cardinal de Lorraine and others in the 1560–80s, the centralized Roman reforms to the chant itself were not replicated uniformly across France. In the province of Reims and those dioceses under its influence, of course, new books were produced with chant revisions that followed the guidance of the 1583 Council.[24] Paris, however, as one might expect, continued to resist the humanist influence of Rome. But while this resistance might seem like simply inertia on the part of the French, the retention of a "conservative" chant repertory, untarnished with Roman reforms, was clearly tied to wider issues of French national identity, internal religious differences between League figures and *politiques*, and a rejection of the Guise humanist agenda.[25]

Chant at the Royal Benedictine Abbey of Montmartre

It is in the context of these wider trends toward adopting the Roman liturgy, rationalizing chant in the name of the Trent and the Counter-Reformation, and embracing late Renaissance humanist impulses, taken together with wider political and dynastic considerations, that we should consider chant at the Royal Benedictine Abbey of Montmartre. As with much of the wider secular church, the process of chant reform at the Abbey began in the early seventeenth century and continued for several decades: in her 1657 obituary of Abbess Marie de Beauvilliers, who oversaw these reforms, Jacqueline Bouette de Blémur describes Beauvillier's arrival at the Abbey in 1598:[26]

---

[23] Guéranger, *Institutions liturgiques*, Vol. 1, p. 498.

[24] See for example the *Sacerdotale vulgo manual seu agenda ... iuxta decretum Concilii Provincialis Anno Domini 1583 Remis celebrati* (Reims, Simon de Foigny, 1607) produced for the diocese of Amiens and the equivalent volume published in 1621 for Laon.

[25] Gastoué describes some modifications to the chant in the early years of the seventeenth century, but the reforms were minor and patchwork in nature; see Gastoué, 'Les Livres de plainchant'.

[26] Jacqueline Bouette de Blémur, *L'Année bénédictine ou les Vies des saints de l'ordre de saint Benoist pour tous les jours de l'année* (Paris, Louis Billaine, 1667–72), Vol. 3, p. 27: "Madame de Montmartre avoit esté contrainte en ces commencemens de substituer la psalmodie en la place du plein chant, à cause de l'effroyable désaccord qui se commettoit à l'Office, bien plus propre à scandalizer qu'à édifier les assistans. Nostre Seigneur luy envoyé en six cens sept une Novice de Fontevraud, qui cantoit comme une Ange, laquelle s'estant donnée à elle, apprit à la jeunesse à l'imiter; elle notta les livres du chœur, & mit la chant en la perfection où il est maintenant."

In the beginning Madame de Montmartre [the Abbess, Marie de Beauvilliers] was forced to substitute psalmody for plain chant because of the appalling discord that resulted during the offices, more suitable for scandalizing than for edifying the nuns. In the year 1607 Our Lord sent to her a novice from Fontevraud who sang like an angel; having received this gift, she [Beauvilliers] taught the young nuns to imitate her [the novice], notated the choir books, and perfected the singing to its current state.

We know that the chant was in a state of flux in the years following 1607, because the Paris manuscript preserves an extensive collection of liturgical works (hymns, Magnificats, Masses, Te Deums, etc.) composed for Montmartre by Antoine Boësset, *maître de musique* in Louis XIII's *chambre*, many of which were based on chant versets or psalm tones that are also preserved in the Paris manuscript, some of them notated in "chant notation," some in standard mensural notation. We also have two later printed sources: the Office chants were published in the *Antiphonier Bénédictin pour les Religieuses du Royal & célèbre Monastère de Montmartre* in 1646 and the Tenebrae chants in *Ténèbres de la semaine sainte pour les Religieuses du Royal & célèbre Monastère de Montmartre* in 1647, collections that preserve a chant repertoire that differs slightly from that contained in the manuscript source, this time notated in the conventional lozenge chant notation.[27] In both manuscript and printed sources, though, some of the chant is closely related to standard Gregorian chant (simply "reformed" or "revised"), while some of it is entirely recomposed.

These bare facts conceal a complex process of reform that can only be understood in the much more specific context outlined below. But it is immediately clear that even from 1607 (as we might expect) rhythm and text declamation were central to the reform process. There are no theoretical chant treatises from the first half of the seventeenth century, but the earliest theorists of the century, Jacques Le Clerc writing in 1665, and Pierre-Benoît de Jumilhac, published in 1673, both defined "plainchant" in the same way, as a type of chant that "consists only of equality of time and of the measure of its sounds or of its notes" – in other words, that was always to be performed in equal note values.[28] On the other hand, in

---

[27] *Antiphonier Bénédictin pour les religieuses du royal et célèbre monastère de Montmartre* (Paris, Louis Sevestre, 1646) and *Les Ténèbres de la Semaine Sainte pour les religieuses de Montmartre* (Paris, Louis Sevestre, 1647).

[28] Pierre-Benoît de Jumilhac, *La Science et la pratique du plain-chant* (Paris, Louis Billaine, 1673), p. 141: "et l'essence de ce chant ne consiste que dans l'égalité du temps et de la mesure de ses sons ou de ses notes …"

"psalmodie" or "chant psalmodique," the length of the notes was to be unequal, Jumilhac and Le Clerc agreeing that the ratio between long and short notes was indeterminate ("it is not possible to determine exactly by what ratio, nor to have a precise measure of this inequality")[29] while disagreeing on the criteria for which syllables in particular were to be lengthened.[30] Nevertheless, even though such definitions date from long after the period in question and should be treated with caution, the fact that an "appalling discord" resulted from the singing of plainchant should not lead us to believe that the nuns were necessarily executing the chant poorly – for if the nuns were inexpert or incompetent, an equal note performance was likely to be more successful. Instead, it suggests that the "appalling discord" was the result of not taking into consideration the prosody of the text itself.[31] The novice who arrived in 1607 presumably did take this into account, and – if we are to believe the story – then reflected this prosody in her revisions to the chant.

But how exactly did this early chant repertory – the first to be go beyond the reforms being carried out in the broader secular church (described above) and the first that we might now call "plain-chant musical" (although this designation is problematic) – get revised, and how are we to understand the significance of these revisions?[32] And how did chant, music, and liturgy more broadly contribute to the Abbey's status and mission as determined by those who controlled it? To answer these questions, we need to appreciate the pivotal role that both the Abbey of Montmartre and the saint in whose honor it was founded – Saint Denis – played in the life of the nation of France, and the symbolism of both for the monarchy.

---

[29] Jumilhac, *La Science*, p. 142: "elle ne se puisse pas exactement déterminer par un nombre certain, ni avoir une mesure précise de son inégalité, ..."

[30] For more on the relation between Jumilhac's, Le Clerc's, and Nivers's conception of chant rhythm, see Davy-Rigaux, 'Le Clerc et Jumilhac'; Patricia Ranum, 'Le Chant'; Davy-Rigaux, *Guillaume-Gabriel Nivers*, esp. pp. 167–244; Denise Launay, 'Un esprit critique au temps de Jumilhac: Dom Jacques Le Clerc, bénédictin de la Congrégation de Saint Maur', *Études grégoriennes*, 19 (1980), 197–219.

[31] Jumilhac, for example, describes how in "psalmodie" every syllable that receives an acute accent or a circumflex in the Breviary should be lengthened (p. 144). But accents and circumflexes were not included in early seventeenth-century editions of the Breviary, only appearing in around 1640.

[32] The term first appeared in 1665, but the degree to which the chant was made "musical" (i.e. tonal and melodic) increased substantially through the eighteenth century; see Amédée Gastoué, *Cours théorique et pratique de chant Grégorien* (Paris, Schola Cantorum, 1917), pp. 84–8.

Montmartre and Saint Denis

The foundation and subsequent history of the Abbey of Montmartre is intimately connected with the commemoration of Saint Denis, first apostle to France, sent by Pope Clément in the mid third century to convert the Gauls, and later taken by the French monarchy as their protector and patron.[33] The first Christians had erected a church (Saint-Denis-du-Pas, close to the later cathedral of Notre-Dame) on the site where Denis had preached with his companions Rusticus (a priest) and Eleutherius (a deacon), a church that was subsequently rebuilt by Childebert, the first Christian king of France. A second church (Saint-Denis-de-la-Chartre) was later built on the site where they were tortured by Prevost Sissinius (at the command of Emperor Domitian) for refusing to worship Roman idols. But it was on the site of their martyrdom, on the "Mons Martis," a hill to the north of Paris on which stood ancient Roman temples to Mars and Mercury, that a "Chapel of Martyrs" was built by the people to commemorate the death of the three companions. Following Roman tradition, Denis and his companions had been executed there by beheading, but the legend recalls that Saint Denis miraculously picked up his own head and walked out to the site of the current Abbey of Saint-Denis, now in the northern suburbs of Paris. According to Hilduin, Abbot of Saint-Denis,

> the corpse of the blessed Dionysius raised itself up, and began – with angelic guidance directing its steps and heavenly light shining all around – to carry in his holy hand the head cut from the body ... And a multitude of the celestial army, praising God without cease in sweet-sounding hymns accompanied his lifeless body ... But also countless throngs of divine spirits seeking the heavens were heard, singing with the melody of incalculable sweetness "Glory be to Thee, O Lord" to which was frequently added "Alleluia."[34]

---

[33] There is no comprehensive modern history of the Abbey of Montmartre. The following account is taken from Abbé Lebeuf, *Histoire de la ville et de tout le diocèse de Paris* (Paris, Libraire de Féchoz et Letouzey, 1883); Jacques du Breul, *Le Théâtre des antiquitez de Paris* (Paris, Pierre Chevalier, 1612); Michel Félibien, *Histoire de la ville de Paris* (Paris, Guillaume Desprez, 1722); Henri Sauval, *Histoire et recherches des antiquités de la ville de Paris* (Paris, C. Moette, 1724); and Maurice Dumolin, 'Notes sur l'abbaye de Montmartre', *Bulletin de la société de l'histoire de Paris et de l'Île de France*, 58 (1931), 145–238. To the extent that the history of Montmartre overlaps with that of the Abbey of Saint-Denis, see Michel Félibien, *Histoire de l'abbaye royale de Saint-Denis en France* (Paris, Frédéric Léonard, 1706); Caroline Bruzelius, *The 13th-Century Church at St-Denis* (New Haven and London, Yale University Press, 1985); and Sumner McKnight Crosby, *The Abbey of Saint-Denis, 475–1122* (Newhaven, Yale University Press, 1942).

[34] Michael Lapidge, *Hilduin of Saint-Denis: The Passio S. Dionysii in Prose and Verse* (Leiden, Brill, 2017), pp. 294–5.

Saint Geneviève later founded the Abbey of Saint-Denis on the site of his tomb, where, in the ninth century, Abbot Hilduin began the practice – controversial yet highly significant into the seventeenth century – of conflating the saint with Dionysius the Areopagite, a disciple of Saint Paul, and with Pseudo-Dionysius, the author of four Neoplatonic treatises.[35] Shortly thereafter, Louis the Pious, who had commissioned Hilduin's history of Saint Denis, began a tradition of devotion to the saint, and over the following centuries Denis became, like Saint Martin, a symbol of national identity and protector of the French monarchy itself.[36]

By around 700 a wooden church (consisting of an upper church and a lower, underground crypt) existed on the hill, resulting in the name being changed to Mons Martyrium or Montmartre.[37] In 944 Flodoard, canon of Reims, describes how the church was destroyed by a terrible storm,[38] but by 1096 the church was described as being spacious and having an altar, a sanctuary, and a cemetery around it. Shortly afterward the church was rebuilt to become a dependent priory of Saint-Martin-des-Champs, and it is at this point that the existence of a "parva ecclesia ... vulgo appellatur Sanctum Martyrorum" or the chapel of the Holy Martyrs becomes clear, becoming a regular site of pilgrimage distinct from the church itself. Finally, in 1133, Louis le Gros and his Queen Adelaide decided to found an abbey on the site, exchanging their possession of Saint-Denis-de-la-Chartre for Montmartre with the monks of Saint-Martin-des-Champs. The monks may have remained, but in any case, a community of nuns moved in under Abbess Adelaide (who had come from Saint-Pierre-de-Reims), succeeded in 1137 by Christine, who was still Abbess in 1147 when Pope Eugène dedicated the Abbey church. Having spent Easter at the Abbey of Saint-Denis, the Pope, assisted by Saint Bernard of Clairvaux and Pierre le Vénérable, Abbot of Cluny, dedicated the Abbey church the following day to Saint Peter and the Virgin Mary. The Sunday after Ascension, Eugène again returned, dedicating the high altar to Denis, Rusticus, and

---

[35] Félibien, *Histoire de la ville de Paris*, pp. 68–9. The tradition continued into the seventeenth century with Jacques Doublet, Dean of the Abbey of Saint-Denis, whose *Histoire chronologique pour la vérité de S. Denys Aréopagite, Apostre de France et premier évesque de Paris* (Paris, Pierre de Bresche, 1646), made the same argument as Hilduin. See also below.

[36] The protection of Saint Denis also extended to the Oriflamme, the banner symbolizing the divine protection of the monarchy, which was housed at the Abbey; see Anne Lombard-Jourdan, *Fleur de lis et oriflamme: signes célestes du royaume de France* (Paris, CNRS, 2002).

[37] Le Beuf, *Histoire de la ville ... Paris*, p. 441, quoting Charles le Chauve, *Liber Miraculum S. Dionysius*.

[38] Du Breul, *Le Théâtre des antiquitez de Paris*, p. 1153.

Eleutherius.[39] From this point onward, major development ceased, Montmartre remaining relatively unchanged until the sixteenth century when, in 1559, a fire destroyed much of the Abbey, leaving – at the end of the century – one of the most important devotional sites in France in physical and spiritual disarray.

It was under the rule of Abbess Marie de Beauvilliers, appointed in 1598 (receiving the blessing of Cardinal de Sourdis in 1601) to restore the Abbey to its former glories, that a number of musical, liturgical, devotional, and political currents would coincide at Montmartre. In particular, the chant reforms that took place under her rule, and the composition of a substantial and complementary polyphonic repertoire by Antoine Boësset, coincided with a politically significant spike in devotion to Saint Denis, and with a takeover of the Abbey by a faction associated with the League and their descendants. Saint Denis had played a pivotal role in the Wars of Religion, adopted as an emblem of French nationhood by both the king and the League, most notably in the climax of the war at the end of the 1580s and into the early 1590s. Louis de Guise, Archbishop of Reims, assassinated by Henri III in 1588 (along with his brother Henri, Duke of Guise), had also held the position of Abbot of Saint-Denis, and on his death, the League had moved swiftly to retrieve the relics of Saint Denis from the Abbey to protect them from the king's forces, leading them from Saint-Denis in procession into the city of Paris itself, where they were held at the church of Saint-Denis for safekeeping. On June 20, 1589, they were again processed through the streets of Paris, this time along with those of Saint Louis, as an act of Parisian and League defiance against the king.[40] Indeed, over the next few years, Paris adopted Saint Denis as the focus of its religious life – his feast was added to the Sanctorale, and pilgrimages to the Chapel of the Martyrs at Montmartre were rewarded with indulgences.[41] Saint Denis – a figure who stood above mere kings – was now held as protector of both Paris (and through it the whole nation of France) and the Catholic Church against the heretical pretender to the crown, Henri IV.

---

[39] Le Beuf, *Histoire de la ville ... Paris*, pp. 442–5.

[40] See Jean-Marie le Gall, *Le Mythe de Saint Denis: entre Renaissance et Révolution* (Seyssel, Champ Vallon, 2007), p. 92; Jean-Marie le Gall, 'Saint-Denis, les Guises et Paris sous la Ligue, 1588–90', *French Historical Studies*, 24/2 (2001), 157–84. For a richly documented overview of this period, see also Joël Cornette, *Henri IV à Saint-Denis* (Paris, Belin, 2010).

[41] A tract on the celebration of the Mass by the noted leaguer and commentator on the psalms, Gilbert Genebrard, invoked Saint Denis's connection to the first apostles; see Gilbert Genebrard, *Traicté de la liturgie, ou S. messe selon l'usage et forme des apostres et de leur disciple sainct Denys, apostre des François* (Lyon, J. Pillehotte, 1594).

Henri equally, though, recognizing the symbolism of the saint, in turn moved to capture the town and Abbey of Saint-Denis in July 1590 with a force of 1,500 men, setting up court there as an alternative strategy to lay claim to the saint's protection.[42] On January 4, 1591, the eve of the Feast of Sainte Geneviève, the League tried to recapture the town, placing their assault under the protection of Sainte Geneviève herself. (Their commander, Aumale, was killed, Henri attributing this to the divine powers of Denis.) Henri continued to make Saint-Denis his effective court for several more years, but as support for the League waned, the Abbey again became a site of pilgrimage for Parisians. Ultimately on July 24, 1593, Henri converted to Catholicism in an abjuration ceremony at the Abbey, an act that effectively ended the Wars of Religion.[43]

Despite the defeat of the League, in the following years members of the Guise family seamlessly resumed their connection with the Saint, who would no longer be seen as a priority by Henri IV or Louis XIII. In 1594 Louis IV de Lorraine was appointed Abbot of Saint-Denis (and Archbishop of Reims), succeeded in 1622 by Henri IV de Lorraine. At Montmartre, the process took a little more time, but was nonetheless complete by the 1620s–30s. During this period the Abbey became a center for those who held ultramontane, pro Roman, often mystical beliefs, inspired by the Eucharistic and Christocentric devotion prescribed in François de Sales's *Introduction à la vie dévote* (1609) and who later formed the circle around Marie de Médicis and would be identified as the *dévots* or the *parti des dévots*.[44]

The process began with the appointment of Marie de Beauvilliers in 1598, a nun from Beaumont de la Tours who was invited to take over Montmartre at the suggestion of Pierre Forget de Fresne, Secretary of State to Henri IV and Marie's brother in law. (Marie herself was a descendant of house of Saint-Aignan, a family which boasted of its royal connections, especially to Louis VI, the founder of the Abbey.)[45] Alongside Forget

---

[42] Le Gall, *Le Mythe*, p. 94.

[43] For the broader outline of the final War of Religion, see Mack P. Holt, *The French Wars of Religion, 1562–1629* (Cambridge and New York, Cambridge University Press, 2005), pp. 123–55.

[44] The literature on the *dévots* is extensive but is generally considered from a political perspective, the *parti des dévots*. But see, for example, Barbara Diefendorf, *From Penitence to Charity: Pious Women and the Catholic Reformation in Paris* (Oxford and New York, Oxford University Press, 2004); Joseph Bergin, *The Politics of Religion in Early Modern France* (New Haven and London, Yale University Press, 2014), pp. 86–111.

[45] Le Gall, *Le Mythe*, p. 487; Diefendorf, *Penitence to Charity*, p. 96; Dumolin, 'Notes sur l'abbaye de Montmartre', p. 190.

(who was Marie's protector in the secular domain), a number of figures with strong League connections played important roles as Marie's spiritual advisors. Initially guided by Dom Didier de la Cour, at the suggestion of the Cardinal de Sourdis Marie then took Benet Canfield as her confessor, one of the most important and influential spiritual and mystical figures of the era, whose *Règle de perfection* (published in 1609 but already in manuscript by 1592) laid out a path toward spiritual growth followed by many *dévots*. When Canfield left France in 1599, he arranged for Ange de Joyeuse, formerly one of the most active figures of the League, to take his role as protector and mentor. Initially loyal to the crown as both a member of Henri III's Congrégation de la Vie Saine and the Congregation of the Knights of the Holy Spirit, Joyeuse later joined the League, leading one of the most famous processions through Paris, playing the part of Christ.[46] Having taken his vows as a Capuchin in 1587, he later moved to Fontevraud before returning to Paris and Montmartre. His daughter, Catherine de Joyeuse, married Charles de Lorraine, Duc de Guise in 1611, and in 1622 she paid for a covered walkway connecting the new Martyrium to the Abbey (see below). Catherine also paid for the *Antiphonier* and *Ténèbres* publications of 1646 and 1647, and Françoise-Renée de Lorraine, Catherine's daughter, herself became Abbess in 1657, succeeding Marie. Finally, numerous other *dévot* figures were associated with the Abbey. Barbe Acarie (later known as Marie de l'Incarnation), widow of Pierre Acarie, one of the sixteen leaders of the League, and a well-known mystic who helped found the Carmelite order in France, lent her support to Marie, as did her extensive circle that included some of the most important figures of Counter-Reformation Paris.[47]

It was under the leadership of such *dévot*, ultramontane figures that the cult of Saint Denis received new impetus in 1611 when, during preparations to enlarge the chapel of the martyrs, an underground vault was discovered containing an altar and cross, together with the words MAR, CLEMIN, and DIO marked on the walls, thought to be the place where Saint Denis had secretly celebrated the Eucharist.[48] Marie de Médicis

---

[46] Francis Yates, 'Dramatic religious processions in Paris in the late sixteenth century', *Annales musicologiques*, 2 (1954), 215–70. The procession is also described in Jean-Claude Fabre, *Histoire ecclésiastique pour server de continuation à celle de Monsieur l'Abbé Fleury* (Paris, Pierre-Jean Mariette, 1738), p. 192.

[47] Diefendorf, *Penitence to Charity*, p. 79.

[48] Du Breul, *Le Théâtre des antiquitez de Paris*, p. 1162. See also *Représentation d'une chapelle souterraine qui s'est trouvée à Mont-Martre près de Paris, le Mardy 12. iour de Iuillet 1611 comme on faisoit des fondements pour agrandir la Chapelle des Martyrs* (Paris, Nicolas, 1611).

Figure 6.1 View of the Martyrium at Montmartre in the later seventeenth century.
Engraving by Israel Silvestre. Bibliothèque nationale de France.

visited the site together with 10,000 people, and the money raised in donations was sufficient to build, in 1622, a dependent priory over the site, a major expansion of the Abbey, and a dramatic symbol, perched high on the hill above Paris and visible across the whole city, of a revival of the cult of Saint Denis (see Figure 6.1).[49]

Music, Chant, and Liturgy at Montmartre

As a liturgical counterpart to the new martyrium, permission was granted by Pope Gregory XV for the foundation of a confraternity dedicated to Saint Denis shortly after the Priory was completed in 1623. Endowed by Marie's sister Anne de Beauvilliers in honor of her late husband, Pierre Forget, "in consideration of the particular devotion and affection that the

---

[49] Le Gall, *Le Mythe*, p. 490. The famous portrait of Richelieu by Philippe de Champaigne preserved in the chancellery of the Sorbonne features the Abbey – of all the buildings of Paris – in the distance. It has been suggested that Richelieu and Champaigne were thus paying tribute to Cardinal de Sourdis, Archbishop of Bordeaux and Marie de Beauvilliers's uncle; see *Richelieu et le monde de l'esprit* (Paris, University of Paris, Académie française, 1985), p. 344.

said Pierre Forget has always borne to the abbey, and especially the chapel built by the first Christians in honor of the martyrdom of Saint Denis the Areopagite," the confraternity elevated the status of the saint (clearly conflated with the Areopagite from its inception) in a way which had not been done for centuries.[50] From the 1620s, then, music and chant were to serve two liturgical cycles and performance venues – that of the confraternity of Saint Denis in the Martyrium, and that of the Abbey Church of Saint Pierre.

In accordance with the *dévot* sensibilities of the Abbey's leadership, the liturgy of the Confraternity, though dedicated to Saint Denis, focused on the celebration of the Eucharist. Beyond the daily Mass in honor of Pierre and Anne Forget, the *Offices Propres* of 1658 spells out the details recorded in the Bull of Foundation for the celebration of the Double Office of the Saint Sacrement each Thursday: at Vespers with the hymn *Pange lingua* and the Magnificat antiphon *O quam suavis*; at Matins with the hymn *Sacris solemnis*; and at Lauds and the other Hours with the hymn *Verbum supernum/O salutaris hostia*.[51] While the Office of the Saint Sacrement was an officially sanctioned liturgy, the slightly later *Cérémonial Monastique* of 1669 also calls for the ceremony (again based on the Bull of 1623) of the Exposition of the Blessed Sacrament during the Octave of the Feast of the Saint Sacrement (known as *Salut* when it took place in conjunction with Compline at the end of the day), and at any other time, a practice that was not officially sanctioned;[52] on the contrary, associated with the *dévots*, and generally perceived to be against the spirit of the Gallican Church, the practice was condemned in the 1620s and 1630s by the Assemblée générale de clergé.[53] According to the *Cérémoniale* rubrics, before the first Mass of the day the officiating priest was

---

[50] *Bulle de confirmation de la fondation du Prieuré du martyre de St Denis*, 1623, Archives nationales de France, L.1031 no. 31: "en considération, de la dévotion et affection particulière quelle et le dict Pierre Forget ont tousiours portée audict monastère, et spécialement la chappelle battie par les premiers chrestiens en l'honneur du martyre de St Denis Aréopagite."

[51] *Offices propres des Saincts de la Royale Abbaye de Montmartre* (Paris, Jean Henault, 1658), p. 221. See also *Mémoire touchant la bulle de la fondation du Prieuré des martyrs*, Archives nationales de France, L.1031, no. 40.

[52] *Cérémoniale monastique des religieuses de l'Abbaye Royale de Montmartre* (Paris, Barthelemy and Marin Vitré, 1669), pp. 411–12.

[53] The history of the rite in France is outlined in C. Cordonnier, *Le Culte du Saint-Sacrement* (Paris, Lethielleux, 1923). According to J.-B. Thiers, *Traité de l'exposition du St. Sacrement de l'autel* (Paris, J. Du Puis, 1673), the practice had been condemned by the Concile Provincial de Malines (1607), the Synod of Viterbe (1614), the Synod of Limoges (1619), the *Assemblée générale du Clergé de France* (1625), the Bishop of Limoges, and the *Assemblée générale du Clergé de France* (1635). The second part of Thiers's book is subtitled 'Où l'on montre que l'exposition fréquente du saint Sacrement est contraire à l'esprit, à l'intention & aux règles de l'Église.'

to remove the host from the tabernacle, and reveal and cense it while "la chantre entonnera l'Antienne *Ave verum*, que le Chœur chantera avec la dévotion accompagnée de la gravité que demande cette action toute sainte." And at the end of the day, at *Salut* (during or after Compline or sometimes Vespers), the host was again to be venerated before being replaced in the tabernacle for the night. In this short but complex ceremony, the host was again censed while "la chantre" began to sing the *Tantum ergo*, *Panis angelicus*, *O salutaris hostia*, or *Ecce Panis angelorum*, which the choir then continued. After many brief sung prayers, the host was returned to the tabernacle.[54]

We can see the musical adornment to the liturgy of the Martyrium (with its explicit role in the celebration of the Eucharist and Saint Denis) and at the Abbey Church itself (with a more broad-ranging liturgy, though no doubt focused toward Saint Denis) in the polyphonic repertoire that Boësset composed and that is now preserved in the Paris manuscript. Perhaps most obvious are a handful of works in celebration of the Feast of Saint Denis itself, October 9. The motet *Pretiosus Domini Dionysius*, a conventional imitative work in the scoring that Boësset typically used – high voices (the nuns), single bass voice (we assume Boësset himself), and *basse-continue* (organ and bass viol) – sets a text celebrating the martyrdom of the saint, the responsory for the Feast of Saint Denis, crying out to Christ in the voice of the saint for safekeeping in recognition that it is through the Eucharistic blood of Jesus that he will be saved.[55]

Pretiosus Domini Dionysius, in agone novissimo dixit: nunc jam Domine per coronam martyrii cum fratribus meis servis tuis suscipe me tuosque. Domine mi tuae custodiae commendo quos ministerio nostro et tibi tuo sanguine acquisisti. Cunctos qui te per nos in nomine tuo petierint ut pollicitus et clementer exaudi.	The Lord's precious Dionysius, in utmost agony cried: now, Lord, by the crown of the martyrs with my brothers, your servant, hear me. O Lord, I commend myself into your safekeeping which by our ministry and your blood I have won. All those who through us in your name entreat you that promise and mercifully, hear us.

The text of the Office Hymn for the Feast of Saint Denis, *Dionysii martyris*, on the other hand, was not taken from the Roman liturgy but – as part of the reinvigoration of the devotion to the saint – newly written, in 1620, by Raoul Parent, an advocate in the Parlement of Paris, known for his devotion to the Saint, and also responsible for commissioning a series of

---

[54] *Cérémonial monastique*, pp. 408–9.
[55] Edition in Bennett, 'Antoine Boësset: Sacred Music', Part 1, pp. 102–5.

Music Example 6.1 Opening verse of Antoine Boësset, *Dionysii martyris*. Paris manuscript, f. 197v–98r.

paintings on his life and martyrdom for the Church of Saint-Benoît in Paris (see Music Example 6.1). Over thirteen verses, the text of the hymn, which first appeared in Jacques Doublet's essay *La Vérité de Saint Denis l'Aréopagite* in 1620, narrates the martyrdom of Denis and his companions, concluding with strophes that directly link the suffering of the martyrs with the suffering of Christ, his cross, and his victory.[56] At the same time, the hymn recounts how

---

[56] Jacques Doublet, *Histoire chronologique pour la vérité de S. Denys Aréopagite apostre de France et premier évesque de Paris* (Paris, Pierre de Bresche, 1646), pp. 487–8; edition in Bennett, *Antoine Boësset: Sacred Music*, Part 1, pp. 186–9. Doublet's tract argued for Denis the Apostle and Dionysius the Areopagite being the same person.

the martyrs overthrew worldly authority, and, strikingly, asks only for God's favor over the three estates of France, not for its monarch.

9. Illos ter Sancta Trinitas	The thrice holy Trinity
Coronis ornat gloriae,	adorns them with crowns of glory,
Post cruces et angustias	and after the crosses and sufferings
Triumpham dat victoriae.	grants them the triumph of victory.
11. Invicta fides Martyrum	By innocent blood,
Per innocentem sanguinem	the invincible faith of the martyrs
Tirannum vincit perfidum,	conquers the faithless tyrant,
Prosternit mundi principem	and overthrows worldly authority.
12. Te summa Deus Trinitas	We pray that you, God and highest Trinity,
Tres nunc Gallorum ordines	show favor to
Precamur semper foveas	the three estates of France
Hos per tres Archi-Martires	through these three arch-Martyrs.
13. Fidem professos aspice	Behold those who professed faith
Forti redemptos brachio	redeemed by the strong arm,
Dionysio auspice	and, under the protection of Dionysius,
Da frui caeli gaudia. Amen.	grant us to enjoy the delights of heaven. Amen.

In scoring and compositional style, this hymn is typical of almost the whole Montmartre hymn repertory – a simple, homophonic setting reflecting the prosody (in this case the accentuation rather than quantity) of the hymn, to be performed in alternatim with a newly composed rhythmic chant melody that is preserved in mensural notation (in what Jumilhac would later call *chant métrique*) in the Paris manuscript (Figure 6.2) and in conventional lozenge chant notation in the *Antiphonier* (Figure 6.3). This and all the other hymn settings illustrate that the practice of hymn singing at Montmartre was rhythmic or "measured" during Boësset's tenure, and since both the melodies (completely unrelated to medieval models) and the polyphony were newly composed, it seems likely that the hymn melodies and polyphonic settings were conceived together, rhythmically, in triple meter, the chants only to lose their rhythmic identity (as with the chants below) when they were incorporated into the *Antiphonier*.[57]

Continuing the Eucharistic theme, the Paris manuscript also preserves a number of works suitable for the Office of the Saint Sacrement or for *Salut*, most likely celebrated in the Martyrium. The Martyrium itself was served

---

[57] For the wider context of performing hymns rhythmically in conjunction with chant see Richard Sherr, 'The performance of chant in the Renaissance and its interactions with polyphony', in Thomas F. Kelly (ed.), *Plainsong in the Age of Polyphony* (Cambridge, Cambridge University Press, 1992), pp. 178–208.

Figure 6.2 Chant for second verse of *Dionysii martyris* (*Ad Gallos missi*) in 3 time and blackened notation.
Paris manuscript, f. 219r. Bibliothèque nationale de France.

Figure 6.3 Chant for *Dionysii martyris*.
Antiphonier Bénédictin . . . de Montmartre (Paris, Louis Sevestre, 1646), p. 503. Bibliothèque nationale de France

by ten nuns who presumably sang the standard round of Offices and Mass described in the Bull of Foundation, but the chapel of Saint Leufroy was served by the clergy of Saint-Germain-l'Auxerrois, who maintained a *maîtrise* of boys in residence there who would also have sung polyphony.[58] So in addition to the Eucharistic works for the nuns that survive by Boësset, such as the through-composed setting of the hymn *Pange lingua*, the *O salutaris hostia*, and the setting of *Ecce panis angelorum* (sung at the moment of elevation), two other works for high voices (in this case we can assume boys) by André Péchon, master of the music at Saint-Germain and the scribe of the Paris manuscript, were probably also performed.[59] Péchon's setting for two high voices and continuo of the hymn *Pange lingua* takes the chant (in this case essentially the medieval melody) and paraphrases it in duet over *basse-continue* (see Music Example 6.2),[60] while his four-high-

---

[58] *Bulle de confirmation, Règlement touchant la desserte de la Chapelle Sn. Leufroy appartenante a Msr. le dit Venerables Doyen, Chanoines et Chapitre de L'Église Royalle et Collegiale de Saint Germain Lauxerroy à Paris*, Archives nationales de France, L. 1031 no. 39. This *règlement* gives a detailed account of the lives and duties of the *maîtrise*.

[59] Boësset settings in Bennett, *Antoine Boësset: Sacred Music*, Part 1, pp. 201–4, 199–200, and 64–5.

[60] There would have been no opportunity to perform a work such as this at Péchon's own church of Saint-Germain-l'Auxerrois; see Peter Bennett, *Sacred Repertories in Paris, 1630–43: Bibliothèque nationale de France, V^{ma} rés. 571*.

Music Example 6.2 André Péchon, *Pange lingua gloriosi*.
Paris manuscript, f. 31r.

voice setting of *Ecce panis angelorum* sets the Eucharistic text in the more old-fashioned imitative polyphony for which he was known.[61]

---

[61] Edition in Bennett, *Sacred Repertories*, 2004, Vol. 2, pp. 17–18.

Music Example 6.2 (*cont.*)

Music Example 6.3 Antoine Boësset, *Stabat mater dolorosa*, v. 1.
Paris manuscript, ff. 215v–16v.

But beyond these works with direct liturgical relevance to the kinds of Eucharistic and Dionysian devotions that the Abbey encouraged, the broader chant repertoire, and the way in which it was reformed or created, is equally significant. Given that the Guises and those who moved in their orbit had been primary movers of humanist-inspired chant reform in the sixteenth century (signaling their affinity with Rome), it is no surprise that their successors (as we will see), having now displaced the king in a religious house dedicated to the saint most identified with France, also chose to adopt overtly humanist techniques. In practice this means that the chant repertoire seems to have been conceived in strongly text-dependent and clearly rhythmically defined manner that – like the archetypal humanist music of France, *musique mesurée* – was based on two note values performed (not just notated) in a simple 2:1 ratio, often resulting in alternating duple and triple groupings. But just as, more broadly, the music of Boësset and his contemporaries gradually abandoned the dependence on this limited rhythmic palette (in the *air de cour*, most notably), so too did the chant at Montmartre, losing this character over time, so that by the 1640s, when the *Antiphonier* and *Ténèbres* were published after Boësset's death, chant was notated in conventional terms, with little attention paid to text declamation or prosody.[62]

Boësset's setting of the sequence *Stabat mater*, for example, effectively a harmonization of a newly composed strophic chant for solo voice and continuo pays close attention to the accentuation (standing in for quantity) of the text, reflecting it in the rigorous application of just two note values and a freely alternating duple and triple measure:

Stabat mater dolorosa, iuxta Crucem lacrimosa, dum pendebit filius

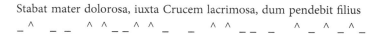

In this alternatim setting, even-numbered verses are to be sung monophonically without accompaniment: Boësset provides music for one of these, likewise adopting the alternating duple and triple groupings, and in his subsequent accompanied verses he modifies the text declamation in the most subtle ways to reflect the prosody.

It is hard to know who compiled the *Antiphonier*, from what models and exemplars, and to what agenda, but certainly the chants that would have originally been performed with careful declamation by the musically trained nuns of Montmartre now appeared shorn of their classical heritage, stripped of almost all rhythmic identity (see Figure 6.4).

If the metrical chants of a sequence (*Stabat mater*) and a hymn (*Dionysi martyris*, though many others are even clearer in this regard) might naturally fall into rhythm (Jumilhac's *chant métrique*), we can nonetheless also find the same rhythmic approach in the psalmody.[63] A chant incipit

---

[62] For the apparent influence of *musique mesurée* on the *air de cour* and its gradual decline, see D. P. Walker, 'The influence of *musique mesurée à l'antique*, particularly on the *airs de cour* of the early seventeenth century', *Musica Disciplina*, 2 (1948), 141–63.

[63] See edition of *Christe remdemptor omnium, Ex patre* ... in Bennett, *Antoine Boësset: Sacred Music*, Part 1, p. 181.

Figure 6.4 Chant for *Stabat mater*.
Antiphonier Bénédictin ... de Montmartre (Paris, Louis Sevestre, 1646), p. 529. Bibliothèque nationale de France

Figure 6.5 Chant for *Et exultativit* in mensural notation.
Paris manuscript, ff. 155v–156v. Bibliothèque nationale de France.

for a polyphonic setting of the Magnificat, notated in mensural notation and copied in the 1620s at the same time as the polyphony, is the clearest example of the original way in which the chant was conceived (Figure 6.5). Using a time signature of C and regular mensural notation in two values, the notation suggests a rhythmic performance, based on the short note as the standard length.

But again, as with the other examples, the later *Antiphonier* version of the *Et exultavit* verset (Figure 6.6) prioritizes long syllables and loses the flow of the text, especially at "in Deo salutari meo," where every syllable, against all the principles of good or classical declamation, is now long.[64]

But it is perhaps the numerous *fauxbourdon*-type settings that most strongly suggest a rhythmic approach to *accentus* chants. Found as either versets for the recitation of psalms or as part of an alternatim Te Deum, these moments of "*fauxbourdon*" carefully notated throughout, have enough harmonic motion, enough "music" to require them to adopt a regular rhythm. The setting of *Credidi propter*, for example (Figure 6.7), is dominated by regular harmonic progressions that require a pulse – alternating between duple and triple measure – and it is difficult to imagine that the chant, when performed for the solo verses, would not have adopted

[64] *Antiphonier*, p. 520.

Figure 6.6 Chant for *Magnificat* and *Et exultavit*.
Antiphonier Bénédictin . . . de Montmartre (Paris, Louis Sevestre, 1646), p. 520. Bibliothèque nationale de France.

Figure 6.7 *Fauxbourdon* (*c.* 1630) for *Credidi propter*.
Paris manuscript, f. 217r. Bibliothèque nationale de France.

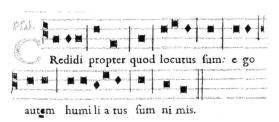

Figure 6.8 Chant (*c.* 1640) for *Credidi propter*.
Antiphonier Bénédictin . . . de Montmartre (Paris, Louis Sevestre, 1646), p. 519. Bibliothèque nationale de France.

the same features. And the fact that subsequent notational realizations of the chant over time lose this feature (alongside all the other examples) suggests that, indeed, interest in declamation was strongest in the early part of the century, but that it subsequently declined. The *Antiphonier* version, for example (Figure 6.8), indicates some details of declamation, while the 1680 version preserved in the Paris manuscript abandons all attempts to indicate syllable length (Figure 6.9).

Figure 6.9 Chant (c. 1680) for *Credidi propter*, v. 2, *Ego dixi in excessu meo*.
Paris manuscript, f. 218v. Bibliothèque nationale de France.

All the evidence thus suggests that Boësset – who must in practice have been the controlling influence over chant and polyphony by the 1620s and 1630s – absolutely intended both chant and *fauxbourdon*, indeed much of the repertoire, to adopt the limited rhythmic vocabulary shared with *musique mesurée*. Boësset was, after all, in many ways the inheritor of his father-in-law, Pierre Guédron's, style of composition.[65] Guédron had sung in the chapel of Louis II de Lorraine, Cardinal de Guise, before his assassination in 1588, and had subsequently served arch-*dévot* Marie de Médicis.[66] His earlier *airs de cour* owed a great deal to the style of *musique mesurée* – essentially homophonic, using only two rhythmic values – and he is even reputed to have composed *fauxbourdons*, which to all intents and purposes must have sounded like unmelodic airs.[67] Boësset's and Guédron's early airs also frequently adopt the alternating duple and triple patterns that emerge from *musique mesurée*, even when preserved in single-voice monophonic settings that were popular around this time. And other works, only ever published for solo voice, such as Denis Caignet's settings of Desportes psalm paraphrases of 1625 (Caignet was one of Boësset's colleagues in the *chambre*), also show how a monophonic line, essentially syllabic, could be performed in strict rhythm, even in the absence of any perceived harmonic implications, and in the absence of a simple controlling meter such as found in the hymns (see Chapter 3, Figure 3.3).[68]

Even more than that, however, we might argue that all music of the time – both chant and "song" – was conceived in a metrical framework that admitted only "whole" note values, eschewing the "expressive" flexibility associated with later chant. Descartes's 1618 *Compendium musicae*, for

---

[65] For the musical relationship between Guédron and Boësset, see Georgie Durosoir, *L'Air de Cour en France, 1571–1665* (Liège, Mardaga, 1991), pp. 221–7.

[66] For Guédron's biography and exposure to musical humanism, see Don Lee Royster, *Pierre Guédron and the Air de Cour, 1600–1620* (PhD dissertation, Yale University, 1972), pp. 50–6.

[67] See Royster, *Guédron*, p. 52.

[68] We know that Mersenne singled out Boësset's text declamation for both praise and critique in the *Harmonie Universelle* of 1636. But in either case, Mersenne conceived of Boësset's text setting entirely in terms of metrical feet; see Marin Mersenne, *Harmonie Universelle contenant la théorie et la pratique de la musique* (Paris, Sebastien Cramoisy, 1636), Vol. 2, p. 394.

Figure 6.10 Arithmetic proportion according to Descartes.
René Descartes, *Excellent Compendium of Music with Necessary and Judicious Animadversions Thereupon* (London, Thomas Harper and Humphrey Moseley, 1653), p. 3.

example, while short on practical musical details, lays out a clear theory of musical time. In the third chapter, "Of number, or Time to be observed in Sounds," he begins:[69]

> Time, in sounds, ought to consist of equal Parts because such are the most easily of all others perceived by the sense ... or of Parts which are in a double or triple proportion, nor is there any further progression allowable; because such are, of all the others, the most easily distinguished by the ear.

Descartes justifies these statements with his "préconsiderables," noting particularly that:

> That proportion ought to be Arithmeticall, not Geometricall. The reason whereof is, because in that there are not so many things advertible, since the Differences are everywhere equall: and therefore the sense suffers not so much labour and defatigation, that it may distinctly perceive all things occurring therein.

In this Arithmetical proportion (illustrated in Figure 6.10), the sense is only required to perceive a single unity to apprehend the difference in each line, resulting in units of time that relate to each other in a 2:3:4 ratio, exactly the way I am suggesting the Montmartre chant was conceived and performed in the years in which Descartes was writing. By contrast, in Descartes's Geometric proportion (illustrated in Figure 6.11), the units of

---

[69] René Descartes, *Compendium musicae*, manuscript 1618; first published as *Musicae compendium* (Utrecht, Zyll & Ackersdyck, 1650); translated into French as *Abrégé de musique* (Paris, Charles Angot, 1668); translated into English as *Excellent Compendium of Music with Necessary and Judicious Animadversions Thereupon* (London, Thomas Harper and Humphrey Moseley, 1653). For an overview of Descartes's evolving relationship with music, see Brigitte van Wymeersch. 'L'Esthétique musicale de Descartes et le cartésianisme', *Revue Philosophique de Louvain*, 4th series, 94/2 (1996), 271–93. See also the discussion of Descartes as he related to rhythm and dance in van Orden, *Music, Discipline, and Arms*, pp. 187–8. Quotation from *Excellent Compendium*, p. 4.

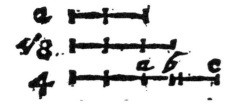

Figure 6.11 Geometric proportion according to Descartes.
René Descartes, *Excellent Compendium of Music with Necessary and Judicious Animadversions Thereupon* (London, Thomas Harper and Humphrey Moseley, 1653), p. 3.

time, indicated by ab and bc, with b (= $\sqrt{8}$) not falling equally between a (=2) and c (=4), are "incommensurable," the term that later chant theorists who argued for a more flexible approach to declamation used to describe chant notation in the 1670s.

In adopting this measured approach to chant and time, which contrasts strongly with that taken at the Congregation of the Oratory (to which I will shortly turn), Boësset was not just following a sixteenth-century musical fashion that had essentially run its course, or pandering to Guise musical tastes, or simply working within the conventional temporal framework accepted by all musicians of the time and outlined by Descartes, though he was probably doing all three. More than that, he was also undoubtedly aligning the music at the Abbey with the even broader conceptual and philosophical framework – essentially still Neoplatonic – embraced by the Guises and their *dévot* allies in the early years of the century. (Although Descartes accepted the Pythagorean numerical basis of time, he rejected its cosmological mystical effects. His reasoning was instead based on the judgment of the senses.)[70] As Dray has shown, the teachings and philosophy of Benet Canfield, François de Sales, and the Acarie circle were all indebted to the writings of the Platonists, the mystical Neoplatonism of Plotinus, and the Christian mysticism of pseudo-Dionysius.[71] Canfield's *Règle de perfection*, for example, calls for an ascent through three stages of contemplation based on the teachings of pseudo-Dionysius (often linked to Denis), Augustine, and Plotinus, and is strongly reminiscent of Pontus

---

[70] Wymeersch, 'L'Esthétique musicale', p. 283.

[71] J. P. Dray, *Neoplatonism and French Religious Thought in the Seventeenth Century* (DPhil dissertation, Oxford University, 1987). See also Jean-Marie le Gall, 'The lives of the Saints in the French Renaissance c. 1500–c. 1650', in Katherine van Liere, Simon Ditchfield, and Howard Latham (eds.), *Sacred History: Uses of the Christian Past in the Renaissance World* (Oxford, Oxford University Press, 2012), pp. 209–29, esp. 225–7.

de Tyard's *Solitaire* treatises, so central to the thought (especially musical) of the *Académie de poésie et de musique*.[72] Canfield also influenced Acarie, Bérulle, and Marie de Beauvilliers, and Beauvilliers herself incorporated Canfield's teachings, together with those of pseudo-Dionysius, into her 1631 *Exercice divin ou pratique de la conformité de notre volonté à celle de Dieu ... par R. M. M. D.*, a treatise, that like Canfield's own, led the reader through the stages required to ascend into conformity with God's will.[73] Even more than that, Montmartre was known as a center for mysticism, fount of the so-called mystics of Montmartre who dispersed across France spreading *dévot* Counter-Reformation spirituality.[74] Saint Denis (and his historical conflations Dionysius the Areopagite and pseudo-Dionysius) thus provided the guiding force for the physical infrastructure, the liturgy, the mystical framework for the devotions of the nuns, and a musical-rhythmic framework in which chant and music could be reformed. Despite being a royal foundation, music did not serve the patron of the Abbey – Louis XIII – but Saint Denis, the Saint Sacrement, and through these the Guises, the *dévots* (including Marie de Médicis), the mystics of Montmartre, and all who tasted the blood of the martyrs.[75]

The Royal Congregation of the Oratory of Jesus Christ, 1611

In many ways, the circumstances surrounding the foundation of the Oratory of Jesus mirrored those of the reforms at the Abbey of Montmartre, in that the group of individuals driving change drew their

---

[72] Yates describes how Tyard's *Solitaire Second* underpinned the activities of the *Académie*; see Frances A. Yates, *The French Academies of the Sixteenth Century* (London, Warburg Institute, 1947), pp. 77–94. See also Diefendorf, *Penitence to Charity*, pp. 96–8.

[73] Henri Brémond, *Histoire littéraire du sentiment religieux en France depuis la fin des guerres de religion jusqu'à nos jours* (Paris, Bloud et Gay, 1916), Vol. 2, p. 453.

[74] The Montmartre nuns themselves later became famous mystics: figures such as Marie Alvequin, Charlotte le Sergent, and Marie Granger were all widely admired in *dévot* circles; see Brémond, *Histoire littéraire*, Vol. 2, pp. 442–84. The network of mystics and ex-Leaguers associated with the Canfield, Beauvilliers, Acarie, and the abbey is explored in Daniel Vidal, *Critique de la raison mystique: Benoît de Canfield: possession et dépossession au xviie siècle* (Grenoble, Jérôme Millon, 1990), especially pp. 63–95.

[75] Le Gall, *Le Mythe*, p. 495: "La prière des confrères s'élève avant tout pour faire triompher une politique dévote, qui place en son centre, non le roi, mais le royaume auquel Denis est totalement identifié" (The prayers of the *confrères* were raised above all for the triumph of *dévot* policies, which placed at their center not the king, but the kingdom with which Denis was completely identified).

influence not from their rank or position of power in the church establishment (bishops, cardinals, etc.) but from their personal, mystical, and charismatic qualities. Founded in 1611 by Pierre de Bérulle, one of the most celebrated Counter-Reformation figures of the age, and loosely modeled on the Oratory of Philippo Neri founded in Rome in 1575, the congregation's aim was to improve the life of the church by the cultivation of the priesthood through "the pursuit of sacerdotal perfection": strongly moved by reading a verse from Psalm 9, Bérulle had decided to found an order celebrating the priesthood, the order instigated by Jesus Christ himself, and thus the "most holy and most necessary order to the whole church."[76] Alongside Bérulle were two other renowned Counter-Reformation figures, François de Sales and Vincent de Paul, together with the Jesuit Pierre Coton (Henri IV and Louis XIII's confessor), and César de Bus. Yet behind all these individuals stood Marie de Médicis, a rallying figure for the *dévots* and influential in numerous other religious orders (including, of course, Montmartre); indeed, by 1623 the Congregation would be described as having been founded by Marie herself. Bérulle himself had been a chaplain at court since 1599 and had come under pressure to found such an order, not just from Marie but from others in her circle. Bérulle's cousin and foremost *dévote* Barbe Acarie (widow of arch-Leaguer Pierre Acarie and spiritual advisor at Montmartre), was instrumental in the process and had already written to Coton in 1606 asking him for his support.[77] Similarly, Cardinal de Joyeuse, older brother of Ange de Joyeuse (who oversaw the reforms at Montmartre) also brought his influence to bear, alongside Bishop Gondi of Paris and Chancellor Sillery. The result was that on November 11, 1611, the feast of Saint Martin (another feast strongly identified with the nation of France), Bérulle and the first members of the society – Jean Bence, Jacques Gastaud (both doctors of the Sorbonne), Paul Métézeau (a famous preacher), François Bourgoing (a *curé* in Clichy, and later Superior

---

[76] Psalm 9:12, 'Proclaim among the nations what he has done'; see Adolphe Perraud, *L'Oratoire de France au XVIIe et au XIXe siècle* (Paris, Charles Douniol, 1866), pp. 38–70, 82. The ideals and rules of the congregation can be found in *L'Esprit de la Congrégation de l'Oratoire de Jésus Christ, et les devoirs de ceux qui sont appelés*, in Pierre de Bérulle, *Œuvres complètes de Bérulle, Cardinal de l'Église Romaine*, ed. Abbé Migne (Paris, Migne, 1856), columns 1270–2. See also Louis Batterel, *Mémoires domestiques pour servir à l'histoire de l'Oratoire*, ed. Paul Ingold and E. Bonnardet, 4 vols. (Paris, Picard, 1902–4); Jervis, *The Gallican Church*, pp. 212–56, for an overview of the other broad reforms and foundations taking place at this time under *dévot* influence.

[77] Acarie and Bérulle had already collaborated in the founding of the Carmelites in France; see Jervis, *The Gallican Church*, p. 251.

General), and Pierre Caron – took up residence at the Hôtel du Petit-Bourbon. On that same day, Madame Acarie and Madame de Marillac (wife of Michel de Marillac, one of Marie de Médici's strongest *dévot* allies at court) came to the community to take communion; and in the subsequent days many others, including Cardinal de Joyeuse, the king, and his mother, visited the community, disrupting their work to such an extent that all spiritual activities were postponed until the Feast of the Assumption.[78] The broad popularity of the order was such that – against the wishes of Madame Acarie – Louis XIII recognized it as a royal institution on January 2, 1612; shortly afterward, on October 12, 1612, the Bishop of Paris approved its statutes; and on May 19, 1613, it received its Bull of Institution from Pope Paul V.[79]

Its membership rapidly growing, and soon finding the Hôtel du Petit-Bourbon too small, the king offered the Congregation the Hôtel-de-la-Monnaie as a home.[80] After some discussion, the offer was refused, Bérulle secretly purchasing the Hôtel-du-Bouchage from Henriette Catherine de Joyeuse, Duchess of Guise, daughter of Ange de Joyeuse, and important benefactor of Montmartre. In the first instance, a small temporary chapel was constructed on the site where, three months later, in May 1616, the Offices and Mass were celebrated for the first time. But this chapel was also too small, and so after the congregation had purchased additional land surrounding the Hôtel, Jacques Lemercier was engaged to design a new church (dedicated to Saint-Honoré) which was begun on July 19, 1621.

The construction of the new church was halted in 1623 by the Marquis de Vieuville, royal superintendent of buildings, because it interfered with the ambitious plans for the expansion of the Louvre.[81] After various unsuccessful interventions from Michel de Marillac and others, the superintendent even obtained an *arrêt* demanding that the church be demolished and the site cleared. Marie de Médicis's indignation had this *arrêt* lifted, but this moment marked the beginning of the royal takeover of the congregation, Louis decreeing in a *brevet* to Bérulle that the Petit-Bourbon and its chapel (effectively the Chapelle Royale) should be demolished (along with the Saint-Thomas and Saint-Nicolas-du-Louvre) and that the church of the Oratorians should henceforth become the new chapel of the Louvre, in a new design to be overseen by Clément Métézeau, and aligned

---

[78] Perraud, *L'Oratoire de France*, p. 44. [79] Perraud, *L'Oratoire de France*, p. 46.
[80] Ingold, *L'Église de l'Oratoire Saint-Honoré: étude Historique et Archéologique* (Paris, Librairie Poussielgue Frères, 1887), pp. 8–10.
[81] Ingold, *L'Église de l'Oratoire Saint-Honoré*, p. 17.

at ninety degrees to the original plan to better fit in with the overall conception of the new Louvre complex.[82]

It is in this decree that Louis declared his patronage of the Oratoire, laying claim to its practices as a symbol of his piety, and steering its mission in an entirely pro-monarchical direction. In return for his patronage, then, the Congregation was required[83]

> to celebrate every day and continually the Divine Office for the benefit of his Majesty, the said lady the Queen his mother, the queen his wife, the Duc d'Anjou his brother, the kings and others of the royal house to come, and the prosperity of this state; that the church founded in that place and house, the priests and people residing there, enjoy all the graces and privileges due to the servants and commensals of the kings . . .

Three arches of the nave were completed by 1625, but construction was then abandoned, the building remaining in that state (apart from some minor additions paid for by the king) until the middle of the eighteenth century, when it was finally completed.[84]

Music and Chant

Louis Batterel, a near-contemporary chronicler of the Congregation, confirms the close relationship between the order and the king: in his biographical entry for François Bourgoing, the congregant who revised the chant (as described below, and not to be confused with François Bourgoing the later superior of the order), Batterel paraphrases the priest, Biblical scholar, and Oratorian, Richard Simon, relating that[85]

> the people of the court, which was still in the Louvre, where Louis XIII ordinarily resided, frequented our church very much. It even became, in a way, their parish,

---

[82] Ibid., pp. 20–1. But for another account of the attribution of the church to Lemercier and Métézeau, see Alexandre Gady, *Jacques Lemercier: Architecte et ingénieur du Roi* (Paris, Éditions de la Maison des sciences de l'homme, 2005), pp. 13–36.

[83] Quoted in Ingold, *L'Église de l'Oratoire Saint-Honoré*, pp. 21–2: "faire et célébrer tous les jours et continuellement l'office divine à l'intention de sa Majesté, de la dite dame Reine sa mère, de la reine son épouse, du duc d'Anjou son frère, des rois et autre de la maison royale a l'avenir, et prospérité de cet état; que l'église commencée audit lieu et maison, prêtres et personnes demeurantes en icelle jouissent de toutes les grâces et privilèges attribués aux domestiques et commensaux des rois."

[84] Ingold, *L'Église de l'Oratoire Saint-Honoré*, p. 27.

[85] Batterel, *Mémoires*, Vol. I, p. 148: "les gens de la Cour, qui se tenait alors au Louvre, où Louis XIII faisait sa résidence ordinaire, fréquentèrent fort notre église. Elle devint même, en quelque façon, royale, et nous, ses chapelains du Louvre."

after the king had declared, by Letters Patent, that he had destined it to be his royal chapel, and us, his chaplains of the Louvre.

Batterel goes on to explain how a new kind of chant was introduced to the order:[86]

There, to add flavor to the divine offices and to adorn them for the better exercise of prayer, M. de Bérulle believed it necessary, in the place of Gregorian Chant to introduce into our church another kind of musical chant, which stands between ordinary chant and music. The performance fulfilled his intentions beyond his expectation. There was an outpouring of all the Court to all our Offices, since when we have been called "les Pères au beau chant."

While Batterel considered that one François Bourgoing of Bourges (not to be confused with François Bourgoing, the later superior of the order) was the creator of this new chant, Hardel (quoted by Batterel) attributed it to an unnamed *premier maître de la musique du roi*, a canon of Péronne, who apparently composed various liturgical items such as psalms for the hours, the Litanies of the Virgin, the *Exaudiat*, the *Rorate*, and the *Miserere*.[87] This music was supposedly performed with the accompaniment of a bass viol by a small choir on the tribune while a larger group of the *pères* responded: such was the excellence of the music that even the musicians of the king attended.[88]

No repertoire of this kind survives. What we do have, however, are two sources by this François Bourgoing, a priest who joined the order on November 26, 1616, and who was charged by the second *assemblée générale* with reforming the chant. The fruits of his work were published in the *Brevis psalmodiae ratio* (which consists of pages titled *Directorium Chori*) of 1634, a volume of notated chants for use in the daily Offices and Mass, prefaced with a short rubric; and *Le David françois* of 1641, a treatise on psalmody published shortly after Bourgoing had left Paris but presumably reflecting his ideas from the previous twenty-five years.[89] Neither of these sources introduce any

---

[86] Ibid.: "Or, pour leur faire gouter les divins offices et les attire aux exercices de la prière, M de Bérulle crut devoir, au lieu du chant grégorien introduire dans notre église une autre espèce de chant musical, qui tient et du chant ordinaire et de la musique. L'exécution répondit a ses intentions au-delà même de son attente. Ce fut une affluence de toute la Cour a tous nos offices, jusque-là qu'on nous appela d'abord 'les Pères au beau chant.'"

[87] Simon, however, saw this new style of chant as originating in secular song. See Richard Simon, *Lettres choisies de M. Simon*, ed. Bruzen la Martinière (Amsterdam, Pierre Mortier, 1730), Vol. 2, p. 68; and for a critique of Simon's account see Philippe Vendrix, 'Pour les grands et les autres: la reforme oratorienne du plain-chant', in Jean Duron (ed.), *Plain-chant et liturgie en France au xviie siècle* (Versailles, Éditions du CMBV, Klincksieck, 1997), pp. 87–96.

[88] Batterel, *Mémoires*, p. 149.

[89] François Bourgoing, *Brevis psalmodiae ratio ad usum presbytorium congregationis oratorii Domini nostri Jesu Christi instituta* (Paris, Pierre Ballard, 1634); and François Bourgoing, *Le David françois ou traité de la sainct Psalmodie* (Paris, Sebastien Huré, 1641).

Music and Chant

liturgical innovations unique to the Congregation, but the way in which they think about chant is significant.

Bérulle had died in 1629, and so Bourgoing's *Brevis psalmodiae ratio* is dedicated to the next superior, Charles Condren. In his dedication, Bourgoing says that he had worked with the choir for sixteen years, implying that he had effectively been the musical director since his arrival in 1616. The *proemium* then goes on to identify the typical problems with chant performance that we might expect, and that the volume is intended to rectify – that syllable length is often ignored – and describes how the psalm *Dixit Dominus* should be performed.

But Bourgoing's solution to this problem goes beyond simply the identification of long and short syllables and verbal instructions for a particular exemplar. Instead, he lays out a whole new system of rhythmic notation not dissimilar to that of Guidetti, though unlike Guidetti's most explicit rhythmic notation, no numerical proportions are involved. As he explains, using his new notation for the versicle and response for Vespers *Deus in adiutorium* (see Figure 6.12):[90]

Also, as it would be for the grandeur of psalm-singing, it is fitting that some syllables be longer than others: accordingly, it is necessary to differentiate the musical notes which show their length: therefore rectangular notes will indicate the long syllables, to which rectangular notes will be added a little dot when the syllables are to be sung or read by someone and need to be lengthened a little, and on the second-to-last syllable of a sentence or phrase. For the notes next to which you see shining asterisks, know that these are especially long, and that the syllables corresponding to them are to be sung with a very drawn-forth breath, as typically happens on the second-to-last syllables of prayers, chapters, and readings.

We assign other note shapes to express short syllables [these are the lozenge-shaped notes, although Bourgoing does not make this clear], or even long ones, although an elegant performance requires these to flow past within a short time. But if, in the flowing of the short syllables, voice [i.e. stress by lengthening] is to be

---

[90] Bourgoing, *Brevis psalmodiae ratio*, pp. 16–17: "Porro ut ad psalmodiae majestatem alias aliis longiores syllabas esse convenit: sic notas musicas, quae earum sunt indices & mensurae, diversis fingere figuris necesse est: quadrangulares igitur longas mensurabant, ad quas, cum cantandae, aut legendae alicui syllabae, paulo divitius inhaerendum erit, ut contingit in penultimis periodorum, & commatum, punctulus adjungetur. Quibus autem asteriscos praefulgentes adverteris, eas scito longissimas, syllabasque eis respondentes productissimo spiritu, ut in penultimis orationum, capitulorum, & lectionum usuvenit esse decantandas. Alias alterius figurae notas brevibus syllabis exprimendis attribuimus, aut etiam longis, qua stamen concinna modulatio breviori tempore fluere exiget. Quod si in ipso fluxu brevium syllabarum vox erit aliquantisper inhibenda in aliqua syllaba, subjecta illi ipsi nota cui adhaerbit punctulus, id indicabit, qui vice sufflaminis effusum cantus cursum in illa syllaba paulisper retardabit."

Figure 6.12 Versicle and Response, *Deus in adiutorium meum intende*.
François Bourgoing, *Brevis psalmodiae ratio ad usum presbytorium congregationis oratorii Domini nostril Jesu Christi instituta* (Paris, Pierre Ballard, 1634), p. 16. Bibliothèque nationale de France.

applied for some amount of time on a certain syllable, a note placed underneath that very syllable, to which a little dot will cling, will indicate that lengthening, which instead of a stopping the flow, will simply slow the course of the chant on that syllable for a short time.

In other words, far from this manner of performance being intentionally restricted to a limited range of well-defined note values, it celebrates the expressive diversity possible in the human voice, relating it to the physical act of performance ("to be sung with a very drawn-forth breath") and invoking the dramatic reading style necessary for readings, prayers and other *accentus* texts (like Guidetti and his forebears). And while the chants themselves relate to the medieval chant repertory in the same way that the Montmartre chants do (i.e. some are trimmed, or modified ["reformed"] while some are entirely new ["composed"]), the manner of declamation explicitly notated throughout the whole of the *Directorium* could not be more different.

Le David françois was published shortly after Bourgoing had left Paris, and his ideas regarding chant seem to have evolved in the years since the *Brevis psalmodiae*, both in musical/textual terms and in the role of chant more broadly. Unlike the *Directorium*, which is essentially a practical guide and compendium intended for the daily use of the congregation, *Le David françois* is framed as an encomiastic tribute to the king – the French David of the title, and its dedicatee – in which King David is set up as both an archetypal musician and as an ideal model for Louis XIII. Yet going beyond the model of David (in a way that I will discuss in the final chapter), Bourgoing also reminds the reader that kings, like priests (which of course they are in the model of sacral monarchy), are especially required to praise God:[91]

... Kings, because they are the living images of this great God who makes them to reign: Priests, because they are consecrated by a completely celestial unction. Kings, because they must imitate JESUS CHRIST, King of Kings, who did not cease to praise his father, and wishes that Kings praise God with him: Priests are also obliged to imitate him as their Commander, since they receive from him the grace and dignity of the Priesthood. Kings, because they have received more and because more is asked of them, are also more obliged to praise God than the rest of mankind.

Despite this emphasis on the Kingship of Jesus Christ, the primary way a king should act was nonetheless through the imitation of David, who in some ways Louis surpassed: David built just one temple, Louis had built many: David built up the clergy, so did Louis. And David founded two new companies of singers and of Portiers – he esteemed the singers because their role was to sing psalms and the praises of God, and he composed melodies to the words of his divine psalms. Louis too was a great musician:[92]

---

[91] Bourgoing, *Le David françois*, n.p.: "Les Roys, parce qu'ils sont les vives images de ce grand Dieu qui les fait régner: les Prestres, parce qu'ils sont consacrez d'une onction toute céleste. Les Roys, en ce qu'ils doivent imiter IESUS CHRIST Roy des Roys, qui ne cesse de loüer son Père, & veut que les Roys le loüent avec luys: les Prestres sont aussi obligez de l'imiter, comme leur Chef, & comme recevant de luy la grâce & dignité du Sacerdoce. Les Roys encore, parce qu'ils ont plus reçue, & qu'il leur sera plus demandé, sont aussi plus obligez à loüer Dieu que le reste des hommes."

[92] Bourgoing, *Le David françois*, n.p.: "David se delectoit à faire des airs qu'il appliquoit aux paroles de ses divins Pseaumes, & en suite les concertoit parmy les Chantes. Et vostre Maiesté, SIRE, qui n'ignore rien, & entre les autres sciences se plaist à la Musique, où elle trouve les plus agréables divertissements, & fait aussi bien que David des airs & des chants ravissans, qui charment, & frappent doucement l'oreille de ceux qui ont l'honneur de les oüir. En somme David après avoir sainctement loué ce grand Dieu en la terre, continue de le loüer heureusement dans le Ciel avec ces Chantres divins, ainsi que fera vostre Maiesté un iour après un long & heureux règne sur la Terre."

David delighted in composing airs which he used with the words of his divine psalms, and then performed them with his singers. And Your Majesty, sir, who is ignorant of nothing, and among the other sciences takes pleasure in music, where he finds the most agreeable diversions, and composes just as well as David ravishing airs and songs which charm and sweetly strike the ear of those who have the honor to hear. In sum, David, having praised God on earth, continues to praise him in Heaven with his divine singers, just as your majesty will one day after a long and happy reign on earth.

The first part of the volume surveys the history of chant and psalmody in particular, quoting the ancient authorities for the various practices of singing the psalms. Bourgoing explains Philo of Alexandria's account of the origins of singing alternatim in two choirs (a practice he claims was introduced by the Essenians), and Socrates's vision of angels who sang songs of praise to the Holy Trinity in the same way; and while it may have been Saint Ignatius of Antioch who introduced this manner of performing to the Christian Church, the ancient practice of reciting the psalms itself was introduced into the Christian church by Jesus Christ himself (as Saint Augustine can attest).[93]

Bourgoing also outlines a brief history of chant itself, pointing out that traditionally there had been no uniformity in its practice. The Church of Alexandria, governed by Saint Athanasius had a chant that was "very simple and heavy, almost without variation, which resemble more a simple reading than a song, which must undergo at least some variation."[94] On the other hand, the churches of the east had a much more varied style of performance, a style that was subsequently taken over by Saint Ambrose for Milan. Although both were homogenized by the reforms of Gregory, Bourgoing is keen to point out that "One can see by that, that the great Saints did not always share the same sentiment, and that one may render glory to God by different means."[95]

Having concluding this first section with a discussion of instrumental participation in the liturgy,[96] Bourgoing dedicates the second half of his treatise to the performance of psalms, beginning with an analysis of the

---

[93] Ibid., p. 22–4.
[94] Ibid., p. 34: "fort simple & pesant, presque sans aucune variation, qui ressembloit plustost à une simple lecture, qu'à un chant qui doit souffrir au moins quelque peu de variation."
[95] Ibid.: "On peut voir par là que les grands Saints n'ont pas tousious un mesme sentiment, & que l'on peut rendre gloire à Dieu par des moyens différents."
[96] Bourgoing declines to describe the "effects" of instrumental music in the liturgy, hoping that an unnamed "grand musicien de ce temps" (probably Thomas Gobert) will take on that task: ibid., p. 43. Gantez describes Gobert as a "maître de Péronne," a description that fits Hardel's recollection in note 87. See Annibal Gantez, L'Entretien des musiciens (Auxerre, J. Bouquet, 1643), ed. Ernest Thoinan (Paris, A. Claudin, 1878), p. 142.

typical faults encountered in performance. The minor or secondary faults – numbers two onward on his extensive list – include a pace of recitation that is either too fast or too slow, and the non-observance of rests, a fault that "takes away the grace and beauty" of the performance.[97] But the first and most common fault, according to Bourgoing, is that singers typically perform the first syllable of each verse long, even though it should generally be short: yet in most situations there are other singers who simultaneously perform it correctly, leading to an "inequality" which ruins the performance. And while the singers should of course respect the short syllable in this particular situation, it is nonetheless also important to introduce longs among the shorts later in the verse "afin de donner plus de grâce & d'ornement a la Psalmodie."[98]

As with the *Brevis psalmodiae*, Bourgoing declares that long syllables must not all be made equally long, but "les unes plus & les autres moins," and he gives rules for the situations in which lengthening should be applied, from most to least. At the lowest level of lengthening, the practice is subtle and spontaneous:[99]

But when it is appropriate to give them a certain little weight, to bring to that syllable some discernment, and some little distinction, which is done subtly by the support of the voice, which does not appear as a dot, and gives I know not what decoration, which ravishes and sweetly charms the ear.

But even at the higher levels of length, the manner of performance should not be highly structured. Again, Bourgoing confirms the principles he set out in the *Brevis psalmodiae* – that these longs relate to each other in a non-proportional manner, or to use the later vocabulary of Le Clerc, Jumilhac, and Nivers, or the near-contemporary vocabulary of Descartes, that these notes are "incommensurable" – "unmeasurable":[100]

This inequality of long syllables should not be considered like the measures of music, which always diminish or augment by strict proportion; but this means that one must weigh them, a bit more, or a bit less, according to the different marks

---

[97] Bourgoing, *Le David françois*, pp. 141, 143, 159.   [98] Ibid., pp. 135–6.
[99] Ibid., pp. 139–40: "Mais comme il est à propos de leur donner un certain petit poids, pour y apporter quelque discernement, & quelque petit distinction, qui se fait subtilement par un soutien de voix, qui ne paroist comme point, & donne je ne scay quelle agreement, qui ravit & charme doucement l'oreille."
[100] Ibid., p. 139: "Cette inégalité de syllabes longues de se doit pas considérer, comme les mesures de musique, qui vont tousiours diminuant ou augmentant de la iuste moitié; mais cela s'entend qu'on les doit peser, ou un peu plus, ou un peu moins, selan la distinction des marques que nous avons fait fabriquer à ce dessein, qui en rendra la pratique fort aisée."

which we have had made for this purpose, which makes their performance very simple.

In order to execute these subtle variations in length, Bourgoing then provides four symbols to correspond to each of the four gradations he has previously outlined: these symbols (in order of length, +, T, \, and '), he claims, would allow a thousand people to sing like a dozen, even if reading from musical notation that does not otherwise distinguish length – i.e. plainchant notation.[101] By contrast, without such symbols the customary faults encountered in performance (all longs equally long, or disregard for rests) typically result in the the listener being barely able discern a single word, an observation reminiscent of the "appalling discord" encountered by Marie de Beauvilliers at Montmartre mentioned above.[102]

Finally, Bourgoing concludes his treatise with instructions for altering text underlay to eliminate melisma when it interferes with syllable length. Clearly modeled on the Anerio/Soriano model, the chant modified according to this practice:[103]

> will be incomparably better, following the correction to the chant made in Rome these days ... But I say that it is certain that, if one suggests this correction, which is so desirable for the ornament of Ecclesiastical chant, various people will find the opportunity to repeat (the ones who have I know not what zeal to preserve, they say) the old ways; and that our fathers were more wise than us: these are their strongest arguments. But one could reply to these great zealots that the fathers of our fathers were also more wise than them, and that the chant was not always in such a bad state, and that it has been reformed in past centuries as much as in our own, and many times, according to Saints Gregory and Leon, ...

In this regard, Bourgoing is clearly a Modern, looking back at the past, seeing its inadequacies, and deciding that a new approach is just as valid. But he sees his mission as fraught with difficulties, arguing that the only solution is for a royal decree, in agreement with the Prelates (who alone have the power to authorize such a reform), to engage those capable to

---

[101] Ibid., p. 163.   [102] Ibid., p. 173.
[103] Ibid., p. 226: "incomparablement mieux, suivant mesme la correction du chant faite à Rome nos iours, ... Je dis donc qu'il est certain, que si on proposoit cette correction qui est tant à désirer pour l'ornement du chant Ecclésiastique, plusieurs trouveroient à redire, les uns par je ne sçay quel zèle de conserver, disent-ils, l'antiquité; & que nos pères estoient plus sages que nous: ce sont leurs plus puissantes raisons. Mais on pourroit répliquer à ces grands zélateurs, que les pères de nos pères estoient aussi plus sages qu'eux; & que le chant n'a pas toujours esté en si mauvais estat, & qu'on l'a reformé dans les siecles passez aussi bien qu'en nos jours & à divers fois, témoins les saincts Grégoires et Léons, ..."

"work on the correction of the chants for the Church," and to make them as uniform as possible.[104]

A Poetics of Royalty

The dichotomy here between two institutions and their approach to chant reflects many much broader changes in the conception of music, rhythm, and language, and two contrasting relationships with the monarchy. At Montmartre, the chant reflected the Renaissance order, a measured music, imitating the poetic meters of antiquity. Boësset's understanding of text setting (certainly in the early days) reflected his musical inheritance and environment – the *airs de cour* of Guédron, the psalm settings of Caignet, the *musique mesurée* settings in Du Caurroy's 1610 *Meslanges*, the neo *vers mesurée* of Nicolas Rapin (Marie de Médicis's poet) – in which musical time itself reflected a numerical and cosmological order. For the Guises who sponsored such efforts, the mystics of Montmartre, and the *dévots* who subscribed to a Neoplatonic conception of the universe, the "effects" of the chant could be harnessed to serve not the king, but France, the Catholic church, and the martyr Saint Denis. On the other hand, at the Congregation of the Oratory, both the institution and the chant itself were explicitly constructed as a mirror of the king himself, whom (despite their *dévot* roots) the Oratorians revered as a fellow priest and a fellow imitator of Jesus Christ. The priests of the Oratory were to serve the king and his court, and the chant they performed was to mimic the song of David, a musician who shared many of the same characteristics as the king. But this song did not imitate the music of antiquity – indeed it specifically eschewed the simplistic nature of antique text declamation (and the very idea of the "ancient") for something much more modern, more spontaneous, expressive, and rhetorical, and a manner of performance that depended on the physical embodiment of the music in the voice. While Bourgoing specifically rejected the idea of single, ideal past ("our fathers' fathers were more wise than them"), Boësset had embraced it, bringing to fruition a final outgrowth of Renaissance humanism before the chant was later "re-reformed" (in terms of declamation if not in terms of pitches) to appear no different to other chant appearing around this time.[105]

---

[104] Ibid., p. 240.
[105] Nivers, Le Clerc, and Jumilhac would all grapple with the same ancients versus moderns dichotomy, seeing equal (i.e. 2:1) performance as old-fashioned and embracing to a greater of lesser extent the freedoms of Bourgoing, whose work, one must assume, they knew. See Ranum, "'Le Chant doit perfectionner'".

These two opposing attitudes mesh in interesting ways with the wider changes occurring in these years as expressed by philosophers and music theorists: as Thomas puts it: "If composers had stopped writing music designed to express the hierarchical intricacies of the universe in order to place more attention on the movement of the voice, theorists also had to develop a discourse that would emphasize the verbal and rhetorical concerns of the new music."[106] Both René Descartes (as we have seen) and the theorist Nicolas Bergier took up this challenge, reflecting, albeit through different priorities, the period in which this transition was occurring and shedding light on contemporary attitudes to chant. Descarte's ideas on musical time clearly evolved after the publication of the *Compendium*, since the affective theories he set out in *Les Passions de l'Âme* (a little later) provide a much more forward-looking model of musical expression (i.e. completely non-numerical, justified instead by the experience of the senses), a model that was adopted by later theorists and that would account for the kinds of comments that Bourgoing made about the physical, rhetorical properties of his chant.[107] Indeed, while I would not argue for any causative link, it is interesting to consider that Descartes was a close ally of the Oratorians, that he spent several years in the early 1620s in Paris with them, and that, having just claimed in the *Compendium* that musical time could only be conceived Arithmetically, he would have experienced Oratorian chant performed in the completely "incommensurable" manner shared with his rejected Geometrical model of musical time.[108] Nicolas Bergier's contemporary theories on rhythm are also instructive. Situating himself between the ancients and the moderns, Bergier sets out a theory in his *Musique speculative* (manuscript, begun in 1603) that distinguishes poetic rhythm from musical rhythm and considers their interaction.[109] Poetic rhythm consisted of only two unchangeable values – long and

---

[106] Downing Thomas, *Music and the Origins of Language: Theories from the French Enlightenment* (Cambridge and New York, Cambridge University Press, 1995), p. 23.

[107] Descartes, *Excellent Compendium*, pp. 1, 5.

[108] Descartes maintained a strong relationship with the Oratorians. The entry for Guillaume Gibieuf in Batterel, *Mémoires*, pp. 233–60 testifies to the connection between Descartes and Gibieuf, and with Marin Mersenne. See also Roger Ariew, *Descartes and the First Cartesians* (Oxford, Oxford University Press, 2014) pp. 26–40. Nicolas Poisson, the French translator of the *Compendium*, was also an Oratorian.

[109] Modern edition and translation into German in Nicolas Bergier, trans. Ekkehard Jost, *La Musique spéculative* (Cologne, A. Volk, 1970). For a broader discussion of Bergier's treatise, see Philippe Vendrix, 'Nicolas Bergier: le dernier théoricien de la Renaissance en France', in François Lesure and Henri Vanhulst (eds.), *"La Musique, de tous les passetemps le plus beau": Hommage à Jean-Michel Vaccaro* (Paris, Klincksieck, 1998), pp. 369–86; see also Kate van Orden, *Music, Discipline, and Arms*, pp. 84–6.

short: but the composers of the present, reported Bergier, prioritize musical rhythm over poetic rhythm "because, attaching and subserving the syllables to the time, rather than the time to the syllables, they make the long syllables much longer and much shorter, so that their longs are not equally long, and their shorts are not equally short." We can therefore see in such an approach to music the same impetus that drove Bourgoing, and the chant of the Oratorians as representative of a new "musical" (rather than poetic or numerical) approach to chant, an approach that would become more and more prevalent through the remainder of the century with the rise of "plainchant musical." At the same time, this new approach at the Oratory subtly realigned the king not with the syncretic models of the past (exemplified by the Montmartre chant) but with a new purely biblical model of kingship, now based on the more affective models set out in Bourgoing's preface – David the expressive poet, or even Jesus Christ himself, the first to sing the psalms in the "Christian" church. It is this model, coming to the fore in the 1630s and informing the next two decades, that is the focus of the final chapter of this study.

7 Succession

The Vow of 1638 and Christ the King

After Louis's success at La Rochelle in 1628, the internal conflict with the Huguenots was effectively over. The peace treaty of the following year, the Grace of Alais, ended decades of religious wars, allowing the Huguenots freedom of worship as equal subjects of the king, while restricting their political and military independence.[1] Yet the Grace of Alais was not welcomed by all – both *dévots* and *bon français* (or *politiques*, those who put French interests over those of Rome) – nor was it a panacea for all of France's troubles. Louis's mother Marie began to resent Richelieu's influence over policy even more, and his brother Gaston also provoked a storm by marrying the daughter of the Duke of Nevers/Mantua. Things eventually came to a head when the city of Casale, in the Mantuan enclave of Monferrato, contested as part of the so-called War of the Mantuan Succession, was again threatened and Louis had to decide whether to intervene militarily. Receiving conflicting advice from Marie and her *dévot* allies (such as Marillac) and Richelieu (himself under the influence of Père Joseph, the *éminence grise*), Louis embarked on another military campaign in 1630, again personally leading his troops but becoming dangerously ill in the process, even receiving the last rites on September 30 after his premature return to Lyon. On his recovery and return to Paris, however, his resolve was strengthened and he confronted Marie on the famous Day of the Dupes, stripping her of her influence and deposing Michel de Marillac.

From this point onward, however, other external issues and the raging Thirty Years' War began to intrude on France's affairs. Louis became involved in a number of external conflicts that could be broadly characterized as defensive (protecting territories just outside the French border), but in 1634 the Swedish and German Protestant League forces were defeated at the Battle of Nördlingen by the Imperial forces of the Holy Roman emperor. For France not to get involved was to leave the whole of Europe open for the Habsburgs, and so in 1635 France entered the

---

[1] A. Lloyd Moote, *Louis XIII, the Just* (Berkeley, Los Angeles, and London, University of California Press, 1989), pp. 199–206.

Thirty Years' War on the side of the Protestants, opening itself up to attack by all supporters of Imperial forces, most notably the Spanish, who started to menace from the Spanish Netherlands to the north. By August 2, 1636, they had crossed the Somme and were threatening Paris. Once again, the kingdom of France was in existential danger and would remain so for much of the remaining few years of Louis's reign. Not only that, Louis was still without an heir, and the prospect of France suffering another succession crisis was most unwelcome.

In these circumstances, as the 1630s progressed, the king's confessional orientation began to subtly shift. As a Catholic monarch now allied with Protestant powers and engaged in a war against another Catholic power (and a monarch who had failed to seize the opportunity to completely destroy the religious and civic privileges of the Huguenots after La Rochelle), Louis was vulnerable to political and religious attack from those not just with *dévot* sympathies, but even the majority of *bons français*. For that reason, it was imperative that his military and political decisions be justified by emphasizing his own status as a devout, even *dévot*, Christian, re-emphasizing his personal virtue and his descent from Saint Louis (in particular the ascetic and spiritual side to his character), and attempting to portray his reign as effectively a theocracy.[2] To some extent, he had already compromised with the *dévots*. Figures such as Bérulle and Saint Vincent de Paul had become influential at court in the 1620s, and the network of famously *dévote* women in the Acarie circle (to which they provided spiritual guidance), together with Marie de Médicis and her allies at court, such as Michel de Marillac, dominated court culture in a manner – personal, introspective, and mystical – that presented a challenge to the "masculine sway of French sovereignty."[3] In the same years, the Jesuit Nicolas Caussin (briefly the king's confessor from 1638 to 1639) had penned his bestselling *La Cour sainte*, a tract published in 1624 and again in the 1640s arguing that the court itself – not just those parts usually understood as having a religious function – was to be considered a sacred institution.[4] In this context, the militaristic and overtly masculine figure of

---

[2] Louis's increasing alignment with the *dévots* is described in Joseph Bergin, *The Politics of Religion in Early-Modern France* (New Haven and London, Yale University Press, 2014), pp. 96–104.
[3] Paul Kléber Monod, *The Power of Kings: Monarchy and Religion in Europe, 1589–1715* (New Haven and London, Yale University Press, 1999), p. 111.
[4] Nicolas Caussin, *La Cour sainte* (Paris, S. Chappelet, 1624), p. 1. Caussin opens the first book with an observation that serves as a metaphor for the whole volume: that the Kings of Judea's quarters were separated from the altar of the Tabernacle only by a wall, through which David had a door installed. As one of "des plus saints Monarques," he was thus able ease his afflictions

David (or his mythological or Roman/Greek stand-in) no longer functioned as an appropriate model for the king despite the danger the nation faced. Instead, attention focused on either David's own devotion as a model for Louis (the strategy adopted by Caussin), on the Virgin Mary, or on Jesus Christ himself, as the object of both Eucharistic devotion (in line with the *dévot* emphasis on communion) and as a model of kingship. Thomas à Kempis's *Imitation of Christ*, translated into French by arch *dévot* Michel de Marillac (published 1626 and again in 1631), captured the spirit of the time with its emphasis on the internal life of the Christian and the sacrament of the Eucharist, and also resonated with the aims of the Compagnie du Saint Sacrement (founded in 1630 and tacitly supported by the king) and the *dévot* movement more generally;[5] so important was this text during the 1630s that a new edition was the first volume produced by the new Imprimerie Royale established by Richelieu in 1640.[6] Likewise, the *Parva Christianae pietatis officia per christianissimum Regem Ludovicum XIII ordinate* (Little Offices for Louis XIII) also published by the *Imprimerie Royale* just before Louis's death in 1643, effectively made public Louis's daily devotional regime and was illustrated with a frontispiece of Louis praying in devotion to Christ himself.[7]

In musical and liturgical terms, the 1630s are not rich in evidence, but the handful of musical works that we can place in that decade do strikingly reflect one of the most important developments of those years – the dedication of the kingdom of France to the Virgin Mary, officially sanctioned in 1638 but presaged from at least 1630. All composed by Nicolas Formé, three sets of works were published or prepared for publication by

---

by literally breaking down the barriers between the court and the tabernacle. See Bergin, *Politics of Religion*, p. 102 for more on Caussin. In a similar vein, Jean Boucher's monumental treatise described how princes had a special duty before all other Christians to live a pious life and fight heresy; see Jean Boucher, *La Couronne mystique ou Desein de Chevallerie Chrestienne pour exciter les Princes Chrestiens a rendre le debvoir a la piété Chrestienne contre les enemies d'icelle* (Tournai, Adrien Quinqué, 1623).

[5] *IV livres, de l'imitation de Jésus-Christ* ... (Paris, Nicolas Gasse, 1626). While the Compagnie du Saint Sacrement was undoubtedly significant (Louis's confessor Père Suffren and his mother were members), in the absence of any record of liturgy or music it will not form part of this study; see Marc René de Voyer d'Argenson, *Annales de la Compagnie du St-Sacrement* (Marseille, Typographie Saint-Léon, 1900), pp. 9–15. D'Argenson reports that members were to read *L'Imitation de Jésus-Christ*.

[6] Thomas a Kempis, *De imitatione Christi* (Paris, Typographia Regia, 1640). In a similar vein, François Bourgoing's *Les Véritez et excellences de Jésus-Christ Notre-Seigneur* (1635) was a series of meditations on various aspects of Christ's life.

[7] *Parva Christianae pietatis officia per christianissimum Regem Ludovicum XIII ordinate* (Paris, Typographia Regia, 1643).

the Ballard house in 1638, the year of both the Vow and of the birth of the dauphin, the future Louis XIV *Dieudonné*: two settings of the Mass ordinary in simple counterpoint, a set of eight Magnificats, and the famous Mass for two choirs *Aeternae Henrici Magni*. Whether in terms of musical conception, or simply the fact that they were prepared for publication that year, all three works can be heard as responses to the new status of France – a kingdom under the protection of the Queen of Heaven and by association the King of Kings, no longer Louis but Jesus Christ himself.

The Vow to the Virgin

The dedication of the kingdom of France to the Virgin Mary was officially promulgated in the famous declaration of February 10, 1638, but Mary seems to have become a particular focus of Louis's own personal devotion long before this. Probably instilled by his first confessor Père Coton, Louis's interest in the Virgin had led him to make a number of documented pilgrimages and dedications. In 1614 he walked on foot to Notre-Dame-des-Vertus-d'Aubervilliers (in the northern suburbs of Paris, not far from the Abbey of Saint-Denis) to ask for protection during the upcoming military campaign in Normandy, one of many such visits.[8] In 1628 he presented a new façade to the church, also visiting Notre-Dame-des-Ardilliers in Saumur on his way back from La Rochelle to give thanks to the Virgin for his successes there.[9] And most famously, the following year he founded the church of Notre-Dame-des-Victoires in Paris, also to give thanks for his victory.[10] But in 1630, recovering in Lyon after his near-death experience, he seems to have taken a significant step toward the dedication of the whole kingdom itself, a letter of October that year declaring that he was delivering himself and his people to God and to "the Empire of the most Powerful Lady."[11]

---

[8] Charles Bernard, *Histoire du Roy Louis XIII* (Paris, Nicolas de Sercy, 1646), livre XII, p. 144.
[9] Abbé Oroux, *Histoire ecclésiastique de la cour de France* (Paris, Imprimerie Royale, 1775–6), Vol. 2, p. 386. See also *Le Mercure françois*, 15 (1628), 708.
[10] Notre-Dame-des-Victoires certainly had an active musical tradition, but the surviving repertory dates from the reign of Louis XIV; see John Burke, 'Sacred music at Notre-Dame-des-Victoires under Mazarin and Louis XIV', *Recherches sur la musique française classique*, 20 (1981), 19–44.
[11] René Laurentin, *Le Vœu de Louis XIII: passé ou avenir de la France* (Paris, O. E. I. L, 1988), p. 94, quoting Archives des Affaires Étrangères, Mémoires et Documents, France, Vol. 828, f. 186v: "l'Empire de la Très Puissante Dame."

Figure 7.1 Simon Vouet, *Le Vœu de Louis XIII*, Charenton-le-Pont, Médiathèque de l'Architecture et du Patrimoine.
Photo © Ministère de la Culture – Médiathèque de l'architecture et du patrimoine, Dist. RMN-Grand Palais/Archives photographiques (Saint-Quentin-en-Yvelines)

The edict mentioned in the letter seems not to have resulted in any particular new emphasis on the Feast of the Assumption (or any other liturgical practice), but it did find expression, not long after this in 1633, in Simon Vouet's striking altarpiece for the church of Neuilly-Saint-Front, sometimes known as *Le Vœu de Louis XIII*.[12] The ambiguous title is

---

[12] Simon Vouet, *Le Vœu de Louis XIII*, for the church of Neuilly-Saint-Front, now in Charenton-le-Pont, Médiathèque de l'Architecture et du Patrimoine. Simon Vouet (1590–1649, *premier*

reflected in the composition of the painting, which takes the form of a *Stabat Mater*: Louis's attention is firmly directed to the crucified Jesus, the body of Christ, and the object of Eucharistic devotion, while Mary, though present, is more a participant in the scene than its object. Beyond that, though, Louis's insertion into the traditional composition on Christ's left side (the hallowed site reserved for John) makes explicit the king's bold claims that his piety and devotion to Christ are as great as that of the apostles.

If the 1630 declaration was not otherwise marked, several years later the imminent danger presented by the Spanish invasion of northern France led to a renewal and intensification of the fervor toward Mary. On May 19, 1636, Richelieu wrote to Louis on the battlefield, describing the devotions that were taking place in Paris and suggesting that "A redoubling of devotion toward the mother of God can only produce very good results."[13] The king quickly replied to Richelieu in the affirmative, but the church more broadly also acted decisively. The Archbishop of Paris commanded the continuous observance of Prayers of Forty Hours across the diocese (each church taking it in turns) from July 10 until January 27 the next year, specifying the recitation of various "Prières pour l'heureux succez des armes de Sa Majesté," beginning with the *Veni Sancte Spiritus* "pour invoquer la grâce du S. Esprit" and including the *Exaudiat te Dominus*, the "prière pour le roy."[14] Although by August 2, the Spanish forces had crossed the Somme and Louis was back in Paris, the city now in a state of panic in expectation of imminent occupation, Louis's armies fought back, pushing the invaders back across the Oise and the Somme, and besieging the town of Corbie, which finally fell into the hands of French forces on November 11, 1636, amid much celebration.

By 1637 Richelieu was working on a new vow (although in essence is replicated the ideas of the 1630 document), and by November 21 that year the Swedish ambassador, Grotius, recounted in a letter that the king had already dedicated both himself and his kingdom to the Virgin, noting that they were proposing to install a new altar in Notre-Dame in

---

peintre du roi 1627–49) was, of course, one of the most important decorative painters serving the French court and nobility in the generation before Nicolas Poussin.

[13] Maurice de Vaulgrenant, 'Le Vœu de Louis XIII', *Revue d'histoire de l'Église de France*, 24/102 (1938), 49: "Un redoublement de dévotion envers la mère de Dieu ne peut que produire de très bons résultats."

[14] *Prières ordonnées par Monsieurs l'Archevesque de Paris pour dire aux Églises où sont les Prières de Quarante-heures: Pour le bon succez de sa Majesté, contre tous les ennemis de son Estat* (Paris, Pierre Targa, 1636).

celebration.[15] But the vow itself was only officially issued on February 10, 1638, with the king signing the *lettres patentes* that placed both himself and the kingdom under the protection of the Virgin Mary in a ceremony at his château at Saint-Germain. Nevertheless, the hostilities continued unabated, and Louis was again forced to continue his advance north. So it was that, on the day of the Feast of the Assumption itself (August 15), Louis found himself in Abbeville. Revisiting the church of the Minims where a year earlier he had (so the accounts went) dramatically and publicly made his declaration to the Virgin Mary at the consecration of the host, he made his own personal devotions in the morning before returning for Vespers and hearing the sermon preached by the Bishop of Nîmes, followed by a solemn procession where his Almoner, Dominique Séguier, Bishop of Meaux, officiated in his pontifical robes.[16]

Shortly after Louis had signed the *lettres patentes* at Saint-Germain, the vow was published as *Déclaration du roy, par laquelle sa Majesté déclare qu'elle a pris la très-Saincte & très Glorieuse Vierge pour Protectrice spéciale de son Royaume* (Declaration of the King, by which his Majesty declares that he has taken the most Holy and most Glorious Virgin as special Protector of his Kingdom). Over twelve pages the declaration explains the motivation for the vow and the practical steps that are to result from it.[17] After a reminder that it is "God who raises Kings on the throne of their grandeur" but that the "malice of the devil" and the "fragility of the age" have created almost insurmountable dangers for the kingdom, the declaration continues:[18]

To these ends, we have declared and continue to declare that taking the very holy and very glorious Virgin for special protector of our Kingdom. We dedicate to her in particular our Person, our State, our Crown, and our Subjects, begging her to

---

[15] Vaulgrenant, *Le Vœu*, p. 52.
[16] H. Dusevel, 'Le Vœu de Louis XIII', in Paul Roger (ed.), *Bibliothèque historique monumentale, ecclésiastique et littéraire de l'Artois et de la Picardie* (Amiens, Duval et Herment, 1844), p. 216: Oroux, *Histoire ecclésiastique*, Vol. 2, 437.
[17] *Déclaration du roy, par laquelle sa Majesté déclare qu'elle a pris la très-Saincte & très Glorieuse Vierge pour Protectrice spéciale de son Royaume* (Paris, 1638).
[18] *Déclaration du roy*, p. 3: "Dieu qui élève les Roys au thrône de leur Grandeur." *Déclaration du roy*, pp. 5–6: "À ces causes, nous avons déclaré & déclarons que prégnant la très-saincte & très glorieuse Vierge, pour Protectrice spéciale de nostre Royaume, Nous luy consacrons particulièrement nostre Personne, nostre Estat, nostre Couronne, & nos Subiects, la suppliant de nous vouloir inspirer une saincte conduicte, & defender avec tant de soin ce Royaume contre l'effort de tous ses Ennemis . . ."

inspire in us a holy conduct, and to defend with great care this Kingdom against the efforts of all her Enemies.

As part of this declaration, a new altar was to be constructed in the eponymous cathedral of Notre-Dame, on which was to be installed a painting showing the Virgin Mary holding the crucified Christ descending from the Cross, with the king to be represented at the feet of Christ and his Mother, offering his scepter and Crown. The Vow was to be commemorated on the Feast of the Assumption (August 15), which was to be celebrated with special solemnity, with High Mass in the morning and then a procession after Vespers in which all the Companies and Corps of the city were to take part.[19]

For the first celebration of the Vow in 1638 (during which the king was in Abbeville), the brief *Mercure françois* account of the event confirms that this is indeed what happened. All the parishes of the city and *fauxbourgs* made their procession after Vespers: the clergy of the Sainte Chapelle processed around the Palace, while the clergy of Notre-Dame made their procession with the civic dignitaries that usually participated in the "Te Deum" (the *cour de parlement*, the *chambre des comptes*, and the *corps de ville*).[20] Archon's report (which may have been a generic description of the annual event rather than of the 1638 ceremony in particular) describes how an image of the Virgin Mary was carried in a general procession around the city with the "Ecclesiastics and Singers of the King singing motets in honor of the Queen of Heaven."[21] At the same time a new prayer was ordained to be sung at Mass in every church in France: beginning with the Antiphon *Sub tuum praesidium* (usually performed in some kind of Marian office rather than the Mass), which implored the Virgin to "deliver us from all perills and dangers," followed by a versicle and response (*Deus iudicium* ... etc., the same as in the *entrée*), the concluding prayer asked the "God of Kings and Kingdoms, moderator and just, who hast pleased that thy only sonne, hath been the sonne of the most happy Virgin Marie, and subject unto her: receave and accept graciously the vowes of

---

[19] *Déclaration du roy*, pp. 6–7.   [20] *Le Mercure françois*, 22 (1638), 289.
[21] There is confusion about where the king was on August 15, 1638. Some accounts record him in Abbeville making the dramatic declaration, others that he made it in 1637. Archon's account implies that he was in Paris; see Jean-Louis Archon, *Histoire ecclésiastique de la Chapelle des Rois de France* (Paris, Pierre-Augustine le Mercier, 1704–11), Vol. 2, p. 779: "On fit un procession générale où l'on porta avec décence une image de la Vierge, les Ecclésiastiques & les Chantres du Roy chantant des Motets en l'honneur de cette Reine du Ciel."

thy servant the most Christian King of France and of his faithfull people, and of his whole Realme."[22] The focus on the Feast of the Assumption was later formalized, because by 1641 Jacques Eveillon's *De Processionibus Ecclesiasticis Liber* contained an order "De Processione vespertina in Festo Assumptionis B. Mariae, pro Rege & Regno," which describes how all the churches of Paris are to make a procession for the peace and tranquillity of the king and his reign, invoking the story of King Hezekia, David's son, who had reconsecrated the temple as an offering to God.[23]

The altarpiece specified in the *Déclaration* was indeed created, by Philippe de Champaigne, and still survives, a bleak and striking composition that evokes the climate of fear in a way that Vouet's image – painted at a relatively secure moment in French history – does not. Unlike Vouet's work, though, Champaigne's composition takes the form of a *pietà* or lamentation, in which Mary is depicted mourning the death of her son and loosely cradling his body: nevertheless, here too Louis's presence in the scene, usually reserved for those close to Christ, visually manifests his claims of piety, and enshrines them publicly at Notre-Dame just as the declaration itself did. Louis wears his full royal regalia and seems to offer Christ (not Mary) his crown and scepter, subjugating both himself and the kingdom of France to Christ as Mary again looks on. A commemorative pamphlet celebrating the altar installation noted this focus on Christ.[24] In a pair of poems dedicated to the portraits of the king and the queen that were displayed underneath the Champaigne painting (in other words, both figuratively and literally at the feet of Christ), an anonymous author describes how "Also, one sees both the one and the other [king and queen] / At the feet of Jesus their good master,/ And of his holy Mother also."[25]

---

[22] *Oraison à la très-heureuse, très-pure, & Immaculée Vierge Marie Mère de Dieu, qui se dira par chacun an, en toutes les Églises de France, en la Messe au iour & Feste de l'Assomption d'icelle Vierge, suivant la Déclaration & Commandement du Roy, publié en l'année 1638* (n.p, 1638). The text is provided in Latin, Greek, French, German, Flemish, Spanish, Italian, and English.

[23] Jacques Eveillon, *De processionibus eccleiasticis liber* (Paris, Matthaeum Guillemot, 1641), pp. 278–82.

[24] *Stances ou prière du Roy sur un tableau offert par sa Majesté à Nostre Dame de Paris, représentant Nostre Seigneur mort entre les bras de la très-sainte Vierge: & sadite Majesté luy présentant à genoux sa Couronne* (Paris, Jacques le Long, 1638).

[25] *Sur les portraits du Roy & de la Royne, qui sont aux pieds de l'Image de Nostre Dame en son Église de Paris* in *Stances ou prière du Roy*, p. 11: "Aussi l'on voit tousiours l'un & l'autre paraistre / Aux pieds de IESUS leur bon maistre, / Et de sa sainte Mere aussi, . . ."

The Vow to the Virgin 247

Figure 7.2 Philippe de Champaigne, *Le Vœu de Louis XIII*, Caen, Musée des Beaux-Arts.
Photo © akg-images

The Champaigne painting was placed near the existing chapel dedicated to the Virgin, a chapel that had been furnished with an elaborate altar and six golden lamps, one of which was a gift already presented by the king at Richelieu's suggestion, on October 9, 1636, the Feast of Saint Denis. Another lamp, presented the day earlier, was given on behalf of the king by Richelieu. Even more spectacular, this lamp, with six chandeliers, was decorated with six angels holding a variety of musical instruments in their hands. Around the base were multiple *escussons* showing the arms of the king, and the body of the lamp – which was five feet in diameter – showed the story of the life of the Virgin. The whole thing was supported by three eagles hung by three chains, and (according to Malingre) was one of the most beautiful pieces of *orfèvrerie* he had ever seen.[26]

Nicolas Formé and the Bride of Christ

We know little of the life of Nicolas Formé, *sous-maître* at the *chapelle royale* alongside his colleague Eustache Picot (they shared the position, each serving for a six-month semester). One of Louis XIII's most highly regarded musicians, he was born in Paris in 1564 and probably received his musical training at the Sainte Chapelle (where he was admitted in 1587), but by 1595 he had been engaged as an *haute-contre* at the *chapelle royale*.[27] In 1609 he succeeded Eustache Du Caurroy, who had died on August 7, as *sous-maître*, serving in that capacity for the rest of his life. Importantly, for much of the period he also simultaneously served in the *musique de la chambre* (although his function there is not completely clear), in this situation apparently serving throughout the year along with his other colleagues there. He died on May 28, 1638, between the declaration of the Vow to the Virgin on February 10 and its first "official" celebration on August 15.

As *sous-maître* for some thirty years, Formé must have composed a substantial body of music, but the only works that have survived are those published or prepared for publication in 1638. For that reason, we cannot claim that these works are typical of his output or representative of musical practice more generally: nevertheless, we might also argue that, at the age of seventy it was these works that he felt most represented his life's work, or were most appropriate at that moment, as he approached the Ballard house with the intention of publishing them. In a contract entered into with Pierre and Robert Ballard on January 30, 1638, Formé agreed to grant the

---

[26] Claude Malingre, *Les Antiquités de la ville de Paris* (Paris, Rocolet, 1640), p. 27.

[27] This biographical information is taken from the introduction to Charles Léon, ed., *Nicolas Formé: Œuvres Complètes* (Versailles, Éditions du CMBV, 2003), in turn taken from Michel le Moël's seminal study *Recherches sur les musiciens du Roi, 1600–1650* (Thesis, École des Chartes, 1954). See also Michel le Moël, 'La Chapelle de Musique sous Henri IV et Louis XIII', *Recherches sur la musique française classique*, 6 (1966), 5–26, and Alexander Robinson, *Musique et musiciens à la cour d'Henri IV (1589–1610)* (PhD dissertation, University of Paris-Sorbonne, 2015).

rights of "three Masses in simple counterpoint, one in four and five voices and dedicated to the king, and two others dedicated to our lords most eminent the Cardinals of Richelieu and of Lyons."[28]

The descriptions of the three Masses in counterpoint correspond to the three Masses that now survive – two in volumes entitled *Musica simplex quatuor vocum*, dedicated to the Richelieu brothers, and a third the famous Mass for two choirs, *Missa Aeternae Henrici Magni, Gallorum Navarrorumque Regis Potentissimi ac Clementissimi memoriae et Ludovici Iusti eius Filii, Gallorum Navarrorumque Regis Christianissimi atque Invictissimi* (Mass to the Eternal Memory of Henry the Great, Most Powerful and Clement King of France and Navarre, and to Louis the Just His Son, Most Christian and Invincible King of France and Navarre), dedicated to Louis himself and the memory of Henri IV. Not mentioned in the contract, but presumably also intended for publication, was a set of eight Magnificats, the Song of Mary that describes her joy at giving birth to Jesus; these Magnificat settings now survive only in manuscript, though in a format that suggests it had been prepared as a master copy for the printers to work from.[29]

The dedication that prefaces the manuscript set of Magnificats clearly alludes to the Vow, highlighting the "ardent affection and reverence that you bear to the Queen of the heavens, protector of Your majesty, your Kingdom, and the Kings your predecessors who have implored her succor,"[30] and suggesting that the preparation for publication – although presumably not the composition itself (these works had probably been in use for many years if not decades) – took place in 1638. It is perhaps possible that the decision to publish was only taken later (even if this plan never came to fruition), after the news emerged that the Queen was to give birth. Certainly, the Magnificat, a song about motherhood, a "queen" giving birth to an anointed one or "Christ," would have particular resonance in the context of the celebrations surrounding the pregnancy of Anne of Austria. (The apocryphal figure Anne was, of course, Mary's mother, so the resonance between the Queen Anne and the Queen of Heaven would have been obvious.)

---

[28] The process by which the works were offered to Ballard is documented in François Lesure, 'Un contrat d'exclusivité entre Nicolas Formé et Ballard, 1638', *Revue de Musicologie*, 50/2 (1964), 228–9.
[29] F-Pn MS fonds fr. 1870.
[30] F-Pn MS fonds fr. 1870, n.p.: "L'ardante affection et révérence que vous portéz a ceste Royne des cieux protectrice de vostre Maiesté, de vostre Royaum, & des Roys vos prédécesseurs qui ont imploré son ayde ..."

Figure 7.3 Abraham Bosse, *Les Vœux du Roy et de la Reyne à la Vierge*.
Bibliothèque national de France

The pregnancy of Anne of Austria, and the subsequent birth of Louis XIV, was certainly significant in this context, because from this point onward the iconography associated with the Vow changed. (It is frequently claimed that the Vow was entered into as a means of safeguarding an heir, but Vaulgrenant has dismissed such claims.)[31] Rather than featuring the crucified Christ, Mary was now pictured either alone or with the baby Jesus. In the contemporary engraving by Abraham Bosse, for example, the vow is now made jointly by the king and queen. In the center, Mary, seated on a throne without the baby Jesus, declares the Bourbon motto "Prae omnibus floribus elegi mihi lilium" (Before all flowers, I have chosen for myself the lily), linking the lily of the royal house with the lily that typically symbolizes the Virgin Mary and reaffirming Mary's dedication to the French monarchy.[32] To the left, the king addresses the Virgin, dedicating his scepter and crown, and praying to her for victory, "Car je combats pour la gloire / De vostre fils et de vous" (because I fight for the glory / of your son and you). On the right, with the future Louis XIV in her arms, Anne too addresses Mary, this time with a more direct acknowledgment of the role she has played in the birth of her son: "Vierge, voicy le cher gage / Qu'il vous a pleu m'obtenir" (Virgin, here is the dear charge / which it has pleased you to obtain for me).

---

[31] Vaulgrenant, 'Le Vœu', p. 56.
[32] For the symbolism of the lily, see Colette Beaune, *The Birth of an Ideology: Myths and Symbols of Nation in Late-Medieval France*, trans Susan Huston (Berkeley, Los Angeles, and Oxford, University of California Press, 1991), pp. 201–25.

Music Example 7.1. Nicolas Formé, opening of Magnificat in Tone 1.
Le Cantique de la Vierge Marie selon les Tons ou Modes usités en l'église, F-Pn MS fonds fr. 1870, ff. 1v–2r.

While the Marian symbolism of the Magnificats could not be more significant, the works themselves are conventional (see Music Example 7.1). Setting the even verses in four-voice polyphony, with the odd verses to be performed in chant, Formé worked his way through the text in loose imitative texture based on short points of imitation and homophony. The opening verse of chant was provided on a separate staff in the source, using three note values, suggesting that chant was performed in a more flexible manner than at Montmartre, but unlike other settings of the Magnificat (such as those by Auxcousteaux published in 1641 or Bournonville in 1625), the chant is not presented in the tenor, nor does it fulfill any other structural or melodic role.

By contrast to the Magnificats, the two volumes of *Musica simplex quatuor vocum* do not make reference to the Vow. They both provide homophonic, *fauxbourdon*-like settings of the Mass ordinary in four voices, set with careful text declamation, using primarily short notes, lengthened where necessary, this time using only two note values. Unlike most of the extant early Mass ordinary settings published by the Ballard house, among them those by Gantez, Frémart, Bournonville, and Cosset (admittedly all from the 1640s), Formé provided each Mass with a setting of the *Domine salvum fac regem*, the first (along with the example in the *Aeternae Henrici Magni* Mass) to be published in the form that would later become ubiquitous i.e. just the final verse of the *Exaudiat* psalm.[33] Although published in 1638, there is nothing to indicate when these two settings were composed: but whenever this was – presumably sometime between *c.* 1600 and 1638 – there is also nothing here to suggest that this was anything other than a continuation of the practice of singing the *Exaudiat* specified in the *règlements* of 1583 and that it continued to be heard as a cry for divine assistance in times of existential danger. Equally unusual in both publications are the two settings of the Elevation text *O salutaris hostia* (the final verse of the Corpus Christi hymn *Verbum supernum prodiens* by Saint Thomas Aquinas), one designated "pour les voix plus hautes" (notated in g2, c1, c3, and c4 clefs), and a different one, unlabeled, in a lower tessitura (using the c1, c3, c4, and f4 clefs). The presence of this *O salutaris* verse as part of a Mass ordinary setting certainly reflects the Eucharistic focus of the court at that moment (and/or the wider market for which this publication was intended) although there seems to have already been a long tradition for performing musical settings of this text at court. Brobeck has identified similar homophonic settings by Claudin de Sermisy and Jean Mouton from the mid sixteenth century, and Du Peyrat's important history of the *chapelle royale* recalls how the second and third lines were modified at court, from "Bella premunt hostilia / Da robur, fer auxilium" to "In te confidit Francia / Da pacem serva lilium"

---

[33] Both collections by d'Ambleville contain a settings of the *Domine salvum fac regem*, but neither in the conventional one-verse form; see Chapter 5 and Charles d'Ambleville, *Harmonia sacra ... cum quatuor vocibus* (Paris, Pierre Ballard, 1636); Charles d'Ambleville, *Harmonia sacra ... cum sex vocibus* (Paris, Pierre Ballard, 1636). For a chronology of Mass publications, see Jean-Paul Montagnier, *The Polyphonic Mass in France, 1600–1780: The Evidence of the Printed Choirbooks* (Cambridge, Cambridge University Press, 2017), appendix 5 (pp. 302–6). For those later Masses that provided settings of the *Domine salvum fac regem* and the *O salutaris hostia*, see Montagnier, *Polyphonic Mass*, pp. 145–6.

(France confides in you / Give peace ...).[34] If that did indeed happen, polyphonic settings did not adopt this text, since the other surviving versions we can associate with the *chapelle royale*, those provided in the *Octo cantica divae Mariae Virginis* of 1584 and 1599, also use the standard text.[35]

Perhaps more relevant is the existence of the high, alternative setting of the text, not a transposition, but a completely different work pitched much higher. Charles Léon has argued that this alternative was intended to provide a setting for performance by nuns – in other words, something Formé composed specially to give the collection a broader market appeal. But it would seem odd if Formé/Ballard only provided one work at this alternative pitch level while leaving the Mass itself untransposed. Instead, I would argue, the presence of this high setting points to an important feature both of these Masses, and of the Mass *Aeternae Henrici Magni* – that they involved the participation of two vocal ensembles at court, the *musique de la chambre* and the *musique de la chapelle* – and highlights the wider significance of this collaboration at the celebration of Mass (see Music Examples 7.2 and 7.3).

We have already seen in Chapter 3 that the *musique de la chambre* and the *chapelle* shared similar duties, both performing in "domestic," paraliturgical contexts – at grace for dinner and lunch, and the *chambre* before Mass – and both being involved in the singing of psalm settings (the Auxcousteaux by the *chapelle*, and the Paris manuscript settings for the *chambre*). But we also know that they collaborated together throughout this period in public ceremonies. As early as 1598 at the "Te Deum" ceremony celebrating the Peace of Vervins we read that:[36]

Those [singers] from the *chambre*, with gentle voices and joined by lute, viols and other soft instruments, were placed on the right side of the altar [the Epistle side] in order, since they were quieter, to be better heard by his Majesty, who had his

---

[34] See John Brobeck, *The Motet at the Court of Francis I* (PhD dissertation, University of Pennsylvania, 1991), pp. 147–50; Guillaume Du Peyrat, *L'Histoire ecclésiastique de la cour* (Paris, Henri Sara, 1645), p. 790.

[35] Again, the *O Salutaris* is not commonly found in the mid seventeenth-century ordinary settings, only becoming a feature after 1736; see Montagnier, *Polyphonic Mass*. D'Ambleville's two volumes are again an exception (possibly because of the Jesuit inclinations of the collection), the four-voice volume providing *Ecce panis angelorum*, and the six-voice volume *O salutaris hostia*.

[36] F-Pn MS fonds fr. 18515, f.160: "Ceux de la musique de la chambre à voix douces et plus grosses jointes à la douceur de luts, violles et autres plus doux instruments estoient du costé droict pour estre mieux entendues comme rendant un son plus bas, de Sa Majesté qui avoit son oratoire de ce quartier là. Ceux de la chapelle, marians leurs voix plus fortes et plus pleines avec les cornets et trompons estoient de l'autre costé vers le quartier de Mgr le légat et se respondoient les deux chœurs d'un fort agréable concert et très harmonieuse mélodie par couplets alternatifs." For a discussion of this event, see also Kate van Orden, *Music, Discipline, and Arms in Early Modern France* (Chicago, Chicago University Press, 2005), pp. 181–2.

Music Example 7.2 Nicolas Formé, *O salutaris hostia*, for low voices.
Musica simplex quatuor vocum (Paris, Pierre Ballard, 1638).

oratory on that side. Those from the *chapelle*, blending their stronger fuller voices with the cornetts and trumpets were on the other side [the Gospel side], towards the Legate, and the two choirs answered each other in agreeable concert and very harmonious melody by alternate couplets.

We also have ample evidence of the two ensembles performing together during the reign of Louis XIII. At the betrothal of the king's sister to Charles I of England in 1625, an account of the proceedings at Notre-Dame reported that the *chapelle* and *chambre* were distributed in the same way, while for the funeral of Marie de Bourbon, first wife of Gaston d'Orléans, in 1627, the musicians of the *chapelle* and *chambre* "sang and responded to each other throughout the whole Mass."[37]

---

[37] F-Pn MS nouv. acq. fr. 819, f.348r; *L'Ordre des Cérémonies observées aux Funérailles & service de feu Madame à S. Denys en France Le dernier Juin 1627* (Paris, 1627), pp. 9–10: "les Musiciens de la Chappelle & de la chambre du Roy, qui chantèrent & respondirent tout du long de la Messe."

Nicolas Formé and the Bride of Christ 255

Music Example 7.3 Nicolas Formé, *O salutaris hostia*, "pour les voix plus hautes."
Musica simplex quatuor vocum (Paris, Pierre Ballard, 1638).

But the account of Angelo Contarini, Venetian ambassador to the Court, describing Mass for the Knights of the Order of the Holy Spirit on January 7, 1620, provides the most tangible description of this musical practice, reporting that:[38]

The Mass was solemnly sung by two groups of musicians: one from the chapel, low, full and sonorous, the other from the chamber, subdued, sweet and delicate: hence

---

[38] P-Pn MS italien 1773, pp. 369–70: "Il giorno dittro, primo dell'anno, pur nella medesima Chiesa il obe con tutti i Cavallieri vestiti col manto, e insegno dell'Ordine, senti la messa sollenemente cantata da due corpi di musica: l'uno della capella, grave, pieno, e sonoro, l'altro della camera di Sua Maesta, sommesso, soave, e delicato: onde questi due Cori cosi diversità d'armonia alleccanco/accellanco, et eccitando i Spiriti, refero insieme la mesta e dileccevole, e maestevole, e devote." Other accounts of the Knights' ceremonies also describe this spatial arrangement; see Thomas Leconte, 'Entre religion et pouvoir à la cour de France: les cérémonies de l'ordre du Saint-Esprit (1578–1661)', in Peter Bennett and Bernard Dompnier (eds.), *Cérémonial politique et cérémonial religieux dans l'Europe modern: échanges et métissages* (Paris, Garnier, 2020).

these two choirs, so diverse of harmony, quickening and exciting the spirits, bring together the sad and delightful, and majestic, and devout.

At the same time, other evidence points to a special role for the *chambre* in these collaborative contexts – performing at the Elevation. In the 1598 account the *chambre* was singled out for its performance alone at the Elevation:[39]

during which the musicians of the *chambre* alone sang an air so sweet and harmonious that it seems as if they were the Angels of Heaven, coming by their celestial song to ravish those present in devotion, and to excite them to holy and celestial meditation of the joy of Heavens and the glory of the Blessed.

And as late as 1665 the *État de la France* specifies the duties of the *chambre* to "sing alone at the altars of repose on Corpus Christi" – presumably some kind of Eucharistic hymn such as *O Salutaris*.[40] While we have no surviving sources for any of the works that might have been performed, and nothing about the repertoires we know separately suggests any kind of pitch or tessitura difference, this description of the "sweetness" of the *chambre*, as opposed to the "low, full" sound of the *chapelle*, together with the fact that the *chambre* was associated with the Elevation or Eucharistic devotion related in the 1598 and 1665 descriptions, suggests that more generally the *chambre* may have had a special relationship with the Elevation, singing it alone, that it performed at a higher tessitura than the *chapelle*, and that, in doing so, it produced some kind of special and desirable effect.

Of course, notated pitch and performed pitch are two entirely separate things, and even if a work appears to be notated higher, it might simply be performed at a lower pitch.[41] But there is compelling evidence that the *chambre* did indeed perform at a noticeably higher pitch than the *chapelle* and that their overall sound was therefore distinctive. Certainly, by 1683 Guillaume-Gabriel Nivers distinguished two pitch levels at court, *ton de la*

---

[39] See Chapter 3, note 18. See also F-Pn MS fonds fr. 18515, f. 160: "pendant laquelle la musicque de chambre seule chante un air si doux & si harmonieux qu'il semble que ce soyent Anges du Ciel qui viennent par leur céleste chant ravir les assistants en dévotion, & les exciter à saincte & céleste méditation de la joye des Cieux & gloire des Bien-heureux."

[40] *L'État de la France ou l'on voit tous les Princes, Ducs & Pairs* (Paris, Jean Ribout, 1665), pp. 104–5.

[41] The most obvious example of this is the notation of music in *chiavette*, a set of clefs implying "higher" performance but actually specifying a transposition down a fourth. Such a transposition, however, would obviously not be applicable in a polychoral work in which a choir in *chiavette* sang together with a choir in *chiavi naturali*; see Patrizio Barbieri, 'Chiavette and modal transposition in Italian practice (c. 1500–1837)', *Recercare*, 3 (1991), 5–79.

chambre du roy being a semitone higher than *ton de chapelle* (not just the *chapelle royale*, but indeed all church organs), which, based on evidence from Mersenne, many other theorists, and the evidence of surviving instruments, was pitched at approximately A−2 (using Bruce Hayne's notation to designate pitch in semitones above (+) or below (−) A = 440).[42] With a resulting pitch for the *chambre* of A−1 (i.e. A = 415) and in the notated versions in which it is preserved, it would be hard to say that the *chambre* repertoire, such as the pieces discussed in Chapter 4, was "high" in any way, but earlier in the century the difference between the two pitches was more significant. In the 1650s, Étienne Moulinié's *Meslanges des sujets chrestiens* of 1658, presumably conceived for performance by an ensemble similar to the *musique de la chambre*, features four works marked with the rubric "Ton de Chapelle" (in distinction to, we must assume, "Ton de la chambre" for the remainder).[43] Since these four works feature a highest note for the *dessus* voice of aa (the rest of the volume goes to gg), the designation "Ton de Chapelle" is presumably a suggestion to perform them at a lower, and therefore more comfortable, pitch. In the same volume, by contrast, there are also six works for which the *basse-continue* part is notated a tone higher than the vocal parts, in this case presumably to lift those vocal parts, notated at a level more suited to the *chapelle*, into a more comfortable range for the *chambre*, since the bass voices reaches down to D.[44] This volume therefore suggests the existence of two pitch standards (*chapelle* and *chambre*) a tone apart in the middle of the century, but evidence from Mersenne suggests that, just a few decades earlier, this difference in pitch was even more pronounced. In the eighteenth proposition of the Third Book of String Instruments in his *Harmonie Universelle*, Marin Mersenne provides a table of string "retours" (returns or cycles) or "battements" (beats) that specify the pitches of Antoine Boësset's four-voice *air de cour* of 1630, *Divine Amaryllis*, the bread-and-butter repertoire of the *musique de la chambre* and similar in most musical respects to the sacred repertoire for the same ensemble. According to Mersenne's text and table, the lowest note of the piece, an F, should oscillate at 96 Hz, giving a pitch standard of A = 480, approximately A + 1.5, creating a difference of A−2 (*chapelle*) to A + 1.5

---

[42] Bruce Haynes, *A History of Performing Pitch: The Story of A* (Lanham and Oxford, Scarecrow Press, 2002) pp. 117, 97–8.

[43] For a discussion of the transposition issue, see Jean Duron, ed., *Étienne Moulinié: Meslanges de sujets chrestiens & motet 'Flores apparuerunt'* (Versailles, Éditions du CMBV, 1996), pp. lxviii–lxix.

[44] Moulinié instructs the performers to sing at the same pitch as the *basse-continue*.

(*chambre*), a much more significant contrast.⁴⁵ Indeed, while Mersenne does not explicitly contrast the *chambre* and *chapelle* pitches, he implies that they were in fact a fourth apart, one of the most common transposition intervals of the early seventeenth century.⁴⁶ The relationship between *chambre* and *chapelle*, then, was not only institutional and liturgical, but also something more – a difference in sound quality that lent special properties to both.

The Mass *Aeternae Henrici Magni*

While Formé's *Musica simplex* settings imply the presence and availability of two unequal vocal ensembles who might share duties at Mass, and while many written accounts of performances testify to these two ensembles interacting in some way, and while we can certainly imagine the *chapelle* and *chambre* spontaneously collaborating in the performance of some of the works from the Paris manuscript or Auxcousteaux's psalms, Formé's most important publication attests to all these practices, prefiguring the musical techniques that would become standard at the *Chapelle Royale* by around 1650–60 and which would endure until the Revolution – the famous Mass for two choirs *Aeternae Henrici Magni*.⁴⁷ Again, no specific mention of the Vow is made in the preface, but there is no doubt that the publication – consisting of the Mass, a setting of the *Domine salvum fac*

---

⁴⁵ Marin Mersenne, *Harmonie Universelle contenant la théorie et la pratique de la musique* (Paris, Sebastien Cramoisy, 1636), *Traité des instruments à chordes*, pp. 142–3. We can also see this earlier higher pitch reflected in the Paris manuscript versions of two Moulinié works, *Congratulamini mihi omnes* and *Flores apparuerunt*. Both appear notated a tone lower in the early version, *Flores apparuerunt* even featuring a bass part that descends to a low C.

⁴⁶ Mersenne, ibid., mentions that *chambre* pitch was based on a four-foot organ pipe at FF. Since we can assume that, almost by definition, *chapelle* pitch was based on an eight-foot organ pipe at CC, the two pitch standards would be a fourth apart, exactly the same relationship that the two keyboards of the contemporary Rucker's harpsichord were pitched at. In the same way that these harpsichords were able to play at two pitch levels, both of which must have been of some utility, it makes sense that the same relationship existed at court. If this were the case, *chapelle* pitch would be about A = 380, a little lower than our current understanding, but comparable to later "classical" pitch. And even if the difference were not so great (and it seems that the seventeenth century saw a gradual diminishing of this distance), the *chambre* was still clearly a "high" ensemble relative to the *chapelle*.

⁴⁷ For a hypothetical collaboration between *chambre* and *chapelle* and for earlier thoughts on the Formé Mass, see Peter Bennett, 'Collaborations between the Musique de la Chambre and the Musique de la Chapelle at the court of Louis XIII: Nicolas Formé's "Missa Aeternae Henrici Magni" (1638) and the origins of the grand motet', *Early Music*, 38/3 (2010), 369–86.

regem, and the motet *Ecce tu pulchra es* – was conceived with the circumstances in which the Vow was made very much in mind.[48]

In choosing to create (or at least name) the Mass in memory of Henri IV – even during the reign of Louis XIII (to whom the Mass was actually dedicated) – Formé was not intending to undermine his patron or to place him in the shadow of his much more dynamic and successful father. Quite the contrary. Just as Chapter 2 showed how the Phoenix was its own parent, self-begotten, the likeness of its previous incarnation, Formé (or those who advised him) was simply identifying with a way of thinking about succession that depended on lineage rather than legal procedure. This connection between father and son was based on Aristotle, but was specifically formulated by the jurist Jean de Terremerveille in terms of the French monarchy in the early fifteenth century. In his treatise on kingship of 1419, Terremerveille concludes:[49]

That a father and a son, although distinct as individuals, may be taken as being just one person in respect to species and nature (because each is a man), and also in the particular nature of the father. The conclusion is proven, for according to Aristotle the semen of man contains a kind of active impressed force derived from the soul of the progenitor and his ancestors; such is the identity of the nature of the father and the son according to St. Thomas.

At Louis's inaugural *lit de justice* the same kinds of arguments were also made, president Harlay pointing out that Louis was the living image of his deceased father.[50] In referring to Henri IV, then, Formé was simply identifying strengths that resided equally in his son Louis and in no way detracting from the king himself. But more than just engaging with the issue of heredity, the Mass also engaged with the practical realities of court musical ensembles, being scored for two choirs, a "high" four-voice choir ("Primus Chorus") scored for g2, c1, c3, and c4 voices, and a "low" four-voice choir ("Secundus Chorus") scored for c1, c3, c4, and f4 voices. The choirs take turns to present text and melodic material, and frequently combine at cadences in a way that is not dissimilar to many of the psalm

---

[48] *Aeternae Henrici Magni, Gallorum, Navarrorumque Regis Potentissimi, ac Clementissimi memoriae. Et Ludovici Jusiti: eius Filii … Missam hanc duobus Choris ac quatuor voc. compositam* (Paris, Pierre Ballard, 1638); modern edition in Jean-Charles Léon (ed.), *Nicolas Formé: Œuvres complètes* (Versailles, Éditions du CMBV, 2003).

[49] See the translation and study of Terremerveille's treatise by Ralph Giesey at regiesey.com, and the introduction in Ralph Giesey, 'The juristic basis of dynastic right to the French throne', *Transactions of the American Philosophical Society*, New Series, 51/5 (1961), 3–47.

[50] Sarah Hanley, *The Lit de Justice of the Kings of France: Constitutional Ideology in Legend, Ritual, and Discourse* (Princeton, Princeton University Press, 1983), p. 248.

settings in Charles d'Ambleville's nearly contemporary collections; although d'Ambleville's choirs do occupy different ranges, they do not emphasize this difference by presenting the same material at different pitch levels in the way that Formé's Mass does.[51] (See Music Example 7.5 for the Gloria from d'Ambleville's setting of Psalm 121, *Laetatus sum*. While both the four-voice and six-voice publications could be used completely independently, they were also cleverly devised so that they could be combined to produce a double choir texture. The example shows this in practice.)[52]

Formé's strategy is most apparent in the movements which present the opportunity for music and text to be repeated – the Kyrie, Sanctus and Agnus Dei, although it does occur in the other movements. At the conclusion of the Gloria, for example (see Music Example 7.5), the musicians of the higher choir (the *chambre*) present the melody and the text in the typical two-voice texture we frequently find in the contemporary *air de cour*, with both dessus and bass parts pitched relatively high (the bass part in c4 clef). Although not specified in the score, we can assume that the lutes and other soft instruments of the *chambre* filled in the harmony to produce a "sweet and delicate" effect. In answer, the low voices of the *chapelle* present the same text and melodic material, this time in a full-voiced texture, requiring no harmonic infill or support and inviting the participation of doubling wind instruments. The melodic material that was originally presented in the dessus voice in the *chambre*, however, is now presented in the tenor voice of the *chapelle*, an octave lower, producing a sound that could be described as "low, full, and sonorous." The *chambre* then repeats its original material, this time harmonized by all the voices, the *chapelle* repeats its material, and the two choirs combine for the final Amen in the same way as in the d'Ambleville.

Although the practice of alternating choirs is often associated with the *chori spezzati* tradition in Italy, it seems likely that the roots of the practice here are grounded in different soil.[53] In the first place, having two standing vocal ensembles available at court, each with its own distinctive and special musical character, and its own role in the court hierarchy, function, and

---

[51] Charles d'Ambleville, *Harmonia sacra ... cum sex vocibus* (Paris, Pierre Ballard, 1636) and *Harmonia sacra ... cum quatuor vocibus* (Paris, Pierre Ballard, 1636).

[52] If only one book was being used, the other versets would be performed in chant.

[53] For other examples of polychoral music in France, see Denise Launay, 'Les Motets à double chœur en France dans la première moitié du XVIIe siècle', *Revue de musicologie*, 40 (1957), 173–95. Launay overlooks the fact that the works for two choirs by Du Caurroy might also reflect *chambre/chapelle* collaborations. The classic study of Italian practice is Anthony Carver, *Cori spezzati* (Cambridge, Cambridge University Press, 1988), but see also Noel O'Regan, *Sacred Polychoral Music in Rome, 1575–1621* (DPhil dissertation, Oxford University, 1988).

Music Example 7.4 Charles d'Ambleville, Psalm 121, *Laetatus sum*, concluding doxology: four-voice and six-voice publications combined.
Harmonia sacra … cum quatuor [sex] vocum (Paris, Pierre Ballard, 1636).

status, naturally invites the composition of works that can exploit this contrast. For that reason, we find accounts of the performance works for three or four choirs outside the court, but for only two at court itself.[54]

---

[54] Launay documents performances for three choirs in Douai in 1631, four choirs in Rouen in 1632, and three choirs at the competition in honor of Saint Cecilia held at Le Mans in 1633, one choir consisting of organ alone, another of viols, lutes, and a few singers' voices, and the third the main body of singers and musicians. See Launay, 'Les Motets à double chœur', and, for a strikingly detailed account of proceedings at Le Mans, see Em.-Louis Chambois, 'La Fête de Sainte Cécile à la cathédrale du Mans, 1633–1784', *L'Union historique et littéraire du Maine*, 2/1 (1894), 343–52.

Music Example 7.4 (*cont.*)

More than that, however, the practice of alternating these two contrasting choirs stems much more closely from the recitation of psalms and the singing of hymns (practices that in turn date back to the earliest days of the church), than it does to the desire for spatial separation and drama (with many more than two choirs) that Venetian composers strived for (as in, for example, the d'Ambleville psalm settings discussed above). Certainly, biblical references to two or more choirs singing in alternation abound, even if in the later church just two choirs became the standard configuration. Psalm 68:27, for example, describes the singing of multiple choirs made up of the tribes of Israel; the prophet Nehemiah describes two choirs of thanksgiving at the celebration of the rebuilding of the walls of Jerusalem; and in Psalm 135 the voices of the people, priests, Levites, and proselytes

Music Example 7.5 Nicolas Formé, conclusion of Gloria.
Mass *Aeternae Henrici Magni* (Paris, Pierre Ballard, 1638).

Music Example 7.5 (*cont.*)

Music Example 7.5 (*cont.*)

sing in alternation.[55] But it is perhaps non-biblical tradition that most aptly explains the practice. In his *David François*, François Bourgoing describes how Philo of Alexandria attributed the origins of psalm singing with two choirs to the practice of the Essenes, a Jewish sect who lived around the time of Christ.[56] Bourgoing gives even more weight to the story of Saint Ignatius of Antioch, who had a vision of choirs of angels singing in alternatim in honor of the Holy Trinity, a practice he immediately introduced to the church of Antioch. Bourgoing did not mention Philon's other discussion of the practice, but according to his *De vita Moses* (published in translation in 1612 by the king's printer Frédéric Morel and well known in early seventeenth-century Paris), after the miraculous crossing of the Red Sea, to give thanks to God, Moses divided the nation into two choirs, one of men, the other of women.[57] Their combined harmonies, low for the men, high for the women, resulted in "pleasant and panharmonic melos."

---

[55] See Herman Gunkel, trans. James Nogalski, *Introduction to the Psalms: The Genres of the Religious Lyric of Israel* (Macon, Mercer University Press, 1998), p. 40 onward.

[56] François Bourgoing, *Le David François ou traité de la sainct Psalmodie* (Paris, Sebastien Huré, 1641), p. 22.

[57] Siegmund Levarie, 'Philo on Music', *The Journal of Musicology*, 9/1 (1991), 124–30.

(The song they sang, the Song of Moses, Exodus 15:1–20, uses language and imagery that would later feature in the psalms.) At the same time, these two opposing choirs represented something even greater:

> Of the two choirs, male and female, standing echoing and antiphonally, ... the male choir shall have Moses for its leader, that is Mind in perfection, and the female choir shall be led by Miriam [Marie in the French translation], that is Sense Perception made pure and clean. For it is right to make music with both Mind and Sense.[58]

We might see this opposition of Mind and Sense (or perhaps "sensuousness" or "sensuality") in the contrasting treatment of the choirs in seventeenth-century France, with the lower choir using fuller, more learned counterpoint, and the higher choir relying more on melody and color to "ravish the minds of those present," as the 1598 account puts it. More than that, though, Philo was, of course, a highly influential Platonist, who, in his attempt to reconcile biblical truth with Platonic philosophy, believed that Plato must have traveled to Egypt to study the works of Moses before writing his *Dialogues*.[59] We can thus see this "panharmonic melos" encompassing the whole universe as a concept borrowed from Plato, in this case the Timaeus. This broader conception of two different yet complimentary vocal ensembles is precisely echoed in the secular domain with the dialogue performed as part of the Balet comique de la reine of 1581 between the *Voute dorée* or "gilded vault" (low music, presumably performed by the musicians and doubling winds of the *chapelle*) and the wooded glade (high music, performed by the singers and soft instruments of the *chambre*) (see Music Example 7.6), where it had the same connotations of complete harmony encompassing the world, in this case the effect heightened by the *musique mesurée* in which it was performed (although this feature therefore diminished any Mind/Sense distinction).[60]

While Formé's double choir technique is an important witness to musical practices that probably occurred much more frequently than we realize, and while it is certainly true that his compositional technique largely eschews the long fluid vocal lines of conventional imitative

---

[58] Translation from Levarie, 'Philo on Music', p. 128. For the French edition see Frédéric Morel, *Les Œuvres de Philon Juif, autheur très-eloquent, & philosophe très-grave* (Paris, Charles Chappellain, 1612), Vol. 2, pp. 1156–7.

[59] For Philo's relationship to Plato, see David Runia, *Philo of Alexandria and the "Timaeus" of Plato* (Leiden, Brill, 1986).

[60] For the text and commentary on the *Balet comique*, see Carol and Lander MacClintock, *Le Balet Comique de la Royne, 1581*, Musicological Studies and Documents, 25 (American Institute of Musicology, 1971).

Music Example 7.6 The dialogue between the Sirens (high voices) and the gilded vault (low voices).
Balet comique de la royne (Paris, Adrian le Roy, Robert Ballard, and Mamert Patisson, 1582), ff. 11v–13r.

polyphony for the shorter melodic and rhythmic fragments later favored by Dumont and Lully, the Mass is otherwise relatively conventional, obeying the standard divisions of text, and not providing a setting of the *O salutaris hostia*. Likewise, the concluding setting of the *Domine salvum fac regem* (with added voices to the choirs) adds little new to our understanding of the genre, other than providing a *terminus post quem* before which the *Domine salvum* (as opposed to the complete *Exaudiat*) was in use in the *chapelle royale*. But the final piece in the volume, not mentioned in the title or dedication and thus perhaps (like the Magnificats) an afterthought, cements the link to the Virgin Mary, the Vow, and the Christocentric inclinations of the court in the 1630s.[61]

---

[61] The title of the volume does not mention the *Domine salvum fac regem*, nor the *Ecce tu pulchra es*, nor does it mention anything other than two choirs of four voices each, when in

Music Example 7.6 (cont.)

The motet *Ecce tu pulchra es*, like the Mass, is scored for two choirs, although in this case a fifth low c4 voice is added to the second choir and the tessitura difference between the choirs is perhaps even more striking than in the Mass. The choirs interact in the same way as they do in the Mass, although they are somewhat more integrated with more frequent interplay between the two blocks of voices (see Music Example 7.7).

reality the *Domine salvum* is scored for choirs of four and seven voices, and the *Ecce* for choirs of four and five voices. We might therefore assume that these works were not originally planned to be part of the publication and that the decision to include them was only made after the title page had already been printed.

Music Example 7.7a Nicolas Formé, opening of *Ecce tu pulchra es*.
Mass *Aeternae Henrici Magni* (Paris, Pierre Ballard, 1638).

The text, presumably selected by Formé himself or by a cleric associated with the court, is taken from the Song of Songs (or Song of Solomon) (see Table 7.1).

Texts from the Song of Songs are generally read as referring to the Virgin Mary, and feature prominently in the liturgy of the Feast of the Assumption. The first lesson at Matins on that feast is taken from the first chapter, and many of the Assumption Antiphons also draw their text from the same book.[62] In this context, such texts are conventionally understood to represent the love of *sponsa* and *sponsus* standing for the love between the Virgin Mary and mankind, or between Mary and Christ.[63] (Such was

---

[62] See Rachel Fulton, '"Quae est ista quae ascendit sicut aurora consurgens?" The Song of Songs as the *historia* for the Office of the Assumption', *Mediaeval Studies*, 60 (1998), 55–122.

[63] Since the Assumption is not recorded in scripture, the creators of the office in the ninth century told the story through the allegorical dialogues in the Song of Solomon. See Fulton, ibid.

Music Example 7.7b Nicolas Formé, second section of *Ecce tu pulchra es*, Mass *Aeternae Henrici Magni* (Paris, Pierre Ballard, 1638).

the importance of Saint Bernard of Clairvaux's sermons on the Song of Songs, from which this understanding is taken, that they were published by the *Imprimerie Royale* in 1642 as the second book alongside Kempis's *Imitation of Christ*.)[64] In this sense, a number of works from the *chambre* repertoire based on Song's texts reflect a devotion to Mary that is by no means unique, but might perhaps have been intensified at court. In *Veni sponsa mea* (see the text in Table 7.2), for example, we hear a direct appeal

---

[64] See Bernard of Clairvaux, *Divi Bernardi operum* ... (Paris, Typographia regia, 1642). The sermons had already appeared in French translation several times in the 1620s.

Music Example 7.7b (cont.)

to Mary, even if, musically, some kind of gendered dialogue is implied by the scoring of the opening refrain.[65]

In Formé's work, however, we see an unambiguous dialogue between Mary and Christ, this time with the role of Christ played by Louis himself. The work itself breaks down into three parts, linked by musical and textual parallelism (see Music Example 7.7). In the first part (7.7a), the speaker addresses his lover, the Virgin Mary, praising her beauty in the conventional terms found throughout the Assumption offices ("Ecce tu pulchra es"). The section begins in the first, high choir, with a distinctive

---

[65] Edition in Denise Launay (ed.), *Anthologie du motet latin polyphonique en France (1606–61)* (Paris, Société française de musicologie, Heugel, 1963)

Table 7.1 Text, translation, and source of Nicolas Formé, *Ecce tu pulchra es* (Paris, Pierre Ballard, 1638)

Ecce tu pulchra es, amica mea.	Songs 1:14	How beautiful you are, my darling.
Occuli tui columbarum, genae tuae sicut turturis; collum tuum sicut monilia.	1:9	Your eyes are like doves, your cheeks are beautiful with earrings; your neck with strings of jewels.
Ecce tu pulcher es, dilecte mi, et decorus.	1:15	How handsome you are my beloved, and charming [and our bed is verdant].
Candidus et rubicundus; electus ex milibus.	5:10	My beloved is radiant and ruddy, outstanding among ten thousand.
Trahe me post te, curremus in odorem unguentorum tuorum.	1:3	Take me away with you, let us hurry, in the odor of your ointment

Table 7.2 Text, translation, and source of anonymous, *Veni sponsa mea*, Paris manuscript, ff. 131v–132v

Veni sponsa mea, veni de Libano, veni coronaberis.	Songs 4: 8	Come, my wife, come from Lebanon, come and you will be crowned.
Tota pulchra es amica mea, et macula non est in te. Veni …	4:7	You are fair my love, and there is no flaw in you.
Occuli tui columbarum. Sicut vita coccinea labia tua et eloquium tuum, ut carmelus absque eo quod intrinsecus latet. Veni …	4:1, 4:3	Your eyes are like doves. Your lips are like a scarlet thread, and your mouth, like Carmel, hidden behind a veil.
Anima mea liquefacta est ut dilectus locutus est. Stipate me malis quia amore langueo. Veni …	5:6, 2:5	My soul went forth when he spake. Comfort me with apples, for I am faint with love.

solo rising gesture on "Ecce tu pulchra es" before the ensemble continues through the same text completing it with "amica mea." This musical material is then repeated by the second, low choir, with the distinctive solo gesture now a fourth lower. The remaining text of the first section is then presented in relatively rapid alternation between the two choirs in dialogue. In the second section (7.7b) Mary in turn responds. Using essentially the same musical material and the upward leap (though now accompanied with another voice), this time on the corollary "Ecce tu pulcher," Mary now addresses her lover who is "radiant," "ruddy," "handsome," "charming," and "one of ten thousand" – in other words, not just the Christ we would expect, but Louis himself, a Christ imbued with overtly masculine qualities. (It is interesting to note that, in the Vulgate text, Goliath described David as "pulcher" [handsome] and "rufus" [ruddy].) A third and final voice, a chorus of children (marked as such in the biblical text) asks to be taken away with one or other of them ("te") "in the odor of your ointment" – with the fragrant lover and Queen of Heaven, or the anointed king of France.[66]

In this the final major work of both Formé's and Louis XIII's life, then, the transformation of the monarchy was now complete. Louis was no longer simply David the Warrior, and certainly not David the Penitent, but now Christ, the anointed lover of Mary, soliciting help from both the God of the *dévots* and from the Mother of Jesus. At the same time, the piece made explicit musical practices (i.e. the relationship between the *chapelle* and *chambre*) that had probably been going on for half a century or more – either un-notated or notated and now lost – and ways of thinking about music that still connected with the Neoplatonic ideologies of the sixteenth century. While I would therefore argue that Formé's Mass was in no way unique in conception, it is certainly the most striking manifestation of the musical, liturgical, and ideological practices of the court that survives. And while Formé's successors must surely have had a much deeper understanding of the history of what went immediately before them than we do (we can only assume that the devastating attrition of musical sources from this period only occurred later), even for them this work and others by Formé held a special place in their understanding of the music of their own time. It is this understanding, and the broader developments during the reign of Louis XIV, that I consider in the Epilogue and Conclusion to this study.

---

[66] Other readings have these words spoken by Mary to Christ (i.e. Louis) crying out for her assumption so that she might join him in heaven; see Fulton, '*Quae est ista*', 107.

Epilogue and Conclusion

Continuity and Change under Louis XIV

As a thanksgiving for the birth of a dauphin, the king did not intensify his devotion to the Virgin Mary. Instead, the Eucharist remained an important focus. In a letter of June 1639, recognizing the great gift that God had given him and noting that the chapel at the *château* of Saint-Germain was somewhat plain, Louis decided to institute a foundation for the perpetual celebration of the Exposition of the Blessed Sacrament.[1] A tabernacle was to be made and placed on the high altar where the "Très-Saint Sacrement de l'Autel" would repose, in front of which was to be placed a large gilded lamp worth 3,000 *livres*. A Chaplain and two Clerks were to dedicate themselves to the devotion to the Saint-Sacrement, saying a Low Mass each morning, after which they were to say "à haute voix" the verset "*Domine salvum fac Regem* &c. & l'Oraison *Quaesumus Domine*" for the conservation of the king, the queen, and the dauphin. At the same time, each evening the Litanies of the Virgin and the *Salve Regina* were to be recited, although not to "musique" or chant.

In the following years, the nation of France achieved a sense of relative stability, with the successful defeat of the Spanish and other adversaries celebrated by several "Te Deums" in Paris and by *entrées* into Perpignan, Lyon, and elsewhere. At his death in 1643, then, Louis would be remembered once again for his military prowess – the New David of former years – and for his Christlike devotion. Thus, according to Pierre Bourgoin's funeral oration, as Louis approached death:[2]

He took communion with such great fervor, he heard the holy Mass which is said every day in his Royal chamber, even responding while receiving the Extreme Unction, having Hymns and Psalms sung for which he had composed the music.

---

[1] Louis's letter is reproduced in Abbé Oroux, *Histoire ecclésiastique de la Cour de France* (Paris, Imprimerie Royale, 1777), Vol. 2, pp. 440–1.

[2] Pierre Bourgoin, *Éloges funèbres de Louys le Iuste sur le parallèle de David vivant et David mourant* (Metz, Jean Antoine, 1643), p. 45: "il communioit avec de si grandes ferveurs, il entendoit la saincte Messe qui se disoit tous les iours en sa chambre Royalle, respondoit mesme en recevant l'Extreme Onction, faisoit chanter des Hymnes & des Pseaumes dont il avoit composé la musique."

Oroux's account is more specific, with the king commanding his valet, one sieur Nielle, together with sieurs Mampefort and Saint Martin, to give thanks to God by singing *Seigneur, à qui seul je veux plaire*, a paraphrase of Psalm 130 by Bishop Antoine Godeau that Louis himself is supposed to have set to music some years earlier, the four of them forming "une èspece de concert spirituel."[3] Looking back at Louis's life, Godeau himself recalled Louis's musical talents:[4] "The late king, of glorious memory, did not disdain to use the perfect knowledge he had of this beautiful art, on four of my psalms, which were printed a long time ago"; not only that, but the king's whole life was "like a harmonious concert of the most august virtues." A few days earlier, according to Archon, Louis had also recited Psalm 121, *Laetatus sum*, to express his joy at his imminent meeting with God, and had prepared himself by reading the Bible, the lives of the saints, and Kempis's *Imitation of Christ*. The day before his death, he received the Eucharist, after which his condition began to decline.[5] As it did, his confessor, Père Dinet, recited the Te Deum, a fact that was noted at his funeral – that just as Louis had heard it sung for his own triumphs, he now wished to hear it sung for God's.[6] The following day, his final passing was witnessed by Dinet himself, together with Vincent (later Saint Vincent) de Paul and the Bishops of Meaux, Lisieux, and Beauvais. At his funeral in Saint-Denis some five weeks later, the Requiem Mass was sung by the "Musique du Roy" (presumably the *chapelle* and *chambre* together), possibly to the setting by Eustache Du Caurroy that may also have been performed at his father's funeral in 1610;[7] and at dinner following the service, the *chapelle* (having sung grace) performed the psalm *Laudate*

---

[3] Oroux, *Histoire ecclésiastique*, Vol. 2, p. 451.

[4] Antoine Godeau, preface to *Paraphrase des Pseaumes de David, en vers François par Mre Antoine Godeau ... Et les Chants corrigez et rendus propres et justes pour tous les couplets par Me Thomas Gobert* (Paris, Pierre le Petit, 1676): "Le feu Roy, de glorieuse mémoire, n'avoit pas dédaigné d'employer la parfait connoissance de ce bel Art, sur quatre de mes Pseaumes, qui on esté imprimez il y a longtemps. Et les plus excellens Maistres ont admiré cette composition. Le pieux divertissement que ce grand Prince y voulut prendre m'est si Glorieux que la modestie m'auroit empêché d'en parler, si je l'eusse jugé plus puissant que toutes mes raisons pour porter ceux à qui je parle, à imiter."

[5] Jean-Louis Archon, *Histoire ecclésiastique de la Chapelle des Rois de France* (Paris, Pierre-Augustine Le Mercier, 1704–11), Vol. 2, p. 786.

[6] Jean de Lingendes, *Oraison funèbre du roy Louis XIII. Surnommé Le Juste, prononcé en l'église de S. Denis l xxij^e jour de Juin 1643* (Paris, Charles Savreux, 1643), p. 56.

[7] Archon, *Histoire ecclésiastique*, p. 790. The surviving exemplars of the *Missa pro defunctis* date from 1636, but scholars have posited a date of composition around 1606 and a first edition around 1610, see Marie-Alexis Colin, 'Eustache Du Caurroy. Un compositeur français aux confins du XVIe et XVIIe siècle', *Acta Musicologica*, 73/2 (2001), 188–200.

Dominum omnes gentes, after which "was heard an infinite number of voices crying 'Vive Louis XIV, Dieu-Donné.'"[8]

Oroux's *Histoire Ecclésiastique* provides us with a detailed account of the religious life of the young Louis XIV as he grew up under the regency of his mother, Anne of Austria, noting the affinity of the mother and son with Blanche de Castille and Saint Louis.[9] Louis himself, however, played almost no part in the spiritual life of the court until he reached the age of twelve, when, on the orders of the Bishop of Rhodez, he was given his own confessor. Accordingly, on October 24, 1649, Louis went to the house of the Jesuits and chose the Superior, Charles Paulin, who decided that Louis should be confirmed shortly thereafter. The ceremony took place that same year, on December 8, the Feast of the Conception of the Virgin, in the chapel of the Palais Royale, and he took his first communion that Christmas, in public, at the church of Saint-Eustache.[10] His coronation in 1654 followed essentially the same rite as that of Louis XIII, although since he had already been confirmed, the Office of Vespers on the eve of the ceremony did not feature this sacrament. Nevertheless, it may well have been celebrated as Vespers for the Holy Spirit, since it featured the hymn *Veni creator spiritus*, sung by the singers of the cathedral and the *musique du roy*.[11] And, following the model of his forebears, Louis XIV was also admitted as a Knight of the Order of the Holy Spirit the day after the coronation.

If the last decade of Louis XIII's reign is relatively devoid of musical sources related to the court, the first two decades of Louis XIV's are similarly, if not more, bare.[12] Yet it is in these years that music historians have conventionally sought out the seeds of the musical and liturgical tradition that seemed to appear fully formed shortly after 1660, that of the performance of a *grand motet* during Low Mass at the *chapelle royale*, the genre that Dumont, Lully, Lalande, Bernier, Mondonville, Rameau, and numerous other composers into the eighteenth century would make canonical.[13] It is not my aim to provide a comprehensive history of this

---

[8] Archon, *Histoire ecclésiastique*, p. 790.   [9] Oroux, *Histoire ecclésiastique*, p. 459.
[10] Oroux, *Histoire ecclésiastique*, p. 461.
[11] Simon le Gras, *Procès verbal du sacre du Roy Louis quatorze du nom* (Soissons, Nicolas Hanisset, 1694), p. 19.
[12] I leave to one side publications by Henri Dumont (*Cantica sacra* of 1652, *Meslanges* of 1657) and Étienne Moulinié (*Meslanges*, 1658), since they were intended to provide versatile repertoires for performance in the religious or noble houses of France rather than being uniquely intended for royal service.
[13] For a conventional exploration of the development of the grand motet see, Thierry Favier, 'Genèses du grand motet', in Jean Duron (ed.), *La Naissance du style français* (Wavre, Mardaga,

transitional moment in history, but it is nonetheless instructive to revisit the relatively well-known (although poorly understood) musical landmarks of this period, and to consider the ways in which the musical and liturgical practices of Louis XIII were, or were not, adopted by those around his son. The creation of the new *chapelle royale* liturgy itself, the subject of an important monograph by Alexandre Maral, is beyond the scope of this study, but in broader terms, it is clear that, while the new genre owed a considerable debt to the musical practices of the previous era, the *grand motet* as originally conceived played an entirely different role in the musical/liturgical discourse, and ultimately in the legitimation of the king's power.[14]

Nicolas Formé had been succeeded as *sous-maître* by Thomas Gobert (1600–99) in 1638, and Jean Veillot joined him at court in 1643. The elusive Eustache Picot also continued in service until 1651, although none of his works survives, nor any Latin sacred music by Gobert. It thus falls to Veillot to act as our case study as we follow developments in the orbit of Louis XIV following the publication in 1638 of Formé's mass *Aeternae Henrici Magni*.

Famously, in his obituary of the composer, Henri Sauval attributes the "invention" of the double-choir motet to Nicolas Formé, describing how, on his death, his works passed to Jean Veillot, who "used them for his profit."[15] Obviously from Sauval's later perspective, Formé's published Mass would have been the only extant evidence of such a scoring at this time, although we have seen that the practice itself (or at least collaboration between court ensembles) was long-established, reaching well back into the sixteenth century. But we can nonetheless trace Formé's influence – as the latest exponent of this tradition – and the Christocentric spirit of the times, in the works that Veillot composed at some point in the following decade. *Alleluia, O filii et filiae* is a setting of the famous Eucharistic hymn for two choirs and strings.[16] There is no designation of *grand* or *petit chœur* (terms

---

2008), pp. 89–113. See also Thierry Favier, *Le Motet à grand chœur (1660–1792): Gloria in Gallia Deo* (Paris, Fayard, 2009).

[14] For the musical and liturgical practices at the *chapelle royale* in the later period, see Alexandre Maral, *La Chapelle royale de Versailles sous Louis XIV: cérémonial, liturgie et musique* (Sprimont, Mardaga, 2002).

[15] Henri Sauval, *Histoire et recherches des antiquités de la ville de Paris* (Paris, Charles Moette and Jacques Chardon, 1724), Vol. 1, pp. 326–7.

[16] Preserved at F-Pn, Département de Musique, MS Rés. F 542. Although the melody of this hymn (text by the Franciscan Friar Jean Tisserand, d. 1494) later became widely known, its first recorded appearances in a polyphonic arrangement are in two important volumes of devotional music, Charles de Courbes, *Cantiques spirituels* (Paris, Pierre Ballard, 1622), modern edition,

first coined by Huygens that would later identify the two choirs in the *grand motet*)[17] in Philidor's much later score (the only surviving source), nor any other indication that one choir is made up of solo voices. But just like Formé's Mass, Choir 2 sings only in full-voiced homophony, is always harmonically complete, extends down to an f4 bass voice, and always doubles Choir 1; Choir 1, however, sings in a variety of combinations of solo, duet, and tutti, extends down only to an f3 bass voice and requires the use of the *basse-continue* to provide harmonic support when the sparser scoring leaves the harmony incomplete. This alone suggests a *chambre/chapelle* collaboration, but the presence of a version of this piece for the *chambre* alone (preserved in the Paris manuscript and probably intended to be sung by the *chambre* at the altars of repose on corpus Christi) that broadly mirrors the overall structure and vocal strategy (i.e. the melody presented in the baritone or *basse-taille* voice) strongly points to this work, and these two groups of singers, as the origin of this "proto" *grand motet*.[18]

Veillot's setting of another strophic Eucharistic work, the Corpus Christi hymn *Sacris solemnis* (probably performed at the Feast of Corpus Christi, 1659, to celebrate the Peace of the Pyrenees),[19] reflects a similar kind of collaboration between *chambre* and *chapelle*, using two choirs and string orchestra to present the seven verses of text.[20] The indications *petit chœur* and *grand chœur* appear for the first time (the score, of course, dates from much later), and presumably suggest, as Huygens had done a decade earlier, that the *petit chœur* was to be sung by soloists. The two choirs

---

ed. Marc Desmet (Saint-Étienne, Publications de l'Université de Saint-Étienne, 2005) and *Airs sur les hymnes sacrez* (Paris, Pierre Ballard, 1623).

[17] The oft-quoted description of *grand* and *petit chœur* clearly derives from the *chambre/chapelle* distinction: "Le grand chœur, qui est à cinq est toujours remply de quantité de voix. Aux petits chœurs, les voix y sont seules de chaque partie" (The *grand chœur*, which is in five parts and contains many voices. In the *petit chœur*, the voices of each part sing alone). See Thomas Gobert, letter to Constantin Huygens, October 17, 1647, in Constantin Huygens, *Correspondance et œuvres musicales de Constantin Huygens*, ed. Willem Jonckbloet and Jan Pieter Land (Leyden, Société pour l'Histoire Musicale des Pays-Bas, 1882), p. 217.

[18] Preserved in the Paris manuscript at f. 146r.

[19] See Denise Launay, *La Musique religieuse en France du Concile de Trente à 1804* (Paris, Klincksieck, 1993), p. 309. According to Loret, three un-named motets by Veillot were performed on June 8, 1659, at the oratory of the Louvre. Since the Feast of Corpus Christi fell on June 12, that year, it seems reasonable to suppose that *Sacris solemnis* was one of them; see Jean Loret, *La Muze historique* (Paris, Charles Chenault, 1655–65), letter 23, June 14, 1659, ed. J. Ravenel and Ed. de la Pelouze (Paris, P. Jannet, 1857–78), Vol. 3, p. 66.

[20] F-Pn, Département de Musique, MS Rés. F 542. Modern edition, Jean Veillot, *Sacris solemnis* (Versailles, Centre de Musique Baroque de Versailles, 2005)(*Cahiers*, 145).

show a significant amount of dependence, much of the *grand chœur* material merely doubling the *petit chœur*, although there are brief instances of independence. While this is a much more complex and sophisticated work than *Alleluia, O filii*, once again the hymn melody is frequently presented in the *basse-taille,* and the overall plan reveals a fundamental conception little different from that of *Alleluia, O filii et filiae.*

If the surviving musical evidence from the 1640s and 1650s points to an emphasis on strophic, Christological hymns, the 1660s saw a return to the Psalm. Composed for the wedding celebrations of Louis XIV and Maria Teresia of Spain, Lully's *Jubilate Deo* received its first performance "after lunch" ("après dinée") on August 29, 1660, at the monastery of La Mercy, perhaps connecting it to the mealtime tradition of performance inherited from the sixteenth century.[21] No mention is made of any *chambre/chapelle* collaboration in surviving accounts, but according to the *Gazette* the motet "was sung by a large number of the most beautiful voices, with the twenty-four violins and other instruments."[22] A second performance for Louis XIV and Mazarin (neither of whom had heard it previously) was given on September 16.

Jubilate Deo is a setting of a centonization of twelve different psalms, a key feature noted by the diarist Loret at its repeat performance:[23]

... Motet rare and melodious,
Worthy, it is said, of the Gods,
Taken from various words of the Psalmist,
And made by the famous [Jean-] Baptiste [Lully],
A young man admirable in his art.

In keeping with the earlier practice we saw in the *chambre* repertoire or the Bouzignac *entrée* motets (though not a practice that would later be typical at the *chapelle royale*), Lully or the librettist made many minor modifications to the psalm texts to make explicit the allusions to the king. The text

---

[21] See John Hajdu Heyer, 'Lully's *Jubilate Deo*, LWV 77/16: A stylistic anomaly', in Jerome de la Gorce and Herbert Schneider (eds.), *Le Grand-motet français: Actes du colloque sur le grand motet français, Saint-Germain-en-Laye, 1987* (Laaber, Laaber Verlag, 1990), pp. 145–54, and Lionel Sawkins, 'Lully's motets: Source, edition, performance', in de la Gorce and Schneider, *Le Grand motet français*, pp. 383–404.

[22] "... fut chanté par grand nombre des plus belles voix, avec les 24 violons & autres Instruments." *Gazette*, no. 105, September 4, 1660, p. 826.

[23] "Motet rare et mélodieux, / Digne, ce disait-on, des Dieux, / Pris de quelques mots du Psalmiste, / Et fait par le fameux Baptiste, / Garçon admirable en son art." See Loret, *Muze Historique*, Vol. 3, p. 245.

of Psalm 97:6, for example, was modified from "Jubilate in conspectu Regis Domini" (Make a joyful noise before the Lord, our King) to "Jubilate in conspectu Regis" (Make a joyful noise before the King), whilst Psalm 121:7 was also changed from "Fiat pax in virtute tua et abundantia in turribus tuis" (Peace be within thy walls and plenteousness within thy palaces) to "Facta est pax in virtute sua et abundantia in turribus suis" (He has made peace in his walls and plenteousness within his palaces).[24]

But it is arguably only when we reach the pieces composed for, and performed at, the new Low Mass liturgy that the *grand motet* tradition can definitively be said to have begun. (The reorganization of the *chapelle royale* in 1663 and the appointment of Dumont, Robert, Expilly, and Gobert as *sous-maîtres* is conventionally taken to mark this turning point.)[25] *Domine in virtute tua*, a setting of the complete and unaltered text of Psalm 20, may well be the earliest extant motet by Dumont, appearing as it does in the 1666 *Livre du Roi* near the top of the list of motets for that quarter.[26] In this case we can certainly finally see a musical work calling to mind the coronation itself, since this psalm was undoubtedly performed as both Louis XIII and XIV processed into Reims cathedral for their *sacre*. (Indeed, we might almost call it a "coronation psalm.") Yet it is perhaps in a final example that we come full circle, revisiting yet also reformulating the musical, textual and liturgical conventions of half a century earlier. Dumont's *Pulsate, pulsate tympana*, which entered the repertoire of the *chapelle royale* in the third quarter of 1670, sets a text from Pierre Perrin's *Cantica pro Capella Regis* of 1665, and again uses the double-choir scoring that had now become standard.[27] In publishing the

---

[24] For a complete analysis of the text see John Hajdu Heyer's introduction to Jean-Baptiste Lully, *Œuvres Complètes*, Vol. 4/2, ed. John Hajdu Heyer (Hildesheim, Paris, Olm Verlag, Musica Gallica, 2010).

[25] See Launay, *Musique religieuse*, p. 314.

[26] See the preface to Henri Dumont, *Grands Motets* (Vol. 4), ed. Laurence Decobert (Versailles, Éditions du CMBV, 1999), xix; Lionel Sawkins, 'Chronology and evolution of the *grand motet* at the Court of Louis XIV: Evidence from the *Livres du Roi* and the Works of Perrin, the *sous-maîtres* and Lully', in John Hajdu Heyer (ed.), *Jean-Baptiste Lully and the Music of the French Baroque* (Cambridge and New York, Cambridge University Press, 1989), p. 56; and Laurence Decobert, 'Henry Du Mont et le grand motet', in Jean Lionnet (ed.), *Le Concert des muses. Promenade musicale dans le baroque français* (Versailles, Éditions du CMBV, Klincksieck, 1997), pp. 127–52.

[27] Pierre Perrin, *Cantica pro Capella Regis* (Paris, Christophe Ballard, 1665). Sawkins, *Chronology and Evolution*, p. 56. It was published in Henri Dumont, *Motets pour la chapelle du Roy, mis en musique par Monsieur Dumont* ... (Paris, Christophe Ballard, 1686). There is no modern edition.

Cantica – a collection of texts explicitly created for the new regime at the *chapelle royale* – Perrin's aim was ostensibly little different to that of the *Académie de poésie et de musique* nearly a century earlier – to recreate the music of the 'siècle des Héros,' music that would invoke the "effects" of Arion, Amphion, and Alexander (who used the sound of music to excite and calm the passions of his court).[28] Thus, according to Perrin, in the sacred domain the composers of the *chapelle royale* should endeavor to recreate the type of music with which David appeased the fury of Saul, and which was then adopted by Solomon and the musicians of the Temple of Jerusalem. But the verses for this music should not use the Latin of Jerome and the medieval church fathers: instead, Perrin took his inspiration from the poetry of Cicero and Horace, which, he claims, had informed the rewriting of liturgical texts in Italy earlier in the century. Nevertheless, since all musicians knew that the rhymed verse of the Italians, Spanish, and French was more suitable for setting to music than the unrhymed Latin verse of the ancients, and since the Hebrew psalms also used a variety of line lengths, Perrin decided that his lyrics would likewise adopt both rhyme and variable line length.[29]

While Perrin's *Cantica* aimed to reflect the multifaceted character of Louis XIV by draping the psalms of David in the garb of classical antiquity, *Pulsate, pulsate tympana* takes this process one step further, adding one additional layer of meaning (see Table 8.1). Using language reminiscent of Psalm 150 ("Sound the trumpet, strike the drum," etc.) *Pulsate* adopts the voice of David, now speaking in "classical" (in practice not classical at all) Latin to celebrate Saint Louis, at once "Un Roy victorieux" and a "Prince très-Chrestien" whose soul, after his death pursuing God's will in the Holy Land, ascends to heaven, where he is crowned in glory – presumably to oversee the kingdom of France and to shine his glory on his namesake and descendant, Louis XIV.

---

[28] Perrin, *Cantica pro Capella Regis*, n.p.

[29] For a discussion of the complexities of Perrin's poetry, see Favier, 'Genèses du grand motet', esp. p. 107, and Jean Duron, 'Les "Paroles de musique" sous le règne de Louis XIV', in Jean Duron (ed.), *Plainchant et Liturgie en France au xviie siècle* (Versailles, Fondation Royaumont, Éditions du CMBV, Klincksieck, 1997), pp. 128–42. Duron describes how the concept of "antiquité medieval" mediated the conflicting trends of modernity vs. antiquity, classical vs. biblical. The issue of modernity is also addressed in Louis Auld, *The Lyric Art of Pierre Perrin, Founder of French Opera* (Henryville, Institute of Medieval Music, 1986), Vol. 1, pp. 11–24, and Vol. 2, pp. 159–60.

Table 8.1 Text and translation of *Pulsate, pulsate tympana*, Pierre Perrin, *Cantica pro Capella Regis* (Paris, Christophe Ballard, 1665), pp. 58–9

Battez, battez, tambour, sonnez, sonnez, trompette,	Beat, beat, O drum, sound, sound, O trumpet,
Un Roy victorieux à la guerre s'apreste:	A King victorious in war readies himself:
Un Prince très-Chrestien pour son Maistre combat,	A Prince most-Christian fights for his Master,
Déjà sonne la charge, & déjà l'on se bat,	Already the charge is sounded, and already combat begins,
Déjà le canon tonne & réduit tout en poudre,	Already the canon thunders and reduces everything to dust,
Et de ce Roy vainqueur, le bras lance la foudre.	And the arm of this vanquishing King launches a thunderbolt.
Par tout règne la mort, la crainte, la fureur,	Everywhere reigns death, fear, fury,
Le carnage & l'horreur.	Carnage and horror.
L'ennemie tombe à terre ou fuit à vaudéroute,	The enemy falls to the ground or flees,
Louys gagne le camp & poursuit la déroute.	Louis captures the camp and pursues the rout.
Bondissez d'allégresse & chantez au Seigneur	Leap for joy and sing to the Lord
Des cantiques d'honneur.	Songs of honor.
Mais, hélas! tout vainqueur il est saisy de peste,	But, alas! The conqueror is seized with the plague,
Il languit, il meurt, il est mort.	He languishes, he dies, he is dead.
Pleurez la cruauté du sort,	Weep for the cruelty of fate,
Pleurez cet accident funeste.	Mourn this fatal accident.
Le corps est mis en terre & l'âme vole aux Cieux	The body is buried in the ground and the soul flies to the Heavens
Pour aller régner en ces lieux.	To reign there.
Déjà sa teste s'environne	Already his head is encircled
D'une prétieuse couronne,	By a precious crown,
Déjà ce généreux Guerrier	Already this generous Warrior
Moissone à pleines mains la Palme & le Laurier,	Reaps the Palm and the Laurel,
Déjà son triomphe s'appreste,	Already his triumph is prepared,
Battez, tambour, sonnez, trompette.	Beat, O drum, sound, O trumpet.

French text trans. Perrin from his own Latin.

Conclusion

The scoring chosen by Dumont for *Pulsate, pulsate tympana*, and the subject matter of Perrin's text, an account of Saint Louis's life in the classicized voice of King David, both point, on the face of it, to at least some sense of continuity with the musical, ideological, and liturgical practices developed under Louis XIII in the first few decades of the century. And yet, I would argue, if we look more critically, Perrin's volume signals a turning point in the role that music and liturgy played in the legitimation of the king's power, a turning point that throws the practices of the earlier period, those of the age of Louis XIII, into sharp relief. Of course, Perrin's poetry did not entirely dominate the *chapelle royale* during this later period – the *sous-maîtres* set complete psalms as frequently as Perrin's texts, if not more so – but his poetry nonetheless appeared in settings throughout the 1670s, and in both Dumont's and Lully's major publications of the 1680s.[30]

When we last encountered Saint Louis we found him returning to prominence in the final years of Louis XIII's life. Featured as a weekly commemoration (Wednesdays) in the *Parvae Christianae Pietatis Officia* of 1643, a book of hours that recorded the king's own devotional routine (see Chapter 7), the single reading for Saint Louis's revised and abbreviated office told the story of his admirable life and noble death.[31] During his first crusade to the Holy Land, many of his men had contracted the plague, and he himself was briefly captured by the Saracens. Liberated shortly thereafter, he spent the next five years converting the infidel to Christianity before returning to France, where he lived a devout life and founded numerous monasteries and hospitals for the poor. Returning to the fray later in life, he journeyed to Africa, but fell gravely ill himself almost immediately, reciting the prayer "I will come into thy house: I will worship towards thy holy temple, and I will confess to thy name" (Psalm 5:8) as he died. By contrast, in the revisions that were made to the office of Saint Louis in the 1620s and 1630s and preserved in the 1636 *Breviarium*, Saint Louis was framed as a model king, a follower in David's line, chosen by God and anointed by Samuel (see Chapter 3). In Perrin's *Pulsate*, however, Louis is an invincible warrior, his entire identity bound up with military prowess (his victories are not even mentioned in the 1640 account), mercilessly pursuing his enemies in a thunderbolt of violence. To the extent that kingship is addressed, Louis is, in passing, the most-Christian king, but his military success and divine kingship in heaven appear to be a greater part of his identity than his earthly reign.

Perrin also places both himself and the act of musical composition at the center of the musical/liturgical discourse. The texts that the composers

---

[30] Dumont, *Motets*; Jean-Baptiste Lully, *Motets à deux chœurs pour la chapelle du Roy* (Paris, Christophe Ballard, 1684). See also Sawkins, 'Chronology and evolution'.

[31] *Parva Christianae pietatis officia per christianissimum Regem Ludovicum XIII ordinate* (Paris, Typographia Regia, 1643), p. 96. Translation in Prosper Guéranger, *The Liturgical Year*, Vol. 5, 'Time after Pentecost' (London, Burns and Oates, 1910), p. 79.

around Louis XIII set to music and performed in his presence were almost exclusively those of the time-honored liturgy of the universal church – typically the psalms themselves (authored by David), the texts of the Mass and Offices inherited from early church, a few later canticles such as the Te Deum (supposedly written by Saints Ambrose and Augustine), and some later hymns ("Charlemagne's" *Veni creator*, for example). While some hymns and texts were penned more recently (most notably, in this context, the hymns to Saint Louis by Isaac Habert), they appeared in the Breviary anonymously and merged seamlessly into the universal liturgy. By contrast, Perrin placed his own voice, and the music dependent on it, front and center, identifying himself not just in the *Cantica* but also in the so-called *Livres du Roi* that "audience" members at the *chapelle royale* were provided with.[32] While he may have claimed to have been engaged in an effort to breathe new life into the psalms by invoking the language of the ancients on David's behalf, Perrin's endeavor was, in fact, driven by musical rather than liturgical or spiritual aims, as he put it, to "take music to the pinnacle of excellence."[33] Composers before him, he reports, selected their own verses, "for the most part, phrases from the Holy Scripture gathered and badly stitched together, and applied to some pious subject or to some solemn occasion, and which are always obscure, forced, sounding bad to the ear and unsuitable for singing."[34] Not for him, then, the centonizations of psalms used by Lully in his *Jubilate Deo*, by the composers of Louis XIII's *chambre*, by Bouzignac in his *entrée* motets, or by Maillard, Mouton, and Costeley in their "coronation" motets. His new verses would surpass those of both antiquity and the psalms: now part of an artistic strategy rather than a liturgical practice, Perrin fashioned his lyrics expressly so that the King could hear his musicians performing "the most beautiful music on earth, as you are the greatest King there."[35]

But Perrins's voice, though vying for the listener's attention, was not the only voice that those present (or those later reading about the event) would have "heard." Both the composer of the music and the performer were often identified, especially when (as they frequently did) the musicians of the *chapelle royale* performed in the presence of Parisian society in the *chapelle* itself or at one of the major churches of the city.[36] A vivid

---

[32] Sawkins, 'Chronology and evolution'. [33] Perrin, *Cantica*, Épistre, n.p.
[34] Perrin, *Cantica*, Avant-propos, n.p.: "pour la pluspart que des phrases de l'Ecriture ramassées & mal cousuës ensemble, & appliqués à quelque sujet pieux ou à quelque solemnité, lesquelles ainsi ont esté toujours obscures, forces, mal-sonnantes à l'oreille & peu propres au chant ..."
[35] Perrin, *Cantica*, Épistre, n.p.
[36] The completion of the new chapel at the Louvre in 1659 was significant in this respect.

testament to the emergence of the public sphere and changing attitudes to individual creativity itself, the *Muze Historique* describes numerous occasions when sacred music was performed in these circumstances, now recounted as social events, with the identity of the performers or composers an important point of interest. We hear, for example of a Sunday Mass at the *chapelle royale* when Thomas Gobert composed a "divine Motet / Music charming and beautiful"; of Lully's motet that was performed by the order of Monsieur Bernard who had a "saintly zeal for these things"; or of a motet for *chapelle* and *chambre* by Jean-Baptiste Boësset, "a rare man / Who with justice one compares / To the Amphions of past times / Being well versed in his art" and a man whose "divin genie" was admired by the whole company.[37] While such descriptions might pay lip-service to the Aristotelian process of *imitatio*, praising Boësset's skill through comparison with authority figures of the past (here Amphion), at the same time they nonetheless reflect a new interest in the unique creative powers of the individual composer and his own "voice."[38]

The fact that the king's singers were now accompanied by strings of the *vingt-quatre violons du roi* abstracted (and distracted from) the liturgical voice even further. Of course, the organ had become almost an equal partner in France, "singing" in its own voice and taking alternate verses of many hymns, canticles, and psalms as an officially sanctioned counterpart of the vocal "choir." But even for the organ, contemporary ceremonials prescribe very strict limits on its liturgical participation: for an instrument associated primarily with dance and that historically had no liturgical voice of its own to suddenly become so central to musical practice (albeit in one very circumscribed domain) speaks to a dramatic change of heart about which voices were permitted in the liturgy.[39] Indeed, we should probably begin to see these events not as "liturgies" per se, but as arenas in which the strategies famously outlined by Elias – the tightly regulated, essentially secular, behaviors associated with the "court society" – could be put into

---

[37] Loret, *Muze historique*, Vol. 4, p. 245, Vol. 3, p. 10. The words "charmant," "belle," and "plaisir" feature prominently in almost all accounts of sacred music.

[38] See Rebecca Herissone, 'Introduction', in Rebecca Herissone and Alan Howard (eds.), *Concepts of Creativity in Seventeenth-Century England* (Woodbridge, Boydell Press, 2013), pp. 1–14.

[39] For the dance dimension to the *grand motet* see Jean-Paul Montagnier, 'Modèles chorégraphiques dans les grands et petits motets français', in Hervé Lacombe (ed.), *Le Mouvement en musique à l'époque baroque* (Metz, Éditions Serpenois, 1996), pp. 141–56; Lionel Sawkins, 'Performance practice in the *grands motets* of Michel-Richard de Lalande as determined by eighteenth-century timings', in Jean Mongrédien and Yves Ferraton (eds.), *Actes du Colloque international de musicologie sur le grand motet français, 1663–1792* (Paris, 1986), pp. 105–17.

effect, or indeed "staged."[40] It is this social dimension, now allied to a new concern with musical aesthetics that could lead to Loret's observation about such an event, that "The Te Deum ravished me / The music charmed me / The large and beautiful company / Caused me infinite joy ..."[41] Here, music's effects are no longer Neoplatonic but Cartesian; in language resonating with that of Loret, Mersenne (probably under Descartes's influence) had concluded by the 1640s that the function of music was now "particularly and principally to charm the spirit and the ear, and to allow us to pass through life with a little sweetness among the griefs."[42] Indeed, even as early as the late 1620s, Mersenne was beginning to embrace the idea of music as an expressive, rhetorical art, rejecting the rigidity of *musique mesurée* in favor of a more natural declamation, without "stopping at the fountain of Hippocrene or at the Tiber, from which the Seine and the Loire do not draw their waters."[43]

But it is perhaps the lack of universality that is most striking about the new musical/textual strategy employed in the *chapelle royale*. If – as I argue we should – we consider Perrin's lyrics and the *grand motet* based on them as at least part of a legitimation strategy, it is a strategy conceived from the center outward.[44] Perrins's lyrics were explicitly created for the *chapelle royale*, not for the nation as a whole. Only a tiny minority would have heard them performed there (Apostolides's "spectacle caste"),[45] and an even smaller minority (the king's musicians) would have uttered them. These lyrics therefore participated in an asymmetrical musical/liturgical discourse – paid artists of the highest caliber presented their art to another

---

[40] Norbert Elias, *The Court Society*, trans. Edmund Jephcott (Oxford, Blackwell, 1983), esp. pp. 78–116. See also Ralph Giesey, 'The King imagined', in Keith Baker (ed.), *The French Revolution and the Creation of Modern Political Culture: The Political Culture of the Old Régime* (Oxford, Pergamon Press, 1987), pp. 41–59, esp. 43–4, 56–8.

[41] Loret, *Muze historique*, vol. 1., p. 440: "Le Te Deum me raviroit / La muzique me charmeroit / La grande et belle compagnie / Me cauzeroit joye infini ..."

[42] See Marin Mersenne, *Correspondance du P. Marin Mersenne*, Paul Tannery and Cornélis de Waard (eds.) (Paris, CNRS, 1932–88), vol. 10, pp. 236–49. Descartes had already declared of music in 1618 that "The Object of this Art is a Sound. The End; to delight, and move various affections in us"; see René Descartes, trans. Humphrey Moseley as *Excellent Compendium of Music with Necessary and Judicious Animadversions Thereupon* (London, Thomas Harper and Humphrey Moseley, 1653), p. 1. See also Brigitte van Wymeersch, 'L'Esthétique musicale de Descartes et le cartésianisme', *Revue Philosophique de Louvain*, 4th series, 94/2 (1996), 271–93.

[43] See David Allen Duncan, 'Persuading the affections: Rhetorical theory and Mersenne's advice to harmonic orators', in Georgia Cowart (ed.), *French Musical Thought, 1600–1800* (Ann Arbor, UMI Research Press, 1989), pp. 149–75.

[44] See Introduction.

[45] Jean-Marie Apostolides, *Le Roi-machine: Spectacle et politique au temps de Louis XIV* (Paris, Éditions de Minuit, 1981), p. 46.

set of elites from whom no particular action was expected in return – certainly, the wider populace of France had almost no contact with this display and could not, in Beetham's terms, demonstrate their consent or approval (especially when the court moved out to Versailles and the "semi-public" events described by Loret no longer took place).[46] In terms of wider dissemination, the most that might be expected is that copies of the *Cantica pro Capella Regis* might make their way out to provinces where they would simply take their place alongside other products of Louis XIV's representational and artistic strategy – medals, engravings of the king's portrait, or accounts of military victories.[47] (It is certainly true that by the eighteenth century the *grand motet* was appearing more frequently in the provinces, but typically as part of a concert series modeled on the *Concert Spirituel* rather than as a part of a liturgy.)[48]

By contrast, we can see Louis XIII embedded in a legitimizing musical/liturgical discourse almost universally accepted and understood across the nation. We do not hear the voice of Perrin, but the liturgy – the voices of David, the other Old Testament prophets, or the Church Fathers – embraced or performed by the people themselves, and, to the extent that music was involved, mediated through (on the whole) unnamed composers and performers whose musical endeavors existed only to serve the divine text (not, as Perrin saw it, the other way round).[49] Such music need not be framed as "the most beautiful music on earth" (although it might "ravish" (seize) the mind of the listener), nor need it "represent" the king as invincible or all-powerful (as *Pulsate, pulsate tympana* did).[50] On the contrary, a verse such as the *Domine salvum fac regem* was premised on the weakness and vulnerability of the king, yet came to prominence as one of the most

---

[46] These are Beetham's "'legitimations' generated by the powerful themselves'; see David Beetham, *The Legitimation of Power* (Basingstoke, Palgrave MacMillan, 2013), p. 19. While it is certainly true that the wider populace of France probably did not "utter" the words of the liturgy either, it was nonetheless clearly celebrated on their behalf.

[47] For the mechanism of "consumption," see Peter Burke, *The Fabrication of Louis XIV* (New Haven and London, Yale University Press, 1992), pp. 151–78.

[48] For the provincial reception of the *grand motet*, see Favier, *Le Motet à grand chœur*, pp. 323–435; John Hajdu Heyer, *The Lure and Legacy of Music at Versailles: Louis XIV and the Aix School* (Cambridge and New York, Cambridge University Press, 2014); and Lionel Sawkins, 'En province, à Versailles et au Concert Spirituel: Réception, diffusions et execution des motets de Lalande au XVIIIe siècle', *Revue de musicologie*, 92/1 (2006), 13–40.

[49] The almost exclusively anonymous preservation of the works in the Paris, Tours, and Newberry/Avignon manuscripts testifies to this lack of interest in the identity of the composer.

[50] That is not to say that composers were not sometimes identified, or that music itself could not be praised, but positive descriptions generally correlate to the sense that the music produced powerful spiritual effects on the listener. See, for example, Chapter 6, note 44.

ubiquitous and distinctive texts (and subsequently musical genres) of the era. Indeed, for the most part eschewing "creative" novelties, it is striking that almost all the liturgical legitimations we can identify during the reign of Louis XIII are similarly "universal" in quality: the liturgy of the *chapelle royale* followed the Roman Rite, modified only slightly with additional hymns and psalms (albeit significant ones); the coronation followed the standard *Ordo*, framed by the standard confirmation liturgy (as part of a conventional Vespers service); the induction (indeed all the ceremonies of the Knights of the Holy Spirit) were effectively unchanged Vespers and Mass for the Holy Spirit; the Vow to the Virgin Mary simply resulted in an emphasis on the Feast of the Assumption throughout the nation; and the *Exaudiat* (and later the *Domine salvum fac regem*) was sung across the French church, essentially reprising its role in the Roman liturgy as the psalm for processions in time of distress, whether performed in the context of Mass, an *entrée* (a long-established liturgy), or a "Te Deum" (liturgically identical to the *entrée*). To the extent that some musical and liturgical innovations were not universally accepted at the time – the early adoption of the Exposition of the Blessed Sacrament, the focus on Saint Denis, or a rigorous application of "measured" chant, all at Montmartre – we can associate these innovations with forces (the Guises) that were at some level hostile to the crown.[51]

It is not therefore the uniqueness or special qualities of the music or liturgy that distinguishes the legitimating framework for Louis XIII. On the contrary, while those around Louis XIV shattered the ancient traditions, entirely decoupling the practices of the *chapelle royale* from the shared experience of almost all the king's subjects, it was this very shared experience, the very universality of this framework that was recognized by those around Louis XIII and which legitimated his power. As God's anointed, the literal or metaphorical descendant of King David, Saint Louis or even Jesus Christ himself, the king served God in both victory and defeat. But whatever the outcome in battle, or however soon the end of times would come, every day the people, the clergy, and indeed the whole of France demonstrated their belief in a system that placed Louis at God's right hand; every day they therefore recognized and accepted that they were subject to his power; and every day they rested safe in the knowledge that ultimately, as the psalmist promised, on the day of tribulation both he and the nation of France would be saved.

---

[51] We might also consider the chant of the Oratorians to be a localized phenomenon, but while their reforms were essentially aesthetic, the unchanged liturgy itself continued to participate in the legitimating process.

Bibliography

Musical Sources (Manuscript and Printed)

Manuscript Collections

Paris, Bibliothèque nationale de France, Département de Musique, MS V^{ma} Rés. 571 [the Paris manuscript].
Tours, Bibliothèque municipale, MS 168 [the Tours manuscript].
Chicago, Newberry Library, Case MS 5136, 5123 [the Chicago/Newberry manuscript].

Printed Sources

* fragment or incomplete

Airs sur les hymnes sacrez, odes et noëls pour chanter au catéchisme (Paris, Pierre Ballard, 1623).
Airs de différents auteurs mes en tablature de luth par Gabriel Bataille. Cinquiesme livre (Paris, Pierre Ballard, 1614).
Octo cantica divae Mariae Virginis, quae vulgo Magnificat appellantur (Paris, Adrian Le Roy and Robert Ballard, 1584).
Octo cantica divae Mariae Virginis, quae vulgo Magnificat appellantur (Paris, Robert and Pierre Ballard, 1599).*
Odes chrestiennes accommodés aux plus beaux Airs à quatre & cinq parties de Guedron et de Boësset (Paris, Pierre Ballard, 1625).*
Ambleville, Charles d', *Harmonia sacra . . . cum quatuor vocum* (Paris, Pierre Ballard, 1636).*
  Harmonia sacra . . . cum sex vocum (Paris, Pierre Ballard, 1636).
Auxcousteaux, Artus, *Psalmi aliquot ad numeros musices IIII, V et sex vocum redacti* (Paris, Pierre Ballard, 1631).*
Beaujoyeulx, Balthasar, *Balet comique de la royne, faict aux noces de monsieur le Duc de Joyeuse & madamoyselle de Vaudémont sa sœur* (Paris, Adrian le Roy, Robert Ballard, and Mamert Patisson, 1582).
Blondet, Abraham, *Officii Divae Ceciliae virgo et martyr Musicorum patronae musici concentibus expressi* (Paris, Pierre Ballard, 1611). Fragment bound into Bibliothèque nationale de France copy of Orlando Lassus, *Moduli*

duarum, vél trium vocum Orlando Lasso auctore (Paris, Pierre and Robert Ballard, 1611).*

Boësset, Antoine, works in the Paris manuscript. Modern edition in Peter Bennett (ed.), 'Antoine Boësset: Sacred Music', *Recent Researches in the Music of the Baroque Era*, 164–5, 2 parts (2010).

Bournonville, Jean de, *Octo cantica virginis matris* (Paris, Pierre Ballard 1612/25).

Caietain, Fabrice Marin, *Airs mis en musique a quatre parties* (Paris, Adrian le Roy and Robert Ballard, 1578). Modern edition in Jane Bernstein (ed.), 'Fabrice Marin Caietain', *The Sixteenth-Century Chanson*, 4 (New York, NY, Routledge, 1995).

Caignet, Denis, *Cinquante pseaumes de David mis en vers François par Philippes Desportes, Abbé de Thiron, et mis en musique à 3.4.5.6.7. & 8 parties* (Paris, Pierre Ballard, 1607).

Cinquante pseaumes de David mis en vers François par Ph. Desportes, Abbé de Thiron, et les chants en musique (Paris, Pierre Ballard, 1624).

Cinquante pseaumes de David mis en vers François par Philippes Desportes, Abbé de Thiron, et en musique, et sur le luth (Paris, Pierre Ballard, 1625).

Caurroy, Eustache Du, *Preces ecclesiasticae* (Paris, Pierre Ballard, 1609). Modern edition in Marie-Alexis Colin (ed.), *Eustache Du Caurroy: Preces ecclesiasticae* (Paris, Klincksieck, 2000).

Meslanges (Paris, Pierre Ballard, 1610). Modern edition in Marie-Alexis Colin (ed.), *Eustache Du Caurroy: Meslanges* (Turnhout, Brepols, 2010).

Costeley, Guillaume *Musique de Guillaume Costeley* (Paris, Adrian le Roy and Robert Ballard, 1570). Modern edition in Henry Expert (ed.), *Les Maîtres musiciens de la Renaissance française*, Vols. 3, 18, 19 (Paris, Alphonse Leduc, 1896–1904).

Courbes, Charles de, *Cantiques spirituels nouvellement mis en musique* (Paris, Pierre Ballard, 1622). Modern edition in Marc Desmet (ed.), *Charles de Courbes: Cantiques Spirituels* (Saint-Étienne, Lyon, Publications de l'Université de Saint-Étienne, Symétrie, 2005).

Coyssard, Michel, *Paraphrase des hymnes et cantiques spirituelz* (Lyon, Jean Pillehotte, 1592).

Dumont, Henri *Cantica sacra* (Paris, Pierre Ballard, 1652). Modern edition in Jean Lionnet (ed.), *Henry Du Mont: Cantica sacra* (Versailles, Éditions du CMBV, 1996).

Motets pour la chapelle du Roy, mis en musique (Paris, Christophe Ballard, 1686).

Formé, Nicolas, *Aeternae Henrici Magni, Gallorum, Navarrorumque Regis Potentissimi, ac Clementissimi memoriae. Et Ludovici Jusiti: eius Filii ... Missam hanc duobus Choris ac quatuor voc. compositam* (Paris, Pierre Ballard, 1638). Modern edition in Jean-Charles Léon (ed.), *Nicolas Formé: Œuvres complètes* (Versailles, Éditions du CMBV, 2003).

Musica simplex quatuor vocum, two settings, one incomplete (Paris, Pierre Ballard, 1638). Modern edition in Jean-Charles Léon (ed.), *Nicolas Formé: Œuvres complètes* (Versailles, Éditions du CMBV, 2003).*

Le Cantique de la Vierge Marie selon les Tons ou Modes usités en L'Église, F-Pn MS fonds fr. 1870. Modern edition in Jean-Charles Léon (ed.), *Nicolas Formé: Œuvres complètes* (Versailles, Éditions du CMBV, 2003).

Jambe de Fer, Philibert, *Les Cent cinquante pseaumes du royal prophète David. Traduits en rithme Françoyse par Cl. Marot, M. Jan Poitevin, M. Sève Lyonnais et autres. Mis en musique par Philibert Jambe de Fer* (Lyon, Jacques Crozet, 1555).

Le Jeune, Claude, *Pseaumes en vers mesurez* (Paris, Robert Ballard, 1606). Modern edition in Isabelle His (ed.), *Claude Le Jeune: Pseaumes en vers mesurez* (Turnhout, Brepols, 2007).

Le Vavasseur, Nicolas, *Airs a III. IIII. et V. parties* (Paris, Pierre Ballard, 1626). *Second livre d'airs a IIII. et V. parties* (Paris, Pierre Ballard, 1629/30).*

Lully, Jean-Baptiste, *Motets à deux chœurs pour la chapelle du Roy* (Paris, Christophe Ballard, 1684).

Macé, Jean, *Instructions pour apprendre a chanter à quatre parties, selon le Plain chant, les Pseaumes, & Cantiques* (Caen, Jean Macé, 1582).

Maillard, Jean, *Domine salvum fac regem*, first published in 1551[24] and 1553[7.] Modern edition in Raymond Rosenstock (ed.), 'Modularum Ioannis Maillardi: The four-part motets', *Recent Researches in the Music of the Renaissance*, 73 (1987).

Mauduit, Jacques, *Chansonettes mesurées de Jan-Antoine Baïf mis en musique à quatre parties* (Paris, Adrian Le Roy and Robert Ballard, 1588). Modern edition in Henry Expert (ed.), *Les Maîtres musiciens de la Renaissance française*, Vol. 10 (Paris, Alphonse Leduc, 1899).

Métru, Nicolas, *Recueil de vers du Sr. G. de Baïf, mis en Musique par N. Métru, chantez en allegresse de l'heureux retour du Roy* (Paris, Pierre Ballard, 1628).*

Moulinié, Étienne, *Meslanges de sujets chrestiens* (Paris, Jacques Senlecque, 1658). Modern edition in Jean Duron (ed.), *Étienne Moulinié: Meslanges de sujets chrestiens & motet 'Flores apparuerunt'* (Versailles, Éditions du CMBV, 1996).

Mouton, Jean, *Domine salvum fac regem*. Modern edition in Edward Lowinsky (ed.), 'The Medici Codex of 1518', *Monuments of Renaissance Music, 3–5* (Chicago, IL, University of Chicago Press, 1968).

Tessier, Charles, Lute Song Manuscript, Oxford, Bodleian Library, Music School MS D 237. Modern edition in Frank Dobbins (ed.), *Charles Tessier: Œuvres complètes* (Turnhout, Brepols, 2006).

Veillot, Jean, *Sacris solemnis and O filii et filiae*, F-Pn, Département de Musique, MS Rés. F 542. Modern edition in Jean Veillot, *Sacris solemnis*, Cahiers 145 (Versailles, Éditions du CMBV, 2005).

Angeli, archangeli, throni et dominationes, F-Pn, Département de Musique, MS V^{m1} Rés. 256.*

Liturgical Books (Anonymous, Manuscript, and Printed)

Antiphonier Bénédictin pour les religieuses du royal et célèbre monastère de Montmartre (Paris, Louis Sevestre, 1646).

Antiphonae quae in solemnitatibus totius anni cum organo solemniter decantari solent in ecclesia S. Ludovici, F-Pn, Département de Musique, MS Rés 2299c.

Breviarium insignis Ecclesiae parisiensis restitutum ac emendatum (Paris, Jean Charron, 1584).

Breviarium parisiense ad formam Sacrosancti Concilii Tridentini restitutum (Paris, Rolin Thierry and Eustache Foucault, 1617).

Breviarium parisiense ad formam sacrosancti Concilii Tridentini restitutum (Paris, Sebastien and Gabriel Cramoisy, Stéphane Richer, and Antoine Vitray, 1636).

Breviarium Romanum ex decreto Sacros Conc. Trid. Restitutum (Rome, Typographia Vaticana, 1633).

Breviarium parisiense ad formam sacrosancti Concilii Tridentini restitutum (Paris, Sebastien and Gabriel Cramoisy, Stéphane Richer, and Gabriel Clopejau, 1640).

Cérémoniale monastique des religieuses de l'Abbaye Royale de Montmartre (Paris, Barthélemy and Marin Vitré, 1669).

Graduale et antiphonale ad usum S. Ludovici domus regiae Versaliensis (1684–6), F-Pn MS lat. 8828.

Heures de nostre Dame, à l'usage de Rome . . . pour la Congrégation Roiale des Pénitents de l'Annonciation de nostre Dame (Paris, Jamet Mettayer, 1583).

Hymni Breviarii Romani S^{mi} D.N. Urbani VIII (Rome, Typis Vaticanis, 1629).

Missale insignis ecclesiae Parisiensis restitutum et emendatum (Paris, Stephanum Vallaetum, 1602).

Missale ad usum Andegavensis (Angers, 1644).

L'Office de saint Louis roy de France, à l'usage de la chapelle du roy à Versailles. Avec des Méditations pour l'Octave & pour les autres Fêtes que l'Église célèbre à l'honneur du S. Roy (Paris, G. Desprez, 1760).

L'Office des chevaliers de l'Ordre du St. Esprit (Paris, Imprimerie Royale, 1703).

Offices propres des Saincts de la Royale Abbaye de Montmartre (Paris, Jean Henault, 1658).

Officium S. Ludovici regis Franciae ac Missae Festorum Annualium ad usum Domus Regiae Invalidorum (1719), F-Pn MS lat. 8831.

Pio III Pont. Max. Pontificale Romanum ad omnes Pontificias ceremonias . . . (Venice, Iuntas, 1561).

Pontificale noviter impressum ... (Lyon, 1511).

Pontificale Romanum Clementis VIII Pont. Max. (Paris, Rolinum Thierry and Eustachium Foucault, 1615).

Pontificale secundum ritum sacrosanctum Romane ecclesie cum multis additionibus ... (Lyon, 1542).

Processionale noviter emendatum et auctum iuxta ritum insignis ecclesie & dicocesis Parisiensis. Quod quidem complectitur et continet ea que in Processionibus per totum anni curriculum sunt cantanda (Paris, Societatem Typographicam, 1588).

Rituale Parisiense ad Romani formam expressum (Paris, Pierre Targa, 1646).

Rituale Romanum Pauli V. Pont. Max. iussu editum (Rome, Typographia Reverendae Camerae Apostolicae, 1615).

Sacerdotale vulgo manual seu agenda ... iuxta decretum Concilii Provincialis Anno Domini 1583 Remis celebrati (Reims, Simon de Foigny, 1607).

Les Ténèbres de la Semaine Sainte pour les religieuses de Montmartre (Paris, Louis Sevestre, 1647).

Angers, Bibliothèque municipale, MS 2103 (fifteenth-century processional).

Tours, Bibliothèque municipale, MS 207 (unidentified liturgical book).

Bibliothèque municipale, MS 204 (processional from Saint Martin Tours).

Bibliothèque municipale, MS 180 (manuscript ritual, late seventeenth or early eighteenth century).

Entrée (in Chronological Order) [Partial List]

Entrée solennelle du roi Louis XIII et de Marie de Médicis en la ville du Mans, le 5 septembre 1614 (Le Mans, G. and F. Les Oliviers, 1614).

Jourdan, C., *L'Ordre, entrée, et cérémonies observées par les habitans de Paris à l'heureux retour de Louys XIII* (Lyon, Claude Cayne, 1614).

Malingre, Claude, *Entrée magnifique du Roy, faicte en sa ville d'Orléans, le mardy huictiesme juillet 1614, avec l'ordre et cérémonies observées en icelle* (Paris, Melchiore Mondière, 1619).

Entrée royale faite en la ville de Poictiers, au très-chrestien roy de France & de Navarre, Louys XIII. & à la Royne sa mère (Paris, Charles Pignon, 1619).

La Royale entrée du Roy, et de la Royne en la ville de Chartres, avec les Magnificences & Cérémonies qui s'y sont observées Ieudy le 26 Septembre (Paris, Iozue Chemin, 1619).

Les Magnificences préparées en l'église Notre-Dame de Chartres, pour les dévotes actions de grâce du roi et de la reine sa mère, de leur heureuse entrevue et de leur aimable réconciliation (Paris, S. Benoist, 1619).

L'Arrivée du Roy, en la ville du Mans le 28 juillet 1620 (Paris, Isaac Mesnier, 1620).

Actions de Grâces de la France, sur la prise, réduction, & capitulation des Villes de Montpellier, Nîmes, Castres, Millaud, Uzès, & autres places Rebelles. Avec le

Te Deum de resiouyssance des fidèles François, pour l'heureux succès des armes du Roy (Bordeaux, 1622).

Harangue au roy, prononcée à Grenoble, le 29 novembre 1622 au nom du clergé ... (Paris, N. Rousset, 1622).

Les Préparatifs ordonnés pour l'entrée et réception du roi, suivant les commandements de MM. les prévôts des marchands et les échevins de la ville de Paris (Paris, Nicolas Alexandre, 1622).

Saxi, Pierre, *Entrée de Loys XIII Roy de France et de Navarre dans sa ville d'Arles, le XXIX Octobre MDCXXII* (Avignon, Jean Bramereau, 1623).

Berton, Thomas de, *La Voye de laict, ou Le Chemin des héros au palais de la gloire* (Avignon, Jean Bramereau, 1623).

Le Soleil au signe du Lion, d'où quelques parallèles sont tirés avec le très-chrétien, ... monarque Louis XIII, roi de France et de Navarre, en son entrée triomphante dans sa ville de Lyon; ensemble un sommaire récit de tout ce qui s'est passé de remarquable en ladite entrée de Sa Majesté, et de la. 1623 (Paris, Jean Jullieron, 1623).

Réception de ... Louis XIII, Roy de France par MM. les Doyen, Chanoines, & Comtes de Lyon ... (Lyon, Jacques Roussin, 1623).

Discours sur les arcs triomphaux dressés en la ville d'Aix à l'heureuse arrivée de très-chrétien, très-grand et très-juste monarque Louis XIII, roi de France et de Navarre (Aix, Jean Tholosan, 1624).

Les Arcs triomphaux érigez à l'honneur du Roy dans sa ville de Dijon (Paris, Jacques Dugast, 1629).

Éloges et discours sur la triomphante réception du roi en sa ville de Paris, après la réduction de La Rochelle (Paris, Pierre Rocolet, 1629).

La Ioyeuse entrée du Roy en sa ville de Troyes ... Le Ieudy vingt cinquiesme iour de Ianvier, 1629 (Troyes, Jean Jacquard, 1629).

Manuscript and Archival Sources

Aix, Bibliothèque Méjanes, MS 272, *Livre de cérémonies de l'Église métropolitaine de S. Sauveur.*

Aix, Bibliothèque Méjanes, MS 276 (Actes de chapitres).

Angers, Archives départementales de Maine-et-Loire, 5 G 1–3 (Diary of René Lehoreau, Angers, c. 1700).

Carpentras, Bibliothèque Inguimbertine, MS 1794 (Notes by Pieresc on *entrées*).

Le Mans, Archives départementales de Sarthe, G 220–226 (Processions at Le Mans cathedral).

Lyon, Archives départementales, 10 G 442 (*Entrées*).

Paris, Archives nationales de France

K 502 (Coronation expenses).
KK 1431 (Record of first meeting of Knights of the Holy Spirit).
Z1a 472 (Personnel of *chapelle royale*, etc.).
L 1031 no. 31, *Bulle de confirmation de la fondation du Prieure du martyre de St.-Denis*, 1623.
L 1031 no. 39, *Règlement touchant la desserte de la Chapelle Sn. Leuffroy appartenante a Msr. le dit Vénérables Doyen, Chanoines et Chapitre de L'Église Royalle et Collegiale de Saint Germain Lauxerroy à Paris.*
L 1031 no. 40, *Mémoire touchant la bulle de la fondation du Prieure des martyrs.*

Paris, Bibliothèque nationale de France

MS 500 de Colbert 54, fonds fr. 7008, nouv. acq. fr. 32 (*Règlement* for the *chapelle* of Henri III).
MS fonds fr. 3994 (*États de la Maison*).
MS fonds fr. 18512 (Listing of *chapelle royale* personnel, 1610).
MS fonds fr. 18515 (Description of ceremonies for Peace of Vervins).
MS fonds fr. 18521 (*États généraux* 1614).
MS fonds fr. 18531 (Index of 'Te Deums' in Paris with psalms).
MS fonds fr. 19140 (Baïf psalter).
MS italien 1773 (Despatches of the Italian ambassador).
MS nouv. acq. fr. 23474 (Processions and 'Te Deums').
MS nouv. acq. fr. 9740 (1585 *règlement* with plan of *chapelle*).
MS nouv. acq. fr. 819 (Ceremonial, 1548–1640).
MS nouv. acq. fr. 7549 (Pénitents members).

Troyes, Archives départementales de l'Aube, G-1613 (Expenses for 1629 *entrée*).

Printed Sources (before 1800)

Actions de grâces et allégresses de la France sur la réduction de la Rochelle à l'obeysance du Roy (Paris, Jules Jacquin, 1628).
Actions de Grâces de la France, sur la prise, réduction, & capitulation des Villes de Montpellier, Nismes, Castres, Millaud, Uzès, & autres places Rebelles. Avec le Te Deum de resiouyssance des fidèles François, pour l'heureux succès des armes du Roy (Bordeaux, n.p., n.d. [1622]).
Biblia Sacra hebraice, chaldaice, graece, & latine (Antwerp, Christophe Plantin, 1569-73).
A Breeve of our Holy Father the Pope to the King upon the taking of Rochell[e] (London, Martin, 1629).

Bref de nostre S. Père la Pape Paul V pour la célébration de la feste de Sainct Louys iadis Roy de France, par tout ce Royaume, Avec le Mandement de Monseigneur l'Illustrissime & Révérendissime Cardinal de Retz, Évêque de Paris (Paris, François Julliot, 1617).

Les Cérémonies royalles qui se doivent faire à la réception de Messieurs les Chevaliers de l'Ordre du S. Esprit . . . (Paris, Isaac Mesnier, 1619).

Le Combat de David contre Goliath, au Roy très Chrestien Louys (n.p., 1618).

Déclaration du roy, par laquelle sa Majesté déclare qu'elle a pris la très-Saincte & très Glorieuse Vierge pour Protectrice spéciale de son Royaume (Paris, 1638).

Discours sur les triomphes que esté faicts le 25, 26, 27 aoust 1613 dans la ville de Paris a l'honneur & loüange de la feste S. Louys, & de Louys XIII . . . (Lyon, Jean Poyet, 1613).

L'Etat de la France ou l'on voit tous les Princes, Ducs & Pairs (Paris, Jean Ribout, 1665).

Histoire des ordres monastiques, religieux et militaires, et les congrégations séculières (Paris, Jean-Baptiste Coignard, 1719).

The Holy Bible translated from the Latin Vulgate. Newly Revised and Corrected According to the Clementine Edition of the Scriptures (Dublin, 1750).

Litanies et prières pour le Roy, et nécessité du Royaume (Rouen, Matthias l'Allement, 1581).

Le Livre des Statuts et ordonnances de l'Ordre du benoist Sainct Esprit, estably par le très-chrestien Roy de France & de Pologne Henry Troisiesme de ce nom (1578).

Mandement de Monseigneur l'Évesque de Paris pour le voyage du Roy (Paris, François Julliot, 1615).

Oraison à la très-heureuse, très-pure, & Immaculée Vierge Marie Mère de Dieu, qui se dira par chacun an, en toutes les Églises de France, en la Messe au iour & Feste de l'Assomption d'icelle Vierge, suivant la Déclaration & Commandement du Roy, publié en l'année 1638 (n.p., 1638).

L'Ordre des Cérémonies observées aux Funérailles & service de feu Madame à S. Denys en France Le dernier Juin 1627 (Paris, 1627).

L'Ordre et les cérémonies qui sont faictes au sacre et couronnement du très-Chrestien Roy de France (Lyon, Nicolas Jullieron, 1610).

Ordre et règlement qui doit estre tenu et observe en la maison du Roy . . . (Paris, Marin le Che, 1651).

Parva Christianae pietatis officia per christianissimum Regem Ludovicum XIII ordinate (Paris, Typographia Regia, 1643).

Prière et oraisons très-dévotes aux Catholiques françois, pour la conservation & prospérité du Roy, avec un paraphrase & brève explication du psalme Exaudiat (Paris, Jean Houdenc, 1622).

Prières ordonnées par Monseigneur l'Archevesque de Paris pour dire aux Églises où sont les Prières de Quarante-heures. Pour le bon succez des armes de sa Majesté, contre tous les ennemis de son Estat (Paris, Pierre Targa, 1636).

Pro restitute regi sanitate: oratio (Paris, 1721).

Psalmi Davidis, Proverbia Salomonis, Ecclesiastes et Canticum Canticorum Hebraicè, cum interlineari versione Santis Pagnini (Paris, Sebastien Cramoisy, 1632).

Les Pseaumes des courtisans dediés aux braves esprits qui entendent le jars de la Cour (Paris, n.p., 1620).

Recherches historiques de l'Ordre du Saint Esprit (Paris, Claude Jombert, 1710).

Représentation d'une chapelle le souterraine qui s'est trouvée à Mont-Martre près de Paris, le Mardy 12. iour de Iuillet 1611 comme on faisoit des fondements pour agrandir la Chapelle des Martyrs (Paris, Nicolas de Mathonière, 1611).

Le Salomon de la France, ou le rapport de nostre Roy à Salomon, en sa sagesse par la iustice, & la clémence (Paris, Pierre Chevalier, 1617).

The Second Tome of the Holie Bible Faithfully Translated into English out of the Authenticall Latin. Diligently Conferred with the Hebrew, Greek, and Other Editions in Divers Languages (Douai, John Cousturier, 1609/R1633).

Stances ou prière du Roy sur un tableau offert par sa Majesté à Nostre Dame de Paris, représentant Nostre Seigneur mort entre les bras de la très-sainte Vierge: & sadite Majesté luy présentant à genoux sa Couronne (Paris, Jacques le Long, 1638).

Les Statuts de la congrégation des Pénitens de l'Annonciation de Nostre Dame (Paris, Jamet Mettayer, 1583).

Les Statuts de la reigle de l'oratoire et compagnie de benoist Sainct François (Paris, Jamet Mettayer, 1586).

Les Statuts de l'oratoire Nostre-Dame de Vie-Saine (Paris, Jamet Mettayer, 1585).

Les Triomphes du très-Chrestien Roy ... Louis le Juste, digne héritier & successeur du Roy Sainct Louis (Paris, Nicolas Alexandre, 1618).

Ambrose, *Apologia prophetae David,* trans. Marius Corder as *Apologie de David,* Sources Chrétiennes, 239 (Paris, Éditions du Cerf, 1977).

Archon, Jean-Louis, *Histoire ecclésiastique de la Chapelle des Rois de France* (2 vols., Paris, Pierre-Augustine Le Mercier, 1711).

Aubigné, Agrippa d', *Œuvres complètes*, ed. Eugène Réaume and François de Caussade (6 vols., Paris, Alphonse Lemerre, 1874).

Bartas, Guillaume du, *La Seconde sepmaine* (Rouen, Raphaël du Petit Val, 1616), trans. as *Du Bartas His Devine Weekes and Works Translated: And Dedicated to the King's Most Excellent Majestie by Iosuah Sylvester* (London, Humphrey Lounes, 1611).

Batterel, Louis, *Mémoires domestiques pour servir à l'histoire de l'Oratoire*, ed. Paul Ingold and E. Bonnardet (4 vols., Paris, Picard, 1902–4).

Bauldry, Michel, *Manuale sacrarum caeremoniarum iuxta ritum S. Romanae ecclesiae* (Paris, Ioannem Billaine, 1646).

Beaune, Renaud de, *Les CL Pseaumes de David, Latins et François* (Paris, Gilles Robinot, 1587).

Les CL pseaumes de David, Latins et François, traduits par feu Mr Renaud de Beaune (Paris, Gilles Robinot, 1612).
Belleau, Rémy, *Œuvres complètes de Rémy Belleau*, ed. Aristide Gouverneur (Paris, Gouvernour, 1867).
Bergier, Nicolas, *La Musique speculative*, F-Pn MS fonds fr. 1359: trans. and ed. Ekkehard Jost, *La Musique spéculative* (Köln, Arno Volk, 1970).
Bernard, Charles, *Histoire du Roy Louis XIII* (Paris, Nicolas de Sercy, 1646).
Bernard of Clairvaux, *Divi Bernardi operum . . .* (6 vols., Paris, Typographia Regia, 1642).
Bérulle, Pierre de, *Œuvres complètes de Bérulle, Cardinal de l'Église Romaine*, ed. Abbé Migne (Paris, Migne, 1856).
Bignon, Jean, *La Grandeur de nos Roys et de leur souveraine puissance. Au Roy* (Paris, n.p., 1615).
Blémur, Marie Bouette de, *L'Année bénédictine ou les Vies des saints de l'ordre de saint Benoist pour tous les jours de l'année* (Paris, Louis Billaine, 1667–72).
Bodin, Jean, *Les Six livres de la République* (Paris, Jacques du Puy, 1576).
Boitel, Pierre, *Histoire générale de tout ce qui s'est passé de plus remarquable tant en France qu'aux Païs estrangers les années 1618, 1619, 1620, ensemble un relation historique des Pompes & magnifiques cérémonies observées a la réception de Chevaliers de l'Ordre du S. Esprit, faits par LOUYS XIII du nom, surnommé IUSTE, Roy de France & Navarre* (Paris, Pierre Billaine, 1620).
Boucher, Jean, *La Couronne mystique ou Desein de Chevallerie Chrestienne pour exciter les Princes Chrestiens a rendre le debvoir a la piété Chrestienne contre les enemies d'icelle* (Tournai, Adrien Quinqué, 1623).
Boucher, Nicolas, *La Conjunction des lettres et des armes* (Reims, Jean de Foigny, 1579).
Bourgoin, Pierre, *Éloges funèbres de Louys le Iuste sur le parallèle de David vivant et David mourant* (Metz, Jean Antoine, 1643).
Bourgoing, François, *Brevis psalmodiae ratio ad usum presbytorium congregationis oratorii Domini nostril Jesu Christi instituta* (Paris, Pierre Ballard, 1634).
 Les Véritez et excellences de Jésus-Christ Notre-Seigneur (Paris, Sebastien Huré, 1635).
 Le David François ou traité de la sainct Psalmodie (Paris, Sebastien Huré, 1641).
Breul, Jacques du, *Le Théâtre des antiquitez de Paris* (Paris, Pierre Chevalier, 1612).
Budé, Loys, *Les Pseaumes de David traduicts selon la vérité Hébraïque* (Geneva, Jehan Crespin, 1551).
Caussin, Nicolas, *La Cour sainte* (Paris, Sebastien Chappelet, 1624).
Chaissy, Gilles, *Glaive de David et de Louis XIII roy de France et de Navarre* (Avignon, Jean Bramereau, 1623).
Comte, Pierre Le, *Les Vœus des bons François sur les victoires de nostre Roy Très-Chrestien & Très-Auguste Louis XIII* (Paris, Pierre Ramier, 1621).
Coste, Hilarion de, *Les Éloges et vies de reynes, princesses, dames et damoiselles illustres . . .* (Paris, Sebastien Cramoisy, 1630).

Descartes, René, *Compendium musicae*, manuscript 1618; first published as *Musicae compendium* (Utrecht, Zyll & Ackersdyck, 1650); trans. Nicolas Poisson as *Abrégé de musique* (Paris, Charles Angot, 1668); trans. Humphrey Moseley as *Excellent Compendium of Music with Necessary and Judicious Animadversions Thereupon* (London, Thomas Harper and Humphrey Moseley, 1653).

Desportes, Philippe, *Soixante Pseaumes de David, mis en vers François* (Rouen, Raphaël du Petit Val, 1591).

Cent pseaumes de David mis en vers françois (Rouen, Raphaël du Petit Val, 1600).

Doublet, Jacques, *Histoire chronologique pour la vérité de S. Denys Aréopagite, Apostre de France et premier évesque de Paris* (Paris, Pierre de Bresche, 1646).

Du Peyrat, Guillaume, *L'Histoire ecclésiastique de la cour ou les antiquitez et recherches de la chapelle, et oratoire du Roy de France* (Paris, Henry Sara, 1645).

Dupuyherbault, Gabriel, *Psaumes de David, traduicts au plus près de leur sens propre & naturel* (Paris, Jehan de Roigny, 1555).

Duranti, Jean-Étienne, *De ritibus ecclesiae catholicae libri tres* (Lyon, Petri Landry, 1606).

Eveillon, Jacques, *De processionibus ecclesiasticis liber* (Paris, Matthaeum Guillemot, 1641).

L'Estoile, Pierre de, *Mémoires-journaux de Pierre de L'Estoile* (10 vols., Paris, Alphonse Lemerre, 1875–96).

Favin, André, *Le Théâtre d'honneur et de chevalerie, ou L'Histoire des ordres militaires des Roys* (Paris, Robert Foüet, 1620); trans. as *The Theater of Honour and Knighthood* (London, William Laggard, 1623).

Félibien, Michel, *Histoire de la ville de Paris* (Paris, Guillaume Desprez, 1722).

Histoire de l'abbaye royale de Saint-Denis en France (Paris, Frédéric Léonard, 1706).

Fleury, Abbé Claude, *Histoire ecclésiastique par Monsieur l'Abbé Fleury*; continued as Jean-Claude Fabre, *Histoire ecclésiastique pour servir de continuation à celle de Monsieur l'Abbé Fleury* (36 vols., Paris, Pierre-Jean Mariette, etc., 1691–1738).

Gantez, Annibal, *L'Entretien des musiciens* (Auxerre, Jacques Bouquet, 1643), ed. Ernest Thoinan (Paris, A. Claudin, 1878).

Garnier, Claude, *Le Te Deum, contre les Athéistes Libertins* (Paris, Daniel Guillemot, 1623).

Génébrard, Gilbert, *Les Pseaumes de David traduits en François avec une explication tirée des Saints Pères, & des Auteurs Ecclésiastiques* (Paris, Guillaume Desprez, 1640).

Traicté de la liturgie, ou S. messe selon l'usage et forme des apostre et de leur disciple sainct Denys, apostre des François (Lyon, Jean Pillehotte, 1594).

Giorgio, Francesco, *De harmonia mundi totius cantica tria* (Paris, André Berthelin, 1545); trans. Guy Le Fèvre de la Boderie, *L'Harmonie du monde divisée en trois cantiques* (Paris, Jean Macé, 1579).

Godefroy, Théodore, *Le Cérémonial de France* (Paris, Abraham Pacard, 1619); Théodore and Denys Godefroy, *Le Cérémonial français* (2 vols, Paris, Sebastien Cramoisy, 1649).

Grancolas, Jean, *Commentaire historique sur le Bréviaire Romain* (Paris, Philippe-Nicolas Lottin, 1727).

Gras, Simon le, *Procès verbal du sacre du Roy Louis quatorze du nom* (Soissons, Nicolas Hanisset, 1694).

Guidetti, Giovanni, *Directorium chori* (Rome, Robert Granjon, 1582).

Guyet, Charles, *Heortologia, sive de festis propriis locorum & ecclesiarum* ... (Paris, Sebastien and Gabriel Cramoisy, 1657).

Habert, Isaac, *Votum regium Davidici carminis paraphrase conceptum* (Paris, Petrum Blasum, 1637).

Pietas Regia Ludovici iusti, pii, triumphantis (Paris, Ioannem Libert, 1623).

Héroard, Jean, *Journal de Jean Héroard*, ed. Eudore Soulié and Édouard de Barthélemy (2 vols., Paris, Firmin Dido frères, 1868).

Hilaire de Poitiers, *Tractatus super Psalmos*, trans. Patrick Descourtieux as *Commentaires sur les Psaumes*, Sources Chrétiennes, 515 (Paris, Éditions du Cerf, 2008).

Hozier, Pierre d', *Les Noms surnoms qualitez, armes et blazons de l'ordre du Sainct Esprit* ... (Paris, Melchior Tavernier, 1634).

Hurault, Jaques, *Trois livres des offices d'estat avec un sommaire des stratagems* (Lyon, François le Febvre, 1596).

Huygens, Constantin, *Correspondance et œuvres musicales de Constantin Huygens*, ed. Willem Jonckbloet and Jan Pieter Land (Leiden, Société pour l'Histoire Musicale des Pays-Bas, 1882).

Jay, François Le, *De la Dignité des rois, et princes souverains du droict inviolable de leurs successeurs légitime: et du devoir des peuples, et subiectz envers eux* (Tours, Mathurin le Mercier, 1589).

Joinville, Jean de, *Histoire de S. Loys IX du nom, Roy de France ... avec diverses pièces du mesme temps non encore imprimées, & quelques observations historiques par Me Claude Menard, Conseiller du Roy, & Lieutenant en la Prévosté d'Angers* (Paris, Sebastien Cramoisy, 1617).

Jumilhac, Pierre-Benoît de, *La Science et la pratique du plain-chant* (Paris, Louis Billaine, 1673).

Kempis, Thomas à, *De imitatione Christi* (Paris, Typographia Regia, 1640), trans. Michel de Marillac as *IV livres, de l'imitation de Jésus-Christ* ... (Paris, Nicolas Gasse, 1626).

Labbé, Philippe, and Gabriel Cossartii, *Sacrosancta Concilia ad regiam editionem* (Venice, Sebastianum Coleti, 1733).

Lebeuf, Abbé, *Traité historique et pratique sur le chant ecclésiastique* (Paris, Jean-Baptiste Hérissant, 1741).

Lingendes, Jean de, *Oraison funèbre du roy Louis XIII. Surnommé Le Juste, prononcé en l'Église de S. Denis l xxij^e jour de Juin 1643* (Paris, Charles Savreux, 1643).

Loret, Jean, *La Muze historique (1650–65)* (Paris, Charles Chenault, 1655–65), ed. J. Ravenel and Ed. de la Pelouze (4 vols., Paris, P. Jannet, 1857–78).

Malingre, Claude, *Les Antiquités de la ville de Paris* (Paris, Pierre Rocolet, 1640).

Marot, Clément, *Cinquante-deux pseaumes de David, traduictz en rithme Françoyse selon la vérité Hébraïque* (Paris, Estienne Croulleau, 1556).

Marot, Clément, and Théodore de Bèze, *Les Pseaumes mis en rime Françoise* (Lyon, Antoine Cercia, 1562).

Matthieu, Pierre, *La Merveille royale de Louis XIII* (Paris, Joseph Guerreau, 1617).
  Histoire de saint Louys, roi de France, IX du nom, XLIIII du nombre (Paris, Bertrand Martin, 1618).

Mersenne, Marin, *Quaestiones celeberrimae in Genesim* (Paris, Sebastien Cramoisy, 1623).
  Questions harmoniques (Paris, Jacques Villery, 1634).
  Harmonie Universelle contenant la théorie et la pratique de la musique (Paris, Sebastien Cramoisy, 1636).
  Correspondance du P. Marin Mersenne, Paul Tannery and Cornélis de Waard (eds.) (18 vols., Paris, CNRS, 1932–88).

Molinier, Étienne, *Panégyrique du Roy-Sainct Louys, sur le subject de la célébration de sa feste* (Paris, René Giffart, 1618).

Morel, Frédéric, *Les Œuvres de Philon Juif, autheur très-eloquent, & philosophe très-grave* (Paris, Charles Chappellain, 1612).

Muis, Simon de, *Votum pro Rege Rupellam oppugnate* (Paris?, 1628?).

Olivétan, Pierre-Robert, *La Bible, qui est toute la Saincte Escripture* (Geneva, Robert Estienne, 1553).

Orléans, Jonas d', *De institutione regia*, trans. Alain Dubreucq as *Le Métier du roi*, Sources Chrétiennes, 407 (Paris, Éditions du Cerf, 1995).

Oroux, Abbé, *Histoire ecclésiastique de la Cour de France* (2 vols., Paris, Imprimerie Royale, 1776–7).

Pasquier, Estienne, *Les Recherches de la France* (Paris, Laurens Sonnius, 1621).

Perrin, Pierre, *Cantica pro Capella Regis* (Paris, Christophe Ballard, 1665).

Perron, Jacques Davy Du, *Les Diverses œuvres de l'illustrissime Cardinal du Perron* (Paris, Antoine Estienne, 1622).

Peyronnet, Arnaud, *Manuel du Bréviaire Romain* (Toulouse, Jean Boude, 1667).

Raemond, Florimand de, *L'Histoire de la naissance, progrez et décadence de l'hérésie de ce siècle* (Paris, Veuve de Guillaume de la Nouë, 1610).

Rivault, David du, *Les États, esquels il est discouru du prince, du noble et du tiers-état, conformément à nostre temps* (Lyon, 1596).

Ronsard, Pierre de, *Discours des misères de ce temps*, in M. Prosper Blanchemin (ed.), *Œuvres complètes de P. de Ronsard*, Vol. 7 (Paris, A. Franck, 1866).
Sailly, Toussaint, *Varia poemata* (Paris, Dionysii à Prato, 1589).
Saint Martin, Simplician, *Histoire de la vie du glorieux père S. Augustin religieux, docteur de l'église* (Toulouse, Adrien Colomiez, 1641).
Sauval, Henri, *Histoire et recherches des antiquités de la ville de Paris* (3 vols., Paris, Charles Moette and Jacques Chardon, 1724).
Savaron, Jean, *Second Traicté de la souveraineté du Roy. Au Roy Très-Chrestien Louis XIII* (Paris, Pierre Chevalier, 1615).
Simon, Richard, *Lettres choisies de M. Simon*, ed. Bruzen la Martinière (Amsterdam, Pierre Mortier, 1730).
Sonnet, Martin, *Directorium chori* (Paris, Sebastien Cramoisy, 1656).
Thiers, Jean-Baptiste, *Traité de l'exposition du St. Sacrement de l'autel* (Paris, Jean Du Puis, 1673).
Thou, Jacques-Auguste de *Histoire universelle, depuis 1543 jusqu'en 1607* (16 vols., London, 1734).
Thou, Nicolas de, *Bref recueil et explication de la messe et du divin service y faict* (Paris, Jacobum Kerver, 1598).
Norma pie vivendi (Paris, Jacobum Kerver, 1575).
Tyard, Pontus de, *Solitaire second, ou prose de la musique* (Lyon, Jean de Tournes, 1555).
Véron, François, *Description prophétique du Roy David de la prise de La Rochelle* (Paris, Jean Mestais, 1629).
Plainte et accusation troisiesme contre tous les ministres (Paris, Claude Morlot, 1633).
Vigenère, Blaise de, *Le Psaultier de David torné en prose mesurée ou vers libres* (Paris, Abel l'Angelier, 1588).
Villette, Claude, *Les Raisons de l'Office, et Cérémonies qui se font en l'Église Catholique* (Paris, Guillaume des Rues, 1611).

Printed Sources (after 1800)

Abbate, Carolyn, *Unsung Voices: Opera and Musical Narrative in the Nineteenth Century* (Princeton, NJ, Princeton University Press, 1996).
Alexis-Colin, Marie, 'Eustache Du Caurroy. Un compositeur français aux confins du xvie et du xviie siècle', *Acta Musicologica*, 73/2 (2001), 189–258.
Allen, John William, *A History of Political Thought in the Sixteenth Century* (London, Methuen, 1960).
Anjubault, Prosper-Auguste, *La Sainte Cécile au Mans depuis 1633* (Le Mans, Monnoyer frères, 1862).
Anthony, James, *French Baroque Music from Beaujoyeulx to Rameau* (Portland, OR, Amadeus Press, 1997).

Apostolides, Jean-Marie, *Le Roi-machine: spectacle et politique au temps de Louis XIV* (Paris, Éditions de Minuit, 1981).

Argenson, Marc René de Voyer d', *Annales de la Compagnie du St-Sacrement* (Marseille, Typographie Saint-Léon, 1900).

Ariew, Roger, *Descartes and the First Cartesians* (Oxford, Oxford University Press, 2014).

Asch, Ronald, *Sacral Kingship between Disenchantment and Re-enchantment: The French and English Monarchies 1587–1688* (New York, NY and Oxford, Berghahn, 2014).

Aubinau, Louis, 'Fragments des mémoires de Dubois', *Bibliotheque de l'École des Chartes*, 9 (1848), 1–45.

Auge-Chiquet, Mathieu, *La Vie, les idées et l'œuvre de Jean-Antoine de Baïf* (Paris, Hachette, 1909, repr. Geneva, Slatkine, 1969).

Auld, Louis, *The Lyric Art of Pierre Perrin, Founder of French Opera* (3 vols., Henryville, PA, Institute of Medieval Music, 1986).

Bak, János (ed.), *Coronations: Medieval and Early Modern Monarchic Ritual* (Berkeley, Los Angeles, CA and Oxford, University of California Press, 1990).

Barbieri, Patrizio, 'Chiavette and modal transposition in Italian practice (c. 1500–1837)', *Recercare*, 3 (1991), 5-79.

Bardon, Françoise, *Le Portrait mythologique à la cour de France sous Henri IV et Louis XIII. Mythologie et politique* (Paris, Éditions A. et J. Picard, 1974).

Baumgartner, Frederic, *Radical Reactionaries: The Political Thought of the French Catholic League* (Geneva, Droz, 1976).

Beaune, Colette, *The Birth of an Ideology: Myths and Symbols of Nation in Late-Medieval France* (Berkeley, CA, University of California Press, 1991).

Beetham, David, *The Legitimation of Power* (Basingstoke, Palgrave Macmillan, 2013).

Belin, Christian, 'Comment se tenir sur un fleuve? Paraphrase et exégèse du Super flumina Babylonis au xviie siècle', in Véronique Ferrer and Anne Mantero (eds.), *Les Paraphrases bibliques au xvie et xviie siècles* (Geneva, Droz, 2006), pp. 343–57.

Bennett, Peter, *Sacred Repertories in Paris, 1630–43: Bibliothèque nationale de France V^{ma} rés. 571* (2 vols., DPhil dissertation, Oxford University, 2004).

'Antoine Boësset's sacred music for the Royal Abbey of Montmartre: Newly identified polyphony and *plain-chant musical* from the "Deslauriers" manuscript (F-Pn V^{ma} rés. 571)', *Revue de Musicologie*, 91/2 (2005), 321–67.

Sacred Repertories in Paris under Louis XIII: Bibliothèque nationale de France MS V^{ma} rés. 571, Royal Musical Association Monographs, 17 (Farnham, Ashgate, 2009).

'Collaborations between the *musique de la chambre* and the *musique de la chapelle* at the court of Louis XIII: Nicolas Formé's *Missa Aeternae Henrici*

Magni (1638) and the origins of the *grand motet*', *Early Music*, 38/3 (2010), 369–86.

'Chant reform at the Royal Benedictine Abbey of Montmartre, 1607–46: The evidence of Antoine Boësset', in William Renwick (ed.) *Chant Old and New* (Ottawa, Institute of Medieval Music, 2012), pp. 189–213.

'The *Entrée royale* and the *Exaudiat te Dominus* in early seventeenth-century France: Evidence from Chicago, Newberry Library, Case MS 5123', in Bernard Dompnier, Catherine Massip, and Solveg Serre (eds.), *Musique en liberté. Entre la cour et les provinces au temps des Bourbons* (Paris, École des Chartes, 2018), pp. 113–26.

Bergin, Joseph, *The Politics of Religion in Early Modern France* (New Haven, CT and London, Yale University Press, 2014).

Bertelli, Sergio, *The King's Body: Sacred Rituals of Power in Medieval and Early Modern Europe*, trans. R. Burr Litchfield (University Park, PA, Pennsylvania State University Press, 2001).

'*Rex et sacerdos*: The holiness of the king in European civilization', in Allan Ellenius (ed.), *Iconography, Propaganda, and Legitimation* (Oxford, Clarendon, 1998), pp. 123–46.

Berti, Michela, 'La Musique pour les *Messe di Francia* à Rome au regard des dispositions pontificales', in Sophie Hache and Thierry Favier (eds.), *Réalités et fictions de la musique religieuse à l'époque moderne. Essais d'analyse des discours* (Rennes, Presses universitaires de Rennes, 2018), pp. 253–72

Berton-Blivet, Nathalie, ed. *Catalogue du motet imprimé en France (1647–1789)* (Paris, Société française de musicologie, 2011).

Bisaro, Xavier, *Guide historique et pratique du plain-chant et du faux-bourdon. France xviie–xviiie siècles* (Versailles, Collection numérique du CMBV, 2017).

Blanchard, Joël, 'Le Spectacle du rite: les entrées royales', *Revue historique*, 305/3 (2003), 475–519.

Bloch, Marc, trans. J. E. Anderson, *The Royal Touch: Sacred Monarchy and Scrofula in England and France* (London, Routledge and Kegan Paul, 1973).

Boilet, Elise, Sonia Cavicchioli, and Paul-Alexis Mellet (eds.), *Les Figures de David à la Renaissance* (Geneva, Droz, 2015).

Bonime, Stephen, 'Music for the royal *entrée* into Paris, 1483–1517', in Mary-Beth Winn (ed.), *Le Moyen français V. Musique naturelle et musique artificielle: In memoriam Gustave Reese* (Montreal, Gros, 1980), pp. 115–29.

Borders, James, 'Rhythmic performance of *accentus* in early sixteenth-century Rome', in Marco Gozzi and Francesco Luisi (eds.), *Il canto fratto: L'altro gregoriano* (Rome, Torre d'Orfeo, 2005), pp. 385–405.

Boucher, Jacqueline, *Société et mentalités autour de Henri III* (Paris, Garnier, 2007).

Bourdieu, Pierre, 'Les Rites comme actes d'institution', *Actes de la recherche en sciences sociales*, 43 (1982), 58–63.

Boureau, Alain, 'Les Enseignements absolutistes de Saint Louis, 1610–30', in Chantal Grell and François Laplanche (eds.) *La Monarchie absolutiste et l'histoire en France* (Paris, Presses de l'Université de Paris-Sorbonne, 1987), pp. 79–97.
  'Les Cérémonies royales françaises entre performance juridique et compétence liturgique', *Annales: Économies, Sociétés, Civilisations*, 46/6 (1991), 1253–64.
  'Ritualité politique et modernité monarchique', in Neithard Bulst, Robert Descimon, and Alain Guerreau (eds.), *L'État ou le Roi. Les Fondations de la modernité monarchique en France (XIV–XVIe siecles)*(Paris, Éditions de la Maison des sciences de l'homme, 1996), pp. 9–25.
Boureau, Alain, and Claudio-Sergio Ingerflom (eds.), *La Royauté sacrée dans le monde chrétien* (Paris, EHESS, 1992).
Brémond, Henri, *Histoire littéraire du sentiment religieux en France depuis la fin des guerres de religion jusqu'à nos jours* (6 vols., Paris, Bloud et Gay, 1916).
Brenet, Michel, *Les Musiciens de la Sainte-Chapelle du Palais* (Paris, Picard, 1910).
Brennan, Brian, 'Augustines "De musica"', *Vigiliae Christianae*, 42/3 (1988), 267–81.
Brobeck, John, *The Motet at the Court of Francis I* (PhD dissertation, University of Pennsylvania, 1991).
  'Some "liturgical" motets for the French royal court: A reconsideration of genre in the sixteenth-century motet', *Musica Disciplina*, 47 (1993), 123–57.
Brooks, Jeanice, 'Italy, the ancient world and the French musical inheritance in the sixteenth century: Arcadelt and Cléreau in the service of the Guises', *Journal of the Royal Musical Association*, 121/2 (1996), 147–90.
  Courtly Song in Late Sixteenth-Century France (Chicago, IL, University of Chicago Press, 2000).
  '"O quelle armonye": Dialogue singing in late Renaissance France', *Early Music History*, 22 (2003), 1–65.
Bruzelius, Caroline, *The 13th-Century Church at St.-Denis* (New Haven, CT and London, Yale University Press, 1985).
Bryant, Lawrence, *The King and the City in the Parisian Royal Entry Ceremony: Politics, Ritual and Art in the Renaissance* (Geneva, Droz, 1986).
Burke, John, 'Sacred music at Notre-Dame-des-Victoires under Mazarin and Louis XIV', *Recherches sur la musique française classique*, 20 (1981), 19–44.
Burke, Peter, *The Fabrication of Louis XIV* (New Haven, CT and London, Yale University Press, 1992).
Canguilhem, Philippe, 'Pratique et context du faux-bourdon et du chant sur le livre en France (XVIe–XIXe siècles)', *Études grégoriennes*, 38 (2011), 181–99.
Canova-Green, Marie-Claude, 'Warrior king or king of war? Louis XIII's Entries into his *bonnes villes* (1620–1629)', in J. R. Mulryne, Maria Ines Aliverti, and Anna Maria Testaverde (eds.), *Ceremonial Entries in Early Modern Europe. The Iconography of Power* (Farnham, Ashgate, 2015), pp. 77–98.

'De Dieu et du roi dans l'entrée solennelle de Louis XIII', in Peter Bennett and Bernard Dompnier (eds.), *Cérémonial politique et cérémonial religieux dans l'Europe modern: échanges et métissages* (Paris, Garnier, 2020), pp. 87–104.

Canova-Green, Marie-Claude, Jean Andrews, and Marie-France Wagner (eds.), *Writing Royal Entries in Early Modern Europe* (Turnhout, Brepols, 2013).

Carver, Anthony, *Cori spezzati* (2 vols., Cambridge, Cambridge University Press, 1988).

Chamard, Henri, *Histoire de la Pléiade* (2 vols., Paris, Didier, 1939–40).

Chambois, Em.-Louis, 'La Fête de Sainte Cécile à la cathédrale du Mans, 1633–1784', *L'Union historique et littéraire du Maine*, 2/1(1894), 343–52.

Chartier, Roger, 'A desacralized king', in *The Cultural Origins of the French Revolution*, trans. Lydia Cochrane (Durham, NC, Duke University Press, 1991), pp. 111–35.

Chevalier, Ulysse, *Repertorium hymnologicum* (Louvain, Polleunis & Ceuterick, 1894).

Chrościcki, Juliusz, 'Ceremonial space', in Allan Ellenius (ed.), *Iconography, Propaganda, and Legitimation* (Oxford, Clarendon, 1998), pp. 193–216.

Church, William, *Constitutional Thought in Sixteenth-Century France* (New York, NY, Octagon, 1941).

Ciliberti, Galliano, 'Musica e liturgia a San Luigi dei Francesi nell'Anno Santo del 1650: nuove evidenze', in Giancarlo Rostirolla and Elena Zomparelli (eds.), *Tra musica e storia. Saggi di varia umanità in ricordo di Saverio Franchi* (Rome, Isituto di Bibliografia Musicale, 2017), pp. 277–94.

'*Qu'une plus belle nüit ne pouvoit précéder le beau jour*': *Musica e cerimonie nelle istituzioni religiose francesi a Roma nel Seicento* (Perugia, Aguaplano, 2016).

Cordonnier, C., *Le Culte du Saint-Sacrement* (Paris, Lethielleux, 1923).

Corianesco, Alexandre, 'Une nouvelle version des psaumes de Baïf', in *Mélanges d'histoire littéraire et de bibliographie offerts à Jean Bonnerot* (Paris, Nizet, 1954), pp. 93–6.

Cornette, Joël, *Henri IV à Saint-Denis: de l'abjuration à la profanation* (Paris, Belin, 2010).

Cosandey, Fanny, 'Entrer dans le rang', in Marie-France Wagner, Louise Frappier, and Claire Latraverse (eds.), *Les Jeux de l'échange: entrées solennelles et divertissements du xve au xviie siècle* (Paris, Honoré Champion, 2007), pp. 17–46.

Cosandey, Fanny and Robert Descimon, *L'Absolutisme en France: histoire et historiographie* (Paris, Seuil, 2002).

Crawford, Katherine, *Perilous Performances: Gender and Regency in Early Modern France* (Cambridge, MA, and London, Harvard University Press, 2004).

Crosby, Sumner McKnight, *The Abbey of Saint-Denis, 475–1122* (New Haven, CT, Yale University Press, 1942).

Crouzet, Denis, *Les Guerriers de Dieu* (2 vols., Paris, Champ Vallon, 1990).

Cummings, Anthony, 'Toward an interpretation of the sixteenth-century motet', *Journal of the American Musicological Society*, 34/1 (1981), 43–59.
Czerniawska, Fiona, *A Study of the Printed Accounts of French entrées, 1610–60* (PhD dissertation, University of London, 1993).
Davy-Rigaux, Cécile, 'Le Clerc et Jumilhac et la question de la "durée ou mesure des sons" dans le plain-chant', *Études Grégoriennes*, 31 (2003), 105–31.
  Guillaume-Gabriel Nivers: un art de chant grégorien sous le règne de Louis XIV (Paris, CNRS, 2004).
Davy-Rigaux, Cécile, Bernard Dompnier, and Daniel-Odon Hurel (eds.), *Les Cérémoniaux catholiques en France à l'époque moderne – une littérature de codification des rites liturgiques* (Turnhout, Brepols, 2009).
Dear, Peter, *Mersenne and the Learning of the Schools* (Ithaca, NY and London, Cornell University Press, 1988).
Decobert, Laurence, 'Henry Du Mont et le grand motet', in Jean Lionnet (ed.), *Le Concert des muses. Promenade musicale dans le baroque français* (Versailles, Éditions du CMBV, Klincksieck, 1997), pp. 127–52.
Delumeau, Jean, *Une Histoire du paradis; Le Jardin des délices* (Paris, Fayard, 1992)
De Marco, Rosa, 'Fleurs d'orange et encens pour la gloire du Roi dans les entrées royales en France', in Peter Bennett and Bernard Dompnier (eds.), *Cérémonial politique et cérémonial religieux dans l'Europe modern: échanges et métissages* (Paris, Garnier, 2020), pp. 181–200.
Descimon, Robert, 'Le Corps de ville et le système cérémonial parisien au début de l'âge modern', in Marc Boone and Maarten Prak (eds.), *Individual, Corporate and Judicial Status in European Cities (Late Middle Ages and Early Modern Period)* (Leuven, Apeldorn, Garant, 1996), pp. 73–128.
Desmet, Marc, 'Introduction: Quelle musique pour les psaumes en vers français?', in Marc Desmet (ed.), *La Monodie du psautier en vers français au xviie siècle* (Lyon, Symétrie, 2015), pp. 1–12.
  'Les Psaumes en vers français de Philippe Desportes, mis en musique par Denis Caignet (1624)', in Marc Desmet (ed.), *La Monodie du psautier en vers français au xviie siècle* (Lyon, Symétrie, 2015), pp. 13–43.
Desplat, Christian, and Paul Mironneau (eds.), *Les Entrées. Gloire et déclin d'un ceremonial: Actes du colloque, château de Pau, 10–11 May 1996* (Biarritz, Société Henri IV, 1997).
Dickerman, Edmund, and Anita Walker, 'The Choice of Hercules: Henry IV as Hero', *The Historical Journal*, 39/2 (1996), 315–37.
Diefendorf, Barbara, 'Henri IV, the Dévots and the making of a French Catholic Reformation', in Alison Forrestal, and Eric Nelson (eds.), *Politics and Religion in Early Bourbon France* (Basingstoke, Palgrave Macmillan, 2009), pp. 157–79.
  From Penitence to Charity: Pious Women and the Catholic Reformation in Paris (Oxford and New York, NY, Oxford University Press, 2004).
Dompnier, Bernard, 'La Saint-Louis sous le règne de Louis XIII. Fête liturgique, fête nationale?', in Peter Bennett and Bernard Dompnier (eds.), *Cérémonial*

politique et cérémonial religieux dans l'Europe modern: échanges et métissages (Paris, Garnier, 2020), pp. 39–66.

Dompnier, Bernard, (ed.), *Les Cérémonies extraordinaires du catholicisme baroque* (Clermont-Ferrand, Presses universitaires Blaise-Pascal, 2009).

Dray, J.P., *Neoplatonism and French Religious Thought in the Seventeenth Century* (DPhil dissertation, Oxford University, 1987).

Dufourcq, Norbert, *La Musique française* (Paris, Picard, 1970).

Dumolin, Maurice, 'Notes sur l'abbaye de Montmartre', *Bulletin de la société de l'histoire de Paris et de l'Ile de France*, 58 (1931), 145–238.

Duncan, David Allen, 'Persuading the affections: Rhetorical theory and Mersenne's advice to harmonic orators', in Georgia Cowart (ed.), *French Musical Thought, 1600–1800* (Ann Arbor, MI, UMI Research Press, 1989), pp. 149–75.

Duron, Jean, 'Les "Paroles de musique" sous le règne de Louis XIV', in Jean Duron (ed.), *Plainchant et liturgie en France au XVIIe siècle* (Versailles, Fondation Royaumont, Éditions du CMBV, Klincksieck, 1997), pp. 125–84.

Duron, Jean, (ed.), *La Naissance du style français 1650–1673* (Paris, Éditions du CMBV, Mardaga, 2008).

'"Ces Mrs ne sont pas trop chargés de Latin": la langue d'église dans les Nouvelles forms musicales du xviie siècle', in Cécile Davy-Rigaux (ed.), *La Musique d'Église et se cadres de création dans la France d'Ancien Régime* (Florence, Olschki, 2014), pp. 175–93.

Durosoir, Georgie, *L'Air de Cour en France, 1571–1665* (Liège, Mardaga, 1991).

Dusevel, H., 'Le Vœu de Louis XIII' in *Bibliothèque historique monumentale, ecclésiastique et littéraire de l'Artois et de la Picardie* (Amiens, Duval and Herment, 1844) pp. 215–17.

Elias, Norbert, *The Court Society*, trans. Edmund Jephcott (New York, NY, Pantheon, 1983); first published as *Die höfische Gesellschaft* (Darmstadt, Hermann Luchterhand, 1969).

Favier, Thierry, 'The French *Grand Motet* and the king's glory: A reconsideration of the issue', in Reinhard Strohm, Ryszard Wieczorek, Robert Kendrick, Helen Geyer, and Zofia Fabianska (eds.), *Early Music Context and Ideas,* II (Krakow, Institute of Musicology, Jagiellonian University, 2008), pp. 188–97.

'Genèses du grand motet', in Jean Duron (ed.), *La Naissance du style français 1650–73* (Paris, Éditions du CMBV, Mardaga, 2008), pp. 89–113.

Le Motet à grand chœur (1660–1792): Gloria in Gallia Deo (Paris, Fayard, 2009).

'Musique religieuse et absolutisme sous le règne de Louis XIV: essai de bilan critique', in Peter Bennett and Bernard Dompnier (eds.), *Cérémonial politique et cérémonial religieux dans l'Europe modern: échanges et métissages* (Paris, Garnier, 2020), pp. 19–38.

Fellerer, Karl, 'Church music and the Council of Trent', *The Musical Quarterly*, 39 (1953), 576–94.

Fenlon, Iain, *The Ceremonial City: History, Memory and Myth in Renaissance Venice* (New Haven, CT and London, Yale University Press, 2007).

'Competition and emulation: Music and dance for the celebrations in Paris, 1612–1615', in Margaret McGowan (ed.), *Dynastic Marriages 1612/1615: A Celebration of Habsburg and Bourbon Unions* (Farnham, Ashgate, 2013), pp. 153–70.

'Sacred legitimation and metaphors of rule: Courtly entries in sixteenth-century Italy', in Peter Bennett and Bernard Dompnier (eds.), *Cérémonial politique et cérémonial religieux dans l'Europe modern: échanges et métissages* (Paris, Garnier, 2020), pp. 285–305.

Filippi, Daniele, and Michael Noone (eds.), *Listening to Early Modern Catholicism* (Leiden, Brill, 2017).

Fisher, Alexander, *Music, Piety, and Propaganda: The Soundscapes of Counter-Reformation Bavaria* (Oxford, Oxford University Press, 2015).

Fogel, Michèle, *Les Cérémonies de l'information dans la France du XVIe au XVIIIe siècle* (Paris, Fayard, 1989).

Folz, Robert, 'La Sainteté de Saint Louis d'après les textes liturgiques', *Revue d'histoire de l'Église de France*, 57 (1971), 31–45.

Foucault, Michel, *Les Mots et les choses: une archéologie des sciences humaines* (Paris, Gallimard, 1966), trans. as *The Order of Things: An Archeology of the Human Sciences* (New York, NY, Pantheon, 1971).

Franko, Mark, 'Jouer avec le feu: la subjectivité du roi dans La Délivrance de Renaud', in Giovanni Careri (ed.), *Jérusalem délivrée du Tasse. Poésie, musique ballet* (Paris, Klincksieck, 1999), pp. 159–77.

Fremy, Édouard, *Henri III pénitent: étude sur les rapports de ce prince avec diverses confrères et communautés Parisiennes* (Paris, Féchoz, 1885).

Fulton, Rachel, '"Quae est ista quae ascendit sicut aurora consurgens?" The Song of Songs as the Historia for the Office of the Assumption', *Mediaeval Studies*, 60 (1998), 55–122.

Gabriel, Frédéric, 'Chanter Dieu à la Cour: théologie politique et liturgie', in Jean Duron (ed.), *Regards sur la musique au temps de Louis XIII* (Wavre, Mardaga, 2007).

Gady, Alexander, *Jacques Lemercier: Architecte et ingénieur du Roi* (Paris, Éditions de la Maison des sciences de l'homme, 2005).

Gall, Jean-Marie le, 'Saint-Denis, les Guises et Paris sous la Ligue, 1588–90', *French Historical Studies*, 24/2 (2001), 157–84.

Le Mythe de Saint Denis: entre Renaissance et Révolution (Seyssel, Champ Vallon, 2007).

'The Lives of the Saints in the French Renaissance c. 1500–c. 1650', in Katherine Van Liere, Simon Ditchfield, and Howard Latham (eds.), *Sacred History: Uses of the Christian Past in the Renaissance World* (Oxford, Oxford University Press, 2012), pp. 209–29.

Gaposchkin, M. Cecilia, *The Making of Saint Louis: Kingship, Sanctity, and Crusade in the Later Middle Ages* (Ithaca, NY and London, Cornell University Press, 2008).

Gastoué, Amédée, *Le Graduel et l'Antiphonaire Romains* (Lyon, Janin frères, 1913).

'Le Chant des Oratoriens: Louis XIII maître de chapelle', *La Tribune de Saint-Gervais*, 19 (1913–14), 121–6, 150–4.

'Les Livres de plain-chant en France, 1583-1630', *La Tribune de Saint-Gervais*, 20 (1914–15), 1–4, 29–33.

Cours théorique et pratique de chant Grégorien (Paris, Schola Cantorum, 1917).

Guéranger, Dom Prosper, *The Liturgical Year*, trans. L Shepherd (8 vols., London, Burns and Oates, 1867–83).

Institutions liturgiques, 2nd ed. (4 vols., Paris, Victor Palmé, 1878–85).

Giacone, Franco, 'Les Lorraine et le psautier', in Yvonne Bellenger (ed.), *Le Mécénat et l'influence des Guises* (Paris, Champion, 1997), pp. 345–63.

Giesey, Ralph, 'Models of rulership in French royal ceremonial', in Sean Willentz (ed.), *Rites of Power: Symbolism, Ritual, and Politics since the Middle Ages* (Philadelphia, PA, University of Pennsylvania Press, 1985), pp. 41–64.

Cérémonial et puissance souveraine: France, XVe–XVIIe siècle (Paris, Colin, 1987).

'The King imagined', in Keith Baker (ed.), *The French Revolution and the Creation of Modern Political Culture: The Political Culture of the Old Régime* (Oxford, Pergamon Press, 1987), pp. 41–59.

Godt, Irwin, *Guillaume Costeley: Life and Works* (PhD dissertation, University of New York, 1969).

Goff, Jacques le, 'Reims, ville du sacre', in Pierre Nora (ed.), *Les Lieux de mémoire: II: La Nation* (Paris: Gallimard, 1986), pp. 89–184.

'A Coronation Program for the Age of Saint Louis: The Ordo of 1250', in János Bak (ed.), *Coronations: Medieval and Early Modern Monarchic Ritual* (Berkeley, Los Angeles, CA, and London, University of California Press, 1990), pp. 46–56.

Saint Louis, trans. Gareth Evan Gollrad (Notre-Dame IN, University of Notre-Dame Press, 2009).

Gonzalez, Sara, *The Musical Iconography of Power in Seventeenth-Century Spain and Her Territories* (London, Routledge, 2016).

Gorce, Jérôme de la, and Herbert Schneider (eds.), *Le Grand-motet français: Actes du colloque sur le grand motet français, Saint-Germain-en-Laye, 1987* (Laaber, Laaber Verlag, 1990).

Guillo, Laurent, *Pierre I Ballard et Robert III Ballard: Imprimeurs du roy pour la musique (1599–1673)* (Liège, Mardaga, 2003).

'Un receuil de motets de Sauvaire Internet (Avignon, c. 1620–1625): Chicago, Newberry Library, Case MS 5136', *Dix-septième siècle*, 232/3 (2006), 453–75.

Guenée, Bernard, and Renée Lehoux, *Les Entrées royales françaises de 1328 à 1515* (Paris, Éditions du CNRS, 1968).

Gunkel, Hermann, *Introduction to the Psalms: The Genres of the Religious Lyric in Israel* (Macon, GA, Mercer University Press, 1998).
Hajdu Heyer, John, 'Lully's *Jubilate Deo*, LWV 77/16: A stylistic anomaly', in Jérôme de la Gorce and Herbert Schneider (eds.), *Le Grand-motet français: Actes du colloque sur le grand motet français, Saint-Germain-en-Laye, 1987* (Laaber, Laaber Verlag, 1990), pp. 145–54.
  The Lure and Legacy of Music at Versailles: Louis XIV and the Aix School (Cambridge and New York, NY, Cambridge University Press, 2014).
Hameline, Jean-Yves, 'Le Plain-chant dans la pratique ecclésiastique aux lendemains du Concile de Trente et des reformes post-conciliaires', in Jean Duron (ed.), *Plain-chant et liturgie en France au XVIIe siècle* (Versailles, Éditions du CMBV, 1997), pp. 13–30.
Handy, Isabelle, *Musiciens au temps des derniers Valois (1547–1589)* (Paris, Champion, 2008).
Hanley, Sarah, *The Lit de Justice of the Kings of France: Constitutional Ideology in Legend, Ritual, and Discourse* (Princeton, NJ, Princeton University Press, 1983).
Haquet, Isabelle, *L'Enigme Henri III: ce que nous révèlent les images* (Paris, Presses universitaires de Paris Nanterre, 2014).
Harran, Don, *Word–Tone Relations in Musical Thought: From Antiquity to the Seventeenth Century* (Neuhausen-Stuttgart, American Institute of Musicology, 1986).
Haynes, Bruce, *A History of Performing Pitch: The Story of A* (Lanham, MD and Oxford, Scarecrow Press, 2002).
Herissone, Rebecca, and Alan Howard (eds.), *Concepts of Creativity in Seventeenth-Century England* (Woodbridge, Boydell Press, 2013).
Higginbottom, Edward, 'French classical organ music and the liturgy', *Proceedings of the Royal Musical Association*, 103 (1977), 19–40.
Holt, Mack P., *The French Wars of Religions, 1562–1629* (Cambridge, Cambridge University Press, 1995).
Ingold, Père, *L'Église de l'Oratoire Saint-Honoré: étude historique et archéologique* (Paris, Librairie Poussielgue Frères, 1887).
Isherwood, Robert, *Music in the Service of the King* (Ithaca, NY, Cornell University Press, 1973).
Jackson, Richard, *Vive le Roi! A History of the French Coronation from Charles V to Charles X* (Chapel Hill, NC, University of North Carolina Press, 1984).
  Ordines Coronationis Franciae: Texts and Ordines for the Coronation of Frankish and French Kings (2 vols., Philadelphia, PA, University of Pennsylvania Press, 1995–2000).
Jacquot, Jean, 'Joyeuse et triomphante entrée', in *Les Fêtes de la Renaissance*, Vol. 1 (Paris, CNRS, 1956), pp. 9–19.
Jacquot, Jean, et al. (eds.), *Les Fêtes de la Renaissance* (3 vols., Paris, CNRS, 1956–1975).

Jeanneret, Michel, *Poésie et tradition biblique au XVIe siècle* (Paris, Corti, 1969).
Jervis, William, *The Gallican Church: The History of the Church of France from the Concordat of Bologna to the Revolution* (London, John Murray, 1872).
Julian, John, *A Dictionary of Hymnology* (New York, NY, Dover, 1957).
Kantorowicz, Ernst, *Laudes Regiae: A Study in Liturgical Acclamations and Medieval Ruler Worship* (Berkeley, CA, University of California Press, 1946).
   The King's Two Bodies: A Study in Medieval Political Theology (Princeton, NJ, Princeton University Press, 1957).
Kauffman, Deborah, 'Fauxbourdon in the seventeenth and eighteenth centuries: "Le Secours d'une douce harmonie"', *Music & Letters*, 90/1 (2008), 68–93.
   Music at the Maison royale de Saint-Louis at Saint-Cyr (Abingdon and New York, NY, Routledge, 2019).
Kendrick, Robert, *The Sounds of Milan, 1585–1650* (Oxford, Oxford University Press, 2002).
Kettering, Sharon, *Power and Reputation at the Court of Louis XIII: The Career of Charles d'Albert, duc de Luynes (1578–1621)* (Manchester and New York, NY, Manchester University Press, 2008).
Kisby, Fiona (ed.), *Music and Musicians in Renaissance Cities and Towns* (Cambridge, Cambridge University Press, 2001).
Ladurie, Emmanuel le Roy, *The French Royal State, 1460–1610*, trans. Juliet Vale (Oxford, Blackwell, 1994).
Lamothe, Donat, *Claude le Jeune, le Psautier Huguenot et la Musique Religieuse à la Cour Pendant les Règnes de Charles IX, Henri III et Henri IV* (PhD dissertation, University of Strasbourg, 1980).
Lapidge, Michael, *Hilduin of Saint-Denis: The Passio S. Dionysii in Prose and Verse* (Leiden, Brill, 2017).
Lardon, Sabine, 'Inspiration biblique et forms poétiques dans les *Œuvres chrestiennes* d'Isaac Habert', in Pascale Blum and Anne Mantero (eds.), *Poésie et Bible de la Renaissance à l'Âge Classique, 1550–1680* (Paris, Champion, 1999), pp. 49–64.
Launay, Denise, 'G. Bouzignac', *Musique et liturgie*, 21 (1951), 3–8.
   'Les Motets à double chœur en France dans la première moitié du xviie siècle', *Revue de musicologie*, 40 (1957), 73–195.
Launay, Denise, (ed.), *Anthologie du motet latin polyphonique en France (1606–61)* (Paris, Société française de musicologie, Heugel, 1963).
   'Un esprit critique au temps de Jumilhac: Dom Jacques Le Clerc, bénédictin de la Congrégation de Saint Maur', *Études grégoriennes*, 19 (1980), 197–219.
   'Le Thème du retour à l'antique et la musique religieuse en France au temps de la Contre-Réforme', in Manfred Tietz and Volker Kapp (eds.), *La Pensée religieuse dans la littérature et la civilisation du xviie siècle en France* (Tübingen, 1984), pp. 814–25.

La Musique religieuse en France du Concile de Trente à 1804 (Paris, Klincksieck, 1993).

Laurentin, René, *Le Vœu de Louis XIII: passé ou avenir de la France* (Paris, Guibert, 1988).

Lebeuf, Abbé, *Histoire de la ville et de tout le diocese de Paris* (Paris, Librairie de Féchoz et Letouzey, 1883).

Leroux, Martial, *Guillaume Bouzignac vers 1587–vers 1643: l'énigme musicale du XVIIe siècle français*, (Montpellier, Presses du Languedoc, 2002).

Lesure, François, 'Un contrat d'exclusivité entre Nicolas Formé et Ballard, 1638', *Revue de Musicologie* 50/2 (1964), 228–9.

Levarie, Siegmund, 'Philo on Music', *The Journal of Musicology*, 9/1 (1991), 124–30.

Lionnet, Jean, *La Musique à Saint-Louis des Français de Rome au xviie siècle* (2 vols., Venice, Edizioni Fondazione Levi, 1985).

Lombard-Jourdan, Anne, *Fleur de lis et oriflamme: signes célestes du royaume de France* (Paris, CNRS, 2002).

Louvet, Jean, Diaries, *Revue de l'Anjou et de Maine et Loire*, 3/1 (1854), 257–304; 3/2 (1854), 1–64, 129–92, 257–320; 4/2 (1855), 130–320; 4/3 (1855), 1–320.

Lowinsky, Edward (ed.), *The Medici Codex of 1518*, Monuments of Renaissance Music, 3–5 (Chicago, IL, University of Chicago Press, 1968).

Lloyd Moote, A., *Louis XIII, the Just* (Berkeley, Los Angeles, CA and London, University of California Press, 1989).

Lublinskaya, Aleksandra, *French Absolutism: The Crucial Phase* (Cambridge, Cambridge University Press, 1968).

Lundberg, Mattias, *Tonus Peregrinus: The History of a Psalm-Tone and Its Use in Polyphonic Music* (Farnham, Ashgate, 2011).

Macey, Patrick, 'Josquin's *Misericordias Domini* and Louis XI', *Early Music*, 19/2 (1991), 163–77.

Maral, Alexandre, *La Chapelle royale de Versailles sous Louis XIV: cérémonial, liturgie et musique* (Sprimont, Mardaga, 2002).

Marin, Louis, *Le Portrait du Roi* (Paris, Éditions de Minuit, 1981).

Massip, Catherine, *Paris, 1600–61*, in Curtis Price (ed.), *The Early Baroque Era* (Palgrave Macmillan, London, 1993), pp. 218–37.

Mayer Brown, Howard, '*Ut musica poesis*: Music and poetry in France in the late sixteenth century', *Early Music History*, 13 (1994), 1–63.

McGowan, Margaret, *L'Art du ballet de cour en France, 1581–1643* (Paris, CNRS, 1963).

Ideal Forms in the Age of Ronsard (Berkeley, CA, University of California Press, 1985).

McGrath, George Warren, *The Revision of the Hymns of the Roman Breviary under Urban VIII* (MA thesis, Loyola University, 1939).

Moel, Michel le, 'La Chapelle de Musique sous Henri IV et Louis XIII', *Recherches sur la musique française Classique*, 6 (1966), 5–26.

Molitor, Raphael, *Die nach-tridentinische Choral-reform zu Rom* (2 vols., Leipzig, F. E. C. Leuckart, 1901–2).

Monod, Paul Kléber, *The Power of Kings: Monarchy and Religion in Europe, 1589-1715* (New Haven, CT and London, Yale University Press, 1999).

Montagnier, Jean-Paul, 'Modèles chorégraphiques dans les grands et petits motets français', in Hervé Lacombe (ed.), *Le Mouvement en musique à l'époque baroque* (Metz, Éditions Serpenois, 1996), pp. 141–56.

'Le Te Deum en France à l'époque baroque: un emblème royal', *Revue de musicologie*, 84/2 (1998), 199–233.

'Chanter Dieu en la Chapelle Royale: le grand motet et ses supports litteraires', *Revue de musicologie*, 86/2 (2000), 217–63.

The Polyphonic Mass in France, 1600-1780: The Evidence of the Printed Choirbooks (Cambridge, Cambridge University Press, 2017).

Mousnier, Roland, *The Assassination of Henri IV: The Tyrannicide Problem and the Consolidation of the French Absolute Monarchy in the Early Seventeenth Century*, trans. Joan Spencer (New York, NY, Scribner, 1973); originally published as *L'Assassinat d'Henri IV: 14 mai 1610* (Paris, Gallimard, 1964).

Mulryne, J. R., Helen Watanabe-O'Kelly, and Margaret Shewring (eds.), *Europa Triumphans: Court and Civic Festivals in Early Modern Europe* (Aldershot, Ashgate, 2004).

Nguyen, Marie-Lan, *Les Grands maîtres des cérèmonies et le service des Cérèmonies* (MA dissertation, University of Paris-Sorbonne, 1998).

O'Regan, Noel, *Sacred Polychoral Music in Rome, 1575–1621* (DPhil dissertation, Oxford University, 1988).

Ortigue, M. J., *Dictionnaire liturgique, historique, et théorique de plain-chant et de Musique d'église* (Paris, L. Potier, 1854).

Palisca, Claude V., 'Bernardino Cirillo's critique of polyphonic church music of 1549: Its background and resonance', in Jessie Ann Owens and Anthony M. Cummings (eds.), *Music in Renaissance Cities and Courts: Studies in Honor of Lewis Lockwood* (Warren, MI, Harmonie Park Press, 1997), pp. 281–92.

Pauwels, Yves, 'La Thème de l'arc de triomphe dans l'architecture urbaine à la Renaissance: entre pouvoir politique et pouvoir religieux', in Patrick Boucheron and Jean-Philippe Genet (eds.), *Marquer la ville, Signes, traces, empreintes du pouvoir (xiiie–xvie siecle)* (Paris and Rome, Publications de la Sorbonne, École française de Rome, 2013), pp. 181–91.

Perraud, Adolphe, *L'Oratoire de France au XVIIe et au XIXe siècle* (Paris, Charles Douniol, 1866).

Pierre, Benoist, *La Monarchie ecclésiale: le clergé de cour en France à l'époque moderne* (Paris, Champ Vallon, 2013).

Quittard, Henri, 'Un musicien oublié du xviie siècle: G. Bouzignac', *Sammelbände der Internationalen Musik-Gesellschaft*, 6 (1904–5), 356–471.

Ranum, Patricia, '"Le Chant doit perfectionner la prononciation, & non pas la corrompre": L'Accentuation du chant grégorien d'après les traités de Dom Jacques Le Clerc et dans le chant de Guillaume-Gabriel Nivers', in Jean Duron (ed.), *Plain-chant et liturgie en France au XVIIe siècle* (Versailles, Éditions du CMBV, 1997), pp. 59–83.

Ravens, Simon, *The Supernatural Voice: A History of High Male Singing* (Woodbridge, Boydell, 2014).

Robert, Jean, 'La Maîtrise Saint-Agricol d'Avignon au xviie siècle', *Actes du quatre-vingt-dixième congrès national des sociétés savantes, Nice, 1965: section d'histoire moderne et contemporaine*, Vol. 3 (*De la restauration à nos jours, histoire de l'art*) (Paris, Bibliothèque nationale, 1966), pp. 609–35.

Robinson, Alexander, *Musique et musiciens à la cour d'Henri IV (1589–1610)* (PhD dissertation, University of Paris-Sorbonne, 2015).

 'Music and politics in the entry of Maria de' Medici into Avignon (19 November, 1600)', in Rudolf Rasch (ed.), *Music and Power in the Baroque Era* (Turnhout, Brepols, 2018), pp. 179–202.

Royster, Don Lee, *Pierre Guédron and the air de cour, 1600–1620* (PhD dissertation, Yale University, 1972).

Runia, David, *Philo of Alexandria and The 'Timaeus' of Plato* (Leiden, Brill, 1986).

Sabatier, Gerard, *Versailles ou la figure du Roi* (Paris, Albin Michel, 1999).

Salmon, John., *Renaissance and Revolt: Essays in the Intellectual and Social History of Early Modern France* (Cambridge, Cambridge University Press, 1987).

Sandlin, Julianne, *Asserting Royal Power in Early Seventeenth-Century Paris: Louis XIII, Maria de' Medici, and the Art and Architecture of Reformed Religious Orders* (PhD dissertation, Florida State University, 2009).

Sawkins, Lionel, 'Performance practice in the grands motets of Michel-Richard de Lalande as determined by eighteenth-century timings', in Jean Mongrédien and Yves Ferraton (eds.), *Actes du Colloque international de musicologie sur le grand motet français, 1663–1792* (Paris, 1986), pp. 105–17.

 'Chronology and evolution of the *grand motet* at the court of Louis XIV: Evidence from the *Livres du Roi* and the works of Perrin, the *sous-maîtres* and Lully', in John Hajdu Heyer (ed.), *Jean-Baptiste Lully and the Music of the French Baroque* (Cambridge and New York, NY, Cambridge University Press, 1989), pp. 41–79.

 'Lully's motets: Source, edition, performance', in Jérôme de la Gorce and Herbert Schneider (eds.), *Le Grand-motet français: Actes du colloque sur le grand motet français, Saint-Germain-en-Laye, 1987* (Laaber, Laaber Verlag, 1990), pp. 383–404.

'En province, à Versailles et au Concert Spirituel: réception, diffusions et execution des motets de Lalande au XVIIIe siècle', *Revue de musicologie*, 92/1 (2006), 13–40.

Sealy, Robert, *The Palace Academy of Henry III* (Geneva, Droz, 1981).

Sherr, Richard, 'The performance of chant in the Renaissance and its interaction with polyphony', in Thomas Kelly (ed.), *Plainsong in the Age of Polyphony* (Cambridge, Cambridge University Press 1992), pp. 178–208.

Somfai, Anna, 'The eleventh-century shift in the reception of Plato's 'Timaeus' and Calcidius's 'Commentary'', *Journal of the Warburg and Courtauld Institutes*, 65 (2002), 1–21.

Spicer, Andrew, and Sarah Hamilton (eds.), *Defining the Holy: Sacred Space in Medieval and Early Modern Europe* (Farnham, Ashgate, 2005).

Spitzer, Leo, *Classical and Christian Ideas of World Harmony* (Baltimore, MD, Johns Hopkins University Press, 1963).

Stankiewicz W. J., *Politics and Religion in 17th-century France* (Berkeley, CA, University of California Press, 1960).

Strohm, Reinhard, 'Music, humanism, and the idea of rebirth', in Reinhard Strohm and Bonnie Blackburn (eds.), *The New Oxford History of Music*, III: *Music as Concept and Practice, in the late Middle Ages*, (London, Oxford University Press, 2001), pp. 360–8.

Strong, Roy, *Art and Power: Renaissance Festivals, 1450–1650* (Berkeley, CA, University of California Press, 1984).

Swanson, Barbara, *Speaking in Tones: Plainchant, Monody, and the Rhetoric of Antiquity in Early Modern Italy* (PhD dissertation, Case Western Reserve University, 2013).

Szpirglas, Jacques, *Dictionnaire des musiciens de la cour d'Henri IV et des maisons princières* (Paris, Garnier, 2019).

Tapié, Victor, *France in the Age of Louis XIII and Richelieu* (New York, NY, Praeger, 1974)

Thomas, Downing, *Music and the Origins of Language: Theories from the French Enlightenment* (Cambridge and New York, NY, Cambridge University Press, 1995).

Van Orden, Kate, 'Les Vers lascifs d'Horace: Arcadelts Latin Chanons', *The Journal of Musicology*, 14/3 (1996), 338–69.

Music, Discipline, and Arms in Early Modern France (Chicago, IL, University of Chicago Press, 2005).

Materialities: Books, Readers, and the Chanson in Sixteenth-Century Europe (Oxford and New York, NY, Oxford University Press, 2015).

Vaulgrenant, Maurice de, 'Le Vœu de Louis XIII', *Revue d'histoire de l'Église de France*, 24/102 (1938), 47–58.

Veltman, Joshua Joel, *Prosody and Rhythm in the Post-Tridentine Reform of Plainchant* (PhD dissertation, The Ohio State University, 2004).
   'Notation and rhythm in the Medicean Gradual', in Timothy Watkins (ed.), *Performance Practice: Issues and Approaches* (Ann Arbor, MI, Steglein, 2009), pp. 15–32.
Vendrix, Philippe, 'Pour les grands et les autres: la réforme oratorienne du plainchant', in Jean Duron (ed.), *Plain-chant et liturgie en France au XVIIe siècle* (Versailles, Éditions du CMBV, 1997), pp. 87–96.
   'Nicolas Bergier: le dernier théoricien de la Renaissance en France', in François Lesure and Henri Vanhulst (eds.), *"La Musique, de tous les passetemps le plus beau": Hommage à Jean-Michel Vaccaro* (Paris, Klincksieck, 1998), pp. 369–86.
Verchaly, André, 'Desportes et la musique', *Annales musicologiques*, 2 (1954), 271–345.
Vidal, Daniel, *Critique de la raison mystique: Benoît de Canfield: possession et dépossession au xviie siècle* (Grenoble, Jérôme Millon, 1990).
Vinay, Dominique, *La Couronne et la lyre: présence du roi David dans la littérature française de la Renaissance* (PhD dissertation, Université François Rabelais – Tours, 2002).
Vivanti, Corrado, 'Henry IV, the Gallic Hercules', *Journal of the Warburg and Courtauld Institutes*, 30 (1967), 176–97.
Walker, Daniel Pickering, 'Musical humanism in the 16th and early 17th centuries', *The Music Review*, 2 (1941), 1–13; 3 (1942), 111–21, 220–7, 288–308; 3 (1943), 55–71.
   'The influence of *musique mesurée à l'antique*, particularly on the *airs de cour* of the early seventeenth century', *Musica Disciplina*, 2 (1948), 141–63.
   'Aspects and problems of *musique mesurée à l'antique*: The rhythm and notation of *musique mesurée*', *Musica Disciplina*, 4 (1950), 163–86.
   Spiritual and Demonic Magic from Ficino to Campanella, Studies of the Warburg Institute, 22 (London, Warburg Institute, 1958).
Weber, Edith, 'L'Intelligibilité du texte dans la crise religieuse et musicale du XVIe siècle: incidences du Concile de Trente', *Études Grégoriennes*, 24 (1992), 195–202.
Weber, Max, *Economy and Society*, trans. Keith Tribe (Cambridge, MA and London, Harvard University Press, 2019).
Wordsworth, John, *The Te Deum: Its Structure and Meaning, and Its Musical Setting and Rendering* (Oxford, John Hart, 1903).
Wymeersch, Brigitte Van, 'L'Esthétique musicale de Descartes et le cartésianisme', *Revue Philosophique de Louvain*, 4th series, 94/2 (1996), 271–93.
Yates, Frances A., *The French Academies of the Sixteenth Century*, Studies of the Warburg Institute, 15 (London, Warburg Institute, 1947).
   'Dramatic religious processions in Paris in the late sixteenth century', *Annales musicologiques*, 2 (1954), 215–70.

The Valois Tapestries, Studies of the Warburg Institute, 23 (London, Warburg Institute, 1959).

Astraea: The Imperial Theme in the Sixteenth Century (London and Boston, MA, Routledge, 1985).

Zak, Sabine, 'Das Tedeum als Huldigungsgesang', *Historisches Jahrbuch*, 102 (1982), 1–32.

Index

Abbate, Carolyn, 5
Abbeville, 245
absolutism, 2, 35–6, 46, 90, 93, 123, 167, 178
Académie de Jeux Floraux, 39
Académie de poésie et de musique, 5, 25–9, 82, 224, 281
Académie du Palais, 34
Acarie, Barbe, 209, 223, 225, 239
Adelaide, queen, 206
Ambrose, Saint, 43, 64, 232, 284
Andromeda, 3, 162
Anne of Austria, 89, 132
    birth of Louis XIV, 249–50
    childhood of Louis XIV, 276
Anointing, 36–7, 42, 55, 62–4
Anthony, James R., 13
Apollo, 3, 5, 25, 39–40
Apostolides, Jean-Marie, 6, 9
Arcadelt, Jacques, 198
Arnoux, Jean, 91, 95
Assumption, feast of the, 132, 226, 244–6, 269, 288
Athanasius, Saint, 232
Attaingnant, Pierre, 68, 172
Attalus, 3
Augustine, Saint, 41, 64, 170, 232, 284
Augustines, Church of the, 76–7
Auxcousteaux, Artus, 118, 125, 253
Avignon, 160, 188

Baïf, Guillaume de, 158
Baïf, Jean-Antoine de, 25–9, 39–40, 61, 82, 99, 107, 157
Bailly, Henri le, 130
Balet comique de la Reine, 4, 141, 266
Bartas, Guillaume du, 41–2, 87
Bataille, Gabriel, 56, 157
Beaulieu, Girard de, 141
Beaune, Renaud de, 38
Beauvilliers, Anne de, 210
Beauvilliers, Marie de, Abbess, 202, 207–8, 224, 234
Beetham, David, 8–9, 287

Bellarmine, Robert, Cardinal, 97
Bergier, Nicolas, 51, 236–7
Bernard, Saint, of Clairvaux, 206, 270
Bérulle, Pierre de, 225–6, 239
Blanc, Didier le, 68
Blondet, Abraham, 60, 146, 184
Boderie, Guy le Fèvre de la, 3, 32
Bodin, Jean, 29–33
Boësset, Antoine, 128–9
    compositions for Montmartre, 197, 203, 207, 212–21
    pitch, 257
Boësset, Jean-Baptiste, 285
Bourbon, Charles de, Cardinal, 34, 77, 95, 141, 200
Bourbon, Henri de, 77, 193
Bourgoing, François, 227–36
Bournonville, Jean de, 13, 146, 183, 251
Bouzignac, Guillaume, 173–7
Bryant, Lawrence, 11, 153
Budé, Louis, 20
Burke, Peter, 6, 9

Caietain, Fabrice-Marin, 27
Caignet, Denis, 107–8, 221, 235
Calvin, Jean, 20, 23
Cambrai, Council of, 199
Canfield, Benet, 209, 223–4
Canticum trium puerorum, 65
Canticum Zachariae, 65
Casale, 191, 238
Catherine de Médicis, 56
Caurroy, Eustache du, 81
    as *sous-maître*, 55, 60
    In exitu Israel, 83, 118
    Meslanges, 108, 118
    Preces ecclesiasticae, 183
    Requiem, 13, 275
    Te Deum, 68–70
    Veni creator spiritus, 57
Champaigne, Philippe de, 246
chant sur livre, 195
chapelle de plainchant, 55

chapelle royale
  liturgy, 110–15, 201
  Mass for the Holy Spirit, 77–80
Charlemagne, King, 3, 57, 156, 284
Charles IX, King, 5, 74
Charles the Bald, King, 37
Charles V, King, coronation, 38
Charles VIII, King, 82
  coronation, 67
Childebert, King, 156, 205
Clément, Pope, 212
Clerc, Jacques le, 203, 233
Clovis, King, 2, 37, 51, 156
Compagnie du Saint Sacrement, 240
Concini, Concino, 50, 88
  assassination, 14, 134, 151
Cone, Edward, 5
confirmation, 55, 57–8
Congregation of the Oratory of Jesus Christ, 197
  chant, 227–35
  foundation, 224–7
Congregation of the Penitents of the Annunciation of Our Lady
  foundation, 140–2
  liturgy, 141–2
coronation, 10–11, 36–7
  and Te Deum ceremony, 179
  Louis XIV, 276
  role of King David, 38
Costeley, Guillaume, 48, 52
Coton, Pierre, 55, 225, 241
Courbes, Charles de, 108
Cyrus, King, 97

d'Ambleville, Charles, 13, 146, 260
David, King
  agent of the Holy Spirit, 5, 15, 42, 44, 86
  anointing, 50, 62, 97, 169
  author of the psalms, 6, 20, 40
  humility, 40, 43, 167
  model of kingship, 5–6, 15, 19, 38, 42, 82, 98, 102, 110, 119, 125, 173, 231
  musician, 25, 41, 45, 90, 101, 103, 231–2, 235, 281
  penitent, 15, 124, 127, 273
  warrior, 7, 15, 19, 43, 90, 101–6, 154, 273
De profundis (Psalm 129), 61, 78, 143–4
  after Mass, 112
Denis, Saint, 14, 91
  companions Rusticus and Eleutherius, 205–6
  conflation with Dionysius the Areopagite, 206, 211, 213, 224
  conflation with Pseudo-Dionysius, 206, 223–4
  feast of, 247
  foundation of Montmartre, 205–10
Descartes, René, 221–3, 236
Desportes, Philippe, 38, 107, 221
dévots, 34, 88, 208, 239
Dionysius the Areopagite, 206
Doline, Nicolas, 57
Domine salvum fac regem (Psalm 19)
  after Mass, 112, 146–9, 252, 267
  in coronation, 48–9, 52–5
  motet, 73, 135
  musical settings, 184–6
  versicle, 52
Dufourcq, Norbert, 13
Dumont, Henri
  Domine in virtute tua, 280
  Pulsate, pulsate tympana, 280–1
Durant de la Bergerie, Gilles, 108

Entrée, 1, 10
  Aix (1622), 162, 169
  Angers (1619), 1, 171
  Arles (1622), 3, 155, 162, 168
  Avignon (1622), 160, 164, 171, 190
  Chartres (1619), 164, 167
  Dijon (1629), 155–6
  Grenoble (1622), 167
  La Rochelle (1628), 17
  Le Mans (1614), 1, 167
  Lyon (1622), 164, 171
  Lyon (1642), 176
  Montélimar (1622), 155
  Montpellier (1622), 171
  Orléans (1614), 157, 171
  Paris (1614), 155, 157
  Paris (1622), 172
  Paris (1628), 156
  Poitiers (1619), 157
  Reims (1610), 51, 54
  Toulouse (1622), 164
  Troyes (1629), 167, 174, 190–2
Eugène, Pope, 206
Exaudiat te Dominus (Psalm 19), 134–49
  after Mass, 112, 138, 252
  in *entrée*, 154
  in *entrée* and Te Deum ceremony, 187–90
  musical settings, 183, 188–9
  prayer for the king, 54, 66, 125, 135, 183, 194, 243, 288

fauxbourdon, 59, 115, 117, 141, 184, 195, 219
Favier, Thierry, 6–7
Ficino, Marsilio, 4, 26
Fogel, Michèle, 11, 153, 178–9
Formé, Nicolas, 12, 55, 60, 84, 119, 240
    and the dedication of the kingdom to the Virgin Mary, 248
    Ecce tu pulchra es, 268–73
    Magnificats, 249
    Mass *Aeternae Henrici Magnae*, 258–68
    Musica simplex, 252
    Nonne Deo subjecta, 118
Foucault, Michel, 9
Francis Xavier, Saint, 160
François I, king, 3, 22, 82, 97
    coronation, 52
Francus, 3

Gaston d'Orléans, prince, 89, 132
Geneviève, Saint, 206, 208
Giesey, Ralph, 11, 65, 153
Giorgio, Francesco, 32
Gobert, Thomas, 277, 285
Godeau, Antoine, Bishop, 275
Gomes, Rita Costa, 9
Gondi, Henri de, Cardinal, 80, 126, 225
Gondi, Jean-François Paul de, Bishop of Paris, 95
Gondi, Philippe-Emmanuel, 126
Grace (*Benedictio mensae*), 90, 115–22
Grand motet, 6, 90
    origins, 276
Granier, Matthias, 55
Gregory XIII, Pope, 196
Gregory XV, Pope, 210
Guédron, Pierre, 56, 128, 221, 235
Guenée, Bernard, 11, 153
Guidetti, Giovanni, 196, 229
Guise, family, 14, 33, 75, 77, 197, 200, 217, 235
    connections to Montmartre, 208

Habert, Isaac, 98–100
Hanley, Sarah, 11, 47
Hector, 3
Henri II, king
    psalms, 22, 126
Henri III, king, 3
    as phoenix, 86
    liturgy of *chapelle royale*, 90
    Order of the Holy Spirit, 74–6
    penitent, 125
    reforms to *chapelle royale*, 111, 143
    Te Deum ceremony, 49

Henri IV, King, 3
    abjuration, 82, 208
    agent of the Holy Spirit, 50
    as progenitor of Louis XIII, 259
    assassination, 46, 110, 123, 146
    coronation, 38, 63, 67, 70, 73
    descent from Saint Louis, 92
    elevation of Saint Louis, 94
    funeral, 48, 57
    wedding, 193
Hercules, 3
Hezekia, King, 246
Hilaire of Poitiers, Saint, 41
Holy Spirit, 58
    inspiration for David, 42, 50
    inspiration for Henri III, 140
    inspiration for Solomon, 134
    inspiration for Te Deum, 170
Huguenots, 102, 151, 238
    psalm singing, 19

Ignatius of Loyola, Saint, 160
In exitu Israel (Psalm 113), 61, 81–3, 116, 118, 132, 144, 191
Innocent II, Pope, 37
Intermet, Sauveur, 160

Jackson, Richard, 11, 47
Jesus Christ, 235, 269
    model of kingship, 231, 240, 273
    reciting psalms, 232, 237
Josiah, King, 37, 51
Joyeuse, Ange de, 126, 209, 225–6
Joyeuse, Anne de, 141
Joyeuse, Catherine de, 209
Joyeuse, François de, Cardinal, 51, 62, 70, 80, 84, 91, 225
Joyeuse, Henri de, 77
Joyeuse, Henriette-Catherine de, 126, 226
Jumilhac, Pierre-Benoît de, 203, 233

La Rochelle, 17–22, 44, 191, 238
Launay, Denise, 13
Le Jeune, Claude, 27–8, 82
League, Catholic, 33, 74, 135, 166, 197
    and Saint Denis, 207–8
Lehoux, Renée, 11, 153
Lemercier, Jacques, 226
Lit de justice, 11, 51, 259
Lorraine, Charles de, Cardinal, 198–9
Lorraine, Charles de, duc d'Aumale, 77
Lorraine, Charles de, duc de Guise, 126, 209
Lorraine, Françoise-Renée de, 209

Lorraine, Henri de, duc de Guise, 200
Lorraine, Henri IV de, 208
Lorraine, Louis II de, Cardinal de Guise, 60, 141, 200, 207, 221
Lorraine, Louis III de, Archbishop of Reims, 52
Lorraine, Louis IV de, 208
Louis IX, Saint, King, 14, 90, 167, 239, 281
   feast of, 91
   model of kingship, 92–4, 283
   revisions to liturgy, 96–101
Louis le Gros, King, 206
Louis the Pious, King, 37
Louis VI, King, 37
Louis XI, King, 74, 82
Louis XII, King, 82
Louis XIV, King
   artistic patronage, 6
   birth, 193
   childhood, 276
   coronation, 276
Lully, Jean-Baptiste, 3, 285
   Jubilate Deo, 279–80
Luynes, Duc de, 89

Macé, Benedic, 60
Maillard, Jean, 49, 52–5, 73
Marguérite, Queen, 57
Marie de Médicis, queen, 14, 62, 132, 209, 239
   coronation, 46
   foundation of Oratory, 225
   regency, 48, 88
Marin, Louis, 6, 9
Marot, Clément, 19, 22
Martin, Saint, 206, 225
Mass of the Holy Spirit, 70–3, 111
Mauduit, Jacques, 27–8, 61, 157
Mersenne, Marin, 6, 28, 82, 157
   pitch, 256–8
Métru, Nicolas, 158, 161
Monarchomach, 29, 123
Montagnier, Jean-Paul, 7, 13
Montmartre, abbey of, 14, 126, 197
   chant reform, 202–5
   foundation, 205–10
   liturgy of Confraternity of Saint Denis, 211–16
   Salut, 214–16
   works of Antoine Boësset, 212–21
Moulinié, Étienne, 13, 132, 257
Mouton, Jean, 49, 52–5, 252
musique de la chambre, 56, 70, 90, 107
   collaboration with *chapelle royale*, 253–8
   Grace, 116
   repertoire, 128–34

musique de la chapelle, 55–6, 63, 68, 90
   collaboration with *musique de la chambre*, 253–8
   Grace, 119, 128
musique de la grande écurie, 57
musique mesurée, 27–9, 61, 82, 108, 199, 218, 266

Nattie, Jehan, 57
Neoplatonism, 24–6, 33, 223, 235
Newberry/Avignon manuscript, 14, 159–61, 188–9
Nivers, Guillaume Gabriel, 196, 233
   pitch, 256
Notre-Dame des Doms, Avignon, cathedral of, 164
Notre-Dame, cathedral of, 14, 61, 68, 147, 178, 184, 205, 254
Notre-Dame-des-Ardilliers, Saumur, church of, 241
Notre-Dame-des-Vertus, Aubervilliers, church of, 241
Notre-Dame-des-Victoires, church of, 241

O salutaris hostia, 61, 252, 256
Olivetan, Pierre-Robert, 20
Oratory and Company of the Blessed Saint Francis, 142
Oratory of Our Lady of Vie-Saine, 143
Orden, Kate van, 12, 18, 30, 49, 154, 179
Order of Saint Michael, 75
Order of the Holy Spirit, 10, 51, 141
   foundation, 74–6
   induction of Louis XIII, 80–7
   induction of Louis XIV, 276
   liturgy, 77
   Mass, 255
   membership, 76
Oriflamme, 77

Palestrina, Giovanni Pierluigi da, 196
Parent, Raoul, 212
Paris manuscript, 13, 129, 173, 184, 203, 212, 215, 253
Paul V, Pope, 226
Paul, Vincent de, 225, 239
Péchon, André, 13, 215
Pentecost, feast of, 44, 57, 74, 76
Perrin, Pierre, 98, 280–2
   liturgy and power, 283–7
Perron, Jacques-Davy du, Cardinal, 115
Perseus, 3, 162
Petit-Bourbon, 197, 200, 226
Pharamond, king, 3

Philo of Alexandria, 232, 265
Picot, Eustache, 55, 119
Pierre, Saint, 206
Pius V, Pope, 200
Plato, 24, 26, 32-3
Pléiade, 3, 23-5, 99
Plutarch, 26
pompilius, 3
Power, legitimation of, 7-9, 283-7
Pré, Arnauld du, 97
Psalm
   1, 108
   2, 122
   3, 82, 127, 131
   4, 108
   5, 108, 283
   6, 108, 126
   8, 130
   9, 35, 225
   17, 19, 47, 106, 122, 189
   18, 106
   19, see *Exaudiat te Dominus* (Psalm 19) and *Domine salvum fac regem* (Psalm 19)
   20, 49, 54, 58, 73, 179, 193, 280
   21, 118, 127
   23, 173
   24, 36
   25, 108
   31, 35
   42, 22
   45, 108
   46, 132, 173
   47, 118
   50, 108, 117, 126, 142, 183
   54, 130
   60, 117
   61, 118
   67, 29, 58
   68, 35, 262
   69, 130
   71, 191
   76, 117
   78, 112, 126, 130, 143
   80, 122
   87, 108
   88, 62, 98
   90, 47
   95, 173
   96, 117
   97, 280
   109, 61, 81, 229
   110, 81
   111, 81
   112, 81
   113, see *In exitu Israel* (Psalm 113)
   114, 117-18
   116, 67, 82
   116), 97, 108, 144, 179, 276
   117, 104-5
   121, 182, 260, 275, 280
   126, 106, 108
   127, 138
   128, 22, 103, 106
   129, see *De profundis* (Psalm 129)
   130, 23, 275
   131, 131
   133, 108
   135, 262
   136, 108, 115
   146, 122
   147, 61
   150, 108, 281
Pseudo-Dionysius, 14, 206, 223

Reims, 37, 51
   Council of, 198, 200
Remi, Saint, 51-2
René d'Anjou, King, 82
representation, 7
Richard, François, 130
Richelieu, Cardinal de, 2, 17, 50, 89, 243
Ronsard, Pierre de, 3, 23-5, 99, 199
Rouen, Council of, 200
Roy, Étienne le, 55, 141

Sabatier, Gerard, 6
Saint-Benoît, church of, 213
Saint-Denis, abbey of, 75, 205, 207-8
Saint-Denis-de-la-Chartre, church of, 205
Saint-Denis-du-Pas, church of, 205
Sainte-Chapelle, 93, 119, 183, 245
Sainte-Marguérite, La Rochelle, church of, 17
Saint-Germain-l'Auxerrois, church of, 13, 112, 215
Saint-Hilaire, Poitiers, church, 157
Saint-Honoré, church of, 226
Saint-Leuffroy, chapel or, 215
Saint-Louis, church of, 95, 100
Saint-Martin-des-Champs, church of, 206
Saint-Nicolas-du-Louvre, church of, 226
Saint-Pierre, Lisieux, cathedral of, 184
Saint-Pierre, Reims, abbey of, 52, 206
Saint-Remi, Reims, church of, 74
Saint-Sauveur, Avignon, cathedral of, 14
Saint-Thomas, church of, 226
Sales, François de, 208, 223, 225
Salmon, Jacques, 141

Salut, 211–12, 214–16
San Luigi dei Francesi, Rome, church of, 21
Santeul, Jean, 98
Sermisy, Claudin de, 252
Servin, Louis, 108, 166
Solomon, King, 37, 50–1, 73, 98, 133, 167
Souffran, Jean, 19

Te Deum, 1, 18, 42, 104–5, 142, 284
    ceremony, 49, 65, 68, 152, 176–82, 253, 274
    in coronation, 48–9, 64–7
    in *entrée*, 151, 168, 170–2
    musical settings, 67–70, 171
    on Louis XIII's deathbed, 275
    paraphrase, 24, 65, 171
Tessier, Charles, 116
Tours manuscript, 14, 172, 184
Tyard, Pontus de, 4, 26, 31, 224

Urban VIII, Pope, 21, 98

Vavasseur, Nicolas le, 184
Veillot, Jean
    Alleluia, O filii et filiae, 277–8
    Sacris solemnis, 278–9
Vendosme, César de, 126
Veni creator spiritus, hymn, 78, 85, 111, 276, 284
Vespasian, 3
Vigenère, Blaise de la, 39
Virgin Mary, 91
    dedication of kingdom to, 15, 240–8
Vouet, Simon, 242

Weber, Max, 7–9

Zoilo, Anibale, 196

CPSIA information can be obtained
at www.ICGtesting.com
Printed in the USA
LVHW061546030821
694430LV00006B/445